MUSICAL
ROAD KILLS

1 – 2 – 3 – 4
"Welcome to my job.
This is what they pay me for.
Welcome to my job.
Sometimes it's fun, Sometimes it's a bore
But NOW, as the first song's under way,
I hope you dig what I'm gonna play
I hope the PA sounds OK.
I don't understand why some people
wanna act like big rock stars
Wearin' their platform shoes to bed,
and drivin' those big long cars
I just sing and talk too much, playin'
this old beat up guitar
BUT I LIKE IT.
I wouldn't do NUTHIN' else,
even if I got religion.
WELCOME TO MY JOB"

CUB KODA

MUSICAL ROAD KILLS

AND OTHER TALES.
SOME WITH MORALS,
SOME WITHOUT

Nevard Tellalian

Quotes from a story about the Hon. Aram H. Tellalian, written by Donald Eng

Originally published in The Trumbull Times, and Used by Permission.

Genre-Music Memoir, Autobiography, Adult

Hardcover 978-1-7320155-0-0, Paperback 978-1-7320155-1-7,

eBook 978-1-7320155-2-4

JUST
AIN'T WRITE
BOOKS

FOR MUSIC

(The author in 2015)

"As someone who has made movies about musicians, I can tell you that Nevard's book has the aroma of certainty, the weight of experience and a sense of humor that only comes from flying by the seat of your pants for a very long time. I would recommend this great read for anyone who would like the unerring view of a touring musician's life and who isn't too delicate to survive it. This life isn't for the squeamish. Would you like to know exactly what fuels the passion for creating and caring? You'll find the answer inside Musical Road Kills"

—Orian Williams- - Award-winning producer for the films Control, England Is Mine, Big Sur, Shadow Of The Vampire and others.

ABOUT THE AUTHOR

(Nevard in 1994)

Nevard Wallace Tellalian, was born in Bridgeport Connecticut, spent her formative years in Trumbull Connecticut, and as a musician, moved back to Bridgeport. Having come from a family who eagerly invited any and all types of music into their lives , the musical passion that Nevard possesses, came forth in her words "before I could walk".

Nevard's main instrument is the piano. She plays the guitar, and has said that she is able to play the blues harp, but don't expect Little Walter. She became a professional musician, band leader, and songwriter when quite young...in the mid Seventies, and continued to make her living at this craft for about twenty five years. Nevard was on the Island label for a time, but we were told "Naah. These things often don't end well." The musician's life contained a large amount of travel. The author was touring when many pioneers of America'a music were sill alive, and playing in many of the same places. Those she knew and learned from included Don Covay, Willie Dixon, Pinetop Perkins, Cub Koda, Muddy Waters, and Terry Southern (a writer, not a musician). The only other well known musicians allowed to be named here that Nevard

knew were John Lennon and Levon Helm. There are a few others inside, but most of them, have "changed" names within the book. This is all that we could get out of her.

*This book is dedicated to four people who were
ablaze with a constant, almost blinding shimmer,
and an unending hunger for life.*

*They walked with arms wide open, encouraging and
PUSHING the aspirations of those who needed it,
as often as they were able.
They willingly shouldered the troubles of others,
over their own.*

*Margo Wallace Tellalian
Judge Aram Hagop Tellalian Jr.
Jeremy John Dennis
Jeff Ross Hyman*

CONTENTS

PREFACE

JEREMY JOHN DENNIS
19 August 1952 – 20 September 2015

This book was finished a long time ago. I know this, because the manuscript was registered with WGAE (Writers Guild of America East) on November 11, 2009. So why is it being finally published now? This is the reason....

After the soul crushing loss of Jeff, I truly did not think I'd be able to stand up again, or to function in any productive way. He had lovingly made me promise that I would not be alone. I had known someone for quite a while, who finally moved into my home. Thinking this was a kind person, I was ignorant of the cost that would be incurred. I will NOT waste life's moments...or YOUR time, with any kind of detailed explanation. FINI.

My parents left this earth during that time (only a couple of years before this book was written) within just a few months of each other, and left a hole as enormous as the sky above.

After this I did not believe that I would WANT to be involved with anyone again. And yet...very soon after November of 2009, an unlikely happening occurred. It shocked my knickers off.

I UNIMAGINABLY met an extraordinarily miraculous human. Jeremy John Dennis captured the heart of my paranoiac and damaged soul. Do you believe someone like me would often meet someone that they'd FIT with? No siree. The chances of that were more than slim. Even more unbelievable was THIS. He lived 5000 miles away from me. He lived across the pond, in West Yorkshire, England, and resided in a small and pretty town...Churwell...in Morley. Jeremy had never been outside of the UK, and yet, his knowledge of an unthinkable amount of things was staggeringly inspiring. This was someone that I could talk MUSIC with. I can remember being in the car with him...me driving and humming tunes. He would suddenly lean over and yell "That's GREAT! Mendelssohn. Violin concerto in E minor, Second movement." Ten minutes later, he would declare "Hoagy Carmichael! 'Rockin' Chair'! The best version of this song was done by Satchmo, ummm, 1929!" And a little while would have passed before he'd come out with…"'Bang Bang You're DEAD'! Dirty Pretty Things. Carl Barat's band. Oh you know…after the Libertines… uhh, was it '97?" Lord, I still can't get my brain around it. Jeremy knew every star and constellation in the sky, and almost every piece of literature EVER written. I think I caught HIS heart, when I asked him if he liked Saki. He knew more American history than we could possibly know here—the name of every single general and battle in the Revolutionary and Civil Wars.

Jeremy had a degree in Architectural Interior Design. He was a supremely gifted fine artist—and adorably funny. Here's a sample of something he'd dashed off to me:

Darling girl …….you sent your symphony unfinished…………you'll get no sympathy from me………finished…..nor swedish………nor denmarkian……….I'll mark you down again…..if you 'do it to me one more time'…………again. ah yes…….James Joyce never wrote a truer word…or several….as I misrecall

Often I am accused of wearing a cowboy hat in the big city…..it is in fact …an Australian bush hat…quite incongruous perhaps …..though lacking corks a'dangling from the brim to deter flies…………. it was made in China…as was my 'Fender' …my coffee table…..the 'baby' talcum powder I put in my socks…..and most probably me………an orientally, digitised doppelganger of Jeremy…….mass produced and packaged in that infernal clear plastic that requires a degree in physics to open without destroying the contents!

I digress….filthy beast, ain't I? Do you….digress….or just plain finesse…..my fine miss…..not fine mess….I prefer a nice mess…….or a nice kettle of fish as dear old Ollie once said…….where is he now I wonder? Playing a purgatorial bunker shot to the unreachable manicured green of eternal bliss? I do hope not……….for myself….I am content to know that I will return to that from which I came….stardust…my love…you and I…and all this whole shebang shall……..when I gaze 'heavenward' and know that on a time….you have looked upon those selfsame twinklers…..yes…I am content….except that you live so much farther south and can look upon those wonders denied to me…you beast! Canopus….Alpha Centauri…and its Omega….Clouds of Magellan………the Southern Cross……..how jolly dare you…………my love…..my serendipity…………..

Did not Mr. Mailer say….'Norman is an Island'? A lesson for all of us to learn…and never remember…to forget?

xxxxxxxxxxxx Jeremy John Donne it one more time xxxxxxxxxxxxxxxx

I may have been living in a hellish place for a long time, but Jeremy was in the same boat. A sinking one at that. He took care of his mamma during her last days, and when she died, he was left with the responsibility of taking care of his dear sister, who is disabled. He had been doing this for almost fifteen years…when he met me. He took on freelance art work-for-hire jobs, but he could only go up the street to the Churwell Club for short periods of time…and run to the grocery store, when needed. The last time I was there was shortly after Jeremy was gone. Got my bum over there, to have an evening celebration of Jeremy's life. I miss them. They

gathered me in their warm loving arms. Most likely would have off'd myself if they hadn't been there.

Jeremy became ill during the last part of his long term of care giving, and when he went to the doctor, he was informed of THIS. "Jeremy, you're still dedicating your life to the care of your sister, aren't you? Do you realize that life is passing you by at an alarming rate? You haven't had a LIFE, Jeremy. You need to find a place that your sister will be comfortable in, and STOP this."

Jeremy began searching for a situation for his beloved sister, and she began to spend weekends away, here and there. It was tough. When we met, he was beginning this process, and we ultimately spent hours on the phone, every evening for about a year, and during this time, we realized we needed to be together. A YEAR was spent dealing with immigration and the process of getting him over here. I won't make you all live through those mind-boggling details. Finally, we got his bum over, and we were married May 15, 2012. It was a date that happened to fit our timeline…until we realized, it was exactly the same date that my Mamma and Daddy were wed. We THEN spent MORE time working on obtaining permanent residency for him. The herculean effort was more than worth it. And for only the second time in my life, I was with someone I loved without measure. Someone who gave a damn about me. The truly bizarre truth of this union was that Jeremy's very nature, brilliance, and outlook was VERY much like Jeff's. I can honestly say I loved Jeremy even more... maybe because the time that Jeff and I had was BEYOND fleeting. Although I was seeing Jeff for about five years, the time we were able to BE together only added up to MONTHS. Perhaps a year.

Right here is where life becomes a shattering nightmare. Jeremy and I were together LESS than a year, when he was diagnosed with a very aggressive cancer. It was as if a bomb had been dropped. We spent the next two and a half years agonizingly attempting to lengthen his life. He showed the same courage, continued kindness and joy that Jeff AND my daddy had shown during THEIR protracted struggles with equally horrible illnesses. All three never gave up. Jeremy endured an enormous and dangerous operation, and before that went through a long and tortuous term of radiation, and at the same time chemotherapy. My poor darling…being from a country where folks don't have much choice in the kind of treatment they will receive, he needed for ME to go to battle for him and search out treatments. Jeff wouldn't let me SEE him when he became very ill—but Jeremy had no choice. He valiantly tried to hide his agony from me.

Eventually, the beast of a disease metastasized. We travelled to Long Beach, California, for another surgery, and to see Dr. Robert Nagourney, the pioneer of a platform in which he can assay the cancer cells. Tissue was brought to him directly from the operating room, and he tested it with a huge amount of combined chemicals. Doing so, allows him to determine what would affect those cancer cells, and what would not TOUCH them. Groundbreaking. Fortunately, he found a combination that would have an effect on the cells that were taking Jeremy's life. Strangely, the Doc and I grew up in the same town. As a kid, I had no inkling that he would grow up to be the genius he is NOW. Bless him. Unfortunately, sweet Jeremy was pretty darn beat up by the time we returned home, and this treatment began. It was WORKING, though. PET scans clearly showed that areas of cancer disappeared, and a couple of tumors shrank by half. My baby became weaker and weaker though. He battled like HELL, but finally ended up in the hospital in September 2015. When it became clear he was declining in a fast way, I needed to fight like the devil, to get him home. I did NOT want my love to have to take his last breath in that damm hospital, and so home he came. It almost killed ME to see that vibrant man looking as if he had emerged from Auschwitz, and his beautiful mass of hair had finally fallen out. Jeremy did not leave this world in a peaceful way. He did not go gently into the night, but he died in my arms…in our bed.

Jeremy John Dennis was a wondrous man; a beautiful man. His voice…both speaking and singing, was glorious, and he sang to me often. Everywhere we went, people thought he was a rock star, which annoyed him — but was enormously fun for me. He loved this country and wanted to see every bit of it. The Grand Canyon, ohh, and he wanted to stand at the foot of the Lincoln Memorial and to read aloud the speech he thought was poetry. I am honored that he loved me. Loved me, and never failed to stand up for me, LOUDLY, whenever he thought I wasn't being treated right. He had stood up to bullies his entire life when he saw them terrorizing people, and didn't care if the crap was beaten out of him. DID NOT CARE. Jeremy was a scrapper. Just like Jeff, just like my daddy. Right must be defended, no matter the personal cost.

Thankfully, there are some things Jeremy was able to experience while he was here. He was able to see an earth-shaking rocket launch, up CLOSE at NASA. God, he loved it. He and I wandered out to the beach one night in June 2012, and with red gels over our flashlights, we searched for a sea turtle dropping her eggs, and finally we spied a huge thing slowly lumbering out of the ocean. It was the most endangered of all—a leatherback turtle, who was as large as a bus. She was over six feet long, and weighed at LEAST a thousand pounds. A shy and prehistoric creature, she let us lie right next to her head, about an inch from our own heads, and we'd stand behind her as well and watch her make her egg-laying nest and drop them all. We then breathlessly watched as she covered every single spot she had touched, and we saw the exhausted beauty slowly make her way back to the sea. We swore she waved goodbye. It was something I never thought I'd see in my lifetime, and Jeremy had never dreamed of.

We finally went on a little honeymoon. It was right after we discovered that the cancer was spreading. I asked, "Honey, where would you like to visit?" And he surprisingly told me…New York City. My first thought was…oh no, the hustle and bustle…would he be able to handle it? But I soon realized, when visiting, we'd never be five minutes away from a cab. And that town has a buzz that no other city in the WORLD has. I booked us into the Waldorf, and when we arrived, darling Jeremy was instantly plunged into a Deco wonderland. One which he loved and I didn't care how costly it was. I didn't give a darn if I ate Ramen noodles for the rest of my life.

About four months after Jeremy went, our darling Asian Leopard Lally died too. She was put to sleep in the same bed that Jeremy had died in. She was my baby…until Jeremy showed up, and then she was HIS. Just as she had taken care of my father during his last days, she cared for Jeremy. I unbelievably saw her lift crunchy food from her food bowl, enter the bedroom, jump on the bed, and deposit the food on Jeremy's chest. *If I feed him, he will be ok, yes?* She would not leave him. I think she died of grief. Thank goodness Jeremy didn't have to witness it. It would have shattered him.

Would you like to know how open-hearted that man was? When we arrived at the hotel in New York, he informed me, "I'm tired, sweetpea…would you lie down with me for a while? I need to hold you, and rest a bit. And after I regain some strength, I'd like to go to see Jeff's street. The one NAMED for him. Can we do that?"

"Sure, baby. Off to the Bowery we'll go." We did just that, and Jeremy took photos. That sign…being the most stolen one ever, was unthinkably high up. I viewed the touching sight of Jeremy craning his neck, and taking pictures. All I could manage to do was to RUN to him, hug him as hard as I possibly could, and cry. I was shocked. This man was so loving, he was willing to painfully venture forth …so that he could take pictures of his wife's dead boyfriend. Lord, he was beautiful. It was the kind of selfless act, he was in fact KNOWN for. Oh HELL…I didn't deserve him.

Merely MONTHS after Jeremy left this earth, his niece…Emily, became ill. Soon it was discovered….SHE had an aggressive cancer. She died not that darn long after. She was only nineteen years old. Her daddy, my brother-in-law, Huw, literally saved my life after Jeremy went. He rushed over here from the UK, and after he returned home, has called me almost every single night since.

Too much loss. Too much. I still sob daily over the loss of Jeremy, and it often makes me cry for Jeff as well…and Emily.

I've been almost a recluse since Jeremy died.

The only thing that is keeping me alive is this book and the foundations it will help support. My deepest desire, my most fervent hope, is that this book will be able to give enough to make a difference, and to save lives. All of the proceeds, NOT just the net proceeds, will go to two places. It will go to the Lymphoma Research Foundation, in honor of Joey Ramone, and to The Robert Nagourney Institute,in honor of Jeremy John Dennis. His lab is called Rational Therapeutics. His momentous and cutting edge contribution to the world of medicine DOES work. It was working for Jeremy, and it may have saved Jeff. His important services are not covered by medical insurance. He is considered to be "Alternative." Are they KIDDING? To me, marching into the teepee and drumming would be an alternative therapy. NOT what Robert Nagourney is doing. It is so very important. WE paid for the assaying of Jeremy's cancer, but that was a drop in the bucket compared to payment for the chemo afterward. Jeremy's therapy would have cost twenty-seven grand. Who ponied up to PAY for it? It was a pharmaceutical company.

I'd like you all to know…it was more than difficult to write about Jeff. I was more than hesitant. I am very protective of him, and of the love we shared. I was even MORE than hesitant to name him—but finally realized he would WANT that, if it would help those who are suffering, and for those who cannot afford the so-called "alternative" yet scientifically COR-RECT services. I AM POSITIVE OF THIS. I was told in no uncertain terms, that the Ramones are now indeed true legends, who in fact inspired an entire generation…and beyond, and FED their musical hunger.

I miss Jeremy, with an ache that will not abate. Lord, he used to DANCE for me. He'd do it almost every single day. Just to hear me giggle. Just to light up my face. Crazy dancing. Romping, glimmering dancing. He always left precious parts of himself scattered about, so that I could gather it all up and knit a beautiful chain to wrap myself in. Wish my mamma and daddy could have met him. Wish I could have met his.

Here is my public Birthday wish to Jeremy, and his answer…exactly one month before he was gone.

"HAPPY BIRTHDAY, MY PRECIOUS HUSBAND. Jeremy John Dennis, you are my raison d'être. you are my courage, when I have not a shred of it. you are my muse, when I'm lacking anything resembling musings. you are my laughter, each and every day. you help me immeasurably, when I am unable to help myself. I LOVE YOU, JEREMY, JAAARY, JAMIE….whatever your name is…I'm lucky you are mine. xoxoxo, your oh-so unworthy wife… Vardzie, Nevard. Jeremy's answer…

Shared this from my wife's site…a week late, but never mind, she's nat-urally a bit peeved because I do not allow automatic postings on my page without vetting them first, for security reasons. Anyway, late or no, I thank you from the deepest depths of my heart, my darling Nevard, still wonder-ing why you took up with an irascible git who ain't fit to lick your boots, although it's an occupation I have taken to with some relish, especially when you spill chocolate sauce and ice cream on them now and then, or sometimes onion gravy or perhaps parsley sauce to which I'm rather parslial…I love you, my little sweet pea, and SHALL do forever, or maybe longer than that…so be prepared, Mrs. Dennit.

(HIS PERMANENT RESIDENCY CARD
ARRIVED TWO DAYS AFTER HE LEFT
THIS EARTH.)

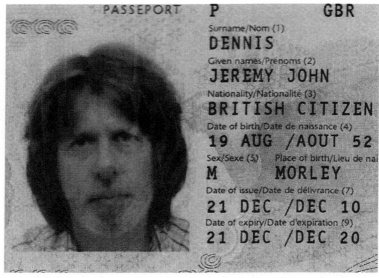

(Up above is my favorite photo… Jeremy's passport)

(Our wedding)

INTRODUCTION

"I don't want anyone to admire
my pants in a museum."
—Fredric Chopin

I've been told…I should introduce myself here. OKEY DOKEY. Hi. My name is Nevard Wallace Tellalian. half Scottish, and half Armenian. I made my living as a musician for many many years. Music has lived in every cell of my being, since I was a toddler. I feel that it was a gift to be able to work at something I had an undying love for. I also feel lucky to have been plying my trade during a time when most of the pioneers of our nation's home-grown music, were still living and playing. Many of them were shucking about on the same circuit that I was rumbling in. I was luckily able to meet and become close to many of them. They were living road maps. I loved them, but most are not with us anymore. It seemed very strange to know many of my male heroes, but to never meet any of the females that I revered. WHY? The reason is… during those years, they would not allow another female to be on the same bill with them. It was written into their contracts. Damn. At least I was able to know some of our more modern musical women. I name some of the musicians that I knew, admired and learned from in this book….but not all that many. For some reason, it feels unseemly to be dropping names with wild abandon. Don't dig it when I SEE it, and didn't want to do it myself. If you find yourself unduly interested in knowing those names, you may contact me…and I'll fork them over to you. This is all that I can promise. AND ON WE GO…

I have written mostly about my experiences in the world of music, and the knowledge I gleaned from my own mistakes, from other musicians who inspired me, and some assorted and sundry musings. Some of these experiences were ill begotten or ridiculous and have been included, in spite of my utter humiliation, as fodder for your amusement. You'll thank me later.

As I take a gander at what I've written in this book, I realize there is a central stream about passion that runs through it all.

One might think because I am from the world of Rock & Roll, and music in general, this would be the reason. That is of course ONE of the reasons. Musicians have a well-earned reputation for randy behavior, and you'd be right in assuming that much noodling goes on in these quarters.

What might be shocking to you, and what believe me is staggeringly shameful for me is the fact that MY life was not brimming over with a nice large number of rompings and fun escapades in this direction. NOT for the lack of want, that's for darn sure, but I was hardly ever SINGLE when I was on the road. Usually there was some idiot back home. There were only a few short windows of opportunity for me to indulge, and you'd think I'd have made hay whilst the proverbial sun was shining.

I attempted to make up for lost time during those all too brief periods, but the experiences I had turned out for the most part to be either yawningly boring, or the stuff that film comedies are made of.

The upshot being, in rock & roll circles I'd be almost considered a virgin. And an embarrassment to my peers…even my female peers, who for the most part don't end up with the big numbers of exploits the boys do. Not a good poster girl here for rock & roll. OK, you can stop laughing now.

I can remember being at the entrance of a rather large party, and next to me stood a very well- known girl in the biz, and let me add….she is a darling woman.

Well, I heard her proclaim, "Isn't it funny when you're somewhere and realize you've screwed every single guy in the room?"

MY dumb answer to this was, "Yeah, I know what you mean. It WOULD be kinda awkward to have my ex-boyfriend and boyfriend in one room together."

"No Nevard, I mean THIS room," she said.

WHAT? I looked around the party room, and there must have been at least fifty guys in there. At LEAST. For the love of Pete! You just GO, girl! How'd you MANAGE that? DAMMM. I'm just pitiful, I am. Oh the shame. Is there an orgy going on in town tonight? Maybe I can catch UP.

But I'm afraid there's a lack of actual good stuff to be had, and the girl at the door of the party probably HAD to sleep with at least twenty before she ran into something worth writing home about. I suppose I just didn't have that patience.

> **Frequent impropriety is a by-product of the rapture and the power without which there would BE no GREAT ART.**

I'm not exactly the font of all fonts of wisdom, or the veritable guru of good music, but I've managed to absorb SOMETHING along the way, and I was told to write it. I was lucky to have four people in my life who taught me about love, courage, and giving…my father, mother, and the two men I loved. All four were illuminated with a light that could not be dimmed. None of them will ever be forgotten by those who came in contact with them, and rightly so. They were inspiring, and their lessons are worth learning.

Many artists (or anyone, for that matter) don't know what REALLY feeds the thirst for knowledge, the creative yearning, and an aptitude for kindness. I hope some part of what I have written might help you along that road of discovery.

VARDZIE ON THE ROAD, OR HOW DO I SURVIVE THESE CLUBS?

Groping War Stories From An Unprepared Girl

The particular tales in this section aren't about the music industry or biz per se, but about some of the real parts of day-to-day, week-to-week survival of a band working on the road, and (chiefly) in the club circuit.

I could tell you of the thousand or so truly splendid and uplifting nights and days that are part of touring, but do you really want to hear how many times people have wept at some ballad I poured out to them? Standing ovations? Enormous venues?

No. You don't. I may relate one if it contains some wacky element, but things of that nature are of interest only to me and the musicians I shared the stage with.

Do you want to hear what makes musicians really, REALLY happy besides playing and creating?

Yes, of course, the admiration and respect of our peers, and our audiences, but MORE satisfying is even a smidgeon of respect from our elders. I can tell you that Count Basie dug me, as did McKinley Morganfield, and Mr. Bassology himself...

I can regale you with the story of the sublime guy who penned "I Stole Some Love" and wrote me a song. Would y'all be in any way interested in these things? I very much doubt it.

I may include SOME info like that, because these are folks I admire, and LEARNED from, and **that** learning is the incalculable gift that gives a musician's life color, but most of these details wouldn't thrill anyone but me. OK...how many TIMES have you read this explanation now? Not many readers would even recognize these artists. Oh, the Count maybe you've heard of, and maybe you'd get something out of my teachings from him. (Do YOU want to know why Freddie Green was never miked? I didn't think so.)

Chances are, only another musician or a serious aficionado of music would recognize any of the other artists I mentioned. They are the only readers who would have any desire to hear that kind of nattering. I don't think there are many lifetime members of the "can't get enough of those musical details" club, so that most likely leaves about five of us who'd want to know.

During the writing of this, I wrote REAMS of music wanderings that are utterly RIVETING to me, but when I read them to friends (even some musician friends), I get a patient but exasperated "What the heck you talkin' 'bout, Vardz? Who's Eddie Bo, and why do I care if he just died, and why are you interested in these things?"

I WILL, however, plug the living HELL out of some of the superb talents I've known. As many as I can fit in, darnit. It would take SIX books to let you in on all of these wonders of nature. Some are still with us, and you'll appreciate their work if you're willing to take the time to look. Unbeknownst to many, these folks have left indelible marks. Again...they are not household names. They SHOULD be, but oh geez...I'm going to go ahead and repeat it again. There is even a large amount of MUSICIANS who respond with blank stares when I speak of them. Can't get my brain around THAT.

Some of the "road" memories I have are pretty darned funny, and some are downright horrid and disheartening. The written note gropes, and other glaring acts of impropriety show a complete disregard for etiquette (boy, that's putting it politely) and I think are experienced mostly by female musicians.

Much of this stuff I eventually became so inured to after a while I wouldn't even repeat it to the band. I have included them, much as I've included a lot of stories, for your entertainment. These are the stories with which I've been regaling mostly my girlfriends for years, who thought my life was one hedonistic walk in the Rock park.

I usually fork them over when they're feeling down and out: "Oh, you think THAT'S bad, huh? Check THIS out, girlfriend."

They are generally lulled into supposing their lives are darned NICE compared to my unbelievable disasters, and they are able to bathe in a relieved feeling of "well...at least I don't have Vardzie's shoddy existence."

So happy to be of help. What do these stories mean to another musician? Routine stuff, baby.

In truth, (except for the physical conditions of clubs in the circuit, and road travel) these distasteful stories are NOT typical…well, apart from the ladies' room debacles.

Most of the time, I have been treated with the utmost respect, and gratefully, at least a degree of regard. Thank goodness, plenty of people DO get me. If the following obnoxious behavior on the part of fans, and non-fans, were more of an every single night thing, I don't know if I would have been able to withstand it.

You need to understand, there has never been exactly a dearth of clubs/venues, what have you, that are geared up to be "musician friendly" and known to the kind of clientele who are hungry for good and different live music.

The really great club scene kind of dried up a while ago, but who knows, maybe it will come back. * (And it HAS come back in some ways…since 2009.)

It's always been a challenge, of course, if you're not playing what is at that moment considered "popular," and I NEVER was. I always thought the whole "top 40" thing started to be a glaringly bad example of the lamentable takeover of art as primarily vendibles. It commenced its headfirst downhill fall at an alarming rate more than ten years before I even hit a stage.

Take a look at the archives of what was on the radio in say, 1964 compared to what was happening when I got in there pitching full time, in the late seventies.

When I started out, the disco era was winding down but still THERE, and after that, large numbers of men in cowboy hats were to be seen in Brooklyn (not an appetizing picture), which was shortly followed by the era of "haircut" bands, and bands who couldn't even follow a basic 1- 4 -5; whose idea of a bass line was just the **one** note there, thank you very much. I DO enjoy primal and raw music, but not when performed by folks who are more impressed with how cool they're looking than what music they are producing.

I do think I've said this before. Plenty of folks had no idea what my band was playing, or why we were playing it. The majority thought we did all originals, which was not the truth. Being the so-called bandleader, I took most of the flack. Didn't usually bother me much, and certainly didn't stop me. My bands didn't find the humor or fun in this as much as I did. Just kept doing it despite everything. For more than twenty years. Had to. I particularly liked playing places that hadn't heard us. Loved being a surprise for people. It kept everything kind of new.

The clubs happily hopped on the six-or-seven-bands-a-night bandwagon at the local scene maker's clubs on weekends, thereby sending club owners a nice loud message. Why should I PAY for a band, when I have these eejit college kids willing to play for nothing? They'll be stockbrokers in a few years.

"Let's see now…if each band brings in just thirty or so of their college chums, then I'll be raking it in at the bar. On the off days, oh YEAHH, let's throw in the DJ's."

This was decidedly a part of the death knell of the "great club" years, and to not put all the blame on the club owners, insurance became astronomically expensive for them…not to mention the growing amounts of big donations to ASCAP.

Even in the heyday of great clubs though, to fill up the calendar, you couldn't just stick to the places you'd be drawing fans, and/or places that are tailored to showcasing the kind of music you bring to the table.

Most musicians need to take jobs that put them in potentially non-friendly atmospheres in order to stay in business. These gigs are many and varied and sometimes a true trial by fire, but a surprising number turn out to be more than bewilderingly peachy.

> *"To escape criticism, do nothing, say nothing, be nothing."*
> *—Elbert Hubbard*

How then did I make a living doing what people thought was an eclectic blend (**they** thought it was indecipherable, I DIDN'T) of music that most people have never heard?

Sheer determination, a dollop of dumb bravado (I betcha they'll love this—who wouldn't?), and the desire to share all the good stuff with audiences was a big help.

A big dose of stubbornness (follow me, I'll MAKE you like it), some ornery head butting, and a shot of imprudent nonsense I always thought was fun to do on any stage made this life possible.

Honestly, I always had an inextinguishable feeling that I was awfully LUCKY to be able to get away with it at ALL.

Heck, when I could get it past them, I'd throw in a Weil song in German, after a crazy rendering of Wicked Pickett, the *Dragnet* theme, a couple that I or a band mate wrote, and if I had a band that could have done it I would have stuck in "Ruby, My Dear."

THIS kind of "fly by the seat of your pants" touring is what makes things rewarding to me, even spurs me on, being the adventurous soul I am. And if you can love and crave the making of the music in spite of or BECAUSE of these terms, then you have found your true self, my friend.

Not many people get a blessing like that, you know. If this is YOU, then embrace it.

"It is much safer to obey than to rule."
—Thomas à Kempis

If, however, you are squeamish, or don't realize that *everything and anything* will happen along the way, if you collapse from a heckle, loud hatred, rowdy drunks, something thrown at you, perhaps even a punch, or worse—total silence; if you expect only the glory and none of the grit, you're in the wrong place altogether. I'd advise you to run. FAST.

If you're thinking of doing it to become wealthy, or attain "big name" stature, or you just think you look GORGEOUS on a stage, you are STILL in the wrong place. Run your butt off.

If you NEED to do it, no matter how bad it can get, if you can stand proudly in the midst of any unholy mess and still find joy in the making of music, you're NUTS, but you are undoubtedly one of us.

If you think a night you are divinely MESHING with your band, no matter if five or fifty thousand are there to hear it, AND you don't care if it's the largest venue on earth or the Laundromat around the corner, then you are in the RIGHT place.

If you're happy when you're pulling an audience into your musical roller coaster, then you are NOT taking a horribly wrong turn. You just dig in and wring the zest out of this life, darn it,

I'm not going to shut up about this, or about where your heart and passion should be, and where it should be coming from. The subject has been tactfully and politely danced around by many artists, but I think it's time to say it a little more forcefully, and I am not afraid to take a stand.

I fully expect to be criticized by not a few, and if you are offended by this outlook, or think it's misguided, it won't bother me. Know what?

FUCK the real world! I want to ride by my coattails all the WAY into the stratosphere and back. In music, not in reason. Our audiences truly don't deserve the self-imposed reserve we display, instead of the hot fever that is IN us. SCREW 'EM.

I used to think the sort of reactions I'm about to describe were entirely MY fault. I guess an audience sometimes thinks I'm more than crazed. Sometimes, they believe I'll swing any which way, and with anyone.

I've been told that I ask for this type of misunderstanding. My stage presence is considered by many to be MUCH too free spirited and impudent. It's been hammered home to me over the years that my performance contained not a small degree of wild abandon, that I have an unfettered, provocative stance and attitude. I guess it's true.

These things have been said in print, and by club owners, agents, audiences, record people, etc. Sometimes it is meant to be flattering, much of the time, a frowned upon criticism, but I have never thought of myself as some sort of vixen type. I simply don't see myself that way, and most times feel a little clumsy more than anything else.

You'll catch sight of me in this book unattractively repeating, "Did I deserve this?" until finally my feverish brain was put at ease by a friend I trusted. It sure didn't help during the first almost twenty years, for gosh sake.

The oftentimes harsh disapproval and punishment I received, accompanied by shaking of heads, rude come-ons, printed slaps, and sometimes physical violence was horrifying to me, but I was incapable of changing what I am.

"The important thing is not what they think of me,

but what I think of them."
—Queen Elizabeth I

Sometimes the unwanted backlash made me feel like a freak, so I'd make an effort to just stand STILL on stage, with no expression or movement. This more than useless attempt can hold me at bay for about five minutes, and then, try as I might, I'll begin to forget myself.

Hair starts flinging about, shoes might fly off, a leg might go around the mic. stand…I may be HUMPING the mic. stand. I don't know. I don't CARE. Sorry, but that's what mic. stands are for. A mic. stand is NOT a place to park your drink holder. YOU, know who you are…dammit.

I'm not aware of a good half of the things I do on stage, and I have always refused to look at any recordings of myself. Don't want to see it.

I can give you an example of a small stage action that's always misinterpreted. During instrument solos, if I don't have a guitar strapped on, I'll sometimes get behind a band mate and hold them close up against me. I like to hear the music coming through them. Their breathing, their heartbeats.

THEY know what I 'm doing, but I can't tell you how many people think I'm copping myself a big old feel up there. Yup, I'm just having my way with my poor band members.

I used to have a boyfriend that would say before I'd head out on a road trip:

"Can't you stop this constant traveling?"

"Uhhh…no, I can't. It's my job."

"I don't like people looking at you like that."

At first I'd respond, "Oh, OK. I understand, but what can I do? It's glued into the performing musician's handbook. How can I stop them from looking at me? Should we blindfold them?"

And he'd always tell me, "You're too provocative. I don't know, you just walk in a room, and it oozes out of you."

WHAT? Not the provocative thing again. And this is a friend?

"Are you talking about on stage, or in real life? It's a parallel universe, you know. I don't like the sound of that oozing thing. Do I seem combative?"

"I'm talking about both."

I didn't know what to say at the time. He made me feel as though I was WRONG…entirely wrong.

I'd know what to say NOW. And by the way, he had a band of his OWN. So why then did he not understand me?

After years of guilt, here's what I believe to the bottom of my boots, and what I'm telling YOU:

ART IS MEANT TO PROVOKE. NOT TO STUN. We don't want to just lead them into the club like the Pied Piper. We'd much rather savagely raise their butts into the air with us, so they will FLY.

If there are some who dislike me, OR the way I sound, or do not understand what I'm doing, and find me more than disturbing, then I'M DOING MY JOB SUPREMELY. Here's what else I should have told that fella, or anyone else who criticized my supposed "irreverence" OR inappropriate BOLDNESS.

I AM being reverent, darn it—this is a living, breathing art…not a eulogy.

I sometimes make chaos on a stage. I can't help it. It's the way I do it.

I am having FUN. I do for an audience what I like done for me.

I go without cowardice and unflinchingly where the music takes me.

And if some of that contains the dynamics (I said DYNAMICS, darn it …LEARN IT) of a BUILDING PRURIENCE, then THIS is the inherent outpouring of that which we are performing for you. The music WILL build, and the performance WILL build…as it SHOULD.

NONE of us are ASKING for anything, except for a hearty "Thanks for the sharing of your souls, your talent, your never-ending enthusiasm and study of your art, and Thank You for entertaining us this evening." AMEN

I am more than aware that the world of music is still in many ways like any other business—ruled by the "boys club." Don't much care. There still exists a double standard, just as my daddy warned me years ago. He was afraid it would hurt me. Sometimes it does, but it's just a part of the life I chose, and to be taken with as much graciousness and humor as I can muster. It doesn't make me bitter. There will always be sympathetic people around to ease the way. I'd like to inform any female who would like to perform music in public: you should expect a certain degree of this, unless you avoid places that are rife with this sort of behavior. And if you're going to do it for a living, I don't quite know HOW you'll manage that.

MY actions on stage, believe me, are that of a NUN compared to many. Certainly compared to the men folk in my line of work. But put a girl on stage at a frat boy/jock-laden college campus thing, or a redneck sort of place with a little too much testosterone filling the air, and it becomes a wolf pack. I'll tell you later about the nice riot I was accused of starting at a college. In a perverse way, I take great pride in that little bit of auditorium damage.

Look, good musicians tailor their performance and what songs they'll do by what they are feeling from the audience. Every time and place is different. A female performer can attempt to be EXTRA careful in likely combustible situations. When faced with a crowd like that, I always try to perform as if I'm singing in my mamma's old Baptist church, for goodness sake.

It doesn't much matter. Often, you simply can't escape the great grimy group grope of the WOLF PACK.

And I'm also not afraid to say…much of what passes for heaven sent libidinous music and actions these days does not come from the passion of music, but from the wallet.

It's not quite as bad as it used to be in the '80s when I was touring at an inhuman pace, but rough places will always be rough places, whether you're a guy or a girl.

PLEASE. ATTENTION, MES COPAINS! I do NOT mean to sound as though guys don't get THEIR share of lumps; of course they do. It's just of a different nature. A gaggle of out of control drunken guys can be just as brutal on a male performer. "Waddya lookin' at, ya music Fag?" Sometimes they got lumps because of ME, much to my horror and chagrin.

I'm giving it to you from a woman's perspective, because I happen to be one, and here we go…

Sometimes, a dressing room can in SOME ways protect a band from the willy-nilly wanderings of drunken fools. Not always though. Nope. In they will come. Even If you have someone posted at the door. And much to my band's dismay, there would always be people coming in to steal beer from the club-given cooler or eat the food off the platter (which could have flies hovering over it) provided for you that evening, if it's that kind of club.

Your dressing room can be an actual room, a kitchen, a curtained off area, a storage room, or a hallway. Lord have mercy, the dressing rooms probably deserve an entire chapter unto themselves.

Most are not charming places. You might be surprised to know, some of the most prestigious clubs have dressing areas a self-respecting rat wouldn't step foot in.

Some have none. Most contain graffiti that still makes me cringe, even after years and years of viewing, but some of it can be SMART, clever, and endlessly engrossing. One of my favorite dressing room scrawlings is "I'd give my right arm to be ambidextrous." There are usually plenty of musician jokes to be read on those walls. COUNTLESS. Wish I'd written them down. Oh boy…there's one about a musician who is unfathomably popular with the general public. Why can't I fathom his popularity? Because every musician knows he's a big load of embarrassment to the WORLD of music. The joke?

"Tootsie has made a recording of well-known jazz masterpieces. He's called it *Round About Mid-Morning*, and one of the best cuts ON there is "Straight, No Changes." If you're a musician you'll be rolling. Big apologies to everyone else that read it and thought, "WHAAAAT?"

The drawings in these dressing rooms can be impressively executed and artistically brilliant—but many would draw a reaction from you not unlike the feeling you'd get in your tummy if you'd discovered at this year's Thanksgiving table that your favorite Uncle Elvin is a child molester.

You become fairly accustomed (if not numbed) to these conditions early in your road career.

And if you can't, you've got absolutely no business being there.

The smell alone in some of these places can be pungent enough to knock out the faint of heart. I mean almost kick your ASS across the room. Sometimes I'd find myself wondering…*just how many guys have peed and barfed in every corner of this place?*

The conditions of the bathrooms, well, let's just politely say if you're worried about your shoes, don't step in there, toots. Your only option was to laugh uproariously. Believe me…you don't want the details.

I've been discussing these things for hours lately with my musician friend Claude (Claudia Bell). She's a great bass player. Funny, we've known each other for eons, but we never really had a chance to discuss this. Turns out, she's had EXACTLY the same sort of experiences as I. Good GOD, I wish we'd been able to hook up and yak about our "road rat" stories years ago. It would have eased much of my anxiety, and I'd be willing to bet, it would have done the same for her. I didn't KNOW many other women back then who were shucking around the same circuit, except Suzy (Stormin' Norman and Suzy), and she disappeared for a while there. By the way Normy, I can't thank you enough for being a mentor. You took me under your wings, and opened my eyes. WIDE.

Tons of places have no bathrooms near the dressing area, so one is forced to use the public facilities. That in itself is not a BAD thing, but it can present another unattractive can of worms. Lamentably, you are then plopped in the middle of the audience in a place you don't want to be meeting them.

You'd better get on your knees NOW, and pray they didn't dislike you too much, or LOVE you too much. They regularly have NO problem with marching right up to you, or opening the stall door that hasn't had the ability to properly close since the late '50s (if there ARE any stall doors) and proudly declare:

"You didn't play NUTHIN' I know. You SUCK. I like that drummer of yers though. He wanna go home with me?"

(I don't know, but I'm sharing a room with him tonight and frankly I'm going to MAKE him, because he's got a cold, and one more night of that snoring is going to send me over the edge. I might smother him with a pillow tonight.)

"Please, darling, by all means go out there and grab that drummer. Isn't he fabulous? You go get him, honey."

Invariably this species of club going MESS will be passed out before I have a chance to shove my drummer in her direction.

Even worse than those who have no use for you at all, can frequently be the "Wow man, you're GREAT" people. I'm talking about a demeanor that surpasses the usual drunk who will natter on till you almost tip over and hit the floor with sheer boredom.

You always TRY to be polite, but sometimes it's not possible. I'm pretty sure my band mates never received THESE kinds of welcoming maneuvers. They would have ended up quivering in the boy bus if they had. They would have assumed a permanent fetal position in a dark corner.

Women are by nature more physical with each other than men, so a hug, and/or a kiss is nothing that makes me feel uncomfortable. The Tellalians HAVE no personal space. I enjoy contact with people.

Sometimes though, the hug would about squeeze the life out of me, or a congenially proffered kiss could be more like slobber, if said slobbered up gal has imbibed more than her delicate system can handle.

The most precarious scenarios in the bathrooms (for ME anyway) are some drunk OR sober girls. Members of this special friendly tribe will recurrently hand out an encouraging, ever-so-polite compliment and then lean right over to smooch at me.

Without fail, I am receptive to an affectionate smooch from males or females, no matter what their sexual leanings may be. What I DO have a problem with, most especially when stupid me never seems to see it coming, are the countless times I will cheerfully pucker up and proffer up my kisser, and then…

Ahh, to have the sudden surprise (why am I always so darned surprised?) of an unmistakable tongue, and a hand or two (sometimes FOUR if their helpful friend is standing by) straying into places you definitely don't want them straying into. FINE if it's a male, and I'm interested in him physically.

What does one do in these situations? Well, you've got to hastily disengage from them somehow—NOT always an easy task if they are determined pursuers of some sugar—and thank them profusely for the kind thought.

"Wow, girl, thanks so much for thinking of me! Really, I'm awfully flattered. The problem is I seem to be addicted to the male parts. Yes, I KNOW, wrong decision there, huh? I'm sorry, just the guy fun parts for me. DARN, if I were gay, YOU would be IT for me. Yes, ma'am. Really…you're stunning, but no, thank you. Thanks for asking though."

And then you've got to run like the devil. If you don't let them down easy, some of them have no problem SMACKING you. I'm not kidding, it's happened to me. There are some tough people out there.

Are you foolishly thinking I shouldn't have let them NEAR me, thereby circumventing the unwanted slobbering or grabbing? No such luck. They'll get you anyway.

Now, if someone is NOT aiming for the unwanted groping, and feels spurned in any way, she can spiral into an unduly insulted and nasty frame of mind.

"HEY, I'm just trying to compliment ya here, girl. What you backin' away for? You too good fer me or sumptin?"

"No, no, just a little gun shy. So sorry."

THEN it can get a special kind of ugly, as they follow you OUT of the bathroom, and into barroom central, baby, whereupon they're more than capable of making a scene worthy of *Who's Afraid of Virginia Woolf?*

It happened so often that, for the longest time, I thought, "Why am I so attractive to gay women? Do I make their gay-dar go off for some reason? Am I gay, and don't know it? What's UP?"

Guess what? When I was talking to Claude the other day, she told me SHE got an equal amount of groping action from women. Is there a sociological study that needs to be done regarding this phenomenon?

I surely have had plenty of gay fans who wouldn't dream of behaving this way. There was a gal pal who seemed to follow us from state to state, and wherever we played, she'd find a chair (even in clubs with no chairs in sight), plant herself right in front of me and SCREAM. She'd scream and scream all night long. Trust me she was a tame one.

There are always memorable fans. Some are memorable in good ways and some in bad. It would take ten books just to describe THEM.

Just off the top of my head, I'm picturing a guy with the Harley insignia tattooed across his entire forehead and dripping down the sides of his face and nose. I can still hear him telling me that he had "inked it" himself.

Good LORD, HOW did he accomplish this? He informed me that he was about to graduate from Nursing school. Exactly who would have HIRED him? HE was a tame one too. I won't even attempt to pass on those who were complete brain shtups.

Truthfully, most people who enjoy your music leave quietly, and you never get to meet or know them. There are those who approach you, who turn out to be dear, dear people and some have become life-long friends. And then there are psycho stalkers, but we'll get to that. Most likely sooner than you'd be comfy with.

I almost forgot the outdoor venues. These can be great fun, unless there's no trailer. Oh, please let there be a trailer. If there ain't, brother, you'll all be dressing in the boy bus (pretty uncomfortable on a ninety-five-degree day), AND you'll be on intimate terms with the porta potties. They're okay for a guy, but I gotta tell you—not so much for a girl. You have to stand on top of the darn thing unless you want to back into the…ohhhh, I'm not even going to describe it.

Let's not think about the muddy conditions. OR the rain. OR the all-too-often ungrounded mic that slams you across the stage in the middle of a song. I'm proud to say, I never missed a note when the shock socked me. THERE'S something to brag about.

If someone were to ask me if I've ever received shock treatment, the answer would be, "Why, yes, I HAVE." I've had enough to keep me out of the dark cellar of depression, where the mushrooms grow, for a lifetime. For free. That's right. FREE fifties-style psycho ward treatments. Like the Ken Kesey play.

Do the sometimes not-so-purty conditions of clubs and other venues sound ugly to you? I've got a fantastic announcement for you.

NO musician escapes this. Male or Female. NO ONE.

Oh, you may get to a level where they put you up more consistently in nicer places (compared to say…three filthy mattresses on a floor, in a room that smells like something's died there not too recently), or you may not have to travel with your band and equipment in the same vehicle as often. The need to load and unload, set up and tear down becomes less and less. That takes some of the grueling part out of constant travel.

But no one escapes the conditions in the clubs. Let me repeat—NO ONE. Sorry, unless you've got your own gazillion-dollar mega "home away from home" vehicle. And most of those folks are not playing these clubs anyway. Or at least not as often as 99.9 percent of us. The rest of us LIVE in these clubs.

Actually…this is hard to believe, but I'm missing it right this minute. Am I INSANE??

I have to tell you, what has always been most alarming (to me anyway) are NOTES passed backstage. They have been an unparalleled addition to my life, and for some unknown reason more upsetting than violent hatred or groping.

It is much easier to WRITE obnoxious come-ons than it is to stand in front of someone, look them in the eye, and let it rip (depending on how stoned they are). So you can imagine what these notes entailed. No, you probably can't.

They were mostly graphic, and about body parts, and what they wanted to do with said body parts. Once in a while I'd find this more than riveting, but most times offensive.

For the love of Pete, I'm a musician, not a stripper. Can you not hear what we are doing up there? Well…the notes were passed on to me. On occasion, they would make me cry. The band couldn't understand this. They wanted their OWN notes.

"Come on, Vardz, you're not taking this stuff seriously, are you? God, you've gotten this enough. Aren't you used to it by now? Why are you letting it GET to you?"

They would always think the note was funny. But I'd tell them, "Don't you get it? I don't want to hear things like this from somebody I'm not IN-TO. Lord knows, I don't HAVE anyone to talk to me like this. Dammit, maybe I won't EVER, but when and if I do I'd most likely burst into FLAMES. So if I ever have a man that's not an IDIOT, all these stupid, insulting, and unwanted notes will be popping inconveniently into my head. Oh fine. Just RUIN my good time."

"Not so good for ya, huh? I'm sorry, Vardzie. I'LL talk to ya like that."

"Oh stop it, you. I've gotta hear enough in the van, coming out of your little potty boy mouths. Good grief. Much obliged for the offer though."

I have an uncomfortable memory. After a show (who knows where), a waitress handed me a mess of folded up bills. "There was a guy here earlier that said he had to leave, but he really liked you and wanted me to give this to you."

I unfolded it and saw the amount. It was five hundred dollars. That was a lot of dough back then, and at any time, a pretty large tip.

Receiving a tip at ALL was an extremely uncommon thing for a musician in those days... unless it was offered in the form of drugs. That would have been a basic everyday occurrence.

To say I was startled beyond belief would be an understatement. I dropped it to the floor like a hot potato, whereupon the band said, "How much is it, Vardz?"

"This is… I don't have the words. It's depraved. It's downright DE-PRAVED. What am I, a hooker? I feel like taking a shower. I ain't touchin' it. YOU all take it."

"Nevard, it's probably his way of saying he LIKES you."

I couldn't deal with it. It felt like it was jammed full of smarmy implications. It may very well have been an innocent display of admiration, but it felt too creepy.

Creepy? Did I say creepy? The big frightening tip paled in comparison to the letters received by agents. All bands must get these, although I haven't checked. I've got to ask around.

More often than not, these letter writers would request a signed eight-by-ten glossy. The letters accompanying the photo demand could range from a ridiculous "Please ask Nevard if she would like to marry me" (very cute coming from an eight-year-old, NOT so cute from a grown-up), to a now and then unsettling "glom on," or obscene missive.

There were a few that belonged to the true "stalking" category.

One of the craziest letters I can recall was a standout. It was written in the teensiest tiniest handwriting I've ever laid eyes on.

"I love Nevard. Please tell Nevard I am thirty-six years old, and I am in college. (OK…WHY?) My college friends (Your WHAT?) and I spend many hours a day devoted to Nevard, (HOURS?) writing letters to TV shows to let them know how great Nevard is, and asking them to book Nevard, so the world will know how great Nevard is. (Your IMAGINARY college friends?) I have been to every Nevard concert in every state. I have driven hundreds and hundreds of miles to see Nevard, blah, blah, blah."

How many times did this person repeat my NAME? The above letter consisted of at least ten pages of essentially the same sort of cloying and frightful drivel. I'm telling you all, I spent the next YEAR looking into crowds and wondering, "Okay, where is the nutter? Does the nutter have an implement of destruction? Is the nutter one of the phone callers threatening to stab me?"

Where did the "stab me" fear come from? Ahh. That came from the newspaper that lamentably printed my ENTIRE name AND the city I lived in. I was in the darn phone book, but not for long, I can tell you.

Just how many Nevard Tellalians do you think there might BE in the Bridgeport, CT phone book? How many in the entire country? The answer to that would be…drum roll (and I'm sure a big surprise)…one. JUST THE ONE. And conveniently, right along with my number, there it was… glaringly sitting there…my address.

This invasion of privacy wouldn't matter so much NOW, as I'm not so active. (ACTIVE? I've been sitting in front of this computer for more than six weeks. By now, I'd welcome a stalker.) But THEN? Holy cow, I was all over the place, almost every day.

I began to reap HUNDREDS of calls from just the one article, running the gamut from "Be my girl, I wanna (whatever) you" all the way to "I wanna KILL you."

One caller was persistent, graphic and violent. His descriptions of the many and varied ways in which he wanted to MURDER me were a tad ANNOYING.

I'm kidding. It was a terrifying experience, and dragged on for such a long time, a detective from the Bridgeport Police Department was eventually assigned to this case. They DID trace the lovely man, and the detective showed up at the threatening guy's door and threatened HIM.

There is not much more the police could do, unless someone caused literal bodily harm. If the thug had actually killed me, THEN there would have been grounds for an arrest. Gee...THAT would have been a help, and THIS man talked about splitting me down the middle in order to pull out my internal organs. NICE. Could I have afforded a big burly bodyguard? That would be a resounding no, so another paranoiac year was spent looking into crowds, and I was scared to death every time I'd find myself in a dark parking lot.

My phone number had to be changed, and boy, did I balk at THAT. It was a big inconvenience, since my phone was a means of doing business. Not as inconvenient as having your guts pulled out though.

OHHHH...almost forgot. After the phone number change, the diabolic man tracked me down AGAIN. Yup, he did, and a few years later, he gave (as a contact) my THIRD new number to his parole officer...who DID contact me...when his parolee went missing.

Aren't you glad I passed that one on? I knew you'd like it. Why don't we put it into perspective?

I am NOT a household name. I wasn't then, and I'm not now.

My probing question is—if UNhuge name Nevard pulled in such an alarming amount of outpourings, then what the heck are the people who ARE household names getting bombarded with?

All I can say is...my sympathy is WITH you. I don't think folks GET it. They seem to think you're spoiled and ungrateful. I'm thinking THEY should get a taste of terror before they judge.

Okay, I've had enough of that nasty subject. Where were we before I took the detour down creepy street?

The NOTES! The goofy notes.

Here's the funny thing (well, not funny to ME at the time): the most memorable and disturbing notes were the ones that had to do with my back end. Stop that laughing NOW.

I must have had some outfits that were a bit snug in the rear for a while or something, (oh alrighty…I AM half Armenian) since all of a sudden, large numbers of those appeared. Some of these notes, I must admit, were screamingly hilarious and written in the most bizarrely formal way. You really had no choice but to keel over with flabbergasted pleasure.

Actually, they COULD have stemmed from one of the most dumb-founding

moments I've experienced on a stage. My band usually played two or three songs before I came on. Some of them liked to sing too, so it gave them a chance to do songs, and it was less awkward than having me leave the stage in the middle of things. During one job, I found myself suddenly needing to use the bathroom. The moment for stage climbing was fast approaching, but dumb ME thought there was time to run for it. Musicians usually tend to this detail shortly before going ON (even if we don't feel like we have to), but sometimes we forget. Is this too much detail for you?

I happened to be wearing a skirt, with a slip under it, and under THAT combo, I was wearing some sort of whacky colored (but very transparent) tights. I had on NO other underwear. Just as I was about to pull up said tights, I heard one of my band mates say something like, "I'd like to introduce you to the girl that can't sleep at night, the girl that makes my life a living hell, the girl who can't stop bumping into walls to save her life, the girl that could be YOUR girl, the girl that can't tell a rock from a hard place, the girl you can't bring home to Mama, the girl… (There were a million of them.) SHE'S BACK FROM THE GRAVE AND READY TO PARTY. She mates, and she kills"…etc., etc.

Up went the tights in a flash, OUT of the bathroom I FLEW, and onto the stage I went. After TWO songs, a girl at the front of the stage meekly crooked her finger at me. I leaned down to hear the unwelcome and surprising news she had for me: "Nevard, your entire skirt is caught up in your tights in the back."

THERE'S a stage moment you don't forget. After the show, I sensibly asked the band if there was a new drug they were inhaling that I wasn't privy to, because how the living hell did they miss the sight of my ENTIRE bum showing? Furthermore, why oh why were they mysteriously unable to SHARE this news with me?

And their infinitely deductive answer was? "I dunno. We thought it was a new outfit or something."

"A NEW OUTFIT? You thought I had a new outfit that left me completely uncovered? This is what you THOUGHT? And by the by, guys, I'm…as usual, commando."

"I dunno. I mean it LOOKED okay."

"It looked OK? You think I'd go on stage…in front of a CROWD with—oh LORD, you boys are hopeless."

Yes, that could have started the goofy rear end notes. Who knows?

A close approximation of how one of these formal treasures would read:

"Nevard, I would like to commend you and the members of your splendiferous accompaniment, for an unparalleled evening of delightful music making. (Is this MY band he's describing??) I would like to particularly make note of your considerable talent as a musician and extraordinary singer. (Aren't you laying it on a bit thick here, bud?) I am aware you most likely receive many invitations of a rapturous nature, and I'm afraid I am about to add to your already overflowing inbox. (Yeah, yeah, pal...okay.)

"I find myself to be quite mesmerized in a general fashion, by the almost offhand manner with which you control a stage, (Okay, am I a modern major general?) and in particular I am drawn to the heavenly sight of your ambrosial derriere. (Ambrosial? Yes, sir, that word was employed.) If you would deign to accompany me to my home this evening or perhaps if you have accommodations more to your liking and, with your kind permission if we can convene at one or the other, I will be most appreciative.

"I would very much like to (uh-oh, here it comes) have you lie on my bed (crouch on my floor, lie in my driveway with a floodlight aimed at you, sit in my birdcage, perch atop a jersey barrier on 95) while facing in a northeasterly direction, OR a southern direction.

"I am sincerely hoping it will then be your pleasure and, undoubtedly mine, if I may EVER so carefully (ineptly, blindly, with the force of ZEUS) use my hands (my antique Foo Dog lamp, my feet, my cat, my tongue, my upright bass, my next door neighbor) to then…"

Hey. HEY! WHO IS THIS? IS THIS WRITTEN BY A NASA SCIENTIST GONE WILD?

I'm assuming you're getting the picture. This is the type of note that, with tons of knee slapping glee, would be passed around après show to the entire crew, wait staff, and all and sundry late night hangers and lowlife.

Most did NOT start off with such a degree of astounding articulation and panache. There were so many notes about my darn bottom, they ultimately prompted me to ask the band:

"Does NO ONE want to turn me around?? Does baby just got BACK? I've got a FRONT too, you know. Hey, is something terribly WRONG with my bum? Way too much bottom talk here. I'm gettin' paranoid. How come you guys don't get these darn things? YOU just get the nice little phone numbers. Why can't I just get the little phone numbers?"

My band was no help. "Well, WE like yer ass. We look at it every night, Vardz."

You'll soon find in many of these stories my various band mates usually attempt to nicely "lay it on with a trowel" with wildly inflated compliments, hoping to placate a hopelessly insecure and frenzied brain. In this case, they were trying to make me feel better, because I had suddenly developed a strange **fear** of my own bum. I became so self-conscious I took to wearing veritable SACKS on stage. There. Now you can't even TELL I've got one. Now what?

The creepiest requests were from couples. My friend Claude says SHE got these too, with approximately the same approach and words. Did they all use a teleprompter?

Did I want to be the filling in their sandwich? Oh HECK no, but I'd have no clue what they were getting at, until they spelled it out. I'd always fall for their "friendly" act.

YOU know, like when someone puts their finger on your shirt and says "you've got a spot there" and when you look down they slam your nose. Like that. I fall for that one every time too. I'm just realizing how utterly DUMB I'm looking in this book. Oh well.

So, the seemingly innocent couple approaches me, and since they're a couple, I'm not suspicious of their motives. It would always start with nice music talk and would then veer into the "We'd love to have you over" sort of thing, and I'd think: "Gee, they are so HOSPITABLE."

After that intro, the description of their home, which is SO much nicer than a hotel would be announced, followed by a caring inquiry of "wouldn't you be more comfortable staying with us?"

Still not getting the drift here, and I always preferred the hotel anyway unless I knew them well.

I'd ask if they had enough ROOM for the band, hoping that would deter them, and THEN they'd start in with "we're not interested in your band...just you."

AND I STILL WOULDN'T CATCH ON. This must have been frustrating for them, the poor pumpkins.

What's the matter with this girl? Is her brain running on empty? Does she not realize we'd like to consume her for DINNER?

Finally, they'd have to come out and say it, and I'd run SCREAMING into the night.

It was usually a guy/girl couple, but sometimes two straight guys.

"We want you to be our girlfriend."

"HUH? What do you MEAN? Both of you? Your actual girlfriend?? You mean a long-term relationship thing? YES? No, no, no, no, no, I think NOT."

SCREAMING into the night.

I don't rightly know what YOUR feelings are, and I'm not especially concerned, but it's too confusing, that three-person thing. I don't believe I'm capable of being absorbed in one person, only to be confronted with ANOTHER person interjecting whatever the heck they're going to interject. I'm too hopelessly uncoordinated and unable to effectively multitask in a horizontal way. It's a useless endeavor, and a lot more giggly than hot.

I was almost ensnared into what might have been an interesting romp. It ALMOST happened during a short time span of "ability to engage in zipless sex." Two fellas had been dancing WILDLY in front of the band all night, flailing about like puppets on a string. After the show, they approached me and wanted to BUY all of our instruments.

More than sensibly, I asked what in the world they imagined we'd be PLAYING with the NEXT night if we SOLD them our instruments. The most important question? Where the livin' HELL would we obtain instruments not easily found, or irreplaceable? How about the Rickenbacher Slide made entirely of Bakelite…including the NECK? Would it be easy to find the electric solid-bodied stand-up bass? How 'bout that nice Selmer sax? Or the old, old Strat? Would this bohunk of a town be carrying THOSE?? Were they eejits? They immediately went into the "We like you. You'll be our girlfriend. YES?" theme for me. Their accents were so indecipherable, I thought only ONE of them was asking for a romp.

Who's the eejit NOW?

The one I mistakenly believed to be my potential date for the evening seemed nice enough, and although I didn't spy the gleam I was always look-ing for, I thought, "Ahhh what the hell. I've just been through an acrimoni-ous and painful break-up, and boy, there wasn't any action going on there for a long time. I'm GOIN' for it."

I trotted back to the kitchen for moment, and the club owner had to TELL me (as usual) who the heck these two guys were. Sorry, only one of their names is coming up in my memory bank, but I wouldn't want to tell you even if I COULD remember. I'm looking like a real stoop in this one. Oh PLEASE…I'm looking like a stoop in every encounter with almost eve-ry person I've ever MET.

Sooo, the owner in the kitchen informed me… the guy (the ONE I be-lieved was inviting me to romp) had recently broken up with—I don't know—SOME kind of royal personage, and the two of them were big ten-nis guys.

Wimbledon, Schmimbledon. I wasn't all that crazy for them, but I'd been feeling pretty lonely, watching my band play around, and here's how my idiot brain worked THAT night: "Well gee; I guess if he's good enough for the duchess, he must be good enough for me. I'm not enthralled, but I'll bet those royal types have their guys tested for FUN proficiency before they'll put a FINGER on them."

Out of the kitchen I pranced, and there they still were. They managed to hurdle their impossible accents, and made their ACTUAL proposal ALL too clear. I was to be the shared stuffing in their duo, and after THAT, they wanted me to meet up with them at the U.S. Open.

I think my incredulous response went something like, "WHAT? WHAT? Not just the ONE, huh? (OK, I want the one that's already been tested, dammit.) What exactly is WRONG with you boys? ARE YOU A TAG TEAM? IS THIS A SPECIAL SPORTS GUY TRADITION? Are ya thinkin' I want to go to a TENNIS game, and then have a seat in the 'I'm waiting to rumble with the tennis player' room? OOPS, I mean the room for those who are waiting to do it with TWO, TWO, TWO tennis players in ONE?? HECK no. Thank you for the invite. Cute accents you two have."

Does the question "WHAT??" seem to be a recurring theme? Not yet? Don't worry, it will be.

"WHAT?" and "WHY?" are ALWAYS my most searing questions.

Coincidentally, they're also my most ineffectual inquiries.

I can cite you a few female couples, which got the standard "thanks for thinking of me" response, but the one I can't comprehend at ALL, was a male gay couple (NOT BI, they told me), which brought on… "What the heck are you THINKING? What in the WORLD would you DO with me? Never mind. Don't tell me. This is more than confusing."

I think we should end this "basest of the base" chapter with one of the three funniest pickup lines that I've had the good fortune to be at the receiving end of. There were not that many that had true hilarity attached to them. Most were fairly standard and fraught with unoriginality.

This delightful gem took place at the Philly Folk Festival. That reminds me of something. Older generation blues men seem to always have a valet with them. I love that. WHY haven't I EVER had a valet? WHY?

Sooooo, we're doing our thing at the folk festival (exactly who thought this would be an appropriate booking I can't recall), and the crowd is little stunned by us at first…sort of felt like Bobby going electric there for a second, but they danced and hollered for us just the same. Bless their adventurous souls.

As we're getting our usual disarray together after our stint, a man comes near me and he says, "Oh girl….gotta, gotta, gotta, gotta, gotta get me some o' that."

He said the word "gotta" so many times I was expecting him to break into a James Brown medley.

OK, I got that, brother, but I'm not sure if you're speaking to me SPECIFICALLY, or are you just doing your own personal RIFF there?

And just who are you? Are you the promoter of this entire event? Are you selling peanuts? Drugs? You a fan? You having a medical emergency with the "get me some" thing? WHAT?

I have to explain to you… It's a FUNNY feeling sort of thing… I mean…being a performer sometimes is. It mixes you up a bit. It's a little odd being around lots of strangers much of the time, and you being the most looked at people/person in any given area you might be performing in or near.

And, YOU—I don't know how to explain this—a lot of times you don't understand exactly WHO is saying what to WHOM, and are you involved in any way? Or NOT?

And exactly WHAT is the meaning of what's being said, and by WHOM and to WHO? You get used to this, but even after years, it can be disconcerting.

Now the man comes closer and declares, "YOU heard me, sistah. I want me some of what you GOT."

Ahhh, now I'm zeroing in on it. He's talking to ME, and he's gotta have him some. Of ME, I mean. I THINK. My comeback to this kind of elegant entrée into my life, is usually one of good cheer. I simply say, "Why thank you" and off they go.

I said to this gentleman, "Nice of you to say so. Thank you." Hey, I'm nothing if not polite. I was brought up right, darn it.

Unfortunately, Mr. Gotta, Gotta, Gotta is not HAVING it. Won't let it go. Says the same thing again, with even MORE gottas, if that's possible, and apparently it WAS.

Now, he's becoming downright bothersome, and I'm doing my level best to ignore him. And he ain't having that EITHER, sistah.

And that's when he comes out with it. Yessireee, he comes out with the line that freezes my feet to the very ground we're standing on.

"YOU gotta come on home with ME, lil' sistah, because I PUTS LOTION ON IT."

Lotion. Lotion. LOTION? My oh my, I just couldn't help myself. Just could not keep my mouth shut. I had to ask.

"Exactly where are you aiming to put this LOTION, sonny? On ME? On YOU? WHERE IS THE LOTION GOING? WHERE?"

"Right on my THANG, girl. Oh, you're gonna like it. Makes it nice and soft."

Lord have mercy, did I hear this right? DID I? Could anyone be so WRONG-HEADED? I had to ask. I shouldn't have asked, darnit.

Too late. By now, I'm laughing so hard, I'm literally banging my head against the side of the stage, and most likely dislodging the performers who followed us. Almost falling on the ground with mirth, I was. The band is pulling me away, but I'm laughing so much, I can barely walk. I finally sputtered, almost SCREAMED at the poor guy,

"Don't EVER say that again. YOU HEAR ME? Never again! THAT'S NOT THE

EFFECT WE SISTAHS IS LOOKIN' FOR!!!"

For YEARS it would only take a band member leaning down and whispering in my ear "I puts lotion on it, Vardzie" for me to completely blow a song. Sometimes two songs. The laughing would bubble up, and once started, was almost impossible to stop. Oh come ON now. LOTION.

(Photo for the cover of a magazine called PREVIEW.
1980something.The author is not happy, because she
was forced to put on makeup.)

A COUPLE THINGS IN MY PEA BRAIN SOME MUSICAL, AND SOME NOT...YET THEY ALL MAKE APPEARANCES OFTEN

HERE WE GO.

Do all of us experience this phenomenon? Please don't tell me I'm the only one.

These events have haunted me. You're most likely going about your business in your usual reckless manner, trimming your bangs, or searching for one of the hundred pens, that cleverly hide when you're not looking. And BOOM.

Here it is baby. It's that memory. Just as if it were freshly baked yesterday.

I WAS KICKED OUT OF THE BROWNIES. I'm not lying. This belongs in the "I've been kicked out of better joints than this" chapter, but being actually thrown out of the Brownies is an experience that still rankles. I don't know anyone else that was thrown out of that organization. WHY ME? I ask myself.

I was eight years old, and wanted to be a Brownie more than life itself. Didn't know the weekly Brownie meetings would be mind-numbingly boring, and pointless. What with the completion of useless tasks in order to win dumb little badges that my mommy didn't want to have to sew on the dumb ol' uniform anyway.

Let's see…there was a badge for sewing (believe me, I could sew a button on at the age of five); there were badges for all sorts of tasks they wanted to infuse into the girlie psyche, none of which I had even a remote interest in. Frankly, I found it confusing that boys weren't expected to know these things too.

They DID have the camping sort of badges as well. You know, how to fold up a sleeping bag (Were they kidding? How hard is it to fold up a sleeping bag? We get a BADGE for this??) and the ever popular "rub two sticks together to make fire" badge. (I'm sorry, but if you're hangin' in the woods, you need to be carrying enough lighters and matches to make Smokey the Bear have a seizure.)

I didn't know any of this when I signed up. Mamma tried to talk me out of it. "Oh, honey, you won't LIKE it. They'll make you stand in circles and hold hands and sing songs." She tried everything to deter me

Here's the thing. I LOVED THE BEANIE. It wasn't the Brownie dress, it wasn't the brownie socks, it was the BEANIE. Couldn't get ENOUGH of the beanie. I'd seen this glorious adornment on the heads of Jewish boys I knew and wanted one perched, just so, on MY head too. I had no INKLING that girls weren't allowed to wear the Jewish beanie anyway. Was this a selfish wish? Probably so, but don't worry, the punishment is coming.

Mommy was right about the whole sordid thing—the standing in circles and all—and even at that age, I couldn't help but wonder why songs for children didn't come out of your mouth nice, and were oddly without melody. Hated being made to sing them, and standing in circles seemed very strange to me.

Here comes the bad part. I learned a new word at school. I was very excited about learning a new word. Had no idea what it meant, of course, but it had a nice ring to it. Really it did. Couldn't wait to show off this new word at the Brownie meeting, which was, sure enough, that very DAY.

Walked to the Brownie meeting after school, marched right up to the Den mother, and with a happy heart and a beaming face, I proudly proclaimed, "Know what, Mrs. Stickindamud? YOU are a cocksucker."

Couldn't figure out for the life of me why Mrs. Stickindamud's face changed. It looked a little scary. No one ELSE'S face changed.

Had something gone horribly awry? Did I do something wrong? Why wasn't she praising me for my new word? Mommy and Daddy always liked it when I learned a new word. Hmmmm.

When I arrived home that day, Mamma told me Mrs. Stickindamud had called her and said, "I am afraid, Mrs. Tellalian, that Nevard is NOT Girl Scout material, and she is not welcome at our Brownie meetings in the future."

Mrs. Stickindamud of course did not go into detail, because then she would have had to actually UTTER the dreaded word. Having no such compunction, little me had no trouble at all repeating the word to Mommy. As soon as she heard what I'd done, my sweet mamma laughed till the tears were rolling down her cheeks. Then she told me what the word meant and I didn't quite get it.

"I don't know, Mommy. That doesn't SOUND bad. Is that a MEAN thing to be doing? Do YOU do that, Mommy? Why is it bad to be doing that?" (It sounded absolutely intriguing to ME.)

Poor Mama had to explain and explain ad nauseam, and it all added up to this....

"Well no, darling, it's NOT a bad thing to do, but it's not something you say in polite company. Most people would take offense. Especially hetero-sexual men. It's something you should only say at home. And ONLY in your bedroom."

Her laughing wouldn't stop. And being the eternal inquisitive idiot, I couldn't stop asking.

"What's a hetersexhel, Mommy? And if it's nice, why would anyone get mad?"

"Oh, Vardzie, just hush up and trust your mamma. Don't say the word."

"OK. Is it all right if I go to my room and say it?"

"Yes, darling, you may go to your room and say it all you'd like. Oh, wait till Daddy hears this one." (More uncontrolled laughing from the Mommy front.)

This all might sound funny to you, but let me tell you—it's a particularly bad memory.

MORAL TO THIS STORY? Please be careful for children. Most of them have kind little hearts, and things spill out of their mouths. Catch the spills, and drink 'em up for them. Just DO it.

HERE COMES MUSIC AGAIN. GUESS I LIED IN THE TITLE.

Here's one that's particularly disturbing to me—and of course an end-less source of amusement for others. I haven't told more than a couple pals this one. It's too humiliating. This story is half nasty memory, and half fabulous music.

Once upon a time there existed a band named FLUB. I don't know, I think it stood for Four Lads and Undeniably Brilliant. Something like that. Shut up, you. Not their real name.

FLUB was the best band in the world. I'm not exaggerating. I mean it. There were countless glowing things written about them, and even more countless endorsements by folks who KNOW what good music is. This band was sometimes called the biggest "secret" in American music. SE-CRET? SECRET? Why a secret, pray tell? There's something about that statement that really bugs me. But I'm not going to go into the sometimes-smarmy world of the "biz" right now.

I'm sure this particular band did fine for themselves, but the idiot pow-ers that be could have made life a lot less of a struggle for them, and not for nuttin'—folks NEED to hear better music. Okay, I'll shut up. Don't think I won't go into this again though.

Here's the setup for this puzzling and haunting memory. I can't recall what year this story belongs in—1982, '83? Don't remember. We did a lot of warm-ups for FLUB that year.

Someone had decided that I would be an appropriate thing to be heard before FLUB hit the stage to do their thing. Lots of dates were set up by my manager or theirs, agents, their road manager, I don't remember.

They were right though. Their fans liked me a lot—loved me in fact—at times demanded encores. Believe me, that's a bunch of fun for an opening act, because LOTS of times it doesn't go that way.

I think their audience liked me because I had the same strange aesthetics as FLUB— was kind of stubborn about doing music that moved me and my band (our own, or covers…it made absolutely no difference to me), and didn't give a hoot what genre it emerged from. And I guess I was pretty funny to them onstage.

For some reason we were also paid well. Warm-up's generally pay doo-dy, and musicians don't like giving up a prospective good-paying night to do them. So far, so good, right?

Don't you worry…Vardzie gets it pretty good, within minutes. Good-ness, this one's hard to get out.

The first time we warmed up for them, finished our set, and I headed off the stage in the direction of my band's dressing room. I'm always the last one to get off stage…where's my water bottle/ guitar/ hat… OCD girl in action. By the time I got off, the backstage area was empty.

Except for ONE man. Leaning against the wall. Staring at me while I'm walking down the steps. Tall guy. Alrighty, I don't know if he was tall. Everyone looks tall to someone that's not more than five feet.

Got to the bottom of the stairs. He's STILL staring. No expression. I head toward the dressing room, the door of which he was standing right next to, and he doesn't STOP staring. Not for a second. Does this man ever BLINK?

I'm fairly sure I'm a halfwit—his demeanor registered in my brain, but not really— and being a friendly sort, I smiled and said, "Hi, there," or something equally innocuous. His response? That would be…NOTHING. Deadpan face. It was like one of those awkward moments when you hold out your hand to shake someone else's and they just leave you hangin' there like a dead something.

THEN it registered. What the heck is wrong with this guy? Oh well…maybe he didn't mean to be rude. Maybe he's distracted and doesn't know that he's being awfully strange.

Look, you never know what's happening in someone's life. They may be going through something painful or confusing and are on autopilot. One shouldn't judge without knowing. It's not right.

A few minutes later, I'm in the dressing room…dressing of course. My band is chattering away like magpies, and all of a sudden it hits me.

Here's the buzz that started in my brain: *Ya knooowww…I sort of LIKE the squinty eyes on that guy… the face too. Mesmerizing interesting face.*

You know what? He seems a bit worn out there. He could almost be kind of…okay, but he looks a little mean. Who the heck is he? He doesn't look too well.

Well, my dears, I didn't have long to wonder. No, I didn't. Left the dressing room to check out FLUB, who was now on stage. I had of course HEARD them before, and I thought the world of them. Who wouldn't? But I'd never SEEN them. I never seemed to have a clue about who was playing in what band, or what they did in said band.

I was too young to go to the bars, and then even before the age of majority set in, I was traveling myself, so I hadn't had the chance to see this band. Live of course is an entirely different animal.

That night, I positioned myself halfway up the stairs so I could see what they were doing. What's the first thing I see? I know you've guessed—the darn staring guy is in FLUB, fer gosh sake.

Having never seen him, I wouldn't have known him if he'd been thrown at my feet. He's not looking at odds with the world now. NOW, he's looking quite gregarious and having himself a good ol' time, he is. Not that this means anything.

We've all gone on and done what's expected of us when perfectly agonizing things are going on in our lives. Sick, grieving, breaking up—it doesn't matter.

We may not be feeling it before we go on, but we do what we need to do to get in the moment, and then we DO it. Every time. And no one knows. You don't let your band down. You don't let the audience down. It's in the job description. Many of the members of my various bands ran to throw up between songs at one time or another.

(Note to budding musicians…if YOU can't swing it when your life is asunder, you've got no business doing it at all. Period.)

Now Mr. Staring Guy is looking even more wondrous to me. He's got the passion. The overwhelming and compelling need to make music. People possessing this sort of fervor can usually recognize a fellow inmate. Actually it possesses YOU. You've GOT to make the music. Don't matter where you do it, or who's there to hear it…it's got to come out.

I can see it in him. It sure ain't for the dough or the easy life for him. He's just putting it out there. They may love him or they may hate him, and it won't ultimately matter. There's no choice. Not for him there isn't. Mix it up and let it fly.

Listen to the music, make it, talk about it. It's like a disease. Like malaria.

I'm also seeing in this guy a kind of wild disregard for his own, well, bashfulness, a sense of childlike wonder and amazement at the sound coming out, and the joy of making it. I can see it in him and know this—because I feel it when I play too.

Oh DAMMMM…he's the male ME. That's what he is. Of course I'm not so darn brilliant, but GOSH….

I quickly forgot the lousy staring, because what I saw was simply glorious. There's no other way to describe it. To me, a band IS the rhythm section. If it moves you where it should, if it hits below your gut like a jackhammer, then they've got it.

Heavenly Gods, that rhythm section…the likes of which I'd never seen! Lookit that bass player… I don't see the fingers walking that much, but it sounds like he's ridin' that thing from the F on that bottom E all the darn way up to the HIGH E on the G—and producing a decidedly beautiful tone, sliding in on a fretted instrument. *Thump*. Popping it. *Thump*. Dear lord…now he's strumming it like a guitar…now the thumb over…that's it, bud…drop out a second to hear that snare. I ASK YOU!!

And what ABOUT the snare? This drummer is doubling up on it, employing every '20s to '40s jazz trick I've ever heard. Is Louis Belson in the house? *Whap. Whap. Whap*. DAMN! Hey there, Dave Weckyl. Look behind you, pal, because THIS cat's got one-armed rolls that'll knock you into the next county. Oh my, look at those nice loose wrists. *Whap. WHAP*. Right behind the beat. Doesn't let up for a SECOND. Great stuff, I tell you.

That's just HALF the band I'm describing here. The others are even more astounding.

I look at the crowd, and they're dancing away, and doing some hootin' and hollerin', and I'm thinking…

How many of you know you are looking at GENIUS? Maybe two out of a hundred? Maybe. Doesn't matter anyway.

I'm sorry; I get carried away describing music. I know some of you are almost snoozing, but I sometimes mourn the loss of enough live music in the world. There are generations now who have never heard it. Sad.

The next time we opened for them, I didn't see the staring FLUB member, and we left right after doing our part. By then I'd convinced the eternally dense-headed me that this man had no idea he'd been rude. SURELY not.

A few weeks later, another opening for FLUB. I'll be snookered, if I didn't mosey off stage that night, and yessirreee…there he is. AGAIN. Hard steely-eyed glaring. How come there's never anyone ELSE back here?

This time, it stopped me in my tracks. I somehow couldn't move. I stared back at HIM, and I've got no idea how long this ridiculous contest went on, but he didn't flinch for a second, just kept scrutinizing me in a ghastly way fraught with… It was pointed, intimidating, humiliating—and I gave in first.

I ran like a bat out of hell, past him and into the safety of the dressing room, the door of which he was almost BLOCKING, so I just about had to push him aside.

And I blurted to my bass player, "That Whatshisface is out there, and he's strange. This is the second time he's stared at me like I'm a bug under a microscope. What did I ever do to him?"

Here's the compassionate response I received.

"Ahh he just wants ya."

"WHAT???"

"He probably wants a lil' bit of Vardzie."

"What the hell's WRONG with you, Tim? BELIEVE me this is not a 'come hither' look; this is an 'I HATE you' look."

"Why would he hate you?"

"This is what I'm ASKING! I don't even KNOW him. Why does he despise me?"

"Naaah…he wants ya. You know how oblivious you are. Remember the guy that licked your ear, and you didn't even notice? Remember that man that was feeling your butt, and you didn't even turn around? God, Vardz, I've heard guys ask you OUT and you're clueless. You're pretty hopeless in that direction, you know."

"OK…YES. I remember the ear thing. All of a sudden my EAR was wet. Was only the ONE ear rained on? How is this possible? It was disgusting. Oh…and about that BOTTOM thing you EEJIT, let me just point out… I was busy conducting some *business* and thought it was one of YOU playing a joke, so I ignored it. And, by the WAY, what possessed you to stand idly by while some STRANGER was feeling my bottom every old which way?"

"We thought it was funny and kind of cool."

"Oh you DID, huh? COOL? How'd any of you like it if I let that happen to YOU? What am I saying?"

"You betcha. I'm waitin' for it. Still say the guy probably wants ya."

"No, NO, NO! What are you not getting here? This is not a ten-year-old sticking my pigtails in the inkwell. I know I'm a little absentminded in these matters, but I'm not TOTALLY lacking a certain amount of normal deduction. Well, maybe you're right. Maybe "Whatshisface" WANTS ME LIKE NOBODY'S BUSINESS and I'll TELL you what he WANTS. He WANTS to grab hold of both my hands, SPIN ME AROUND HIS HEAD TILL' MY ARMS POP OUT OF THEIR SOCKETS, THEN LET GO, AND WATCH AS MY HEAD SCREWS ITSELF INTO THE CEMENT FLOOR, AND I COLLAPSE LIKE A BROKEN RAG DOLL.. That's what he WANTS."

We left right away that night too. Good thing, because I couldn't bring myself to watch FLUB anyway. And let me tell you…Whatshisface sure wasn't looking so wondrous to me any longer. Not a bit. Just mean. I was confused.

Next opening comes along. It was always great warming up for them. We'd started to see a lot of their fans at our shows, and that was nice too. This time, I asked my bass player to NOT exit the stage without me.

This time there were a few people milling around in back. Yup, there's Whatshisface, but I didn't look up. Nope. I'm no stoopie. I kept my head down, grabbed the bass player's hand, and he pulled me toward the dressing room. My knees were shaking.

I swear I could feel that cold squinty gaze.

We got in the door, and my good old comforting bass player said, "God, you were right, Vardzie. He zeroed right in on ya, and he did NOT look friendly."

Yes. Tim, I know. I KNOW.

So this is THREE times now? I called a friend of mine, and confided. He said, "Wow, that's weird. I know that (can't remember what) of theirs. I'll call and ask why Whatshisface would be doing something like that, and would he please cease and desist. Maybe he's got some sort of problem with you, Vardz. Maybe he's just bananas."

"NO. You outta your mind?" Would you want your mommy calling the playground bully's mommy? HECK NO. I hadn't even told but ONE person in my band. It was embarrassing. Made my pal promise he wouldn't call.

By this time, I was dreading any more bookings with FLUB. My calendar told me there was one more coming up. Okay, I could take one more.

NOW, I was speculating and whirling like an FBI agent. What could be wrong with Whatshisface? Or is it ME? What's wrong with ME?

Do I somehow deserve this obvious derision? Am I really bad? Maybe I'm really that bad and shouldn't be on a stage anywhere in the hemisphere. Is this what he's trying to tell me?

Naah…couldn't be THAT bad. I mean there be folks Whatshisface probably admires who think I'm okay. I do believe we've got some musical pals in common, and THEY don't think I'm horrible. Uh-oh…could it be they are just exceedingly polite? Wait a minute now…I know his best damn friend. Someone whose musicianship NO ONE would ever question…and he comes to see us often, and sits IN with us.

Guess what, Mr. Glaring Guy. You're a TAD more seasoned than Nevard here. Let's see… I've been a road rat for about four years—you've been going at it for what? Maybe FIFTEEN years with this lineup, and altogether, I don't know, TWENTY years?

I'm still pretty wet behind the ears here. So even if I AM amazingly bad, why wouldn't you be a nice person and offer up some pointers or sumptin'? Or just leave me be in my awfulness? I'm just saying.

If you hate me that much, why wouldn't you simply request my absence from your sacred freakin' FLUB shows? Is it more FUN to make someone like me scared?

A couple of months later, the last evening with you-know-who came up. THIS time our dressing room was a little hallway with a couch in it, which led to THEIR dressing room. So of course they had to march through ours to get to theirs.

I'm not obsessively modest or anything, but I sure don't like the thought of being caught standing in my underwear, or lack of it, with strange people hanging about.

I was used to my own band. I mean it's not possible to share almost every living moment with folks, and not become a little blasé about things like that. We were together far more than we were with any of our significant others, that's for sure.

Right at the top of my already reeling head was the frightful thought of the now downgraded to decidedly not-very-nice Whatshisface coming by—Superb! Perhaps he'll just slap me upside my head this time—which of course he HAD no choice but to DO (the passing by…not the slapping).

And so he did. (The passing by…not the slapping.) The rest of FLUB and their assorted and sundry companions meandered back and forth. Not that THEY were particularly friendly (well, except for the smiley drummer, who I have a strange feeling, would smile at DRAPERY). But they weren't actively mean or anything.

Eventually of course he came on through. And of COURSE I looked up at the wrong moment. (Again…why, why, WHY do these things happen to me, and how many times have I said the word WHY in this chapter?) Yes, indeed I did. I looked up.

He slooooowwwly sauntered on by, and managed to concurrently sneer at me. SNEERED, I tell ya. Talk about some multitasking. I'm applauding right this minute. Walking AND sneering. Well done. Sorry I'm being snotty. Just makes me so mad.

Well, this is certainly off the subject, but I must tell you, dear readers, I just heard

from my editor, who very reasonably said something akin to, "There is no END to this story. Is that how you plan to leave your reader? With no END?" I had to admit there IS an end, but it's even stranger than the rest of the story. I suppose I should

relay it. What the heck...it's not as if you know who I'm talking about, so here goes.

After the Flub guy (the one who had been unbearably awful to me for eons)

passed by with his sneer, I figured that was the end of it, and he was positively done

with me at that point. One would THINK so, but NOOOO. About ten minutes after

he'd strolled by, he came BACK. I was sitting on the couch, still wondering what the livin' HELL was wrong with that guy.

Suddenly, he was standing directly in front of me. He reached out, grabbed my arms, and PULLED me off the couch. I think I was so frightened I may have been shaking. FLUB boy then put his damned arms around me, and planted a positively full tilt kiss on me. Shook me to my core. It may have been the hottest kiss I'd EVER experienced. Good God, I can't think about it NOW without turning up the air conditioner. And THAT is the true end to the story. Never saw him again. Frankly, I don't think it's a conclusion that is any more satisfying than the end with NO conclusion, but here's what I've got to say to HIM.

Why does the memory of you haunt me? Good question. There must be a trillion people who have hated me through the years, or at the very least just didn't "get" me. In print, out of print, in the biz, out of the biz, and many not too shy to tell me. "I'm just not getting' you." "I hate you." A very highly regarded bluegrass picker absolutely detested me. Why someone thought I belonged on a bill with him remains an unsolved mystery, but he complained loudly. I was mighty raucous and loud, he thought. Didn't faze ME.

Okay, here's a horrifying one. For goodness sake, Cab Caloway *hated* me. And I think he loved EVERYBODY but me. Well...can't say our band

BLENDED with Mr. Caloway. Who cares? I sure didn't. And I liked him a lot.

Why would just **one** person's reaction to me be something so painful? Two reasons I think. The most looming being…this guy was older and more experienced than I, and I ADMIRED him. Admired his talent so very much. I'm kind of tearing up just thinking about it. Thought he was a stunning musical phenomenon. Still do, but all these years later, can't bear to hear him. I'm a moron.

I'm talking to YOU now. You big galoot. If you are any kind of man at all, you should buzz up, and act NICE, to make up for your hurtful behavior. What the heck were you THINKING

there, bud? Have a little courage and do the right thing. Okay, but don't yell at me. I'm still scared of you, so please don't make me cry again.

MORAL of this story??

JUST BE NICE. CAN'T PEOPLE BE NICE TO EACH OTHER? BECAUSE THERE'S— WHAT? TOO *MUCH* LOVE AND CARING GOING AROUND? CAN YOU SPARE IT, PEOPLE?

My love of Shakespeare is deep. I know I'm not cool. I'm not a scholar or the world's greatest writer by ANY stretch of anyone's imagination. I haven't read and picked apart every play and sonnet he wrote, and haven't spent large amounts of time on the study of his immense genius.

I began to read his prose at a young age, simply because I discovered him hanging about on the bookshelf in our living room. I didn't understand most of it then and would tire of the reading after a fairly short spell.

It was a struggle to try to interpret his mysterious prose. I had never seen Elizabethan English before, but in spite of that struggle, his words felt delicious and majestic when I gave voice to them, and I can tell you with CERTAINTY something I will dare anyone to contradict.

William Shakespeare was and IS one of the greatest musical geniuses that ever lived. Do you think that's an outrageous statement? After all, he was a playwright and a poet….not a musician, right?

Perhaps, but there was never before (the mid-fifteen hundreds), and never will be again, ANYONE in prose or poetry, who will come within miles of his sublime outpourings. And they're as beautiful and as rhythmically right on as any great piece of music. Arranged to be voiced and performed that way.

He was a man who encompassed the entire scope of the human condition in his language and in the sound and rhythm of his words. In every line and every single syllable, he revealed our very souls.

He did it in blank verse...iambic pentameter to be exact. It sounds like this: ba BUM ba Bum, ba Bum, ba Bum, ba Bum. Like our hearts beating. Like 4/4 time. Except in prose, not measures. TEN syllables in every line, in pairs of two called feet, and the rhythm depends on which syllable is stressed in each foot. And pentameter means there are five feet to each line.

He knew how to manipulate the downbeats as well, our Will did, and he'd reverse them, mix them up a little when he was dealing with sinister things, or mournful, or anxious themes.

And within that phrasing, that pattern, there's room for unlimited improvisational interpretation for the reader, or speaker. When it's done right, baby, when it's slammed just so—it sounds like the best rockin' you ever did hear.

This is probably why I was drawn to it even if I couldn't understand all the language.

I must tell you this is not a DEAD PROSE.

Do you know how many words Will Shakespeare literally made up? I DO mean made up. Words never uttered before... words we're still using. Addiction. Bedroom. Laughable. Amazement. Blushing. ZANY.

That just blows me away. Shakespeare made up the word zany. What is even more astounding to me (maybe not to you...you could be asleep by now) are the PHRASES and descriptions that he wrote almost FIVE CENTURIES ago that are STILL in use. So, William Shakespeare went quite a long way in the actual CREATION of our language. This is amazing stuff, man. Here's just some of the seemingly trillion.

Lay it on with a trowel. Mum's the word. Star-crossed lovers. Night owl.

Fair play. A sorry sight. Good riddance. Heart's content. Come what may. Fight fire with fire. One fell swoop. Wear your heart on your sleeve. Like the dickens. Eaten out of house and home. Fool's paradise. Lie low. Wild goose chase. Send him packing. There's method in my madness. Make

your hair stand on end. Love is blind. Vanish into thin air. Strange bedfel-
lows. In a pickle.

ARE YOU AMAZED? I sure am. That's just a few of them. How many
of these phrases have we heard in songs? LOTS. The things I've been telling you about him are the very reason scholars are fascinated, bewitched,
and never grow tired of this writer.

Did I not start out to tell you a story? Well then, here it bloody well is,
and not a moment too soon.

One year I heard tell Morris Carnovsky would be giving a Shakespeare
class at a local university. Morris Carnovsky was considered one of the
greatest if not THE greatest King Lear of the twentieth century.

I had to sign up. I didn't care if I couldn't act my way out of my own
front door. Good GOD, y'all—MORRIS CARNOVSKY. I had to HEAR
him!

What I failed to consider was that I would inevitably be asked to perform the Shakespeare, not just sit there like a lump and LISTEN to the
great Morris, which is exactly what I had hoped with all my heart to accomplish.

I went to the classes and found myself in heaven. The voice, the rhythm,
the words. I was mesmerized. As an added bonus, Mr. Carnovsky was a
living doll, just a darling man. Full of fun, and at that time in his seventies,
finally the right age to play Lear.

And he did it for us. Oh yes, he did. I almost passed out from sheer
bliss. I'd never heard anything like it, and not on a stage, mind you, but
barely a foot in front of me.

Carnovsky's deservedly acclaimed and history-making King Lear was
shaking me in my seat, resonating with a roaring and disheveled madness
that would have shattered the rafters in the sturdiest of barns.

And it was music. I'm TELLIN' you…MUSIC.

He told us fascinating but sad stories of the entire Joe McCarthy fiasco,
and the House Un-American Activities Committee.

Morris Carnovsky had been caught up in that, and was blacklisted in the
industry, as were a great many writers, actors, musicians, government employees, and even our own Armed Services. People like Leonard Bernstein,
John Garfield, Aaron Copland, Orson Welles, and Artie Shaw. Many lost
careers, some found themselves in prison.

Two of the founding members of the Group Theatre were Morris Carnovsky and his darling wife Phoebe Brand. They didn't work for quite a while after they were named as Communists by Elia Kazan in 1951.

His face would turn red at the very mention of Richard Nixon or Bobby Kennedy. Enough of the history.

The REAL historical event took place, when your pal Nevard stood up with her carefully prepared soliloquy. I had been assigned the famous Lady Macbeth speech, (uttered before she was going off to stab Duncan to death) and after taking a trembling and deep breath I started...

"The raven himself is hoarse

That croaks the fatal entrance of Duncan

Under my battlements. Come, you spirits

That tend on mortal thoughts, unsex me here,

And fill me from the crown to the toe top-full

Of direst cruelty! Make thick my blood;

Stop up the access and passage to remorse,

That no compunctious visitings of nature

Shake my fell purpose, nor keep peace

Between the effect and it! *Forswear me*

That thou enrobe my willful mantle in

Thee, to whom I owe much, is lost upon,

To have it be starved o'er a hot temper

Neither crippled in these laws for the sport,

Than to either defend thusly or be

Married I fear..... "

All of a sudden, I hear the great Carnovsky clear his throat...

"Ummm, little one..."

(He always called me "little one")

"Yes, sir?"

"Please come here."

He pats his elderly Lear lap, and I notice his wife Phoebe is chuckling now.

"DO have a seat for a moment, little one."

"Yes, sir." I proceeded to have a seat on the proffered lap of one of my heroes, my arm around his neck, and I'm thinking..."Ohhh how sweet are Morris and Phoebe here. Great actors of the century though they are, they want to put me at ease."

"Little one, I'd like to tell you, Phoebe and I think the world of your father, and we have thoroughly enjoyed YOUR company these past few weeks, haven't we, Phoebe?"

"Oh yes, Morris, Nevard has been a delight, and we love to hear her laughter and see that smile."

OK…NOW I'm thinking, *why do the Carnovskys know Daddy? And how come I get to sit on the Carnovsky lap, and they're talking about my smile?* I often am asked to sit on laps…because I'm sort of little, I guess. As a kid, I had sat in the great BB King's lap, and will forever be honored and grateful.

"However, as delightful as you are, little one, may we ask at what point in your SOLILIQUY did you STOP speaking the Shakespearean TEXT??"

WHU WO.

"Well, sir, my memory of the correct lines completely left me, right after the line 'nor keep peace between the effect and it!' So I sort of uhhhh…ad libbed."

Phoebe is beyond chuckling now. She's choking on some yucks there. As for me, I'm backpedaling like a sum' a bitch.

"And uh…didn't I do the iambic thing? Did I get the rhythm right? I know it's probably not the correct thing to do, but I put in all the Shakespeare–like speech I could think of, and well…you know…I couldn't just STOP. Doesn't the show HAVE TO go on? At all costs? That's what I was led to believe in the Mickey Rooney, Judy Garland movies. HEY, didn't you love Mickey's PUCK?"

If you look above at Lady Macbeth's speech there, you can see exactly where I start my shameful Elizabethan gibberish. It is not what I said that day—how in the world would I remember THAT? But it is similar, and a big plate of highfalutin' nothing.

I believe my only pal in the room at this point is Phoebe Carnovsky, who is viewing me as even MORE delightful now, because she's got her hand over her mouth, and I can hear a distinctive SNORTING sound coming out.

Morris Carnovsky of course had the last word on the travesty I had visited upon his class (the class who remained deadly silent throughout this entire episode….because now they were trembling in their boots, knowing THEIR speeches were coming up)….Morris's last words were:

"Little one, little one…WE DO NOT AD LIB SHAKESPEARE!"

"Yes, sir"

And then he muttered under his breath, "Wasn't Shakespeare, but nicely executed bullshit. "

I have to say, this experience was one of the unforgettable highlights of my life. To SIT upon the KNEE of one of the GREATEST Shakespearean actors of our time, and to be personally reprimanded! Does life GET any better than that?? What a gift.

He did ask me one thing a month later, before the classes ended.

"Little one....why did you come?"

"Because I had to HEAR YOU, of course."

"I see. Thank you." He beamed from ear to ear.

Moral to this story?

THERE IS NONE. But I believe we're wandering into music again...

There resides a pitiful memory in my head, regarding the spoken word—I've got the memory of a sieve. Hell, I can't even recall lyrics to songs I'VE written. But in one respect I was correct. The show does have to go on...in one form or another. I for instance am a good lyric mumble bumbler when the need arises. It's all "Louie Louie" to me.

Musically, however, I'm an elephant, and never forget. I remember to the note most every melody, line, riff, I've ever heard, along with the other parts in any given piece. Can reproduce them vocally, and can pick them out on piano.

In some ways this is unfortunate, because I do not sight-read with the greatest of ease. That's saying it politely. When I was five, and took piano lessons, I simply listened to the teacher play the piece, and when he left, I just went ahead and played the darn thing from memory. If there were parts I couldn't recall, I would laboriously read it off the sheet one time, and then I was on my own.

When the guy showed up the next week for my lesson, I'd play the piece, and pretend I was looking at the music. He would turn the pages at the proper times, but I had no idea what those pages contained, or where in fact, we were.

I managed to fool a few teachers, but did myself a great disservice. To this day, if I have to read, I resort to…let's see now…Every Good Boy Deserves Fudge, so that note there is an A flat.

Here's something you might find odd. ONLY if you're not a musician.

I played at ONE wedding reception. Surprisingly, couples would constantly ask my band to do so. My assessment of their mysterious desire to have their holy union musically blessed by MY band? In all probability they must have been so crocked, their inebriated ears heard "Proud Mary" instead of "Somebody's Gonna Get Their Head Kicked In."

After these inappropriate "play at our wedding" pleadings, I'd always blurt, "Ok now, have you TRULY thought this out? Let me assure you we won't be playing the darn bunny hop, or the cut the cake thing, or the bride's first dance with Daddy, or ANYTHING like that. YOU might like us, but for GOD'S SAKE, think of your FAMILY!" The one and only wedding we DID play, (for probably the only guy in the world that HAS a family that could stand my shenanigans, and lack of "wedding like" tunes) was David Hull's wedding. Ahhh…you don't know who David Hull is? Open your ears budding (or not so budding) musicians and music lovers.

DAVID HULL HAPPENS TO BE ABOUT THE BEST BASS PLAYER IN THE WORLD.

I'm quite sure he's been mentioned in numerous publications as one of the ten best bass players in America. No one can come close. There are only two other bass players that I can think of. Umm Leo Lyons, and Joey Spampinato…and frankly, even THOSE miracles aren't IN the HULLAPALOOZA universe. NOPE. LEND me your EARS citizens.

Who has David played with? A more accurate question would be—who has NOT had the honor and pleasure of working with David? May we begin with the startling fact that he played at Jimi Hendrix's funeral? Boy, when I got wind of THAT, it thrilled the bejesus out of me, because it makes David seem unbelievably old compared to outrageously youthful ME… until I remember…he started out at an unthinkably young age. Was he TEN when he began playing with Buddy Miles? MUST have been. Does the startling fact that an experienced R&B Master chose a young lil' white boy from Stratford, CT to take the bass seat in his band tell you SOMETHING about David's Bass prowess? There's not enough room here to list the long and impressive discography and credentials David is lugging around with him. What other albums has David been on? Sure, the Buddy

Miles Live "Chages" album, ohh The Joe Perry Project's "Have Guitar Will Travel", Detroit boy…Ted Nugent's "Weekend Warriors" album. Who else has been lucky enough to have David Hull spend time with them? Joe Cocker, Jon Butcher, James Montgomery, Arthur Lee and Love..(the Vindicator album), and I don't know WHO all else.

Google the LIFE out of David Hull (but leave some of him for the rest of us, will you?). Do yourself a favor, and DO IT. Your starving ears will thank me. Let me know if you've ever heard bass solos like THAT. He's a BASS MONSTER, and as if that's not enough, he's got a high-ranking spot on my list as one of the most caring and generous people I'VE ever known. Bless him.

David Hull was a huge inspiration to me, and if you're lugging any good taste around with you, he'll be a big inspiration for you TOO. The entire Hull family is wildly talented and musical …gosh…Chris Hull, Peter Hull…Hulls GALORE. I think they contracted the fever from their music teacher grandma, and their daddy, Gene Hull, a gifted sax player (flute and clarinet too). You can rightfully ask once again…who the heck hasn't GENE played with? Buy his book, *Hooked On A Horn* to find out.

I must tell you about the uproarious night I met David. I don't reckon he remembers it, so I'll be reminding him in the near future. I was a young 'un. (What year was it…'78?) As usual, I'm sort of fuzzy…let's see, was your band called The Dirty Angels by then? I'm not sure that one could rightly call it a MEETING, but it occurred at the Shaboo. I accidentally wandered into HIS band's dressing room, instead of my own. Let's just say, they scared the bejesus out of me. They looked as though they were wearing eyeliner, and had tons of big hair, and lots of leather.

They acted mighty sassy toward me. I think David was wearing velvet. He's the first male I ever saw donning velvet. I can't begin to tell you how much this impressed me.

As usual, I was completely unaware of David's LEGENDARY bass playing status, and had no knowledge of the UNIMAGINABLE amount of projects that have benefited from his talent. Guess when Vardz became slowwwly aware of this? That's right…pretty much yesterday. OK, I'm exaggerating, but not too much, and for UMPTEEN years I thought, "Damn. DAMN that David is the BEST. He just KILLS me. LISTEN TO THAT…BOY…I'm just sayin'…DAVID HULL. OK? OK? Does anyone else KNOW this?" I was sometimes surprised to discover …upon mentioning David's mind-blowing bass playing to a new band mate, they would display a look that said "ya THINK?" You've already heard one of my "I don't know nuttin' bout nobody" tales, but believe me, it is an unfortunate and recurring theme in my life. The truth is…David like my other "plugees" isn't known by NEARLY enough people. MILLIONS have heard him. SOME just don't know WHO they be hearing. Now YOU know.

Whilst I've been running off at the mouth, did you people run to check out The Dirty Angels? David? Other band involvements? How about White Chocolate? GROUNDBREAKING music. Listen to a song called "Debris" if you want a hint of David Hull's funky, funky beginnings. THEN give yourself over to the little ditty "Tell Me." And tell ME what big hit-making guy had his musical brain rearranged by David and his pals. Can't guess?

In years to come, he advised me on any number of things, helped get rid of my migraines, and oh yeaaaahhhhh… I forgot about the weddings. Here we go.

Dave hired my band to play at his wedding. One of the only FUN weddings I've ever encountered—with all those crazy and musically creative Hulls sitting in. The union didn't last all that long. Do you think it's because of his terribly misdirected choice of a wedding band? Coincidence? Naaaahhhh. I'll bet David is awfully glad I was nowhere in the vicinity of the nuptials when he joined hands with the lovely woman he's been happy with for years.

WHERE ARE YOU, R & R HALL OF FAME? IT'S ME, VARDZIE. YUP, THE ONE WITH THE BIG MOUTH. THERE'S A GIFT WALKING WITH US. WITH THOSE OF US WHO HAVE CHOSEN THIS PATH. HE'S BEEN HOLDING OUR HANDS, INSTRUCTING US FOR YEARS.

HE'S HERE TO SHOW US HOW IT'S DONE.

HOW IT'S DONE NICE AND DIRTY,

AND HOW IT'S DONE TO CAPTURE THE WINGS OF ANGELS.

YOUR LIL' HALL THERE NEEDS HIM.HE'S THE MAN. THE MAN WITH THE BASS

DAVID HULL

Thanks for your time.

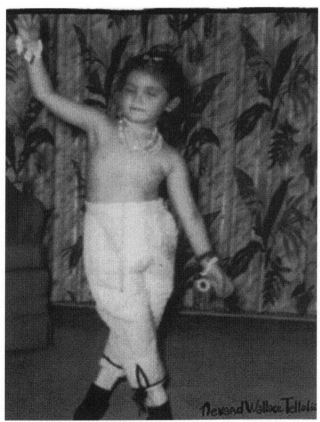

(The author at 3 1/2 yrs. belly dancing with a strange look of rapture on her
face. Most disturbingly, her diapers are looking bulky through those jammie
bottoms. OH for the love of...well,for the love of mamma's
costume jewelry, apparently.)

FUN WITH THE TELLALIANS

I'd be in possession of incalculable wealth, if I were handed a dime each time someone said to me "Do you KNOW how LUCKY you are to have parents like yours?"

Yes, I DO know how very lucky I was to have two such luminous presences to light my way. THAT is incalculable wealth.

My father would often jump on the phone with my friends and offer wise advice during their rough times. His most astute advice to LOTS of my girlfriends usually contained the following words.

"Well, he's NO DAMNED GOOD, that's all, honey. You've GOT to get away from him. NO…don't speak with him about ANYTHING. Sweetie, this is an unpredictable situation, and we have no idea how he'll react. If he calls, tell him to speak with your lawyer. This is why a lawyer is called a MOUTHPIECE. Hahahaa. Let him do his job, love, will you? Call me if you need anything. I've lived a helluva long time, and I can tell you…HE'S JUST NO DAMNED GOOD!"

Whenever my girlfriends and I have equally thorny problems in our lives, this is our battle cry. "He's just no damned good, honey." That's all.

I first heard this phrase when my father regaled us one night at the dinner table with the story of a woman he'd represented. SHE ran her husband down with her CAR. He got her off. Yup.

"How did you get her OFF, Daddy??"

"Why it was self-defense."

"Self-DEFENSE? What? She was IN A CAR. Waddya MEAN self-defense?"

"Oh, I don't know. He was a liar, a cheapskate, and he continuously beat her. He was just no damned good, honey. That's all."

We laughed till we cried.

How can I possibly begin to describe the revelry, the affection, and the unprecedented and bold lack of propriety present in the Tellalian household? The above words are only a SHORT description of my parents, the duo helms of our house. Just have to dig in and start, I guess.

My father received an honorary doctorate from a university, and the other keynote speaker for that day was Kay Redfield Jamison. She is an extraordinary woman, being the author of THE seminal book on Manic Depression, *An Unquiet Mind.*

We don't need to go into her many and impressive affiliations with many impressive places…let's just note she'd been chosen by *Time Magazine* as a "Hero of Medicine." So, I'm thinking, boy, this woman's no slouch, yes?

Well, I'll be darned if Professor Jamison didn't march right up to me at the après commencement tea, and declare, "Do you KNOW how LUCKY you are? Your father is the most ADORABLE man I've EVER met."

I replied with my usual aplomb, "You BETCHA, sister." And when I looked into her eyes, I saw the exact shimmer and empathy that was always present in my father's. Yes…she had recognized one of her own.

My dad had a collection of medicines that would astound a pharmacist. The trouble was every single one of them was at least ten years old. If you informed him over the phone that you had bronchitis, you'd get this response.

"Oh well, sweetie, we can fix that right up. I have a perfectly good bottle of Ampicillin here….let's see…1976. Yup, still good. I'll be right over with it."

This conversation would have taken place in **1994**. Do you have a tummy ache? DADDY'S got you covered all right.

"I'm looking at a nice little 1981 Compozine, that should do the trick, honey. I'll be right over. What do you MEAN not good anymore? Let's see….it smells just FINE. If it's good for the third world countries we're selling it to, it's OK for us TOO. This is some great VINTAGE STUFF, dammit. I'm coming over."

"Daddy, it's not like WINE you know. It goes BAD for gosh sake."

No amount of coaxing would deter Daddy from delivering the goods from his stash of great medicine. Finally, Mommy made him throw most of it out when he was ninety- two. "Well, that's just a WASTE, Mommy. A WASTE!"

Although my folks were immaculately proper, and dignified in many ways, they were (most especially for THEIR generation) markedly lacking in ANY pretension, and in fact, right beneath the surface lurked an una-bashed and innocent wantonness, a voluptuousness that could, and WOULD burst from their outer shells at any given time. We were a physi-cal family; hugging and kissing and holding was the norm, and we were vo-cal about our love for each other. The folks told me that as soon as I was able to walk, I'd walk up to strangers and smooch away at them.

When any pal of mine comments on MY proclivity for immodesty, I al-ways point my fingers…all of them, right at my parents. I was informed at their feet.

When you're a child, you think everyone else is growing up just like YOU are. You believe the conduct in YOUR home is completely in sync with the behavior and the beliefs in every OTHER kid's house. RIGHT? Well, let me tell you, when I became old enough to visit other families on my own, I was plunged into culture shock. I'm STILL in shock.

I'd like you all to take a look at the photo on page 58 of this book. There's a picture there that is a good representation of ME, at the tender age of three and a half.

My folks entertained a lot. I mean a LOT. In those days, it didn't take a lot of dough to party, and almost every week there was a BASH of one sort or another going on at the Tellalian abode.

At an alarming young age, I began, with no prodding whatsoever, to pour myself into a pair of satin quilted pajama bottoms, slip into some slip-pers, stick my hair in a bun, and ambush my mother's ample supply of cos-tume jewelry with which to adorn myself. Other than those items, I BE NEKKID, child.

I would then run to the den, CAREFULLY place El Bakkar's *Port Said* album on the old hi fi, and as gingerly as any tot CAN…I'd place the needle on it. Then, I'd RACE to the living room, the backyard, or wherever the festivities might be centered. Sometimes I'd have my brother set up LIGHTS ahead of time, so the revelers wouldn't MISS the sight of Vardzie belly dancing her little heart out.

Where in the world I got the crazy notion that I would be some great entertainment for those parties, OR the idea that to dance half undressed was a mighty fine thing to do, is a riddle that's up for grabs y'all. It sure wasn't the folks' idea, but they yelped with encouragement, just as they would for the next eighty YEARS.

Who KNOWS what their assorted pals thought of my earnest outpourings of artistry.

The folks always had a diverse mix of pals hanging about—from every walk of life, and every occupation and interest—and somehow they all seemed to enjoy each other. Perhaps it was because they all had something in common. They all were in possession of a discernible spirit. They had a sense of sharing and if necessary, SHOULDERING for each other, whatever life delivered to their doorsteps. You can add a big dollop of rejoicing in there. These were people who savored and appreciated. They were ALIVE.

There was no such thing as a closed door in our house. Okay…maybe when the folks were romancing, but even THEN, no locked door. We lived in a tiny ranch house, and by the time I came along, the folks had added a little knotty pine den.

There was HUGE acreage, but a small house. Acreage my mamma would lovingly fill with an enormous amount of lovingly tended plant life. There was one bathroom in the house (until I moved out, and they added another one).

We would all dress, undress, enter, and exit the bathroom and bedrooms, with no thoughts of shutting a door. This one bathroom was visible from each of the bedrooms, so every morning Pops would be in there (on his throne if you will) with the daily newspaper AND the door wide open, broadcasting any item he thought would be of interest to the rest of the family, or items that were of interest to HIM. If he happened to run across a piece he'd consider might be particularly exciting to any one of us, he would yell out, "Vardzie girl, come here, come HERE! I've got an exceptionally scintillating article here, and I have a hunch… Yes, yes, I think you'd find this an informative …"

"OK, Daddy, just a second. I haven't finished putting on…"

I (or whoever was on the receiving end of Daddy's outstanding find) would scoot to the bathroom and take a seat on the edge of the bathtub, right across from Daddy.

We'd then be knee to knee with him, as he held court and shared with us the info he'd unearthed, as if it were an archeological find. THEN, a lengthy analyzing would take place, and the possibility of running to grab a reference book for verification was NOT out of the question.

As I grew into my teens—usually an age when modesty kicks in—I still did not feel uncomfortable being in any stage of undress around my parents, and I was used to seeing them buck naked throughout their lives.

They weren't ALWAYS nekkid… I mean they didn't go out of their way to be disrobed. The folks never came to the dinner table with no clothes on, but they had no trouble going about their business without self-consciousness.

I STILL have a tough time with the task of closing the bathroom door when guests are in my home, but can sometimes remember to do so if there's a male around. Some of my girlfriends have been taken aback by this rash abandonment over the years. I'll just step into the bathroom, or begin to change my clothing and keep on talking to them. "GOD, Nevard, do you have ANY sense of modesty?"

"Well, sure I do. I wouldn't behave that way around strange men, or in PUBLIC, but sheesh, you're a GIRL. What do ya do in the 'one dressing room' stores? You never went to the Y? What happens to you in a locker room? Do you become paralyzed? I don't get it." I feel unabashed with band members as well, if I've known them for a while. They're family too.

I've often wondered WHERE Aram and Margo acquired such a forward thinking philosophy. My father was born in 1913, to an old country Armenian family, who sure as HECK didn't act that way.

My mother was a farm girl, the oldest of thirteen, and I imagine having fifteen people in a teensy house wouldn't exactly engender a great deal of shyness, but I'm sure the kids never saw THEIR folks undressed. They were strict Southern Baptists. No drinkin', no smokin', no nuttin'. They were used to nature though, and nature HAS no modesty.

You can imagine what my mother's folks must have thought when the recently wed Margo Wallace brought her new husband Aram Hagop Tellalian Jr. home to Macomb, Mississippi. Good LORD…not only a Yankee, but a FOREIGNER as WELL!

The first time they visited the Mississippi contingency of our family, Aram and Margo attended a flag-raising ceremony. First the Stars and Stripes went up, but when the Confederate flag flew up a pole and unfurled itself in front of a baffled Aram, he turned to Margo and in a loud voice (Daddy wasn't capable of anything BUT a loud voice) he posed this question: "What the HELL is THAT flag, Margo?"

During the same visit, the folks attended a big Wallace celebration, and let me tell you, the Wallaces KNOW how to celebrate. Aram drank cup after cup of the fruit punch being served.

He'd imbibed his tenth cup, when he finally asked his bride, "Margo, I keep DRINKING and DRINKING this stuff, and I'm getting a stomach ache, but I'm not feeling a THING."

Her laughing retort was, "No, and you WON'T, honey. There's nothing IN the punch."

Daddy was a Northern Congregationalist and had no IDEA there would be no booze at ANY Baptist gathering and was unaware that Mississippi was a dry state in those days. In the years to follow, he'd bring a flask.

He and Uncle Gordon (and I don't know who else) would sneak behind the barn for a snort as if they were teenagers. They'd also sneak back there to have a smoke. He carried on this habit into his eighties.

The Wallaces took him into their hearts pretty quickly, and oh Lord, Daddy loved them too and enjoyed taking off to see them more than he loved trips to any exotic locale in the world. He LIVED for that catfish fishin' (the REAL, not farmed catfish) and wolfed down those boiled peanuts like crazy, he did. He looked forward to their visits to Connecticut too (even though there was no sacred catfish fry or crawfish eatin' involved). Just as Margo had become an honorary Armenian, he became an honorary Wallace.

I used to accompany them when I was a kid and wanted to be with my kin, but when I started making my living as a musician it was impossible. I missed out on a lot of fun, hanging out with my grandparents (Onie and Parshall), all my darling aunts, uncles, and cousins. I missed seeing THEIR kids grow up too. I need to make up for lost time.

I have a couple of old favorite Daddy stories my friends have recalled. Here's a rather tame one.

Daddy loved his old BIG Lincoln. I think it was circa 1974, the last year they made them as big and heavy as a ship. He drove it until it couldn't be fixed anymore, so Pops was forced to get a new one, and he HATED the new car. "Damned thing is like a tin CAN. It's a piece of CRAP."

"Daddy, stop that cussing."

"All right, Margo. Dammit."

My friend Doug took a little drive with Pops, shortly after the horrendous new car purchase. Well….not actually NEW. The Tellalians have never been "brand new" car consumers.

They were coasting along on the highway, and my friend inquired if this new vehicle was a V6. Daddy said, "Gosh, who KNOWS Doug? Let's just see what it can do!" Whereupon he FLOORED the thing. I'm told the car accelerated so fast, the G force could be felt. Just as they hit a speed of a hundred or so, Daddy exclaimed, "OH, well now, here is our EXIT. Let's see how this veritable pile of junk does in a nice quick turn!" He proceeded to WHEELIE his way onto the exit, while muttering about the shabbiness of modern vehicles.

Daddy was almost ninety years old when that cozy little move was executed. He'd call me every single day from a cell phone while he was driving (driving FAST) just to say, "Hi, sweetie, how's it going? I'm on 95 right now…have a meeting in Essex…."

It scared the dickens out of me, especially the dialing part, and I'd yell into the phone, "DADDY, can you just watch the ROAD and NOT CALL me until you GET somewhere?" Didn't faze him an iota. He did it until he was ninety-two.

EVERYBODY was scared to drive with my father. Most of the people he knew have funny and terrifying "driving with Aram" stories to tell. That reminds me. Whenever my friend Tony gave me a lift, he'd call it "Driving Miss Crazy"…and people are afraid to get in the car when I'm driving as well. HOW COME?

Years and years after I moved out of my parents' house, my father was looking for something or other in my old closet and happened upon a dusty joint. That evening, he said to me on the phone, "Sweetie, this afternoon, I found a MARIJUANA CIGARETTE on the top shelf of your closet."

"Holy cow, Daddy, I'd say that joint would be about twenty years old."

"So I SMOKED it."

"You…YOU WHAT, Daddy? You SMOKED it? You did NOT."

"Well, yes, I DID, Vardzie. I smoked it, and I think you'll find the results of my experiment very interesting. It didn't do a THING for me. I didn't feel a THING. I can't understand WHY the marijuana would APPEAL to anyone, because I may as well have smoked some CARDBOARD."

"Oh for goodness sake, what kind of effect were you expecting to GET from twenty-year-old pot? Would you like me to get some FRESH pot for you to try?"

By this time in my life, I hadn't smoked pot in over fifteen years, so I didn't quite know where I'd GET some, but I'm sure I could have asked around and come up with a nickel for him. How much would a nickel have COST? Not a nickel anymore, that's for sure. How much would you get for five bucks now, maybe a thimbleful? I'm out of the loop.

"Oh no, sweetie, there's no need for THAT. I would be perfectly capable of obtaining some marijuana if I were inclined to try it again."

"Daddy, WHERE would YOU get the MARRY WANNA? At the office? The Courthouse?" He's gotta be kidding, right?

"Don't you worry about ME, Vardzie. I could have SOURCES."

Sources? What SOURCES could my seventy-year-old popsie HAVE? It boggles the mind. Every time I picture him in that little suit of his, toking away on the ancient pot, it cracks me up.

My mamma and daddy retained their sense of WONDER. The posture they displayed was childlike, their little heads coming forward, hungry for information, and wanting to learn something new. They were intrigued by everything and anything.

I sometimes found their itinerary of seemingly endless "third degrees" to be an annoyance, but then the recognition of something UNTHINKABLE would stop my impatience in its tracks. I needed to LEARN from this, because someday, I wouldn't HAVE these two miracles to lead the way to tireless enthusiasm. Who the heck ELSE will CARE this much? This behavior had a great deal to do with MY interest in others, and sadly they passed this third degree leaning…down to me.

One of the most unusual things about them was a perplexing tendency to constantly run into celebrities, and many times they'd have NO idea who in fact these people WERE. We'd all tease the poor things about this strange aptitude.

When the Tellalians encountered these people, the same rules they applied in their home came into play, often with unheard of results. There was NO such thing as censorship in the Tellalian household, and there was NOTHNG that wasn't allowed to be up for discussion. No subject was too mundane, too insignificant, or too private. They went where animals, plants and minerals fear to tread.

Two years ago, I was packing for my move to Florida, after they both were gone. I was faced with, and I'm not exaggerating, a good two HUNDRED plus pounds of Tellalian memorabilia. I had time to sort through some before leaving Connecticut, but It wasn't until recently I finally began to delve into the entire mountainous pile.

I went through photos that spanned the entire twentieth century, and beyond, and found pictures of things they'd never TOLD me about. One photo showed the folks sitting on a couch, highball glasses raised, laughing it up, and having a fine old time. Between them sat a cute, plump redheaded woman, holding the same sort of libation, and leaning against my mommy.

Boy, she looks familiar. Ah GEEZ, that's Beverly Sills. That's who it is. It's Bubbles. Now WHERE would they have been partying with HER?

In another photo they were with Dr. Jonas Salk, the inventor of the POLIO VACCINE. Annnd where in the world were they hanging with HIM??

Just this year I ran straight into a photo of my father having lunch with Clare Boothe Luce…gazing at her as if he'd have liked to consume HER for lunch. It's from a newspaper and looks as if it's the '40s. Did he help her write *The Women*? Naaah.

When I was approximately eight years old, the folks and I were driving around Manhattan, and that day, another bothersome family trait, namely our nonexistent sense of direction, was on full display. Yessiree, we were lost as usual.

My Dad was NOT a male who was afraid to ask for directions, so we stopped the car right in the middle of the street in order to hail down the first friendly face we could latch onto. Lo and behold, moving steadily toward us was a man in lime green bell bottom pants. The pants are a standout in my brain, because at the age of eight, I'd never seen the likes of them before.

My pops flagged this poor guy down, like an elephant hunter in the wild.

"Hello there, young fella. Sorry to disturb your, ehh…delightful midday perambulation. If you'd be so kind, we're having a problem navigating our way to a destination that seems to have avoided our radar. If you have a couple of minutes, we'd be awfully grateful for your help."

The green bell-bottomed man was of course charmed by my amiable daddy. He cheerfully leaned into our car window and said that "Yes, sir" he would be more than happy to lend a hand. What followed was Daddy's usual barrage of questions.

"Now, is that a northeast or northwesterly direction? Does blah-blah street lead into blah-blah street, which I recall is a one way blah, blah? And the Triborough Bridge, I'm assuming, blah, blah. Hey, young fella, are there any new restaurants blah, blah. Would you like to join us, because we'd love to have you, wouldn't we, Mommy?"

After a good FIFTEEN MINUTES of conversation with this infinitely patient victim, Daddy FINALLY thanked him, and asked, "May we give you a lift somewhere?"

And he answered, "No thank you, sir, I'm all set, thanks."

As we sped off, Daddy commented, "What a NICE young fella, eh, Margo? Vardzie? He was PALE though. So PALE! Did you notice?"

"Daddy...it was Andy Warhol."

"Who? Andy who? Who's THAT, love?"

And my mamma piped in, "Andy WARHOL, honey. YOU know, the Campbell Soup man."

"Oh sure, the Campbell Soup. NICE kid. PALE."

If my father had known this before we took off, the poor man would NOT have escaped a benign kidnapping by the Tellalians.

Daddy would have had ol' Andy in the car, and whisked away to dinner before he could have uttered "Baby Jane Holzer," and THEN he would have gone to TOWN. "Exactly how LONG does it take to PRODUCE a soup can image, and how many to turn a profit? Is this a lucrative process, young man, because I think ANYONE ...now tell me, why did you pick the soup can? Why not a box of PANCAKE mix?"

More than coincidentally, many, MANY years later, I was at a Warhol shindig. I was almost paralyzed by the more than distracting sight of big, BIG amounts of various powders flying up the noses of some of the people attending. People who possessed the (capable??) hands in which our "State Of The Union" rested. Ahh well...we've all got to grow up and face the truth sometime. I guess it was MY time.

Late one evening, my parents arrived home from a dinner party. "We met a FASCINATING musician this evening," my father said, "and he performed a few pieces of his music. I wish you'd been there, Vardzie, you would have been... His name? I think it's RAY VEE SOMETHING."

"Do you mean Ravi Shankar, Pops?"

"Why yes. YES. That was his name. We thoroughly enjoyed him, didn't we, Margo? Nice young fella. Indian. He played a large stringed instrument. WHAT was it, Mommy?"

"DAD, that would have been a sitar he was playing."

"YES, Nevard, that's IT. Are you familiar with that kind of music?"

"Well, I'm sure as heck familiar with Ravi Shankar, Daddy."

"Ahh, I SEE. So he must be popular, because he was completely unknown to US. Do you know what's astounding? There were women, who quite obviously follow this young fella around. Now what puzzled ME, is this. The MUSIC he plays is ENJOYABLE, but..."

" Oh GOD. What did you ask him, Daddy? WHAT? OHH boy."

"Well, nothing of CONSEQUENCE, Vardz. I simply commented on the wonderful sounds he was able to produce, and told RAYVEE that it reminded me of the Armenian tones played on the OUD. Such a restful sound. So I asked him...given the SOMNABULENT NATURE of your music, how in the WORLD do you keep those WOMEN of yours AWAKE long enough to enjoy ANY of their ample delights?"

"Holy crap, Daddy."

"Stop that swearing, love. It is NOT attractive language."

"DADDY, please don't tell me you asked Ravi Shankar those questions."

"Well SURE, I did, honey. You never LEARN things, unless you ASK, do you?"

Unbelievable. I wish I'd been there to see the reaction. I have no idea what Mr. Shankar must have thought of my daddy, nor did I ever find out what ANSWER he'd given to my errant parent.

There wasn't a THING you couldn't discuss with my parents. Dinner table topics would include subjects I imagine would be deemed inappropriate in most homes. Dinner was a time to learn, and to inquire.

They taught me all about sex, while enjoying Mommy's chicken piccata. They discussed DEVIANT sex, while chowing down on salad. Drugs were an open topic, and they were aware of any dabbling of mine. Politics along with dessert. History, horticulture, literature, music, it was all fodder for mealtime education. I relayed every happening in my life, unless I was keeping horrible behavior of someone I was seeing from them.

When I was a kid, my father sat me down to inform me about the inequalities between men and women.

"Vardzie girl, you've been raised in an environment of acceptance, and I'm sure you're aware, sex is a natural part of life, and something to be enjoyed. Mommy and I were both very active before we met, and you'd be surprised to know…Margo's participation in this area surpassed my own.

I'm telling you, because I want you to be aware of what you are going to run up against when you're launched into the world. Even though you're used to hearing a nonprejudicial view of men and women, you need to know—the double standard is still alive and well. I don't want you to get hurt, sweetie."

I asked him why it didn't bother HIM that Mommy was so active. Know what he said?

"Because I'm not an IMBECILE, darling. Most men are. I ENJOY your beautiful mommy's wild side…she'd have been pretty boring without it."

And then he'd sing me to sleep with "Scarlet Ribbons" or the "St. Louis Blues," as he always did. What a gift to give your daughter. I knew my father was pretty special even then, but it wasn't till years later I realized what an extraordinary man he had been.

My mother was movie star beautiful. In public, she had every hair in place, was immaculately and tastefully adorned, soft spoken and warm, and extremely polite. If required, she could be as formal as all get out—an ability she passed conveniently along to her daughter. I'm able to "clean up" for Sunday company as well.

As soon as she got to know you though—which didn't take too long—she'd let LOOSE. You can ask any friend of mine that knew her. In fact, she LOVED a dirty story more than anyone I've ever met. We'd all scurry around to find the most outrageous jokes and stories we could get our hands on, things that would make ME cringe, just for the exhilarating experience of seeing those eyes of hers open up wide, and hear her giggle like a schoolgirl.

The trouble came when Mamma attempted to repeat these stories or jokes. She'd tell them a lot at home, but it was when she'd try to recount them in restaurants that all hell would break loose. QUIET restaurants…and she'd invariably end up getting the punch lines ALL mixed up.

So there we'd be in a public place, and Mamma would begin the recounting of the oh-so-admired dirty story, and the endings usually came out like this. "Oh, DADDY, I forget. Did the sum a bitch man get his dick stuck in the…?"

Daddy would try to remember. "No, love, I think the stick was in his ass, and THEN his dick was…"

Can you picture it? My father suited up, my mother looking like the Historical Society lady she WAS, with the LOUD filth pouring out of their seemingly genteel selves, and every table in the vicinity would be attempting to inch away from us. This was sort of an every week event.

When I was a child, I'd tack onto my wall every single poster that came with an album. We all did that, right? Who knows what I had on those walls. I did have a poster of up of a completely leather clad musician. Why can I distinctly recall that particular one? Here's what my Daddy astutely observed one fine day after studying the guy in all his leather finery decking my wall.

"Who's that? Boy, what a horsey face. He has a very horsey-looking face. OHHH, sure from that band. I like them, Vardzie. What…what…WHAT's that in his PANTS?"

This poster was a full-length one, and I must admit, as soon as my father pointed this out, those leather pants looked a tad overstated to me too.

"Well, that's not NATURAL, Vardzie girl. Oh no, I'm telling you that is not natural. Is he EXCITED? What the hell is he excited about…he's just STANDING there. And even if he WAS excited, I'm TELLING you, that's just not RIGHT. Well, I think any young lady he'd bed down would be very disappointed upon opening THAT package. That's just false, that's what it is. Here, let me show you the kind of thing we get in our mailbox every day."

Daddy went to get a flyer of prosthesis things, and showed me this, all the while talking about the bad fake stuff in the pants tragedy.

A few months after he took notice of this offending poster, I went to see this band, with my friend Carole Laskey. Maybe it was because they hadn't had a number one hit yet or maybe they HAD… whatever the reason, they didn't seem to be too popular at that venue.

Our hometown boys, the Wildweeds, were warming up and got a great reception, because well… they WERE great, with Al Anderson et al, but I think only Carole and I dug the overstated leather pants band. REMEMBER, CAROLE? They received a lot of boos, resulting in the "deflated pants now" guy flipping the bird between every song. When he picked us up, Daddy had gotten a look at the band and was quick to point out the "horsey face" aspect, and the lack of big pants action that was evident on stage, but we had a great time.

Let's fast forward to a few years later. Mommy, Daddy and I were sitting at a gate in Heathrow Airport. There we were, sitting and chatting, and Daddy all of a sudden exclaimed loudly, "Hey, isn't that, uh, WHAT is his NAME, Mommy? Never mind. VARDZIE, isn't that OLD HORSE FACE right here?"

I looked up, and standing less than a foot in front of the nosy Tellalian noses was INESCAPABLY "he of the overstuffed pants and horsey face". I was aghast at the sight of this man standing there in line, almost on top of us.

Of course he had HEARD, Daddy. Well, SURE he had, and being the only rock star type of person standing there, he knew it was HE that was being talked about. Oh no, WHY was Daddy's voice so loud? The poor flabbergasted man's head spun around and he stared at us. I uselessly tried my level best to SHRINK into the seat, so I wouldn't be associated with this embarrassment. His face clearly said...

"Whaddya MEAN horseface. Fuck you." Oh, it was a saaad moment, and the only thing that kept racing through my mind, over, and over, and over was—"Oh God, please don't let Daddy ask about the pants. DON'T let him ask about the SPINAL TAP TROUSERS, PLEASE!"

I'm informing you all right now, if that line hadn't moved along right quick, there's no doubt in MY mind, my un-edited father would have had NO problem asking, "You KNOW young fella, my little girl Vardzie...yes, here she is...has a photo on her wall, and I must INQUIRE, and I'm sure VARDZ would like to know as well...wouldn't you, sweetie...just WHAT exactly did you have RESTING in those pants of yours?"

Being the music lovers that we assuredly were, my father accompanied me to lots of concerts before I was old enough to go unattended. As a matter of fact, when I was a REAL tyke, maybe seven, Daddy and I went to see the Beatles play at Forest Hills Stadium. He LOVED it, in spite of the fact that you could barely hear a NOTE they played, and they looked like little ants in suits.

He loved the SPECTACLE of it. Daddy was riveted by the weeping girls, the helicopter, the binoculars we'd brought that were constantly grabbed from us by the weeping girls. He was like Pearl Buck, conducting a sociological study. We WERE frustrated that we couldn't hear them too well, because we were huge fans. Daddy loved those early Beatles songs and thought the songwriting was great.

I can be equally fearless when it comes to imposing my largely ignorant and usually endless amounts of wonderings on the unexpected. ESPE-CIALLY if I'm in any way interested in something they've accomplished, or curious about why they have NOT accomplished things. I've inherited the curiosity gene, I guess mostly from my father, but my mother had her moments too. None of us would limit these interrogations to hugely known folks. I'm giving you two "young" ones I promised you. They're a couple of the most awkward outbursts from ME, and positively the stupidest. No…I'm wrong. There are a few MORE glaringly bad ones later.

Here are two of MY most inane questionings. I must have been about fourteen when I traveled to Paris to spend a couple of weeks with my Aunt Fifi (we called her Feef), who lived on Rue Saint Honore. This was an EX-OTIC and exciting thing for little me. I'm not exactly a world traveler.

Aunt Fifi was not my real aunt, but a close family friend from Bridge-port, Connecticut. When exactly she moved to France, I've no idea, but of course Fifi COULDN'T have been her given name. SHE was an exciting person to be with, a real character. She taught me to drink Pernod, a liquid I thought was cool, because it turned white when you added water (ahh shush…I was fourteen, all right?). She also taught me to smoke strong French cigarettes. Not so good there, Aunt Feef.

Feef was in her sixties by then, sloshed much of the time, and she amazingly had not one but TWO boyfriends living with her. Two gorgeous Arab boys.Imagine how exotic THAT must have been to witness. Not only was she a million something years older than her boyfriends, but Aunt Fifi was all but crippled by arthritis by this time and could barely walk. Her poor fingers were all twisted up, and her back was outwardly deformed by this disease as well.

These facts beg the question…WHY were these two young boys interested in Feef? Money? Nope. Aunt Fifi had run through her trust fund by then, and these two guys were supporting HER. While I was visiting, I saw them FIGHT over who would get to share her bed on any given night, and they'd bicker about which one of them should serve her dinner, or any other little task they could wrangle over. They sure didn't give ME any notice, I can tell you that. Soooo, WHY?

I'll tell you why. Aunt Fifi had that SPARKLE. She had the same "THING" my parents were filled with. She was mesmerizing. What kept my mommy and daddy eternally young, interested, and infinitely alluring to everyone they met was this same thirst for all that life had to offer.

Back to the story. Every month, Feef would have a Sunday afternoon soiree, or as they used to call it...a salon. In truth, they were booze-filled BRAWLS she hosted, and everyone including the Paris artsy set showed up. This is why I ran into Francois Truffaut at the one party I was able to attend.

For those of you who don't know who Monsieur Truffaut was...he was an immensely gifted French filmmaker. How come I recognized him? Because he was IN one of his recent movies. As soon as I saw him, I was of course ELATED. I mean I had QUESTIONS. Course I did.

"Monsieur Truffaut, boy, I sure do love your movies. *The 400 Blows.* Wowie what a THING! I think my favorite is *The Wild Child,* Monsieur Truffaut. It's based on a real story, right? A kid brought up by wolves? WOW. So, was it YOUR take on nurture versus nature, or..."

"Merci, call me Francois. You 'ave SEEN my films?"

I looked younger than my age, so Mr. Premier French Filmmaker was probably thinking..."How does this ten-year-old KID know my films?" He politely told me what he could. His English wasn't THAT great, and my French wasn't much better. I must have seemed pretty strange to him, to say the least. God, I really AM a moron...and coming up right now, is when my idiocy REALLY showed.

"Sooo you know that Jean Paul Belmondo, right? Course you do...he was in...I don't know...he was in LOTS. Know what? I LOVE his nose. LOVE that NOSE of his. Is that his REAL nose? I mean was he BORN with the nose, or did he get into a FIGHT or sumthin'? Is it a FAKE nose? Gee, I need to SEE the Belmondo NOSE. You think he's hanging about somewhere? Can we give him a BUZZ? That's a nose you have to EXAMINE. You know...up CLOSE I mean."

"I, I don't KNOW, uhh, Jean Paul's NOSE, eh?"

Could I be more of a PLANK HEAD? Jean Paul Belmondo's NOSE? Does this remind you of Daddy's "what's in the pants" questions?

This story reminds me of the time I saw Eddie Cochran on Tom Snyder's late night talk show. He didn't ask Eddie something that would be pertinent to his contribution in the world of rock and roll...you know, maybe, "Eddie, what was it LIKE to be in on the very beginning of that world?" No, no, upon hearing that Eddie had opened a boutique, Tom's big question of the evening was, "Eddie, Eddie, where do you think the word boutique COMES from? Boutique. Boutique. That's something to think about! BOOOOTEEEEEEK."

All righty there, Tom, I was FOURTEEN. What was YOUR excuse? I loved his show because of stuff like that. I also LOVED Joe Franklin (You fashion clothing out of walnut shells? YOU ARE THE BEST walnut fashion designer in the WORLD), and adored watching late night host Stanley Siegel as he pranced about the stage, using the camera as his psychiatrist. Oops. Off topic again. But Stanley reminds me of the next story. Those who are familiar with him will know why. It's a secret, OK?

The last time we saw Aunt Fifi alive, she came back to Connecticut for a visit, and yes sireee…the boyfriends were tagging along, carrying her luggage, and carrying on over HER. She died shortly thereafter, of cirrhosis. Still miss her.

My other nutty run-in when I was a tyke, took place during a weekend spent with my Aunt Annette Parlink, at her apartment in Manhattan. She had a teensy walk-up on Park Avenue at the time. Like Fifi, she was not my real aunt, but Mommy's best friend since WWII. She was a wonderful woman…and just as wayward as Mommy and me. Why did these two stories occur while visiting the "aunts"?

I was eleven years old…I think. Aunt Annette and I went downstairs to her neighbor Luba's apartment for something. Luba was a family joke of sorts. She claimed to be a Romanian Princess, but we all thought she was just a semi savvy con woman. She seemed to know about everybody who was anybody in the hip intelligentsia scene, and MOOCHED off of everybody who was anybody as well. In today's world she'd be called a scenester, or poser.

In we went to Luba's, and there was a naked man sitting on her couch. Luba said, "Oh hi, Annette, this is Timothy Leary."

Timothy Leary? HOLY COW. Timothy LEARY. What did your friend Vardzie do at the age of eleven? Yup, I just plopped on Luba's couch next to the naked Acid King.

"Mr. Leary, Mr. Leary, do you think I'm too YOUNG to take the LSD?"

Oh for crikey sake. He was probably so stoned he saw TWO eleven-year-old heads bobbing around in front of him and had no CLUE what I was asking. His profound answer?

"Uhhh. Uhhhh. Uhhhh. UHHHHHHHHHHHH. I GUESS. UHHHHHH. OK."

Now THERE's some sage advice for you.

Oh lord have MERCY, I just thought of yet ANOTHER positively mortifying lack of loopage story. This unattractive story played out in 2010. I got on Facebook, and found THIS.

November 19, 2010

Chip ------ Do you remember Terry Southern? He liked your act!!

Nevard Tellalian And I liked HIS act! Ohh I was thinking about Terry the other day. How could one FORGET? God, I adored him... dry wit, a wee bitter. Damn he was hypnotizing. My kind of guy. He was a lunatic who lived on the lunatic fringes and was usually well into his "cups" when we'd visit après show. Once in awhile, Terry would blurt..."When I wrote...bla, blah". He'd always get the same response from me."Get OUT Terry. You did NOT."

"Yes I DID."

"Shut UP."

If that wasn't stoopid enough on my part....it gets worse.

Almost every time we played at the club where Terry would come to see us, I'd toodle off to a club worker's house to crash for the night. One night we chatted for so long, we had to actually CLOSE the place. It seemed to be Terry's turn to provide an overnight for me. Where were my BAND mates that night? DUNNO. Gone.

We get to his house, and we manage to tumble in. He's three sheets to the wind and fixing his five hundredth drink in the kitchen whilst I'm THROWING three sheets on his couch. Noticed his large library, with one shelf of nice leather-bound volumes. Forgot the sheets and began looking at them. SOMETHING'S beginning to seep into my brain. Finally I took a gander at the inside back of one ...and whose face was unblinkingly there? SURE! It was Terry of course.

"Ter? Hey TERRY."

"WHAAAAT?"

"FER GOD'S SAKE...you're TERRY SOUTHERN"

"Yes. I know. I fuckin' KNOW who I AM Nevard."

"So you DIDN'T TELL me?"

" I DID tell you, ya little FUCKER."

"Jaaysus Terry. YOU WROTE EASY RIDER."

"Yes I'm AWARE of that. CRAP."

"EXCUSE me...why didn't you TELL me?"

"I DID tell you. YOU FUCKIN' CRAZY BITCH."

"DID NOT."

"You want a bourbon??"

Does it GET any more stoopid than THAT? Don't think so. *Note…2017 It was only a YEAR ago, when I found, that Terry is on the cover of the Sgt. Pepper album. Really; Terry. REALLY? Don't have any idea who Terry was? Don't blame you. He wrote an enormous amount of things. Books, articles, screenplays. *Dr. Strangelove Or: How I Learned To Stop Worrying And Love the Bomb*, *2001: A Space Odyssey*, *The Magic Christian*. Go and google that creature, if you've got an itchin' to. I feel lucky to have known him…to have been able to enjoy that enormous and fascinating brain of his…and absolutely incredulous that he was a fan.

One of the most endearing things about my parents was that they came out to see the band until they were in their EIGHTIES. How many parents do you think did THAT?

When they were younger, they'd travel far afield, especially if they had friends they could visit who lived near a venue where I might be appearing. They'd pop up in NYC, Vermont, Maine, Philly...oh lots of places. Of course they would come out to local clubs too, like Toads in New Haven, or any outdoor summer job, but as they aged, they couldn't hang in the larger clubs close to home. Places like that really had nowhere to SIT, at least not in the vicinity of their stages. It was just too much for them.

When I needed to fill up my calendar, I'd play at local dives, and I do mean DIVES. Places that had doormen named Tiny, who weighed upward of four hundred pounds, and would be shirtlessly stalking about the joint (I'd always insist on putting MY person on the door).

I'm talking about unbelievably seedy and often mob-owned places. Places in which the barroom brawl of the evening was just as entertaining as I was. Places where I'd see the owner grab his girlfriend by the hair and start banging her head on the bar. Places where I sometimes had to physically defend myself. Places where they'd ask, "Who's that? Is that a cop? I don't like cops."

And I'd answer, "No. Cool it, OK? Not a cop…just a fan."

Some of these "buckets of blood" clubs (as my daddy called them) were my FAVORITES. You can't BEAT a good dive. YOU JUST CAN'T. And you can be sure that most of the folks are there to see YOU, because otherwise they wouldn't be there, now would they? One of the saddest sights in the world to see (for a musician, anyway) is a great dive attempting to turn itself into a NON-dive club. This NEVER works, and it's always a pitiful thing to witness.

These are the places where the folks came to see me in their later years. ALL of these dives had tables and chairs. Ya can't expect the drunks to STAND all night, can ya? My sweet parents loved a good dive too. Go figure. They would just have a BALL watching their raucous and infinitely LOUD daughter, with her LOUD band. Didn't matter to them. That's our girl, go get 'em! The atmosphere didn't faze them.

One of these places had an owner that had been jailed a number of times, and was absolutely connected, if you know what I mean. Sometimes he'd get pretty snookered by the time the band was getting ready to go on, and we'd see him waving his gun about behind the bar. His pals would haul him to the back room, and one of the patrons would take over bar duty.

This bar owner almost passed out the first time he saw my father, who was a well-known judge, walk into his joint. I believe he had a flashback, and thought he was IN the joint. Poor thing.

The folks would drag their friends to these places, too. Sometimes they'd go to the SYMPHONY, and then come to hear me. WITH the friends. Most of their pals enjoyed themselves. Once I saw a chair FLY over Dr. Miller's head. He's not all THAT much younger than my folks. I called him the next day to apologize profusely, and he told me they'd had a WONDERFUL time and would return soon. "Reminded me of when I was in the Army," he said.

Once in a while, my parents would bring in friends that were decidedly NOT appreciative. I can recall a British couple they dragged with them one night…let's call them the Smythe-Browns. MRS. Smythe-Brown was a delight, and would roll with anything. MR. Smythe-Brown was another story. He was a stiff, parsimonious little man. My beloved Jeremy would have called him a "big girl's blouse." We were playing in a small club that night, so we were using my P.A., and the stage was already set up when I went over to sit and visit with the folks and their friends. I'd always have a pre-show visit with them in these places…not like a huge place, where you're not seen before you play.

So there we were, Mommy, Daddy, the Smythe-Browns all with their drinks, and they were facing the stage. (Funny, a LOT of dives have great stages.) Mr. Smythe-Brown sat there for a good long time inspecting the stage set-up. He could CLEARLY see the amps—the big ol' Marshalls, the SVT, and he could also see the SOLID BODY electric guitars sitting on their stands, right under the lights. And he could see the equally solid-bodied BASS sitting there big as life.

Mr. Smythe-Brown, after taking in the items placed on that stage, very DELIBERATELY turned to me, and with a definite and NOT misinterpreted smirk on his face, he divulged the following opinion (OK, picture the accent and his little Hitler-like mustache). "I THINK THE ELECTRIC GUITAR IS AN ABOMINATION. AN ABOMINATION."

My cheerful reply was, "Oh, do you? DO YOU, Mr. Smythe-Brown? That's great. Just GREAT, because I have some TERRIFIC news for you. YOU, sir, will appreciate our musical stylings more than anyone in this room. I can GUARANTEE it. Yes, you will. Cheers!"

I then walked back to the kitchen/dressing room, where I encountered the band, and said, "I wantcha to CRANK IT UP tonight, boys. I want you to CRANK IT UP TILL THEIR FREAKIN' EARS BLEED."

"Really, Vardz? This is not a huge club, you know. You sure?"

"Oh, yes indeedy. I've never been surer of anything in my life. CRANK IT."

Within a very short time, I was happily watching Mr. Smythe-Brown's eardrums explode. Mommy and Daddy didn't see that anything was amiss.

Know what folks? I'm patient. Very patient, but I do not like mean people. Don't fuck with me. That's all.

I used to love introducing any given song (usually something raw and frenzied-sounding) as a tune written by my Uncle Jay. I have no idea why this seemed to excite most audiences. The announcement would invariably pump the crowd up into an almost delirious state, and most times the whole place would begin to CHANT in the middle of the song.

"UNCLE JAY. UNCLE JAY. UNCLE JAY. UNCLE JAY." They'd usually do this, for a good five minutes, and often right through the next song. I still can't figure out why this got them going. Was it the SOUND of the words…Uncle Jay? If you've got a band, why don't YOU try it? Let me know what kind of results you get. Maybe I unwittingly hit upon some kind of cosmic universal sound. UNCLE JAY.

The band and I were always so proud to have my parents hanging in a club. Sometimes I'd flounce up to the stage and say, "OK, y'all, PARENTS IN THE HOUSE! Clean show. I SAID SQUEAKY CLEAN SHOW." Did we in fact manage that feat? Naaah.

The crowd seemed as thrilled as we were to have them there. They'd bring them drinks, hover over them protectively, call them Mr. and Mrs. Nevard (the folks got a BIG kick out of that), and a gang of them would ALWAYS walk them to their car when they were ready to go home. Surprisingly they'd usually make it till near closing time. Damn, they were cute.

Their lives weren't all fun and games. They went through some agonizing and trying times…some really tough things that would have felled many. They never lost their courage, their laughter, their need to help others. We all need to learn that. ALL of us.

I think my favorite memory of having my parents in clubs was the sight of my precious Mamma, walking into any old dive in her mink coat.

In she'd come draped in the mink, and I'd say, "Mamma, Mamma, this isn't the sort of place you'd be wearing MINK, for gosh sake."

Her answer? It was always the same.

"Oh honey, it's all right, this is Mommy's CASUAL mink."

(My parents)

REGRETS AND LESSONS

"If you seek happiness – believe.
If you seek the truth – inquire."
—Nietzsche

My father became very ill in 2007. He was ninety-three years old. He behaved the
same way that my two loves, Jeff and later Jeremy, behaved, and was joyful until the day he left this earth.

My folks had a few neighbors and friends, who never let them down, and their outpourings of devotion were a huge gift.

There were also those who showed utter coldness, and a more than stupendous degree of selfishness. It was unfathomable. It was untenable.

My parents were regrettably and brutally aware of this, but never lost hope until the very end. They believed that some degree of inherent goodness and compassion would eventually win the day.

It did not.

They tearfully asked only for love and attention, as they knew there wasn't much time left and their pleas were met with icy masks, and derision.

This was an unspeakable hurt they could not understand, and so I had to watch as their hearts were broken, and in my father's case, while suffering almost unendurable pain.

Toward the end, they had the pleading look of animals being tortured: trusting animals not able to speak the language of human cruelty. So they didn't understand.

I don't either. I was told with annoyance, by a friend "That is YOUR choice to be there."

My CHOICE? My choice, to watch the light go out of a loved one's eyes? NO, I was there because it was my obligation and my HONOR to serve them.

Heartless and rude behavior is often tolerated without a peep from those of us who recognize naked and crude mercilessness when we see it. Why without a peep?

It is because of this—when you are already grieving, and in shock, anyone can run over you like a steamroller.

I am alone, but I'd rather not be within the vicinity of venom. I think there's a Spanish saying that loosely translates into something like this: "BETTER ALONE, THAN BADLY ACCOMPANIED."

My Uncle Bob and Aunt Jean are firm believers in Karma. What goes around comes around. I'm not sure I buy it. I've seen too many loathsome people happily going about their business while leaving a path of destruction behind them, and they don't seem to be dropping in their tracks from any kind of just dessert.

It is not easy to see the light slowly dim in the eyes of someone you love with a depth that is bottomless, and all encompassing. Someone whose physical presence you can't fathom going on without.

Can you remember what I said about animals? They DO know more than we: an immeasurable amount. My Asian Leopard hybrid had accompanied me to my parents' house. She parked herself on my father for hours, and would not move. Every single day. She guarded him, kissing his fingers and gazing at him. This is NOT a lap cat. Oh, she was utterly affectionate and wanted to be with you, but she was not a domestic animal: ALWAYS busy and on high alert. You couldn't pick her up without getting that stiff arm thing—"What? I've got things to DO!"

Lally sitting on Daddy day and night was strange enough, but here's the crazy thing: two days before my father went into the hospital, she sat on him with her tail sticking STRAIGHT UP IN THE AIR. For TWO days. We knew then, the end must be near, because SHE knew.

The day he died (and how pray tell did she KNOW this?) she wasn't there. She immediately took her place on the pillow next to Mommy's head. Daddy's pillow.

The animals KNOW.

**ALWAYS ABIDE BY, AND RESPECT THE
INSTINCTS OF ANIMALS. THEY ARE
NEVER WRONG. THEY UNDERSTAND FAR
MORE THAN WE.**

"THERE ARE MORE THINGS IN HEAVEN AND EARTH, HORATIO, THAN ARE DREAMT OF IN YOUR PHILOSOPHY."
—William Shakespeare

I discovered during this painful time, and times after this loss, that I seem to be the owner of a talent I'd never been aware of. I'm good at helping people die.

I did it for Daddy, later for Mommy, for my Aunt Ellie, for my love Jeff—but only on the phone because he would NOT allow me to see him decline—and finally for sweet Jeremy. I laid down with them. I held them, felt their tenuous and stubborn clinging to this physical life, wept for them, and helped to ease off their mortal coil.

The first was my father. I told him how much he was loved, my tears dropping on his face while he patted me. I said I couldn't bear to say good-bye, but I wanted him to go.

"You can go, Daddy; you need to NOT be here and in pain like this. Not in this frightful twilight. Please, I don't want this for you, Daddy. Don't be scared. I'll look after Mommy. Promise you'll always be with me?"

He nodded, muttered yes, and tried to kiss my head.

And I said, "You've said Mommy and I were your greatest joys, but you'll never know…you taught me how to care. How to LIVE. Lessons I'm just NOW beginning to understand. You taught so many, by words, and deed. I want you to know. Please go, Daddy, you can leave knowing you damn well did a great show. Just like you taught me. You know when to make an exit.

"You will NOT be forgotten. I'll make sure. You did what you came to this earth to do. Your task was to see justice served, and to love. I will keep my promise to you. I'll do my best to let NO ONE forget the holocaust. I will open my mouth at every opportunity. "

I said a bit more and held him close then somehow knew he was going to hang on until I left. He did not want me to be in the room when he died. He did not want that memory for me.

I reluctantly went home, and as soon as I got in the door, I received the call I'd been dreading for years.

REGRET: During this time I also discovered that people will let you down—or worse, turn against you. If YOU have people in your life that display this kind of cruelty, DO NOT think they will have a miraculous "epiphany," and somehow become human. They won't. EVER. My regret is in hanging on to this hope for much too long, and with it, a bitterness of the damage done.

LESSON: Please, don't make my mistake and waste any of life's precious and fleeting moments on those who don't give a crap. Don't let them take the savoring of LIFE from you. Let it go. Let THEM go. Get them the heck out of your life. I'm doing just that.

If you RESEMBLE the people I described…well, first of all, you're most likely too self- absorbed to even recognize yourself, probably not capable of any kind of self-examination, and think you're a pretty swell person. In the unlikely event that you DO recognize yourself, may I, with no one's permission simply say:

YOU ARE TAKING UP TOO MUCH ROOM ON THIS PLANET

(Daddy's WWII I.D., and daddy with Ike)

I'd like to pass on one more Shakespeare thought. I lost both of my parents, within just a few months of each other. I am quite aware of my astounding luck in knowing them. To have had two remarkable spirits to touch for so many years was a gift most people won't get.

The loss of them was a cataclysmic one, and it pulled me to a place that had no light. Grief can be a physically lacerating ache that coldly slams into the very part of your being that distinguishes who and what you are. When they went, they took a large part of me with them.

The only written verse I've ever come across that clearly expresses the precise and horrible turning of the human brain when hit with something almost unendurable was of course penned by William S.

It's a well-known writing, and most would agree he bravely pushed his head directly through our ribs, INTO our essence, and pulled out the bloody truth. For some reason the following words helped at a time when nothing else could have reached me.

If you have had a loss, whether it's a death, a breakup with a longtime loved one, or if you have a giving heart that has been ruthlessly trampled by someone you trusted, (which invariably will occur numerous times during your life…especially if you're trusting), these words will describe your feeling of hopelessness as well.

Tomorrow, and tomorrow, and tomorrow, Creeps in this petty pace from day to day,

To the last syllable of recorded time;

And all our yesterdays have lighted fools The way to dusty death.

Out, out, brief candle! Life's but a walking shadow, a poor player

That struts and frets his hour upon the stage And then is heard no more.

It is a tale Told by an idiot, full of sound and fury,

Signifying nothing.

The above words aren't true in the sense you think they might be. They ring true when we're in the throes of distress, but we ALWAYS LEAVE A FOOTPRINT. All of us affect others' lives in larger ways than we can imagine. I know my parents left huge footprints, and their ripple is still resonating today with thousands.

Our society has become fairly numbed and calloused regarding our fellow human beings. Less and less, people know how to even be a good friend.

My friend Dawn often says, "Where are the good people? Where are the people who have a conscience? "

I always answer, "Sweetie, we must learn to be on our guard, because there are ARMIES of graceless monsters out there…to the left, to the right, behind, and in front of us. The song was wrong. The love we give, sure as HELL ain't the love we get.

That's the cynical me speaking—and like many of us, I have been defeated by loss, betrayal, misplaced trust and loyalty.

The feelings eventually ease, and the human heart will most times heal, and does forget, but it is in the forgetting that we are opened up yet again.

Resilience, hope, and a sense of humour will hopefully win out, and eventually the old optimism comes back.

REGRET: Too much time was wasted on those who did not deserve that time.

LESSON: The truth lies somewhere in between. Be loving, but be more cautious about where you park your trust.

RELIGION AND BELIEF

Since we're on the subject of grief and behavior… Do I believe in a hereafter? Do you care?

For the record, yes, I do think there's some sort of afterlife. I'm more or less a skeptical sort. I should have been born in the "show me" state, although I can't recall what state that IS exactly. I never THOUGHT people hung around after they were gone, but I've experienced things through the years that simply can't be explained. Let's not go into it.

Do I believe in God? I believe something we'll never be able to comprehend MUST have created this world, although I don't know what that IS. I have only to look at the glories of this earth, to tell me this.

When I see the enormity of the ever-changing ocean, when I see the prehistoric sea turtle

laboriously dragging her nine-hundred-and-fifty-pound self up the beach on a moonless night, laying her eggs in the very same place she was hatched years ago, yes, I'm staggered.

When I see the formidable Florida panther casually wander by, shoulders slowly rolling, as powerful and as graceful as a dance, when I see a lightning storm, or hear the quiet noise of a forest, I know it was created by something.

When I come face to face with the profundity of the miracle of life, whether it be human or animal, when I encounter kindness, laughter, music, and passion, I know there's a miraculous thing happening.

I'll call it God, because I don't know what else to call it. I don't think of God as a "someone" sitting somewhere.

Perhaps God is some sort of energy that made this world, and godliness is in the way we TREAT each other. If we're able to give of ourselves, and display compassion for fellow living creatures, and our planet, is this not religion? Darned If I know. I remain open on this subject, and I guess need to accept the hindrance of ignorance.

I DO know that to be unappreciative of what we have, or to be blind to it, and to waste it, is to SPIT in the face of God—WHATEVER that may be.

I think Hinduism is a lovely concept, but believe it was born (as many religions are) out of socio-economic need. How else, to get the hungry masses to behave themselves, and not revolt, if not to promise them a better life the next time around?

That brings me to the ever so attractive idea of reincarnation. What a GREAT idea! Boy, I'd love to believe that one. Get to come back and take the ride again! I don't know though... Have you ever noticed that every single person you've heard talking about their past lives were always something exotic in the previous ones? How did they manage this?

They were an Egyptian slave who helped build the pyramids.

They were a London prostitute cut to ribbons by Jack the Ripper.

They were the first person to go over Niagara Falls, or Houdini's assistant.

They were a witch, wrongfully drowned in Salem, a Queen, or a medieval sorcerer.

They were a knight at the roundtable, a wit at the N.Y. Algonquin Round Table.

They were beheaded in the French revolution.

I have **NEVER** heard anyone proudly announce:

"I grew up in Newark, pumped gas for forty years and being used up like a soggy tissue, I decided to drop dead."

Or "I was a housewife in Peoria, attended the PTA regularly, made loads and loads of cookies and then keeled over at the ripe old age of eighty."

The jury's still out on that one. Are you asking for these opinions? In MY head you are. I don't like hypocrisy wherever I run into it, so I'm not thrilled about any clergy urging me to vote for anyone. Hey, if you want to get in the game, pay the taxes OK? Nor am I tolerant of the intolerant.

REGRETS: that the darned preacher at my Daddy's service thought it was a great idea to point out to the hundreds there, that my father hadn't been to church for YEARS. Lock up the cakehole Rev. He was a LIVING church.

PSYCHIC? I DON'T THINK SO

After moving to the state that is now my domicile, while out and about, I spied a woman all gussied up in gypsy garb sitting at a card table. She was doing palm and tarot readings. I had never experienced any sort of psychic readings, and thought it would be tons of fun.

I ponied up the fifteen bucks she was charging, had a seat, and thought there would be merry laughter about this experience for many moons to come.

"Would you like a palm reading, or a tarot reading?"

"Let's do BOTH!" She was handed the extra ten bucks, leaving the wallet bare now, but I thought…what the hell.

"Give me your right hand first, please" (I thought they did the LEFT hand.)

"Why are you here? Are you a professional?"

"Huh? Are you asking me if I'm a hooker? Why shouldn't I be here?"

"I'm asking because I know you ARE a psychic. Did you think I wouldn't see? Are you here to look at the competition? It's OK if you ARE. I just wanted to know."

"WHAT? I'm a WHAT?"

"You really don't know, do you?"

"KNOW WHAT???"

"You lost both of your parents recently. They're with you."

"Yes."

"You're an artist. Music. Visual arts. You're a writer. Do you teach?"

"Yes, I'm a musician, and I draw and paint. I'm not a writer. I'm a reader. I used to give piano lessons."

"You have the dreams."

"**WHAT**? Dreams? What dreams? Well…I guess I have dreams. It's no big deal though. It's kind of stupid, really."

"What are the dreams?"

"Seeing as you're the psychic here, you must be referring to the dreams that come true, right? I've always had them. I'M not psychic though. It's not like a TV show. I don't dream about people being killed or where they're buried, for gosh sake."

"WHAT are the dreams?"

"OK, GOD…I've never had a dream about someone I don't KNOW. It's usually mundane things. I'll dream I'm opening the front door in the morning, and the paper hasn't been delivered. When I wake up, I'll go for the paper, and sure enough, it won't be there. Things like that."

"I do dream when someone I know has died, or it'll pop in my head if I'm awake, and I usually dream when someone I know is in trouble, or troubled, and I'll call them. Is this a big deal? I'm TELLING you, I've always done it. I don't think twice about it."

"When did it start?"

"Since before I could speak."

"Did your mother have the dreams?"

"Yes."

"Was she from the South?"

"Yes. How do you KNOW this? I always thought the dream thing was normal. Mommy used to talk about it casually, like… I was planning to go to Stop and Shop for some nice bananas, but they don't have any ripe ones today. It never seemed CREEPY. I guess I've always assumed everyone does it to a certain degree."

"No. They DO NOT. And it doesn't feel creepy, because you were born with it. You got it from your mother. That's usually how it's passed. You should be teaching. Let me see your left hand. You're very physical, aren't you?"

"Teaching what? The dreaming thing? " She nods. "That would be a heck of a short class—Thanks for coming. I have dreams. Maybe you do too. Class dismissed. And you're REALLY off base with the physical thing. I love to swim, but don't know HOW to play Football."

"That's not what I mean. You have an intense, um… appetite. Of a…what's the word…of a certain nature."

"Prurient?"

"Yes. When did it start?"

"Since before I could speak."

She's nodding again. "It comes out of you. I felt it when you walked in my booth. It's arousing. We need to do the tarot cards."

"Well, I am fairly, um…lustful, I guess. What do you mean 'comes OUT of me'? Someone once told me something similar, and I didn't like it much. So are you saying everybody can tell I'm a bit…I don't know… This is embarrassing. And WHAT—am I ABNORMAL? "

"Yes. You are. But it's nothing to be afraid of."

Nothing to be afraid of? While she's shuffling away, or whatever it is they do, I turn to my friend, and tell him I don't care what she says…I'm feeling very uneasy. He thinks I should stay. OK. But I'm NOT psychic, and there's nothing coming OUT of me. No, SIR. She starts pulling cards out, not that I'd know what they meant.

"You're not arousing yourself. Actually, you are (WHAT? Are you crazy, lady??), but you are also giving it off like sparks. It's compelling. It's seductive. It is abnormal in this respect. Most people don't have that sort of turmoil. They are not in touch with it. If they do, many don't recognize what to do with it. I don't see it that much but when I DO see it, it's most often in artists. Not always, but usually. Do YOU recognize it in others?"

"I'm sparking? Crap. I know I SCARE people sometimes. I don't understand that. How could I scare someone? You make me sound like I'm MEDUSA or something. OK, LOOK, I play music, and music brings out desires like that. ESPECIALLY if it's loud and has a driving beat. So unless you're not a very…let's use your word "physical" person, I don't know how you can miss it. It's why musicians get that kind of attention. It goes with the job. Everybody gets it. I've already HAD this conversation with someone."

By this time I'm thinking, alrighty, this gal has guessed I have dreams. Big deal, and she thinks I'm a sexy musician type. Big deal again. There are

MILLIONS of us. Isn't she going past our allotted time? God, now I'M starting to feel a little scared.

"Yes, I'm sure you're intimidating to some. I'm not talking about being onstage. I'm talking about you, ANYWHERE. Your essence. The font of your creativity. Isn't that why you paid me? To tell you about yourself, and to give you guidance? You already know these things. I asked if you recognize it in others."

"Essence? Sounds like a bad movie. OK, yes. Yes, I've seen it. Not a lot, but it's always in their eyes. I think I know what you're getting at here, and you're right—I've always known, but it's hard to put into words. I've met some women that had it, and that was great…made me feel like not so much a freak. Only one man I've really BEEN with possessed that look in his eyes. The first was brief; the other was for a while. I get a glimpse of it in others from time to time. I've seen it in a few couples; that's always lovely to see. It gives me hope. Who knows how many people have that look? It's not like I've met everyone in the universe, for gosh sake. I don't GET to meet lots of good ones."

"Whose eyes did you first see it in?"

"My parents. This conversation is beginning to sound familiar to me. I had this discussion with Mommy after Daddy died. You think I should teach? Can you TEACH that? I DID try to pass some of this on to band mates, girlfriends, other singers who wanted me to teach them how to sound soulful, boyfriends…most of them don't really get it, and they think I'm nuts, so I don't talk about it anymore."

"You aren't nuts. It's something you were born with, and recognized through the example of your parents. And maybe someone else?"

"Yeah. Someone taught me. That was the first encounter. That's when I began to put it together as a whole. To understand the circle. And then, as I told you, only one other. I loved him. Deeply. It's been pretty dismal since then, I can tell you."

She turned over another card, and said, "It was no mistake. They were sent to you."

"ARE YOU CRAZY or something? Who? That first guy? The second one? How do you know what I'm talking about? What do you mean SENT? Who the hell SENT this to me? WHAT, was it some kind of cosmic PRESENT?" Now I'm feeling like something in *The Omen*.

She ignores my question. "And what IS it you understand? Where does creativity come from?"

"Hey, isn't our time up? Oh lord…OK. OK. It comes straight from our libido, and geez, most people need to get THAT right; it pours into our passion, whether that's a passion for something in the arts or anything else. There's the short version. Now you think I'm crazy too."

"No. Not crazy. You're quite sane, and you've got it ABSOLUTELY RIGHT. By the way, I'm curious. You saw it in your parents. They were active in that way in their later years, weren't they? "

"Sigh…yes. Right up to the end. I want to thank you for taking so much time with me. I always thought what I felt and believed was true, but no one has ever really discussed the whole shebang with me. Thank you for that. It really is a comfort to me. Thank you." I leaned over to give her a hug, and take my leave. She really DID make me feel better in some ways. Except for that psychic business, and frankly, I couldn't wait to get out of there.

"Wait. I'm not done. It's important."

"What's important?"

"You HAVE to TEACH it. The long version. It's what you're meant to do, besides making music."

"WHAT? By what device would I be teaching a philosophy that most likely NO one will subscribe to, OR believe? I TOLD you, I've tried with friends, and THAT was difficult. What the Sam HILL. It did NOT for the most part light any bulb in THEIR heads.

"Look, this is not something that's comfortable for me to talk about. I don't think it's something comfortable for most people to HEAR. It would be a foreign subject for most. They'll think I'm a crackpot."

"What am I supposed to do, start by telling people they're probably lousy lovers, and they need to start THERE, and then hit them over the head with the rest of it? WHERE would I be teaching this, in a classroom at the local Adult Ed place? Who would want to KNOW?"

"When you first came in I asked if you were a writer. You have to write it."

"I told you, I'm not a writer. Maybe a couple of funny stories here or there for my girlfriends, but that's it. And WHO would be READING it?"

"It doesn't matter. It will find its way to those who need it. You tell stories to your girlfriends? Put them in. You know more than you think. Your father was a great raconteur. Please do it."

"I'll think about it, though it sounds like loads of work for nothing. Thank you so much, again."

As I was leaving, I wondered how she knew Daddy was a great storyteller. GOD. And I'm NOT psychic. Spooky.

NO REGRETS…yet.

LESSON: If you have knowledge you think might be helpful to others, don't be greedy and lazy. Pass it on.

STAND UP FOR YOURSELF!

I'm going to tell you about the most tormenting regret I have, but before I delve into THAT veritable manifesto, I should relate the bizarre happenings that were occurring when I ran smack dab into it.

An especially chaotic time was unfolding in a stupefying way. I was in the midst of music BIZZ troubles, and my current band lineup was beginning to fall apart.

Here's a MINI LESSON within this lesson (you know, like a play within a play). Amongst other sundry idiocies, I was going through the end of a pretty long-term relationship—a relationship with someone I had cared about, who was in the throes (and had been for a long time) of something I couldn't help with.

He was spiraling down FAST. The strength to completely end it NEEDED to be mustered, but having been brought up in a family that NEVER gives up, and never loses hope, it was more than difficult for me to come to terms with it. I was in fact hindering a lot more than helping. This kind of relationship would repeat itself AGAIN, in a few years; and I did the SAME darn thing, with even more painful and disastrous results. Sometimes it takes us more than once to learn from our own blundering idiocy, and stubborn hope.

REGRET: DO NOT TRY THIS AT HOME.
You will waste moments, days, YEARS of your
life that can't be relived. TO NO AVAIL.

LESSON: Don't waste your loyalty in madness.
What you think is selflessness is hiding
senselessness. You can't help. BELIEVE this as
if your very life depended on it, and LEARN
from my failing. You will be vilified and smashed
harder than you ever thought possible. By people
who won't even give a backward glance.
Sometimes the human heart cannot heal. TAKE
HEED.

Boy, that scenario was pretty lousy, but I was concurrently dealing with label-signing dilemmas, time spent recording and, to me, not enough time playing. The record company part was a confusing sink hole. A label that I liked wanted me, but it was strictly a blues label. Although there ain't no white girl can sing the blues like me (sorry to be so blunt, it's still true), my interest in doing "nothing but the blues" was nil.

That situation stubbornly repeated itself when a well-known band was looking to replace their long gone front man, and planning on doing an exclusively roots blues thing.

The numerous hits they'd had were of course blues based (what ISN'T?), but they were more definitively a rock band. I guess I didn't think they would be sticking to just one genre, so I didn't speak up. I also didn't particularly want to be compared to their former high-profile front man.

That attempted "mating" if you will, had a keystone cop quality to it, as most of my ridiculous adventures do.

My manager having been at one time THEIR manager thought it would be a great thing for them to have me. I remember meeting with some of them. I thought they were loads of fun and perfectly amiable.

Sure I did, but one of the times they came out to see me, something entirely different kicked in. My contrary thinking reared its unruly head, and I sort of…well, I purposely sabotaged what I didn't want to do. You want BLUES? Ya want the pure STUFF? OK, Bessie, Wolf, Son House. Here's some Muddy, Mr. Dixon, and just a little more Bessie. Oh and here's a speed metal version of "Bali Hai." There we go.

I was acting like an imbecile. I even had a shot of whisky before I went on. I think I did that only a few times during my life. I was just unabashedly CRAZY. I don't recall what I did on that stage, but my band loved it.

The other band clearly did NOT. I could see their faces. "DAMMM is this what she's going to do with US? Oh, no, no."

When I happily (for them) descended from the stage, I casually ambled over to their table and proceeded to "accidentally" spill an entire soda directly into the lap of one of those nice guys.

I'm not really sure, which band member it was, but I THINK that I adroitly managed to render his magical area more soggy than anything else.

If my poor victims are reading this, any one of you, I need to APOLO-GIZE. I am truly shamefaced and feel badly. What I did was an unforgivable waste of your time. You are nice people and didn't deserve my asinine behavior.

I should have told you I wasn't interested in ingesting a strictly blues diet, and I SURE as heck should have had the courtesy to have asked at least one of you, "Are you thinking about putting anything else on the plate there, Bucky?"

On top of the preceding involvements (things that take a musician away from what he/she loves the most—namely MUSIC), I was going broke pretty fast. I was soon to be hustling like all get out to make ends meet.

Another puzzling thing was going on during this time period. There used to be an awful show on TV, a kind of predecessor of the equally awful one that's on now. *Star Search*. THAT'S what it was.

Their obviously confused producers had gotten it into their heads a certain somebody would be perfect for their show—that certain somebody being of course me. They called my manager. They seem to have called, if I remember, numerous times.

They were hounding him. These producers couldn't seem to understand quite how much I wouldn't have fit in, that I wasn't someone who would be warbling while gazing winsomely at the camera and donning a pinafore and crinolines.

Nope, they wanted, wanted, wanted me. In one sense I didn't want to be caught naked or dead on that show, but in a perverse way, I was itching to go right ahead and let the frightful mistake occur.

The man I'll be telling you about soon thought this would be more than a scream.

You want me? You GOT me. NOW whatcha gonna do with me? My manager, of course, wouldn't let me go and have me some serious laughs—the old "kiss of death" thinking. It would have been a hoot, because they'd never run into the likes of me.

I had recently finished putting in a lot of studio time, doing rough cuts for the label I did sign with, but was not happy with the direction it was taking.

For the purpose of getting this pre-production stuff out in a timely way, they were hell bent on using, of all things, a drum machine. GOOD GOD. This was a tough concept for me to swallow. My musician self was rebelling against such a nauseating idea. They did not want to deal with the always problematic drums.

If you're reading this, you might not know it really DOES take a while to set up, mic, and get the sound you're looking for on drums, but if you don't want to take the time required, it's just LAZY and sloppy, and I don't think a drum MACHINE belongs on a recording anyone will hear. ONLY on a song you're writing in your living room.

Other musicians were brought in, and some were excellent journeymen, but all followed the producer's vision exclusively. None of these sessions sounded a bit like any band I would ever get NEAR…well, it didn't sound like a band at all. My actual band members were highly insulted by this situation—who could blame them?—and it didn't help matters.

I'm not going to tell you why this all went down. Not only because it would bore you to tears, but if I relayed the details, I'd probably have a litigious contingency coming out of the woodwork at an alarmingly rapid pace. The only thing I can say in my defense was that I was working within a situation that wasn't, all in all, a good scene. Not telling you how. Still no excuse for me.

I simply had no choice in the matter. None. I shut up, and did what I was expected to do. Anyone familiar with this business will have an inkling of the kind of circumstance I found myself in (many having found themselves in a similar trap) and would rightly deduce in cases like this:

The power goes where the money is. ALWAYS.

**REGRET: Stand UP for yourself, no matter what
you think may be at stake. I did NOT, and ended
up with something I cannot stand behind with
any sort of conviction. This does not apply only
to music, but to every situation in your life.**

**LESSON: When dealing with those who have no
conscience, or compassion, PROTECT YOUR
INTEGRITY. CALL THEM ON THEIR
MANIPULATION. Oh, they'll smack you down,
and when you're down there, they'll kick your
teeth in on their way out the door. Hard. NOT
TO WORRY, because YOU, my darling, can
look at yourself in the mirror.**

This next story takes place in 1975 and '76. I'm going to tell you about
some musicians and one in particular. They were a band. No, they were two
bands. WHAT THE HECK DO I KNOW??

I'm in the dark about what personal or musical dynamics were happening between the people involved in these bands, and for the most part unaware of events, and what sequences they might fall into. I sure as shootin'
don't know what the truth of their lives was during this time period, and
can't honestly claim ANY right to an opinion.

Having just given you a long-winded dissertation on my usual lack of
"loopage", I'm going to forge on and do it anyway. Call me crazy, but I like
to see credit given where it IS DUE.

This one is for you, Craig Bell, Cheetah Chrome, and Peter.

My pops had a secretary for over twenty-five years named Mary Nisbet.
She was Aunt Mary to me, and once in a while if I couldn't find work elsewhere, I'd help her out in the office. I wasn't out playing music yet. Aunt
Mary was a riotous woman, and she'd always taken an interest in my musical fever. I was in the office doing Aunt Mary chores one day in '75. She
told me her nephew little Peter who lived in Ohio was also a musician. "I'm
going to tell my sister to pass your address along to little Peter. He loves
music." She always called him "little Peter," so I always THOUGHT of
him that way. Aunt Mary must have still seen him as a ten-year-old. Some-

times I'd slip and CALL him little Peter, but it didn't seem to faze him. He'd just say, "YES, Aunt MARY" and chuckle.

A few weeks later, I received a package in the mail. Contained therein was a 45 and a note that said something like:

"HI! I'm Aunt Mary's nephew Peter. She told me all about you. Would you be my pen pal? Just finished this single with my new band. Please tell me what you think of it. I'd really like to know. Please don't be afraid to give me your honest opinion, OK? Do you think I should keep going?

Love, your cousin by default, Peter"

I pulled the album I was listening to off the turntable, which was most likely Etta James. I had to hunt around for that darn plastic thingie but finally found it and slapped little Peter's 45 on there.

I put the needle on and stood back. Three seconds later, I was propelled into the living room sofa bed like a discarded doggie bone. I careened into it so HARD I broke the thing. I BROKE THE SOFA.

I played that 45 of Peter's at least twenty times that day. My roommate, Connie, came home in the middle of this marathon, and said, "What the HELL is THAT?"

I think I was able to utter, "Huh? Oh...little Peter."

When I finally emerged from the haze, I scribbled off a note to Peter. It contained only four lines.

"My dearest cousin by default Peter,

HOLY SHIT. HOLY FUCKIN' SHIT. Should you keep going? DON'T FUCKIN' STOP! FUCK, I JUST BROKE THE SOFA. FUCK, I LOVE you, Peter. SHIT.

Kindest Regards, Nevard

Engraved on that innocent-looking 45 was a song called "Thirty Seconds Over Tokyo."

Aunt Mary's nephew, little Peter, was in fact a guy named Peter Laughner, and his "new" band was called PER UBU. The sad reality is, not many remember him. I do. I remember him all right. That 45 changed my LIFE.

Oh, I'd heard Peter's influences, and thought they were OK, but what he'd casually passed on set off a STORM in my brain. THIS was something charged with a power I'd never experienced. Well...you all just go and give it a listen and tell ME what you think it must have done to the head of a kid who was swimming in American roots music. GOD, there was so much power there I wanted to run screaming out of my apartment and have at it with the first man I ran into. Of course what I ended up doing was making a tuna casserole with Connie.

Peter and I spoke on the phone a bit, and he sent me a tape of the band he'd been in before Per Ubu. I'm surprised I didn't break another piece of furniture. THIS was even MORE life changing; it was a cluster fuck. It was FERAL. I think Peter received the same note I'd sent when I heard the 45, with another line of "HOLY FUCKIN' SHIT" added. The name of THAT band?

ROCKET FROM THE TOMBS.

Darn it, go look them up. Look them up NOW. Is there anybody reading this who might think their favorite band is pretty tough sounding? Go listen to the REAL tough stuff. Do you know what this music felt like to ME when my Etta James-loving ears got wind of it? I'll tell you right now.

I FELT LIKE I WAS BEING HAD BY A WILD ANIMAL WITH BIG, BIG DROOLY TEETH AND RAZOR SHARP CLAWS. SAVAGE AND CONSUMMATE BRILLIANCE.

Getting' the picture?

What songs? " Final Solution," "Ain't It Fun," "Muckraker," "Sonic Reducer" amongst others. Thousands of bands have covered them. Thousands. I don't know who wrote what, so I need to be filled in. Craig, did you write "Final Solution"? Yes, Claude just told me you co-wrote that one, and "Muckraker" was yours alone. Peter had told me he was the sole author of "Ain't it Fun"...the jolliest self-annihilation song ever written.

Along with the superb music, Peter would send me reviews he'd written. He passed these on, and talked to me about his friend Lester, who he admired. I, however, was NOT a Lester admirer. Peter was a great interpreter of styles and could decipher the influences in any piece of music. I think this must have annoyed some folks, but he never meant it in a bad way. He was always so filled with the rapture of music, and never full of himself. I loved him for it. I don't think he ever knew what he really WAS. I don't think he was aware that Rocket From The Tombs surpassed his music heroes, and he never realized just how FEROCIOUS they were.

Strange, I played that 45 and tape for every person I knew. For the most part, I got blank stares in return, or negative responses. OOPS sorry, not pure anything. DARN music SNOBS. They're everywhere, I tell ya.

Peter and I came face to face only once, sometime in '76. He came over to my place in Bridgeport, Connecticut, and was as full of the same eagerness and funny innocence that he'd showed in the first letter he'd written. We had a great time visiting. I can remember Peter making an ALMOST play for me that day. Oh I can tell you…I would not have been adverse to this idea…yet Peter was much too high too pull ANYTHING resembling that sort of thing..off. The only thing I can remember of our conversation is me blurting, "Ah Lou, Lou, Lou, LOU. FUCK, I think you're BETTER. Shut your cakehole, Peter."

There was something wrong with him though. Something I wasn't able to hear over the phone, although I did often notice when he was high. He seemed antsy, not comfortable in his skin. He didn't look well, and there was suffering in his eyes. Peter was surrounded by sadness.

Peter. I didn't know he'd be dead within a year. He was only twenty-four. I'd known this "cousin" for such a short time, but he felt like family. Aunt Mary's little Peter, so full of talent, and he'd given me a GIFT I could never repay. He didn't have to take the time. He wanted so much to share. I'll never forget the day he died, and Aunt Mary called to ask when I'd spoken to him. It had been a few months before. We cried together.

Did you see who I dedicated this to? Peter of course, but also Craig Bell and Cheetah Chrome. They were BOTH in Rocket From the Tombs.

OK, this is becoming MORE than perturbing. This is ANOTHER story that's displaying a STUNNING "duhhh" factor on my part. When Peter sent me that tape, it only had song titles on it, so was I in ANY way aware of who the band members of Rocket From The Tombs might BE?? NOPE.

Why don't we just scoot forward a few years. Cheetah formed a band called the Dead Boys, and I thought, "Huh…isn't it nice to hear them doing those Rocket numbers. Boy, that would sure make Peter happy." Did this in ANY WAY tip me off? Course it didn't.

Scoot forward a little more in time, and my band lineup included a guitar player and drummer who are brothers. Their names are Steve and Mike (or as I call him, Bam Bam) Tanski. GREAT musicians they both are. They had been playing with—guess who—Cheetah before they came to me.

I must have found out THEN, right? NOPE. What are you THINK-ING? Not till YEARS later did I realize that Cheetah WAS in Rocket From The Tombs and ON that tape. Lordy.

Is that dumb enough for you? NO? Good, because I'm about to become even MORE plank headed. Craig Bell had a couple of great bands in Connecticut (where I lived), and I really dug the Saucers and the Bell System. I thought Craig and his honey, Claude, were wonderful folks. Sounds lovely, yes?

Move over for the "Nevard's in a COMA moment." A few years ago, I heard someone talking on the phone with Craig. I heard Peter's name, and I perked right up... "Craig knew PETER? Wow, I didn't know THAT." Still didn't catch on...thought he just KNEW Peter...not PLAYED with him. Oh MY.

ALL THOSE YEARS I didn't know? For almost THIRTY YEARS? So I was an admirer and thought Craig was so nice, but for thirty years I DID NOT KNOW the part he'd played in blowing my HEAD OFF in 1975? Can we please forget I said anything? I'm making believe.

Peter told me Rocket From The Tombs had started out in '74. WHAT, WHAT, WHAT? Who ELSE was doing anything that came CLOSE in '74 OR '75? Who else was sounding quite THAT raw? That rough? Who the heck ELSE came close to that tough sound? Let me tell you who. NO-BODY. They had indisputably created a bridge between sparse, lean rock, and art rock. That in and of itself was a consequential donation to the world of music, but in '74, this perfect integration flew over the heads of the un-wary. Most did not recognize what a defining moment it WAS. There are many bands who have recorded those songs over the years. "Ain't It Fun" was covered by Guns 'n' Roses, and thousands of OTHER bands. I don't know the names of the other guys in that band, but I'd just like to say ONE THING. OK...TWO THINGS.

Perhaps you haven't run into one of the fifty times I've told you—there aren't all THAT many truly revolutionary moments in Rock and Roll.

WISE UP ROCK and ROLL HALL OF FAME.
WISE UP.

I DON'T CARE IF THEY WEREN'T
TOGETHER VERY LONG.

I DON'T CARE IF THEY WERE TOGETHER
FOR JUST THE THIRTY SECONDS IT
TOOK THEM TO GET THE HECK OVER
TOKYO.

ROCKET FROM THE TOMBS WAS ONE OF
THOSE MOMENTS.

INDUCT THEM NOW.

Thanks so much for your time.

REGRET: Could I have helped Aunt Mary's
beloved Peter? No. Even though we talked and
were pals for a short while, I was on the outskirts
of his life. If those who were really IN his life
couldn't help, what could I have done? Still, I feel
guilt for not digging deeper. I commented, when
I saw him that one time, but I didn't pursue his
pain, then or later. I STILL miss your spirit,
Peter.

LESSON: RECOGNIZE AND SAVOR THOSE
RARE MOMENTS OF INSPIRING
OUTPOURINGS IF YOU ARE LUCKY
ENOUGH TO CATCH ONE ON YOUR
TONGUE LIKE A SNOWFLAKE. CHERISH
THEM. CHERISH THOSE WHO ARE A
PART OF THAT WONDER. LISTEN.
LISTEN. LISTEN.

PS. I'd like to thank you Richard Lloyd. You are of course certifiably
crazy, and will pull the nicest of folks right into the ditch with
you…but you've been awfully sweet to me lately… and I need to tell
you this. I ADMIRE GREATLY the way you took on Peter's guitar
work on that Rocket From The Tombs Redux album. You did

MORE than play parts that were representational of Peter's fierce and raw style...you seemed to actually CHANNEL him. You BE-CAME Peter....long enough to put his very SOUL down on that re-cording. Bless you Richard. I BOW DOWN.

(Jeff Ross Hyman, aka. Joey Ramone)

JEFF AND NEVARD I

NOTE:* this writing has not been changed since 2009. Jeff's public name is not used. You'll find THAT on the cover of this book, and as you must be aware by now, Jeff was known more commonly as Joey Ramone. "The Ramones" wielded a lot more influence in musical terms than I was aware of, and as for Jeff/Joey, NO ONE will ever be able to re-create that voice. EVER. I was hesitant to name him, but was finally given this piece of wisdom..."If you REALLY want to make a difference, you MUST name him." Still not believing it was needed, I did something my brother in-law Huw asked me to do...and I found myself on YouTube. I did something I've never done. I typed in "songs about Joey Ramone". The results were beyond startling. There were HUNDREDS of songs with the name Ramone in them, and a large percentage were about Joey Ramone, which almost made me blurt out a politically incorrect "Lennon-like" saying..."CRIKEY! He's bigger than JESUS." It sure does look that way...and I'm not even counting the hundreds of tributes to him. I've never seen anything like it. Certainly, the Ramones DID change the face of popular music....but this was more than stunning. I never look for Jeff on the internet, because invariably photos and clips of him looking very ill, will appear. He never wanted me to see it, and it crushes me when I catch a glimpse. During the writing of this, things about Jeff that I'm not sure are known, were danced around. There are also things that Jeff did NOT want to be spoken about, and so I have been silent about them. Below, are the writings from 2009...with just a few things I've added recently.

I have a sad regret in my life. Regret I haven't been able to resolve until these past few months. It's a big one. It's about a relationship, a romance, a deep love, and it is about someone I feel protective of. The telling of it, although it has some funny moments, feels immensely private, and freshly painful. After twenty years.

I'm not going to name him. The following writings are the only DE-TAILED descriptions of a genuine relationship that I've put in this book and it is because it was a monumentally defining one.

I was hesitant to write about this man. I realize he will be known to some. At the time, I'm pretty sure our involvement was unknown to everyone but US. We were

seeing each other for about five years.

I don't know if "seeing" is the right word, because we weren't able to see each other nearly enough, and it was painful and frustrating for us both. We had never defined the parameters of our attachment, until the very end, but despite our inability to categorize what exactly we HAD, thankfully, we were unceasingly able to show how much we loved each other.

Just before writing this, I finally spilled this relationship to someone who I'd known since we were toddlers, and he coerced me into writing about Jeff.

His name was Doug Hovey, and he was a dear friend. He had known Jeff...and we had the following conversation... "What do I call him, Dougie?"

"Call him Jeff."

"Well, it IS what I called him. Why should I write about him? I don't know, it would hurt. You tell ME. I think you know lots more than I do, about parts of his life."

"I feel very strongly about this Nevard. I know he'd want you to tell."

"Well...he said something vague the very last time I spoke to him, but he wanted our union to be private, and maybe it should remain that way."

"No. He would want the people who cared about him to know that he was able to experience what the two of you had. They felt sorry for him. He'd WANT them to know."

"Oh. Well, if he had wanted them to know, wouldn't HE have eventually told them? Wouldn't I be betraying a trust?

"Sigh. You don't know, Vardz. I believe he was afraid that whatever it was he had with you would be ruined, or you'd be taken from him. He probably thought you'd become the "new" thing to be goaded about. Also, I don't think he met many people like you, or had a chance at any sort of relationship with them if he did."

"What do you mean like ME? For god's sake, Jeff wasn't exactly an un-known in certain places. You told me just a minute ago… he was mobbed in his stomping grounds. I'm sure he had plenty of relationships."

"I don't think so. Not like that. No one would have EVER pictured you two together. Different worlds, and you're so…I mean, well…pretty con-ventional, but you had everything in common. Spoke the same language. I don't think you realize how strangely alike the two of you were."

"No…I knew how much we resembled each other. Conventional? Nev-er thought I was THAT strait-laced. Sooo Jeff wanted me because I was the most boring girl around? Great. I've been keeping these memories at bay for a long time. Are you saying maybe I can bring some comfort to those who actually cared about him? There are so many things I never under-stood. I never could watch that documentary. Don't think I ever will."

I met Jeff, where else—in a club. As usual, I have a hazy recollection of the exact time (the very end of 1989, or the beginning of 1990), but I know it was when a band lineup of mine, bizz things, AND a relationship I should have ended long ago were strolling on quicksand. I was doing fewer jobs with my band, and missed having a full calendar, so I'd sit in with vari-ous friends' bands as well.

What this club might have been? I know it was somewhere in NYC, and I'd gone to hear a friend. I know I sat in, because it was the only time Jeff ever saw me on a stage. Jeff was sitting at a table with a musician I knew. I thought it might have been the iguana-topped Lone Star, or maybe Tramps on 15th. That's where I'd usually run into that musician, but those clubs were defunct by then. It was Kenny's.

I know that I was there to see my pal. I know HE was friendly with this musician. He was Mr. History of American music.

In any case, after I did two songs, I got a glimpse of the musician and went over to say hi and visit with him a bit.

I was thrilled to see him there, being a HUGE admirer, and he had al-ways been gracious to me. Whenever I saw him, he'd ask, "Anything I can do for ya, kid? I like what you do. Let me know."

I'd always reply, "No, I'm fine. I've got an OK manager now, so things are looking up a little."

He'd say, "Yeah, I know. Bullshit. Don't you trust them. You're too young to know. He'll hurt you. They all will. You let me know." I thought that was an amusing comment at the time, because I didn't think I was all THAT young. Like HELL, I wasn't.

He was MORE than right, and I should have listened a lot closer, because this was a man who'd seen the whole messy business from the inside out, and right from the beginning. And if anyone knew, it was he. He was present from the inception of rock and roll, and had more than a large hand in creating it.

His name was Pete, and I'm grateful I was there that night, because this was the very last time I was to lay eyes on him.

He'd mean nothing to most of you, but he meant an awful lot to me. He was an important part of music history. Every time I ran into him, I felt amazed that such an incredible man was still on this earth, and I could SPEAK to him. To me, it was like running into Abe Lincoln sitting in some dive, just HANGING. When the world of music lost him, it was an IMMENSE loss.

I don't know if he and Jeff had arrived together, but they seemed to be acquainted, and I can say with certainty that Jeff would have considered him to be an even BIGGER deal than I did, and that's saying a lot. After talking for a while, I was introduced to Jeff.

Here I go again, sounding like a dolt… but I have to fess up. I had no cable TV during this time period. I clung to that rusty antenna on my roof until the broadcast channels refused to come in, so there wasn't much TV going on in my house.

I had no CD player until, I think it was 2000, about the same time I obtained a computer. I never bought tapes or albums (except old albums at tag sales or Goodwill), so friends used to burn tape copies for me. Mostly my girlfriend Jody.

I'm trying to convey to you…I rarely knew what a band LOOKED like, unless I had seen them live. I didn't know what instruments various members of most bands PLAYED, or what their NAMES were either, unless it was old music, or I'd hear the guys in my band talking about someone. They'd show me articles about particular musicians occasionally, but music magazines were not something I bothered to buy. I was on the move, and not all that thrilled with the pop music that I was hearing. I wasn't aware of music mags I WOULD have liked. I had two copied tapes of Jeff's band, without photos or liners.

So there you have it. It was only because Jeff's last name was mentioned during the introduction (and I wasn't even sure I heard THAT right) that I had any idea who he might be affiliated with. His last name WAS the band's name. And the last name of every guy in the band, which I thought was funny. At least I knew THAT much about them. I didn't know their first names... Sleepy, Grumpy, Dopey...whatever.

I smiled at him, and said, "Hey, you're in the BLANKS then, right?" That wasn't their real name...just what I'm calling them.

He smiled back and politely answered, "Yeah, I am."

"Oh. OK. Know what? I love your band." Which was the utter truth. "I always pop you on when I'm cleaning my house."

His smile got bigger. Gosh, I thought that smile could light up a CAVE. "Thanks. I'm a big fan of YOURS now. You're a great singer. Umm...you put me on when you're, uhhh, CLEANING?"

"YES!"

Jeff clearly thinks this is amusing, because his smile is growing. "OK, I wanna hear YOU when I'm vacuuming too."

"No, no, not while I'm VACUUMING. I wouldn't be able to hear. It's when I'm DUSTING."

For some reason, he thinks this is even funnier. "DUSTING? I'm help-ing ta what...DUST at your house? So, then I wanna put ya on and dust with you too."

"Yeah right."

"What?"

"You're a GUY. You're not dusting ANYTHING. You're not dusting the DUST."

"Ya got me there."

It was starting to get louder, so we began to lean in closer, and I'm get-ting the distinct impression that Blank guy thinks the idea of someone cleaning to the sound of his music is more than peculiar. In no way, does this deter me from asking him what I really wanted to know.

"What exactly do you play?"

"What? You wanna know what I play? What I PLAY?"

"Yes."

"You don't know...you don't know WHAT I PLAY? YOU DON"T KNOW?" (OK, how many times is he going to repeat this? I feel embar-rassed now.)

"No. I'm sorry. Really sorry. I've never seen you. Someday, I'll get out."

"You've never, uhhh, SEEN me, huh?" (OK, am I insulting him?)

"No. I swear I will though. Next chance I get. Really."

"I PLAY DRUMS."

"Ahh. Great drumming there. Nice judicious use of the high hat. How can you keep up that tempo LIVE? Damn."

Now, he's laughing at me outright. I don't think he's laughing with me. Nope, he's laughing AT me. Pete is looking quizzically at him, and starts chuckling TOO.

"Thanks," he says between seemingly uncontrollable giggles. What did I SAY? What's so FUNNY? OK, drummers are SPECIAL. (How many drummer jokes are there? Two thousand?) But they're not THAT funny. Jeff and Pete have a big joke going and I'm not privy to WHATEVER it is. And it's on me.

Jeff finally stops laughing, leans in more, and is not smiling now. He's looking at me. Closely. At least it FEELS like he is, because here's the thing. Jeff has bangs that hang almost below his eyes. And underneath that almost eye-covering hair, he's wearing sunglasses. In a dimly lit club. In spite of the fact that I have no idea what I'm looking at, I'm beginning to feel a definite stirring.

He leans in even further, and he's making me squirmy. I'm really feeling it now. Oh geez, what's going on here? Is this guy coming on to me? I'm getting confused and I can't distinguish what look he might have on his face.

"Where do you live?"

"Connecticut. I live in Connecticut."

"How far is Connecticut?"

"Little less than an hour." (Why is he talking as if I live in a foreign country?)

"Yeah." Still gazing, he is, (well, at least he SEEMS to be) and I'm starting to feel like I want to kiss him. I'm probably blushing. What's happening here? This is a baaad self-conscious feeling.

"Would you, uhhh…could you, uhhh…maybe give me your number? I really like you…umm…I like you a lot."

"Welll, I don't know…." I never gave out my phone number. Would usually say, "No, you can give me YOUR number." But good God, I'm starting to heat up over a guy's face I can't even SEE, and he did come in

with someone not unknown to me. At least I think he did, so I'm guessing
he's not the Zodiac Killer.

"Please?"

"Maybe. I have to see your eyes."

"What?"

"I SAID I need to see your EYES."

Without hesitation, he pushes up his glasses.

Oh no. Oh NO. Crap. I'm plummeting at a most alarming rate. I'm taking a big header here. Suddenly I can hear my voice. It sounds oddly far
away. My voice NOW has a mind of its own:

"Have you got a piece of paper?"

"Yeah."

I scribble out my number on some crumpled thing Jeff pulls out of his
jacket, and I hear him say, "You wanna come with ME a minute?"

"OK."

Jeff turns to the songwriter. "PETE, I'm, uhhh, takin' her out for a little,
OK?"

And he gets the reply, "I can SEE that. You two are plain as DAY."

I start to get up, surprisingly knock-kneed at this point. And then he
goes and does it. Puts the final nail in.

HE STANDS UP.

I had no idea. NO IDEA.

Oh. Bloody. HELL. He's TOWERING. He's just big, darn it. Skinny,
but HUGE. I couldn't help being pretty impressed with the commanding
intensity that was Jeff. I was LONG gone by then anyway, but I wasn't altogether immune to THIS startling aspect:

"Gimme that pen. I'll write my number on your arm. Your hand. I'll
write my number on your ASS, OK?"

I don't think Jeff realized that I was at this point swooning, and pretty
much a done deal. DONE. FINISHED.

He took my hand, and I stumbled out after him, stumbled because I was
quite literally stunned. His legs seemed to be as long as my entire body. I'd
never SEEN anything like this. I think I came up to his waist, which set me
whirling, because then I couldn't stop STARING in the vicinity of…oh
GOD…and then we were outside, where it was relatively quiet.

I followed for a second, and when we stopped in a darker area, Jeff
backed me into a wall. I guess he was a lot stronger than his skinny self

looked, because he lifted me up like I was nothing, until my face met his, and wedged me against the wall. I felt like I was so far off the ground, my nose might start to bleed.

I can remember almost EVERY word of our stupidly lengthy exchange. Who made it stupidly lengthy? Yup, that would be me.

Thank goodness he could speak, because I was by then fairly speechless. He told me what he wanted, and all I could get out was jumbled nonsense.

I would have agreed if he'd said, "I'd like you to dress up like Frank Langella and if you could look through the bottom of a couple of shot glasses and then get up on a mechanical bull for me while reciting Only God Can Make a Tree, I'd be much obliged."

I'll tell you what he said, and what I was now only able to THINK in my bewildered state. What I was capable of was mere head nodding, and something that wouldn't have passed as any known language.

"Why you looking so scared? I like that."

"Huh?"

"You're beautiful. You know that?" (I'M BEAUTIFUL? ME? No, no… YOU'RE the beautiful one here, God, look at that MOUTH.)

"I'm feeling different bout ya, OK? That sounds like, ummm, like a line, you know? I mean, I know it does, but I never…FUCK …I don't know. I don't KNOW. How 'bout you?"

"Yeah."

"Yeah?" (OK, communication is off to a rousingly coherent start here. But it seems he's as smitten as I am.)

"Uh…I don't know how ta say this…" (Well, DON'T then. Just kiss me.)

"Every girl I ever met, or I've been with, wanted to mother me. I don't WANNA BE MOTHERED. I don't WANT it. That OK with you?"

"Yeah." (Wow…he's DEFINITE about this. He almost YELLED it, so it must be awfully important to him. Fine with me. Whatever you want. You got it. No mommy HERE, big fella.)

"You SURE?"

"I'm on board." (HOLY COW. I'll take you whatever way you WANT me to take you.)

"REALLY? You OK with that?"

"Yeah. You're in charge. OK? YOU." (What are you not getting here? I'll be your ANYTHING)

"You want to be my chick? You wanna be my babygirl?"

(OK…except THAT.) "Put me down."

"Huh?"

"Please put me DOWN."

Jeff set me on the ground, and now HE is speechless. I, however, having just heard something distasteful come out of that pretty mouth of his, have rediscovered the English Language, and find I'm suddenly not only ABLE to speak, but can't seem to STOP myself from speaking volumes.

"You are astounding. I was DOWN for the COUNT, but you just LOST me. **I** don't care what your friends call you when you're out on the street. Romeo or Casanova, to me you ain't NOTHIN' but a lowdown beat. Can ya DIG it?"

"Whaaa?" (Oh geez, Poor Jeff.)

"You have altogether NO inkling, do you? Ahh darn it, pick me up again. I can't talk to you from here. Thank you. Can you see me, Jeff?"

"Yeah."

"Look at me…really look. Am I wearing pleather? Fake fur? Anything trendy? See any makeup on me? Are my eyebrows shaved off and painted in all skinny? Feel my face, Jeff. Go ahead, rub my eyes. My eyelashes. Anything coming off? What do you feel?"

"Uhhh…your skin is, uhhh…soft. Oh…your eyelashes are all kinda soft. I can kiss 'em?"

"Yeah, you sure can. Feel my breasts, Jeff. Go ahead."

"Yeah?"

"Go right ahead. Real?"

"Oh yeah, real. Can I put my face…"

"Yes, you can. Feel my bottom, Jeff. Tell me what you feel."

"You sure? SHIT."

"Do you feel any panties there, Jeff? Panties that might be purple and crotchless? No sir. Not in public, anyway, that's for sure. Go ahead, move your hands where they want to go."

Not so easy for me to find any words now, because Jeff is getting a little busy, and I'm having trouble focusing, but I need to get this straight, because I see something in HIM that's worth the trouble.

"I would be more than thrilled to be your babygirl. I'd love to be your SWEETIE, your BITCH, or your personal CUNT. It would excite me no end. What I will NOT be, Jeff, and what I will NEVER be is a CHICK. Not for ANY guy. Is that what you're used to, Jeff? Chicks?"

"Yeah, sure, sometimes I guess. You don't, uh, like that word, huh? How come?"

"Because for one thing, it smacks of a kind of contemptuous attitude toward females that says they are fairly disposable and lacking in depth. It's a not so flattering and pretty shabby view of a woman that's indicative of the IMMATURE POSTURINGS of a FUCKING SCHOOLBOY. I don't want a schoolboy, Jeff. I want a man. Let me ask you, how long does it take them to get bored with you and start the MOTHERING thing?"

Jeff was silent for a moment. "WHAT? WHAT? Uhhh. I guess not too long ...aww CRAP. I'm not gettin' complaints though." He was starting to look affronted.

"No you wouldn't be getting complaints. I'm guessing they're mighty dazzled by your cool leather-jacketed self, and any attention you might give them. I'm getting the picture here. You don't want to be mothered. That's loud and clear, so then TELL me, when the mothering starts, how long does it take for YOU to get bored?"

"Same thing. OK? Uhhh, not long."

"Jeff, I'm sure you could have all the CHICKS you want. They're plentiful as hell. Just like I could have the insipid, fawning and scene-making idiot boys back in that club. That's usually what I meet, and what's for the most part throwing its moron self at me. I'm not the female equivalent of them.

I'm NOT looking for a toss off. I can get it anywhere, and the prize in the Cracker Jack box means nothing to me. I don't HAVE popular affectations, Jeff. I'm not hip, not cool, and not capable of it. I've got no patience with airs."

"I already know I want ya. I mean I know what you're sayin', and I'm agreeing. Yeah. OK, go ahead. Need to, ummm, do some little hanky PANKEEE."

"Ohh...can't think straight. I'm wanting you and willing to follow. There's no one I've ever met that was WORTH following, but I think you might be. If you want yourself a chick, Jeff, I'm begging you, PLEASE move ALONG, and leave me be. I don't need to get slammed."

"Hey look...I, uhhh, you're not what...I mean...that's why...I...I...don't SAY that word hardly. So why did you give me your NUMBER then?"

"Well, you're a big boy there, but gosh, do you know what's in your eyes?"

"I dunno, nothing?" (Oh Lord, how do I tell him? He doesn't KNOW?)

"Dammit, Jeff, I almost FELL in them. You have a truckload of determination. DETERMINATION. And you're a loving guy. It's obvious. CURIOSITY. That's what you've got. A need for big gulps of LIFE. God, you remind me of my folks. OK, that's weird. Why did I say that?

"You're SMART, Jeff. I mean really smart. You've got the excitement for creating. It's NOT all that common, Jeff. Do you KNOW why I want you? It's that SUBSTANCE and PASSION, Jeff. You're FILLED with it. You're not trying, it's just THERE. Playful and hot, you are. You AWARE of it? You need to be shown maybe? You have it. It's in your eyes. I've never felt it that strong. Hardly ever give my number. Never WANT to."

" Are you sure you're talking 'bout ME?"

"Maybe you're used to being one, but you're not a little school kid, Jeff; I wouldn't want you if I thought you were. And I'm sure not Alvin Lee. Not your mamma either. No THANKS. You WANT me to be your baby-girl? You're gonna have to work for it. You can just do what I TELL you to do. IF you can take me, IF you can make me beg,
you'll OWN my ass. And you SURE as HELL can."

"Yeah. THAT'S what I want. NOT gonna mess with ya, babygirl. I sure wanna own your ASS though. I want to (now HE'S sputtering)...umm...OK. So who's gonna, uh, own MY ASS?"

"That would be me, Jeff. ME."

Finally, his smile comes out again. I feel like the SUN is shining.

"Yeah... You've got some big words. Kinda turns me on. YOU'RE brilliant. SOOOO you'll be my CUNT, **huh**?? I like that."

"Yes. My pleasure."

"Yeah?"

"Yeah."

"Yeah?" (Are we singing a BEATLES song here? Come ON, gimme some sugar.)

DAMN. When Jeff kissed, as the saying goes...you STAYED kissed.

"I should, uhhh...get back, Jeff. Pete is in there."

"Yeah, all right. Don't tell anybody? Promise me." (Boy, he's bossy.)

"OK."

"I'm walkin' you to the door, and I'm takin' off. Tell Pete goodbye, OK? I'll call ya."

"Yeah." (I've lost language again. Has this man rendered me incapable of any intelligible SPEECH?)

Just before I slip back in the door I hear:

"Babygirl?"

"Yeah?"

"I'M NOT THE DRUMMER."

I was halfway back home, when the last thing Jeff said popped up. Not the DRUMMER? HUH? Why would you lie about…well…what DIF-FERENCE does it make? Is THAT what the joke was? Years later I got it, and Jeff soon figured out that I wouldn't have cared if he'd told me he was playing the PAN FLUTE in a Lawrence Welk tribute band. I would have fallen just as hard.

There was one more thing I realized. And it was a doozy. I still had someone living with me. It had been a heartbreaking relationship for a good while. He was such a nice guy, but I knew it had to end. He needed more than I was capable of giving. I wasn't helping him, but didn't yet have the courage to make him go. How could I not have TOLD?

I was downright shaken by my first encounter with Jeff, felt staggeringly off kilter, and taken over. He'd continue to elicit those feelings for about five years, and beyond. I had wandered into foreign territory. My swift and strong reaction to him confused me. I wasn't used to being swayed that easily.

You'd surely never have called me a rabid fan of his. I didn't see him as some sort of mythical creature, and as you know, I had no idea which guy he was in his band (a fact he laughed about for EONS until I threatened to smack him one). I was contentedly unaware of the fact that he WAS almost mythical to some.

Normally, I wouldn't be impressed by someone like Jeff staking me out. It's not an uncommonly unflappable outlook in my world, especially if you were a weekly darling of the artsy crowd in ANY large hub for a while.

By this time in my life, I'd been off the turnip truck for some time, and like most musicians who get around, had been hit on by people with a lot more "visibility" and clout than Jeff was ever in possession of. Or so I thought…until…one YEAR AGO.

This is not the place to tell you about the nasty "I'm a big name, so I KNOW you'll want to sleep with me" syndrome. Lord, once some actor (two SECONDS after having been introduced to me) actually said out LOUD, "I'll bet you want to fuck me, right?" Wow…THAT'S nervy. STILL can't believe it.

And my response was something like, "OK, that's a big NO. But if I HAD, you would have blown THAT thought right out of my head, you conceited twit." I think mostly females are subjected to this. It's not nice, and was most likely the reason I blew a gasket over that "chick" allusion.

Now if Pete had asked for my number, THAT would have been astounding and flattering. HE was mythical to me.

Reading this over, I realize how utterly HARSH I was to Jeff. I don't know why he didn't run. When the person I was discussing this with…Doug, heard that I'd confronted him about the "boring" and "mothering" aspects, he was shocked.

"Are you kidding me? You said THAT to Jeff? I think you unknowingly pushed every anxiety button the guy HAD."

He told me about something cruel that had happened to Jeff. Something he suffered and obsessed about for YEARS, and anyone who knew him well would see that button. I still feel wretched about it. It wouldn't be the last time.

Jeff and I met at the right time in each other's lives. He'd obviously had it with the mothering, and I was exhausted by an alliance in which the ground kept moving under my feet, and I watched my back constantly.

Jeff soon made it plain that HE wanted to be in control, and extraordinarily dominant. It was a relief to me, and seductive.

When I went back into the club that night to visit with Pete, he said, "He's one of the few."

"One of the few WHAT?"

"One of the good guys. No bullshit there."

Well, if PETE said so, it had to be.

There's only one thing I've learned about this sort of love and it is this: that I truly know nothing about it. It shows up in every imaginable fashion. You cannot predict when or how it will appear. It can come at you like a tornado, and you won't care if you're essentially buried. Or, it can gently nudge you and then release you quietly, leaving no imprint at all.

I got a call from Jeff at four that morning.

"Did I wake you up?"

"No, you didn't wake me up. I haven't gone to sleep yet." (Wouldn't a musician KNOW this?)

"Hey, do I, uhhh, SCARE you?"

"A little bit. "

"I'm sorry. No. I'm not really." (I hear him chuckling) "Night, babygirl."

Click. That was it. Damn. I hadn't told him I wasn't living alone.

Jeff called couple of days later, and the guy living with me was right in the living room, where I took the call. And he was very high.

"Who's on the phone, Vardz?"

"Nobody."

Jeff could hear that along with my discomfort, and says, "Yeah. Go ahead. TELL him."

So I told him. "It's Jeff Blank."

The guy develops a big smile, and says, "Cool. Hey, why don't you tell him to come over?" WHAT? Jeff had obviously heard this statement, and he's laughing a bit. I'm not seeing the humor. What a stupid situation.

About a week later he rang up. "I wanna to see you, babygirl."

"Hey, Jeff... Do you actually know my NAME?"

Pause. And then this soft talking, sometimes mumbling guy gives it to me.

Tough, strong, and forceful. No mumbling. I hear him take a breath. It sounds angry.

"YES. I know your name, NEVARD. I know who your manager is. (He correctly names him). I know you have the two brothers in your band. I know the label you're with. I know what's happening there. I know you're sweet. I know what you can do. I know what that bastard fuckin' #*##* did to you. And if I run into HIM, he's a <u>DEAD</u> man. I know who your FATHER is. I know I wanna be with you. What I WANNA know right NOW, NEVARD, is WHEN are you gonna THROW THAT FUCKIN' GUY THE HELL OUT?"

HOLY... I still hadn't TOLD him. Hadn't had time to.

"How do you know...I mean...how...?"

"Because I DIG ya, and I made it my BUSINESS to know. Whaddaya think of THAT?"

"I don't know. I think I LOVE you."

Oh GEEZ, did I just SAY that? A veritable David Cassidy song? Do I mean that? Yes, I think I DO. Did I have to SAY it though? Do I have ANY self-control left?

"Yeah. You DO. You LOVE me all right. I KNOW that. Know why?"

"No, Jeff, I really don't."

"Cause you're already MINE. I gotta go take care of business. When I get back, he'll be GONE."

I didn't know what to say. He was taking over. I was reeling. All I could give him was silence. And then I heard, "When's the last time you, uhhh...I mean, ya know. Oh fuck, when did you last sleep with him?"

"A while ago, Jeff. Quite a while ago."

"I'm rejoicing here. I AM. I'm FUCKING REJOICING. You gonna...fuck. You gonna break my heart, babygirl? ARE YA?"

"No. I'm going to take care of business too."

"OK."

He hung up. I'd soon find out, that Jeff wasn't ABLE to hang up with me, unless he said the last words. He did it in person too. Sorry about Jeff's potty mouth if you're offended. I liked it...didn't bother me. If it unduly bugs YOU I can't help you there, and I won't describe him as something he wasn't.

Here's another thing I realized. Jeff was calling me from phone booths. He always did, and always would. Maybe he had a phone card in later years. I doubt it...can't see him keeping track of any phone card. Sometimes he'd call collect, and when he came over, he didn't often use MY phone either. He made calls from (guess what) the PHONE BOOTH on my corner. WHAT would he have done if I'd lived in the woods?

Recently I realized he must have used phone booths, due to a shared accountant, and in any case, he wouldn't want my number to show on his phone bill, or on anyone else's. Good GOD.

The guy did move out. How did Jeff know all about me? I never did ask, thinking it would be a touchy subject.

HOW? How in the world did Jeff know those things? The only explanation that makes

sense would be this. The guy that was still living in my place was pretty snookered

many evenings. He has no memory of this, but I'm thinking it's likely that Jeff called, asked questions, and he would have answered them. I've also been told a band member of his had heard that I was hanging out with Jeff, or at least knew him. Frankly I don't care anymore. It does, however, give me another view of Jeff's life that was pretty ugly. This wasn't true of the guy that was living with me, but I believe that Jeff had fans who would be wanting to MEET him a lot more than they cared about the possibility of Jeff screwing their girlfriend. (Something he would never have knowingly done in any case. Jeff was much kinder than that sort of behavior would imply.)

I think a large part of Jeff's world was uglier than I'd ever imagined. When I realized what a sheltered simpleton I must have been…it was pretty darn humbling, but I realize now that he loved me and didn't want me to see.

Doug, who had filled me in earlier on parts of Jeff's life that I didn't have an inkling about, told me he once had a firsthand glance at what Jeff lived with. He ran into Jeff one night and began walking down the street with him. Passing clubs, he saw him HOUNDED by his rabid fans in a seamy way, by people with an agenda.

"Holy shit. It's JEFF BLANK. Hey, Jeff, I'm playing tonight…you come in and listen. COME ON. What's wrong, you can't come in? Come on, man."

They were relentless, a bit mean sounding, and all thought they'd further themselves through Jeff. He'd quietly say, "OK, you know…sure I'll come in for a drink."

It was awful to watch, because Jeff was so nice, and the worst of the hounding people obviously thought being seen with him would give them some sort of street credibility.

Jeff wasn't exactly a "fade into the background" guy, being almost freakishly tall, and looking like the Punk God he was considered to be. At least he was in many circles. Not mine. I wasn't IN any circle. I'm not a joiner.

His band never had a big hit, even in their heyday, but would be described as cult-like legendaries, having spearheaded a movement, the sound of which eventually trickled into pop music, in a watered down way, as always happens in these cases.

When I first heard them, I thought their sound was crisp, primitive, and driving. It was a refreshing thing in the midst of over-produced corporate glop. I wouldn't have called them versatile musicians, but they did ONE thing SUPREMELY, and they did it in a powerful, extremely virile, and screamingly breakneck way. I know now guys LOVED them. Every college kid loved them. And they were known for being loud. They was BIG with who they was BIG with. And a worldwide influence. I never realized HOW huge they were, and how MEGA huge NOW… until…God…two days ago. This sound familiar? It should by now.

Jeff was the front man of this band, the heroic poster boy for a generation of disenfranchised kids, many of whom unfortunately thought THEY could have a great band too, since it didn't take a whole lot of chord knowledge to play this sort of pared down music.

I say unfortunate, because the spawning of a stupendous amount of "I look so cool, but I can't play worth shit" bands was born out of this movement. And many of them—unlike the originals—sported a musical snobbishness and a self-deceiving quality that convinced the eejits that they actually sounded great, had a degree of talent, and were terrific songwriters as well.

What these wrong-headed people thought (and probably still think) upon listening, is this. You wouldn't need a huge amount of musical knowledge to play this music. It would SEEM so but this type of music was in fact a lot trickier to play with any degree of command than they'd ever imagined.

If you actually ARE a musician, you can identify it in a SECOND. You can clearly hear the precise timing and execution it takes to pull off this sort of sound. One little flub, one tiny pull off the beat, and the whole darned thing could collapse like precisely lined up dominoes that have been given a mere tap. It can go by too swiftly to catch up to it.

An ability to write songs that were as brilliant? Good luck with THAT task.

GREAT bands, GREAT practitioners of this ilk, and styles born of it (and there ARE many of them) are masters of this kind of delivery. What may sound like a slobby garage style to many is in fact a carefully crafted, endlessly honed and practiced art.

It's much like the old blues and jazz artists who sound to the uninitiated like they're barely and tentatively hanging together by a gossamer thread, but it's SWINGING dammit, and how are they DOING that? Sloppy, but PRECISE. You all get what I'm getting' at here????

I don't care what it's GOT. It's HOW YOU PUT it TOGETHER.

Sorry to say, what the aforementioned "it's gotta be easy, right?" quasi bands were attempting had not only been DONE, but had been done extremely well, thanks so much, by artists who wrote songs with actual HOOKS, and who were either well versed in other genres, or were eager enthusiasts of other forms of music. Not all of these wannabe bands were bereft of musical capability, but a sizable amount of them were.

Those of you who either knew Jeff, or knew of him, will have already recognized him, because the description of Jeff's public persona can only lead to Jeff. He was something rare.

He was an original.

How did I find out what he indeed DID in his band? We were talking one evening on the phone before he'd visited. I was listening to his voice, low and lush sounding, and it hit me: "Jeff, I don't know what else you play, and I know you're not the DRUMMER, wise guy, but I'll tell ya one thing. YOU SING."

"What make you think THAT?"

"Because I AM a singer, and I can hear it. I can HEAR where your voice is coming from. It's right from your diaphragm. The resonance is unmistakable. You're a GREAT singer, Jeff. DAMMM, now I have to go dig out that tape and listen again. Why would you HIDE that from me?"

"I don't know. I thought it was funny. I just, um, you know… I didn't wanna ummm…"

At the time, I thought the reason was the following (I was wrong), and I think this will tell you something about singers. For many musicians there's a stigma attached to a singer or a front person. (Used to be, you weren't even allowed in the union.) Lots of folks think you're not really a musician, which in some cases might very well be true. Not in MY case, I can assure you, and not in Jeff's case either. He WAS a musician, and a great songwriter.

My friend Doug thought Jeff might have been intimidated by my voice…may have thought he didn't possess the chops I had. I'm not buying it. Jeff was my biggest fan, always said he was proud of me, and certainly knew what I thought of HIS singing.

"Ohh, Jeff…you've got such a different TONE."

"Aww yer fuckin' NUTS. YER the one with…"

Back and forth we went. You may not know this, but MOST singers don't like their own voices. I usually cringe when I hear my own, but I loved Jeff's. LOVED it. His voice was beautiful and his style was entirely his own. No one will ever be able to recreate that voice in a believable way. EVER.

I would have soon found out he was a singer anyway. He was excited beyond belief when he found out I had vaporizers in my home. He asked nervously before he first came to stay, "So…vaporizers, huh? Not HUMIDIFIERS?"

"No. Humidifiers are CRAP. Bacteria and big droplets falling to the floor before they can moisturize the air. I've got VAPORIZORS. Why don't I just say it again, Jeff. I'm a singer too."

This was something only another singer would understand. Folks who don't have to sing a million songs six nights often think you're in some way babying yourself too much, or you're a frail and flower-like creature. NOT TRUE.

DUCK! THE UNIVERSAL SINGER'S LAMENT IS COMING STRAIGHT AT YOU.

They don't get it. A voice can go out pretty quickly. Any cold can settle right on the vocal chords causing them to swell, and the bottom notes disappear, soon to be followed by the top notes (you'd think it would be the other way around). If you try to force it, it can COMPLETELY go, and you can do permanent damage to your INSTRUMENT.

A loss of elasticity can end your career quickly. Singer's nodes mean surgery to shave them off, and there's NO guarantee of vocal restoration.

These things are FRIGHTENING for someone who makes their very LIVING with their voice. Most of us have gone through steroid therapy numerous times to take down swelling, rather than miss jobs.

Human vocal cords were built to withstand just so much. If your voice GOES, whether from sickness or over usage, it means two weeks of enforced voice rest. Singers have a lot of fear. "If I can't sing, I'm taking money from my band's pockets and trashing our 'reliable' reputation."

A singer can feel the onset of a vocal meltdown long before the rest of their band can tell a THING. If you SAY something, they might think you're an IDIOT. You avoid dairy before shows. It creates too much phlegm (singers live in a world of phlegm), and it makes for sticky vocal cord rubbing. You should drink lukewarm water to keep things sliding, and not cold water, which would be like putting ice on a hot radiator.

You sure as heck shouldn't be drinking booze during a show (not regularly) or it will dehydrate the whole mechanism. God help you if you snort some coke or blow before singing your thirty songs on any given night. You'll be so numb, you could be lacerating your instrument without feeling a thing, and it won't register in your altered little pea brain until it's too late.

The basics have to do with breathing, and learning to sing from your diaphragm, or the power will be coming from the wrong place. You'd never be able to sustain the pace of touring, and constant over usage. You'll blow those bad boys out FAST. If you're doing a large number of belting songs (which Jeff and I WERE), it can be even trickier to keep a voice in good shape.

You have to be careful not to overuse your voice before a show. If other members of your band sing, problems like this are not so looming. If you're carrying the load, these are the facts you have to live with.

NOW we're approaching the confounded MONITOR issue. Every singer gets SO sick of this one, they just about want to bang their heads through the grill cloth of their guitar player's Marshall.

Monitors are speakers on stage, aimed at the musicians. You'll see some hiding your musician pal's feet (there are different systems NOW, but that's what WE had to deal with). In a large room, or outdoors, the sound technician controls what the crowd hears, and in part what those on stage hear. Singers can't hear themselves unless they're loud enough in the monitors. That's the short, short version. For detailed instructional studies of stage set-ups and sound things, you'll have to catch me in a chatty mood.

Many times, a singer will plead for MORE MONITOR, PLEASE, and finally end up with placating murmurs. "Yeah, OK…fucking singers…"

MONITORS are the bane of vocalists, and some people don't get it, and we singers are not getting what they don't GET. The two prevailing thoughts are—"If you can't hear yourself, you can't sing on key." OR "A singer can't get enough of the sublime sound of their own golden-throated warbling."

This is NOT the case. Good singers don't need to hear themselves to stay on key. We SHOULD be able to feel the right notes. Hey, there fretless bass player, YOU know where YOUR notes are, don't you? If you don't, then slap those frets back ON there. Slap 'em on FAST.

A not so great singer will drift off key like a semi on a slick highway, no matter how many monitors they're surrounded by. I can stay solid if I hear the first chord of a song, even if those around me fall apart. A good singer CAN. You want vocal massacre? Take two guitars that aren't in tune with each other. Oh HELL…which one do I follow? OHHHHH. Come ON now.

The real monitor problem is this. If you can't HEAR yourself, you'll sing louder than necessary. It's a knee jerk reaction that can't be helped. And THAT will ultimately blow that voice out after a few nights. (*2017 note…I saw an early clip of the Beatles recently…at perhaps Shea Stadium. The stage was of course huge, as was the crowd. Guess what. NOT ONE MONITOR. Well that makes us all seem pretty spoiled, DOESN'T IT?)

SOOOO…good monitor or bad monitor, thirty to forty-odd songs a night can take a hell of a toll. I've got one little suggestion for any singer. If your voice is going through a rough patch, don't EVER whisper. It's more damaging than screaming. I mean it.

ARE YOU HEARING US? GIVE US THE MONITORS.

Oh boy, I did the generalizing again. There are some GREAT sound technicians out there. I've met many. I can recall one particular sound guy that worked in a great club. Joyous Lake. Best sound guy ever. First time I wandered in, I was ridiculously young, and warming up for Sonny and Brownie, a couple of blues greats. It must have been close to the end of that acrimonious pairing, but they were still sharing the same stage. I asked the club owner about the befuddling configuration of the house speakers.

"Why have you got over a hundred of those teensy weensy speakers mounted all over the place in the ceiling…like the solar system?"

"Because it makes the sound come down like falling rain."

"WHAT? Oh my GOD!"

A club that cares about music is rare. There ain't a lot of them around anymore. I climbed on stage for the sound check, and although I couldn't SEE him, the sound man kept asking if I had enough monitor. At the end of it, he called out to me, "Are you nice and comfortable there?"

What the blazes did he just ask? Am I COMFORTABLE? Did the soundman just ask AM I COMFORTABLE? " HELLO there…can't see you, but…will you MARRY ME? I MEAN IT. Let us just go to that darn Elvis chapel, and DO THE DEED. NOW.

KNOW WHAT, MR. SOUNDMAN? I WANT TO HAVE AS MANY OF YOUR LITTLE SOUND PEOPLE BABIES AS I CAN POSSIBLY POP OUT. YOU HEAR ME? I WILL GLADLY VOLUNTEER, AND

DEDICATE THE REST OF MY LIFE TO THE TASK OF COM-
PLETELY REPOPULATING THE SOUND PERSON POOL. THAT'S
RIGHT. LOTS OF SOUND TECHS CARRYING YOUR "BEST
SOUND GUY IN THE WORLD" GENES. JUST CALL IT MY MOD-
EST CONTRIBUTION TO THE WORLD OF MUSIC. OK? OK? "

His mastery didn't end there. While I was onstage singing, and enjoying
his comfy monitor, I began to hear a low voice. Where's it coming from?
What IS that? It was HIM. The SOUND GUY…murmuring encouraging
little things to me THROUGH the monitor.

"That's right." "Uh huh." "I'm lovin' it." It was a little disconcerting at
first. Am I having a religious awakening? And then it was hard to get
through without giggling. But ultimately, it was soooo fabulous.

Is he still there? Doubt it. Is the CLUB still there? I have to track him
down and make a call. THANK YOU. THERE MUST BE COUNTLESS
FANS OF YOU. There SHOULD BE.

Let's all not forget to track down and call those who have made a difference, took the time to care when they didn't have to…the GOOD ones.
OK? I have a list of mine…gotta get busy.

That's my singer's tirade. Any singer who read it is saying, "Boy, you're
my PAL, Vardz." Any non-singer is too comatose to comment. (If you're a
Beatle, you're thinking "What're ya goin' ON about?")

If you're someone that worked with Jeff, maybe you'll have a better understanding of what an overworked voice faces. You don't want to let anyone down, and those who don't get it think you're a whiney SISSY, and
have no problem letting you know it.

Jeff was serious about singing. There's no denying he was a skinny thing,
but he had the diaphragmatic muscles to prove his dedication. We did vocal
warm-ups together, and when he let a breath out with pressure, I can assure
you his tummy was as hard as a rock below his ribs. Just like mine. Oh, you
thought he had no training? He sure as heck did. OK, I'm done with the
singing rant.

<u>UNSUSPECTING JEFF HANGS WITH THE TELLALIANS</u>

I've got two "Jeff meets the elder Tellalians" scenes that still slay me. My
touring had slowed, but Jeff's seemed to be revving up to an inhuman pace.
We only got to visit the folks twice together.

He rang me up. I think it was the first Christmas Eve we came upon after we'd met. It could have been the second one. I suggested he should hop on down to my folks' and be with us.

You would have thought I'd invited him to climb the Matterhorn with me.

"I have like a thing here going tomorrow and, um, so um, maybe after that? Uh, I don't think… They live in the fucking suburbs? I don't think I can."

"They live in Trumbull, Connecticut, Jeff. What. You SCARED of the suburbs? You'd enjoy them."

"Listen, babygirl, I don't think your parents'll like me, right? So here they are faced with ME? I'm not the guy your father wants you bringing home. I mean… He's somebody kinda important. Shit, they'd hate me. HATE me. They wouldn't fuckin' approve of ME."

"Oh lord, my folks are used to all sorts of sloppy musician types. You wouldn't even turn their heads. Hate is not in their vocabulary. Mommy would especially love you."

"Naaaah. Oh yeah? Why?"

"Mommy loves tall guys. She's TINY. She'll want to keep you. May never let you go home."

Abject FEAR in Jeff's voice now. "Wow, that's a bit um…ARE YOU KIDDIN?"

"Of course I'm kidding, but you got it GOIN' brutha."

Now, I'm hearing a little laughing on the other end of the phone.

"So, um, maybe tomorrow night or… OK and, um, do I, um, have to wear like…"

"Jeff, wear a DRESS if you want. Just give me a ring if you make it. I'll be home, or at the folks."

"All right. So are you SURE they'd LIKE me? You fucking SURE? Maybe I could take a cab. They're gonna think I'm a little, um…EXTREME."

"Yes, I'm sure. You're pretty lovable, you know. I can pick you up."

I gave him my folks' phone and address. I knew deep down he wouldn't want to face the entire Tellalian GANG, but by golly, he showed up a day later.

I was at my parents', helping them put things away, and Jeff called. He was at the station, and I told him I'd pick him up, but he wasn't having it.

He managed to get off the train and in that cab without making Jeff trouble, and showed up that evening looking like he was being chased by a nightmare.

"So, is everybody gone?" Bless his pea-pickin' heart. I was awful proud of Jeff that day.

"Of course they're GONE, Jeff. It's not Christmas anymore."

He was immediately escorted into the kitchen by me, where I'd been helping my mother clean. She started right in.

"Hello, dear, are you Vardzie's friend? Weren't you coming for Christmas? That's all right, we've got plenty of leftovers. What would you like, honey? I made a good batch of sweet potato this year, and stuffing, and some shrimp, and a nice cranberry mold. You know cranberry is VERY good for your urinary tract. You make sure to add that to your diet. You look a little thin, sweetie. Why don't you sit? What would you like to drink? How about some iced tea? I just brewed it up this morning."

I thought Jeff looked as if he was about to have a seizure of some sort. Kept looking from me to Mommy, and back. Guess he couldn't quite grasp the fact that Mommy wasn't fazed by the "JEFF" he had carefully put on for the folks.

Jeff had arrived in FULL stage regalia, and I almost fell into the banister with the violent laugh that burst out of me when I opened the door. Actually, I almost SHUT the door, because he was nearly unrecognizable to me. I had NEVER seen him dressed this way. The evening we met (in that club) he was clothed in a plain leather jacket, and the Jeff hair thing was merely SEMI happening. It was the only time I'd seen him look even REMOTELY "rock-like," and it was a pretty subdued and common "street" look.

The only Jeff I EVER saw would be wearing a button-down shirt, T-shirt or sweater, and pants that weren't all THAT ripped up. His hair was usually in a ponytail, and hardly any bangs hanging around his face. When it was cold weather, he always had on the same goofy parka. The Jeff I was used to appeared as if he had lived in Vermont his entire life, made maple syrup, and hung out with cows. Gosh, he would have looked at home in clogs.

OHHH NICE big try there, Jeff, I thought, as I gazed at him in Mommy's kitchen. Jeff was sporting jeans so tight they looked painted on, and so ripped in the crotch area they were almost x rated. Oh, and his bum was just about coming out of them. His T-shirt didn't quite make it to his pants, and boldly exclaimed something like "FUCK YOU, ya ARSEHOLES" and the artfully arranged Jeff bangs were about covering his entire face. Pretty funny looking. His leather jacket had all sorts of things attached to it. I think he was wearing two studded belts, kind of resting near the X-rated crotch area of his pants, and they had an entire hardware store hanging off them. Puttin' 'em to the test, huh, JEFF?

He's a little scared of Mommy, and says, "Yeah, Mrs. Tellalian, I like cranberries. Umm...cranberries are GOOD, ya know? Yeah. Mold. OK. Cranberries. CRANBERRIES. Thank you. "

Now, Mommy is leaving the sink area, and walking directly toward him, and it's spinning Jeff's head. Mommy, who used to be five feet tall, is now in her late seventies, and no more than four eleven.

"You can call me Margo, sweetie. Oh goodness. Oh goodness gracious, you are a TALL young fella, aren't you?"

UH OH. Mommy has registered the big boy factor (knew it would come to this) and a flirty gleam is now present in her still-gorgeous eyes. She's movin' in on him, is my fearless Mommy, and when she's fairly UP AGAINST him (and Jeff seems frightened yet hypnotized), she moves in for the kill. The Mississippi accent is coming out. Poor guy, he hasn't got a chance.

"Honey, why is that HAIR in your face? It's HIDING your face."

And that's when she demolished him.

This alluring woman, like a small tornado, singularly focused on the nearly fainting Jeff and actually performed the famous MOMMY SPIT move. You know what I'm talking about. Oh yeah.

She LICKED HER THUMB, and proceeded to valiantly reach way, way up to get at the long, rangy, great big music god's bangs, and she was just too small to reach. Did this stop Mommy?

"Come here now, darling, and let me fix that for you."

Jeff did as he was told. NO ONE disobeyed MARGO. Not even Daddy. So he dutifully bent over, and was literally baptized by the glorious Mommy-spit-carrying thumb, as she SWEPT the infamous hair from his face.

"There now. Isn't that better? Oh yes. MUCH better. I can see your face now. Doesn't that look better, Vardzie? I don't know how you kids can stand the hair in your faces."

At this point, I'm having trouble getting any words out, because Jeff's stunned gaze was so funny. It was beyond funny. So beyond funny, I almost did a pee pee on the floor.

Margo firmly sat his hangin' out butt at the kitchen table (after she admired him a little more). Mommy was a beautiful and bold woman. If she saw a man thing she took a cotton to, she had no compunctions about squeezin' him any old way she wanted, and clearly she was diggin' on Jeff there, because she was ALL over his stuff. Lord have mercy, it was a moving thing to see.

The next thing I hear is Mommy imploring, "Sweetie, how can you see a thing? You're indoors. You don't need sunglasses indoors. I can't see your EYES."

"Yeah, but Mrs. —um, Margo, I can't quite see, I mean…."

"Honey, I can't see your EYES."

She fixed a plate for him, and as I was leaving the kitchen, to see if I could help Daddy put away chairs and such, I viewed the sight of Jeff wolfing down Margo's Southern dishes, his carefully planted bangs gone, no glasses so he can't see a thing, and Mommy is now giving her famous vitamin C speech.

"You eat all that sweet patata now, it's FILLED with vitamin C. Did you know it's the only vitamin we can't store in our bodies?"

I looked once more before exiting, and Mommy was PETTING him, and as God is my witness, I think I heard Jeff purring. Now he was Margo's special PET. How come Margo got to mother him? Damm.

After a while a dazed Jeff wandered into the living room. He didn't know it yet, but he was about to have an unforgettable Daddy Tellalian experience.

"Hi there, young fella. What's your name now? Are you a musician like Vardzie? Yes, of course you are. What gigs have you done lately? Have a sampling of your work on you? I'd love to give it a listen."

"Uhhhh, yes, sir. Yes, sir. Gigs? Gigs?"

"You can call me Judge. Yes GIGS…you DO them, don't you? Well, I'm reasonably sure you MUST have some gigs lined up, don't you, Jerry?"

"Pops, it's JEFF." I know this is a useless insight to give Daddy, but I try anyway. "Jeff has lots of gigs, Daddy. I don't think he's got any music on him."

"Yes I do, Judge. You have a tape player?" (What a show of bravado THAT was! Such a dauntless guy.)

"Well, I don't KNOW. Perhaps we DO. Sweetie, have we got a tape player? I'd like to hear what this young fella does. You know, Jer, we're all ardent students of music, we Tellalians. I taught Nevard her first tune on the piano. 'St. James infirmary' wasn't it, sweetie? What instrument do you play? Vardzie, would you be so kind? Fetch that whatchamacallit player for us."

"Popsie, the boom box is in the music room. No, it's not a BOX…it's a radio with the tape player in it. I'll get it. His name is JEFF."

"Of COURSE it is, love. Right, Jeff? You know, young fella, sometimes my girls talk to me as though my BRAINS are exceeded only by my GOOD LOOKS. Jesus Marion JOSEPH, I may not understand that washing machine Margo always wants me to load, but I make a DAMNED good omelet, Jer. What would they do without THAT astounding talent?"

I'm coming back with the boom box in hand, and I can hear my mamma from the kitchen.

"DADEEE. You stop that cussing. Jeff will think you have NO manners."

Can I in ANY way describe Jeff's countenance at this point in time? It was a cross between a sort of bewitched infatuation, abject confusion, and yes…he was starting to GET it.

The joy was beginning to burst out of him. You could plainly see, he was feeling the limitless affection that lived in my parents. The CIRCUS that was the Tellalians. And Jeff LOVED a circus.

Goodness… teensy, proper Margo bossing him around, petting, flirting, effortlessly REMOVING his trademarks (except for those "half on" pants, and I don't think he'd have balked at that EITHER), and then faced with the, distinguished Judge Aram, in his neat Brooks Brothers suit, replete with perfectly tied tie, who was over eighty years old, and amusingly repeating the word "gig." His Honor couldn't for the LIFE of him get his NAME straight but was interested in him in a focused and genuine way. He wanted to HEAR what he did and was jovially SPARKLING in his direction.

Oh, and Margo was curiously worried about Daddy's potty mouth being offensive to HER special new friend. Jeff almost crumpled at that one.

Jeff gave me a tape, I popped it in the boom box, and Daddy listened intently, with his brows knit, as he always listened. Jeff was nervous. His body movements gave him away—legs furiously moving back and forth. Always did when he felt threatened or uncomfortable. He didn't have to be. My dad always knew what was good. At any age.

After about five songs, I turned it off.

Daddy was quiet for a minute—it always took him a while to absorb things—and Jeff didn't know what this meant. He seemed PETRIFIED, as though the Judge might throw him out of his HOUSE any second now. I knew better.

Suddenly, Pops slammed both his fists on the arms of his chair, and in that ENORMOUS Judge voice he said, "DAMMIT, that's remarkably ROUSING MUSIC! That's ENERGETIC and CATCHY. Yup, it's CATCHY. I LIKE that, young fella. I like that, Jer. What are you playing? OH…you're SINGING? You're a SINGER like NEVARD? ExCEPtional voice you have there. Very different style…and DEPTH. You have DEPTH. Brother Bob would like YOU in the choir.

"Vardzie, why don't YOU do some of the songs Jer does? They're ROUSING. Woke me the hell up! I have to tell you kids though. I can't understand A WORD either ONE of you sings. I always ask Nevard…dammit, why can't you ENUNCIATE?"

"Uhhh, Daddy…Daddy. I think Jeff's music lends itself to precise enunciation even LESS then my stuff. It wouldn't sound right."

"What? Not SOUND right? Is this true, Jer?"

" Yes, Judge. It would begin to sound…ummm…stilted. It wouldn't move the right way. I mean along with the music. I'm happy—glad you like my music, Judge. I didn't think it would be your cup of tea. Your musical beverage of choice."

"Oh sure…it's GREAT. I believe I see what you mean about the movement. About the words. I SEE. Why didn't you ever tell me this, Vardz?"

"I HAVE told you, Popsie. I tell you every time you come out to see me. You've forgotten."

If Jeff's face was memorable BEFORE Daddy heard his tape, it shined with a sort of AMAZEMENT right after the listening. It was as if he'd just been presented with a number one hit. WITH A BULLET. And he HAD.

Oh, it didn't end there. Not by a long shot. Mommy called him into the kitchen again. "JEFF? You're such a STRAPPING fella. I can't REACH to put away my casserole dish. Thank you, dear." Did Mamma say STRAP-

PING? Had anyone ever called Jeff STRAPPING? Almost did another pee pee.

Every guy under SIXTY was a "young fella" to my folks. Neither one of them could remember Jeff's name. They could never remember anyone's name. Daddy often called me Ellie—his SISTER's name.

Jeff was beckoned into the hallway where Daddy pitifully implored, "Jer, can you reach this recessed light bulb up here? Can't MOVE the damned thing." OF COURSE HE knew Jeff DAMNED WELL could reach it.

How many Tellalians does it take to change a light bulb? NONE. They always find someone taller to do it for them.

We left Jeff in the hallway with Daddy, and I caught snatches of Daddy playing his usual five thousand questions...and then...well, then I heard Jeff ask the judge what he'd been yearning to ask. Jeff wanted to hear about the Nuremberg Trials ever since I told him about my father's involvement, becoming general counsel, and just how much he was involved in those trials.

"Judge, you collected all that stuff, all the evidence...and ummm...I'd like to know..." And Daddy told him. They talked till midnight, out in the kitchen. I'm sure there were pistachios involved.

Mommy and I settled in on the bed, reading and watching TV. I began to get a little selfishly antsy, because I hadn't SEEN Jeff in a while and wanted a little bit of his lovin'. But I KNEW how much Jeff wanted to hear...to know...and I'm so glad Daddy was able to provide.

He was happy to. It was his honor to tell the story to someone it would mean so much to. He told me that. Told me Jeff was warm and loving. As if I didn't know.

I did walk down the hall one time while they were visiting. The kitchen was open to the short hall that led directly to their bedroom.

I heard and saw something that I didn't understand. I heard Jeff say "I won't, Judge. I PROMISE. I won't."

I looked into the kitchen. Daddy was holding Jeff's hand in both of his. Jeff's white hand was resting in Pops's darker Armenian ones, like a dove. Jeff's head was down, looking at the table. I backed out, and neither one of them saw me. I didn't know what it all meant, but I'd see the truth in a few years.

Mommy finally called a halt to their talkfest. "Aram, it's time to wind down, these kids have to go HOME now. Are you two cleaning up the MESS you're making?"

Pops must have sensed Jeff's fear when they first met. Before we left that evening, he made it plain, POINTEDLY plain that he was absolutely comfortable with the knowledge that his much-beloved and only daughter was about to bring Jeff home with her, and into her bed. Standing at the door and saying our farewells, Jeff stuck out his hand to say goodnight to Daddy. He wasn't expecting the Tellalian embrace.

My dear father took Jeff in his arms and held him, patting his back. He then grabbed hold of both Jeff's hands in his, and with that loving twinkle that would not dim until his last day on this earth, my gentle daddy gave Jeff a wink. "Take our girl home now, and make her happy. I think you know how to accomplish THAT feat, young man. Hop to it."

I know that Jeff felt infinitely honored by that particular trust: a trust that was smilingly and willingly placed into Jeff's open arms by my Pops. He had a hard time believing it. Not I. And Jeff was the only guy I ever brought around that my Pops didn't vocally entertain doubts about. I think Jeff hugged my pops at LEAST three more times before we walked out the door.

If Daddy saw real compassion in someone, he fully trusted them with his most precious loved ones. He knew who to love, and who not to love instantly. This was a man who had looked unflinchingly into the eyes of evil incarnate. So he KNEW. Always.

Jeff was crazy about my parents.

"Oh, babygirl, so lucky. You know how lucky? I mean, they're really something. And you …JEESUS…you got to GROW UP with that. So ya know, I can see YOU better, right? I can't believe 'em, can't quite, uh, take 'em IN. Judge and Margo. The Judge and Margo.

"SHIT. I love 'em. You know…I don't think I ever saw people with all that… oh I don't know…they're MADE of SOMETHIN'. Wow, babygirl, it's like some covering ENERGY, I mean I …it's kinda ENCOMPASSING, you know? I wanna go LIVE with 'em. So you think they like me? Ya know what, babygirl? When we were goin', I felt like the Judge GAVE you over. He gave you ta ME, right? DID HE? The Judge is PROFOUND. He's like a MYSTIC or something. He's a GOO ROO. WOW."

"Yes, he DID, sweetie. They can SEE you, Jeff. Mamma wouldn't have been half in your PANTS, and Daddy wouldn't have yakked with you till midnight if they couldn't. Everybody wants to take them home in their pockets. You could just about eat 'em with a spoon."

"Shit, your father's BRILLIANT. And, um, he doesn't make you feel…I mean you don't feel STUPID around him. I never met another human being like him. We can … we can come over again, right?"

We made it over there only one more time…and it wasn't for a lack of desire to visit.

The second time we visited, they of course put Jeff through the light bulb-changing obstacle course again, with Pops asking his questions…

"LOOK, Margo! Jerry, what does the filament actually LOOK like? Should we look? How does the socket differentiate the negative from the positive do you think? Jer, why do the recessed light bulbs burn out more quickly? I wonder why the lightbulbs outside seem to last longer. Hey, young fella, why do we have power surges in this day and age?"

Mommy fussed all over him again, telling him jokes, and asking if HE had any good stories for the Tellalians, stuffing him with food, and the four of us ended up all lined up like dolls, lying on the King-Sized-Mommy-and-Daddy-Bed, watching a new tape Pops had. Armenian music. Passing Mommy's popcorn and orange segments around.

"You know, honey, I didn't put ANY butter on that, so it's good for you, and not fattening at all. Have you been getting your vitamin C? Have some more orange."

"Mamma, I don't think Jeff has to worry about the calories in butter."

"Oh, well, let's see…YES, you COULD stand to gain a little."

Now, Mommy is rubbing his chest.

"Daddy… don't you think Jeff looks better without that HAIR? Oh…look, your feet are hanging off the bed. Is that uncomfortable?? I can put a pillow…"

"Yes, I can SEE that. Jeff, you know Margo is quite taken with you. Mommy, dammit, just leave that poor boy alone, will you? Jesus Marion Joseph, you're going to wear the kid OUT. What in heaven's name will Vardzie be left with by the time you're done with him?"

"Oh, Aram, Jeff is a YOUNG fella. I think he's got enough to go around. Don't you, dear? You can handle a little roughing up. Stop that CUSSING, Aram"

"Uhhh…sure, Margo…ummm, I can handle it."

"Hey, Daddy, tell Jeff about that DATE Mommy didn't show up for."

This was a story I used request at LEAST twice a year, just to hear them go at it. It never WAS resolved. Sure did stir 'em UP though. Every time.

"Ohhh, well, Jeff, I was stationed in D.C. for a while, and Margo was living right near Washington Square, in New York. We had a date to meet. Dammit, I had to hitch a ride in some lieutenant's PUDDLE JUMPER and then make it over to Grand Central. Do you know what she DID, Jeff? She STOOD ME UP at Grand Central Station. Was it 1943? Dammit we had a date to meet under that CLOCK. I think Mommy had something on the side. Yes, she DID."

"Don't you START that now. Jeff, don't listen to Daddy. I WAS there. I waited for HOURS. He had some other BABE…that's what HE had."

"No, SIR. I was THERE. Jeff, I was the one waiting, and I had some nice BOOZE too. Do you know how difficult it was to find good booze in 1943? You know, Jeff, we'd add a little shot of ACQUA VELVA to the drinks. It gave them a ZIP, dammit. A nice ZIP. You can still make up for that ABOMINABLE weekend, Mommy "

Jeff is now looking at me and mouthing incredulously, "**ACQUA VEL-VA**?" And I'm nodding and laughing.

"Oh, now JEFF — speaking of weekends, what GIGS do you have lined up this weekend? Anywhere we can come to see you? We've got the opera coming up this Saturday, but it ends early, so we can come along to hear YOU. We'll have some other folks with us too. Sometimes we go to those BUCKETS OF BLOOD when Vardzie's playing in one, after the opera. WE have a GREAT time, don't we, Margo? Have some more popcorn, Jeff.

"Boy this is just a PANOPTIC show. What a terrific and sweeping account of the musical heritage of Armenia. Do you like those TONES, Jeff? What exactly would one call that particular scale? Listen to THAT music, kids. Hey, Mommy, come HERE."

"STOP that, ARAM. Oh all right. You're just not happy until you stir me UP like a catfish with a hook in its mouth."

Jeff gets to see them smooching for a while… Popsie grabbing Mommy's bottom.

"Uhhh, Judge, I think I might be GIGGING in Montana this weekend."

"Ahhh, Montana." (I have no idea WHERE he was headed. I'm just making up Montana.) "Well, Jeff, we would unquestionably enjoy seeing your Montana gig, but I believe that would be a mite far for us to wander. Gosh DARN it, would have been FUN, right, Margo? You're going to have to let us KNOW when you'll be closer. ROUSING music. I remember."

"Daddy, will you boys bring these plates out to the kitchen, and clean them up? If you're still hungry, I have some NICE FiGS in the fridge. Don't you two get into that chocolate drawer."

So off they went for another three-hour chat.

As soon as they took off, Mommy said, "You just love him, don't you? I can tell. He's a good boy. Be careful, Vardzie…you love so deeply. Daddy and I worry for you."

"Oh, Mamma, please don't. Jeff is tenderhearted. I don't think he'd ev-er…I don't know. I guess you NEVER know, but yes…I love him. Heaven help me."

"Well, you just enjoy him, Vardz. Mommy can see how he looks at you. You know, he looks at you as if he can't believe you just dropped from heaven for him."

"He does? Really?" I found this hard to believe.

After Jeff met my Mamma and Pops, and saw how they were STILL all over each other at their age, he was pretty inspired. Who wouldn't be? I don't think he'd ever seen anything like it. "They ALWAYS been like that, babygirl?"

"Yes, always. EVERYONE asks. I get a little tired of answering."

"I wonder. I mean if we were maybe TOGETHER more. You think we'd, like, still be, ummm, all OVER it? You think? Yeahhhh…I know we WOULD. We fuckin' would. And even at that age too. Yeah, um, babygirl? All right, you know what?? Uhhh, they…I mean…they sort of REMIND me of US. They're like US, OK? You see it too? You SEE it?"

"Yeah, they are. JUST like us. Look in their eyes. Don't you remember? I told you the night we met?"

"No, no, uhhh…**Oh**…YEAHHHH."

Jeff knew where the passion for living and creating came from.

I asked my friend Doug yesterday if my folks ever mentioned Jeff. He told me…as a matter of fact they did. He was standing around with them on a Christmas day, just a couple of years before they died. They were re-membering all the friends I'd bring by on past Christmas days.

Mommy piped up. "Oh, I loved that tall boy of Vardzie's. You know, I couldn't see his EYES. I had to get that HAIR out of his EYES for him. The poor kid. Such a nice boy. I just don't understand you kids."

"Oh sure…great young man. Loved his outlook…bright fella. Margo, he was a MUSICIAN. You know, like Vardzie. That's why he had the HAIR (as if this explained the **still** not quite understood STUFF in Jeff's eyes. They just couldn't get OVER it). Margo, we've seen messier hair than THAT. Nice, nice kid. Sweet kid. So pale. I miss him."

I understand Mommy's head was shaking back and forth during this whole conversation, and Daddy looked a little sad. Thank goodness they didn't ask where Jeff was. I don't think I would have had the heart to tell them. I think my Daddy knew.

I'll be telling you again in Daddy's chapter. He and Jeff developed a close bond. Pops would sometimes casually mention, "I heard from your friend Jer last night. Had a nice talk. He's quite an interesting young fella. Did you know that, Vardzie?"

"His name's Jeff, Daddy. Yes, I know he's interesting. What did he call for? I mean what were you talking about?"

"Oh, you know…this and that."

I wish I knew then what the heck they spoke about. I can finally guess at some of it. Did the Judge help Jeff in any way…with legal or general advice? Did they discuss me? Most likely. They were both protective and thought they knew what was best for loved ones. Bossy men. Bossy, bossy men. Did Jeff just want to reach out and touch the Judge? He WAS pretty enamored of him. They were both capable of chatting for hours about an unlimited number of things. I knew Jeff had their number from that first time we were with them. I never mentioned the "Judge" calls to Jeff and have no idea how many times they spoke on the phone. If I knew Jeff at all…I'm thinking a lot more than a few evenings were passed between the two.

It's a curious thing—I never told a soul when I was seeing Jeff. I must have blocked this out. I DID tell one person…one girlfriend, a few months into the relationship. I'm sorry, Jeff…but girls always have to tell ONE girl. It's a built-in thing. I wish I hadn't, because it seemed that, unlike me, she knew exactly who he was. She could not for the life of her imagine what sort of appeal he would have for me. I couldn't imagine why she had no compunctions about SLAMMING a man I was enraptured with.

"Vardz, what do you see in this guy? He looks... well...this is not a good-looking guy. He's weird-looking. Scary. God, you have bad taste in men. I wouldn't get NEAR him."

I was dumbfounded by the vehemence she displayed, and I wasn't ever able to forgive her for it.

"EXCUSE ME? Jeff is a fascinating, wonderful person."

"Yeah right. I wouldn't want to be caught in a dark alley with him." After a heated exchange, where I told off this contemptible woman, I never spoke to her again. Her rather violent response to Jeff's very BEING, however, gave me pause, and a not so nice view of another side of what must have been his life.

A performer's life is always split into fragments—public, and private—especially the kind of performers Jeff and I were. Different types of music and performing styles, but we were essentially the same. Many times those fragments can be at war with each other.

We elicited the same strong reactions from people. They wanted to kill us, or were captivated by us, they were either hot for us, or completely cold, and we suffered the same professional burdens, and chain reactions resulting from it. We had both at times inspired violence, and riots...once for me, and more for him.

WHY? Well, I think I'm getting it now. I guess on a stage, we gave off a "no holds barred" confidence. Despite our naturally congenial "Come on in, we wanna share this good stuff with you" attitude, we also owned a blunt FUCK YOU stance. I've mentioned...many were SCARED of our public personas, which was bewildering to us BOTH, because WE were so scared during much of our OFF stage lives.

I didn't even KNOW I had that stance until, gosh, I can't tell you how many friends told me they were intimidated and downright frightened of me until they knew me for a while. Jeff told me people were afraid of HIM too. We never really understood that. This puzzled me, because Jeff was eminently friendly and approachable. To anyone.

I finally got an answer to the question I'd been fretting over for YEARS. (Did I REALLY ask for repugnant behavior from audiences?) Jeff helped me with that, and it's what finally put my obsessive mind at ease.

How many times have I gone on about it in this book? Geez, GIVE IT UP, VARDZ. Well, I DID want to pass along semi comical, screwy experiences, and wanted to describe in general what goes on in the world I inhabit.

I remember what Jeff had to say on the subject, and despite what that psychic lady tried to tell me, it meant a **lot** more coming from him, a man I trusted. I'll tell you what came out.

Jeff was always after me to get a new lineup together, and couldn't stand it that I was taking a little hiatus. Bless him…he was so encouraging always. But I was tired out from the whole scene.

"But, NEVARD, you need to be OUT THERE singin'. I wanna, uh, SEE you again, ya know? I mean I like how the, uh, the guys look at ya. Makes me wanna fuck ya right in FRONT of 'em."

"Oh, Jeff, I'm just beginning to remember what I always loved DOING before all the stuff got in the way. I'd almost forgotten. It feels good, always has…makes me fly. I don't need an audience. And what do you MEAN about the stupid guys? You only saw me ONCE, for about ten minutes."

"Yeah, I KNOW. I was ONE of the stupid guys that night."

"You're just ridiculous. Hey Jeff…would you tell me the truth if I ask you something?"

"Yeah, course."

I asked him about the thing I'd always been berated for and almost beat UP about for years. I felt Jeff would know the truth, if anyone did, and he'd tell me.

"Do you think I'm too provocative on stage? I mean…God, do I ask for the assholes? The vampire-like grasping or the hating?"

"WHAT? Well…yeah, um, you're provocative, all right. Um, sure, yeah, you radiate yer, uhhh, KEESTER all over TOWN, babygirl, but I don't know, you're, um, I don't know…yer not like a scary alien SPACESHIP with things EMANATING out of ya. Like you're searching for unsuspecting VICTIMS to practice your DEVIANT experiments on. And talkin' bout deviant, babygirl, you know what I wanna DO to you today? Um, I'm DIGRESSING.

"It's not like you're a Jesus on the CROSS painting on VELVET, ya know, with some bad brushwork and those RAY THINGS shooting out of yer head, or the, umm, STIGMATA comin' out ON ya. Naaahh… except the stigmatas I'M leavin' on you every chance I get. It's my hobby. My HOBBY, Nevard.

"HEY, what's that strange thing on Nevard? That a hickey? NOOO, it's just her JEFF STIGMATA. Ya know what I mean? It's like... a MIRA-CLE...and it might be dripping my SPIT. It just APPEARED. Fuck. We NEED ta take the PHOTOGRAPH for the papers. Like when a POTATO grows into....ohh a Herbert HOOVER head.

"HE'S GOT THE WHOLE WOOORLLLD IN HIS HANDS, THE WHOLE,,,,"

Jeff is SINGING now, and clapping along. "Uhh. Jeff. JEFF?"

"Sorry. Provocative...PROVOCATIVE. I like that word. So what's fuckin' wrong with THAT? OK.OK...**NO,** you don't, like, do it on PUR-POSE or anything. Aww, yer not a DUMMIE, NEVARD. I mean, ya KNOW you got that thing just like I do.

"It doesn't look like yer WANTIN' the ASSHOLES or you're BAIT-ING anybody. Naaa. You're doin' yer THING. You're, ummm, natural. It's ORGANIC...that's it—ORGANIC. It's NOT your FAULT, baby. You think YOU'RE to BLAME fer that CRAP?"

"I've been told many times, I am, and have had to defend myself."

"WHO SAID THAT TO YOU, NEVARD? IT'S NOT TRUE. NOT TRUE. Fuck THEM. You BETTER not buy that, babygirl. I WON'T have you BUYIN' INTA that SHIT. You KNOW I get the same THING. It's the same freakin' crazy people... I mean, I'm like just STANDIN' there. I hardly MOVE, all right? So uhhh, whaddya think? You don't have to APOLOGIZE. You know what I'm sayin'?"

"Wow...you don't MOVE? Geez, Jeff, you must be really SOME-THING. You don't move? Doesn't the music make you MOVE?"

"Well sure, yeah. But if I MOVED too much, I'd be fallin' all OVER the fuckin' STAGE."

"Huh. Just STAND there. Huh. You must be just BEAUTIFUL up there, because you're 'bout the most beautiful man I've EVER seen in my living room. HOLY CRAP....you must be a FORCE, Jeff."

"What're you BLIND? I'm STUPID lookin' I just get it because...you know, 'cause I'm UP there. Like we just talked about."

"Oh, Jeff...no. I'm not blind. You're beautiful. I've never SEEN you UP there."

"Ahhh...ya didn't KNOW me when I was real geeky."

"Jeff, you're still geeky. Trust me. I wanna see photos."

"You mean like when I was younger...uhhh, NO WAY."

"Yeah. Come on. Oh, YOU would have been my SWEETIE when we were kids, Jeff. I would have been ALL OVER you."

"Yeah? You woulda FUCKED me?"

"Well, I was kind of shy, and a late bloomer, but if I'd known YOU…YUP, I WOULD have. Absolutely. Would've loved you no end."

"REALLY?"

"NO doubt in my mind. You come here. Show me whatcha GOT, big boy."

"Yes, M'AAM."

I felt much better about the "provocative" thing. That was always a thorn in my side. An albatross too heavy to carry. Thank you, Jeff.

Some of the dialogue I just put there for you is an example of a Jeff "tangent." He'd veer off any given subject…right into a mirth-filled RIFF. I can remember hundreds of them. The way his mind worked was always nothing less than staggering to me. CRAP. He's taking over my book. Probably wants to.

As far as I knew, during those years, there was no real purpose to our furtive behavior. I wasn't encumbered by any big relationship, and I don't reckon Jeff was seeing anyone seriously either. I think he was too kindhearted to have pulled THAT off while we were together, because what was between us went pretty deep.

His band and people he worked with had no idea, nor did any friends— he told me that, and went to great lengths to assure this. Jeff didn't want me anywhere near them.

I don't think his family knew. I think if Jeff had told anyone, it would have been his mom, but I've got a feeling he didn't tell her either.

Why were we so secretive? The only real discussion Jeff and I had concerning this DOES indicate what I FINALLY found to be true: his fear took over due to past experiences, and toward the end Jeff let a bit more of THAT out. I think in later years it was only a part of Jeff's almost obsessive desire to keep me away from others.

"Jeff, WHY are we so clandestine? What, are we WATERGATE here? I mean…I'd hate to burst your bubble, should you HAVE one, but it's not like you're the freakin' PRESIDENT or anything, and I'm even less the president than you. I'm maybe a Cabinet member…maybe. I don't believe, the *National Enquirer* would be racing to press in order to breathlessly an-nounce, 'WOWIE…Nevard and Jeff are doin' a THING.' Who would care? I can't think of anyone who'd have a reaction that would be anything but NIL. They'd only think 'Hmm…well, THAT's an odd coupling. Interesting.' Who cares?

"Here's something unusual, and I have to admit it does NOT make me feel so good, Jeff. I don't know YOUR PHONE NUMBER! You don't think that's rather ODD? I know casual acquaintances' phone numbers. I know my MAIL BOY'S number. What's wrong with THAT picture?"

"Well, if you called at my place, eventually people would KNOW and FUCK, babygirl…I haven't, uhh, you know, I mean… I never like thought this thing OUT properly. What's fuckin' WRONG with me? What if you have an EMERGENCY? What if something BAD happens to you? How would I KNOW? HOW WOULD I KNOW? Shit."

"The answer to that one, Jeff, is you WOULDN'T know. WHAT…should we get me one of those medical bracelet things? So I could push the button right before I fall under the freaking BUS? You could have it hooked up so you'd be CALLED, but I wouldn't know your precious NUMBER. How 'bout THAT?"

"OH! All right, yeah. That could, um, it could be the SOLUTION. Yeah. OK, so ya know, I'm gonna look into that because…that would be a PERFECT answer, cause I worry ya know. I WORRY a LOT allright? A LOT. Ok. Ok, good."

"NOT good, Jeff. Not so good. I was only KIDDING. I'm not going to be wearing the SCREWY BRACELET. And how would you be reached in another STATE, or COUNTRY? Oh lord, you are a PIXILATED man, you are."

"Well, but, um, for HOME. No, huh? No? You sure, cause, babygirl, I could finally have some peace, and then I'd KNOW you're safe…Oh FUCK, no bracelet, huh? Hey, wouldja… LOOK, they might have…a necklace with the button. No? OK, allright. OK."

"That's right, that would be NO. I don't know WHAT you're thinking. I'm going to walk around with a Jeff LEASH? What's with the paranoia? I don't REALLY care, except—is there something I'm MISSING, Jeff? Are you LIVING with someone? Because if THAT's the case…I'm not getting involved in something MESSY, Jeff. If there's something like that going on, you'd better come clean. I mean NOW."

"NO, no, babygirl. Nevard, I AM NOT living with anybody. SHIT, you think I'd do… THAT'S what you think of me? FUCK…I gave ya no choice...so I guess you'd HAVE to think SOMETHING. I can't, uhh, explain because I mean, what you're saying is...kinda RIGHT."

"You THINK so?"

"It's just, I just, I, I WANNA KEEP **US** JUST FOR **US**. I NEED you ta be JUST for me. I HAVE TO. So I need to keep it that way. I'm sorry, Nevard. I KNOW...I know it makes you feel weird. I'm sorry, I'm sorry, I'm SORRY. I love you. I'm never gonna mess with you. I KNOW it sounds like utter shit, all right? But you KNOW me. Please. Come on...please.

NEVARD, JUST LET ME HAVE THIS. OK?"

He was so frightened. I felt badly even bringing it up, so I never questioned it again. How do I know he was being truthful? I guess I don't, and wouldn't ever want to believe he wasn't.

I followed where he wanted me to go, and was more than happy to provide whatever haven he needed. He sure as heck was worth the trouble. I needed it too. Maybe just as much.

So, DID he take me...like I told him he HAD to? Did he make me beg? Did he own my ASS? You bet he did. Within minutes. Between long beautiful kisses. He got me. Never loud, always low and demanding.

"Want some more? WHAT? Did you SAY somethin'? Are ya giggling? Think it's

funny? HUH? Ya think you can take ME, little girl? Want me ta plough you straight through the floorboards? Oh, I CAN, all right. Ya won't be standin' fer a week. Ya WANT it? You heard me. Ya gotta ask me NICE. That's it. Wanna hear it. Again. I said AGAIN. I wanna hear ya BEG me." Boy, what a sublime man. To be continued...if ya BEG me.

MUSICAL PONDERINGS

GET out of the WAY. Here it comes…the infamous Hunter S. Thompson quote! Sorry, but when one uses a quote written after 1922, permission must be obtained. This quote is difficult to track down. It was eventually used in a book by Hunter, but it wasn't about music. It was written about the TV Industry. The LAST sentence however, has NO known author. It is actually is a modern urban cyber myth.

The quote starts with a description of a hellish world peopled by degraded musicians, and ends with the punch line sentence that Hunter did NOT write. "There's also a negative side." NOW YOU KNOW.

There are three kinds of snobbery existing side by side in the music world. They're all despicable.

You'll find the first kind of snobbery hauled around by some of the supposed "in" folks, the intelligentsia, if you will. Journalists, or any sort of media actually. It's in some radio folks, and you run into bagfuls of it in fans. On occasion, I've seen it in fellow musicians, and THAT'S a nasty thing.

There's also a mountain of folks that do not in ANY WAY resemble the snobs I'm about to describe. They are generous and selfless supporters of artists, who work tirelessly attempting to help musicians they admire attain the recognition they deserve. They are NOT the folks I'm describing.

The people below are another type of animal altogether.

There are those who like to HOARD good artists. Sort of keep a band to themselves and their like-minded community. They like to feel they OWN them. The ultimate snobs don't want the entire population to hear their band. Oh HECK no, they want them to be THEIR special band/artist.

Most people are simply not COOL enough to enjoy their favorite artist, and by golly, they don't want to lose that special identification that states: "I belong to the exclusive club of WOWIE band fans, and you don't."

Oh, these elitists would DENY it with their dying breaths, but if the truth be known, they'd prefer their favorite artists to NOT have more exposure, and God forbid they have a HIT. They feel fine when other artists lift "their" band's sound and get tons of air play. After all, THEY'RE cool enough take note, and they can righteously proclaim just how APPALLED they are.

When I hear the word "Cult" used to describe any band, I KNOW there are selfish snobs lurking about. I had some myself and can recognize the signs.

Snobs that answer to this description are too clever to show their true colors, but in spite of their "You're the BEST" cover, you can spot them. (Especially under black light.)

I'm spilling the proverbial beans about their natures, because I would like aspiring artists to recognize them. I'm just saying, notice who they'd be, and give them a WIDE berth if you can.

Try not to hang about with them, or YOU'LL begin to believe you are a rare flower that couldn't POSSIBLY be appreciated properly by the unwashed masses. It's WRONG thinking, so please don't fall into it.

Most of you have run into this attitude on the street level.

"Wowie USED to be my favorite band, but they sold out, and NOW I hear them on the RADIO." WHAT? I guess they're not special enough for you now.

You'll ALWAYS hear the "never sell out" routine from any number of fans. My response was always: "Well, I'm not changing who I am for ANYBODY, if THAT's what you're asking, but SOMEBODY had better buy me soon, because I've got BILLS piling up, pal. Are you offering to subsidize me instead? Are you an eighteenth century KING who can support a musician in your royal court? May I send my bills to YOU? What's your address? By the way, I have no health insurance, so when I'm hit by a bulldozer tomorrow, you'll be footing the bill, right? You don't WANT me making dirty lucre, RIGHT?"

I'd like to pose a question. You DO NOT want your favorite artist to make a living? Let me get this right.

Are you a plumber? This is what you do for a LIVING? How about if I'd like to be your exclusive customer? I don't want you to be a plumbing away at anyone else's house. Do you think you can pay your mortgage, or keep food on the table with my twice a year plumber call?

How many times have you heard THIS one? "We just found a great new restaurant, and we hope no one else finds it. They'll ruin it for us." So, you'd like your new favorite restaurant to go out of business, would you? You'd like to see nice hardworking people out of work? NICE. You're lovely.

I know another type of snob to add to the lineup. Exactly how many early Beatles fans do you think were aware of the artistry they were listening to? Did they know our American-born rock and roll had been eagerly ingested and spit back out in a way that was NEVER heard before? Did they SEE a shining moment of musical metamorphosis in those crisp songs, and their perfect lil' middle eights?

Some of them DID, but most did not. They were just four cute guys with haircuts and Nehru jackets, and their music made them feel HAPPY. It doesn't matter. **You don't HAVE TO UNDERSTAND HOW IT'S DONE in order to love it, to be MOVED by it.**

I described a band earlier in this book, and I pondered how many in the crowd saw the genius that was shining on that stage. I'm sure not all that many did, but **IT DOESN'T MATTER.**

Most likely only a musician, or an avid student of music would have recognized exactly what they were doing, but you don't need to be able to pick apart good art to enjoy it.

There is an abundance of musicians that don't WANT the general audience to see what's behind the curtain. We don't WANT you to see how we make it happen, the mechanics of it, and the bare bones.

We'd rather let it wash over you like a glorious mystery. You can ENJOY it more that way. Like a magic show.

It IS always flattering when someone CAN see it, and we appreciate any awareness of our proficiency, but we don't need that recognition from the world.

And HERE is someone WHO'S GENIUS is MORE than visible.

Cub Koda. I said CUB KODA. Time to plug him. He was a generous and shining talent...a larger than LIFE talent, who lit a smoldering FIRE beneath a huge number of willing musical asses. He belongs to that rarified group of "musician's musicians" (as most of my "plugged ones" do), but I believe it's time for YOU ALL to know him.

HE'S the man who once shouted at me, "Give 'em all the GOOD shit, Vardz. Fuck, you GOT the good stuff, so GIVE it to 'em.

FUCKIN' GIVE IT. Whether they WANT it or NOT. **They ain't diggin' it? FUCKIN' GIVE IT TO 'EM AGAIN! YES. I SAID AGAIN!!**"

So I did. Hey…I know how to take direction.

I went to his site today and read a few Cub stories. Someone described a show in which he did exactly THAT. The same darn song, repeated four times.

He could expertly wallop a number of instruments but was most widely admired for his singular work on guitar. Not only was he a guitar MASTER in every dusty corner of American music (outlink the Link, outroy the Roy, outtamp the Tampa), CHILD, he could make that thang SCREAM. You don't often see an instrument handled with such an astounding degree of offhanded, seemingly effortless artistry.

HOW COME the fingers don't seem to be moving? Just the one HAND? OH OK…I'VE SEEN that LITTLE HARMONIC TRICK. Ohhhh…come ON now…behind the back and upside down, NOOO…not over the head…down towards the butt. CRAP…here comes the darn thing between the legs…JAAYSUS.

I can still see it—the flash of color and chrome twirling UP. Twirling up in the air, like a drunken rocket. And then beginning the long spiral downward.

To be caught by those beautiful hands.

Precisely in position.

I can see his finger pulling the note as it lands. With unhesitating authority. Gotta tell y'all, Cub was the LOUDEST guitar player I've ever run into. And I ain't talking about his amp. No eleven there. No sir. Nope.

OK, stop kissin' that sky, Jimi. Get on your KNEES, and KISS Cub's

HEM.

Was Cub a diva? Oh HECK yeah. Had to be done, and done RIGHT every time. BUT…he was an indestructibly affectionate and concerned man, even in the midst of his own sufferings. And funny, FUNNY.

I wanted to believe HE was indestructible too, and in a way, I was right.

Michael "Cub" Koda was only fifty-one when he left this earth in 2000, but what he left US was precious and enduring.

I knew almost before I began writing this book that the lyrics in Cub's song "Welcome To My Job" belonged on the very first page. His words reflect the heart of every dedicated touring musician that's ever been.

Cub Koda HONESTLY did NOT give a DAMN if he was headlining in a coliseum or rockin' it out in a dive. And believe me, he did both with EQUAL relish. He'd give it his all, and give it anywhere. NOTHING ever stopped him from rocking, sharing his knowledge, or his gigantic enthusiasm. He eagerly parted with every bit of it for anyone who cared and was smart enough to zealously grab for it. THAT IS THE **MARK** OF A TRUE GREAT. These very same traits apply to the rest of my beloved "plugged ones" too. And MORE, there wasn't ROOM to plug.

He was one of the greats, and like most folks belonging to that breed, you can NOT pin his music down. It's everything. Cub Koda may very well have been more stuffed with music than ANYONE I've ever known...well, perhaps the NEXT one is just as musically stuffed. And honored to have known him, I AM.

You might not know his name, but his song "Smokin' in the Boys Room" should ring a bell. His band was Brownsville Station, and the tune was later covered I THINK...by Motley Crue, and was a hit again. It first split the airwaves in '73, but I'm here to tell you LOUD AND CLEAR that was only a smidgen, of an inkling, of a teensy TASTE of what Cub TRUTHFULLY was.

That Detroit boy was stickin' his inquisitive nose into the blues before most white Americans knew it existed. He took over the great Hound Dog Taylor's seat, when he left this earth. Oh GOD..listen to Cub Koda and the HouseRockers. How about his band, The Points? Lend an ear to that raw acoustic album *Box Lunch*. Oh HELL, listen to everything he ever DID. He once said he was "somewhere between a cult figure, and rock and roll legend."

Steven King hailed Cub as "America's GREATEST house rocker." Right on. I'd be a willing member of that club any day.

Cub was a great writer, student, and archivist. He wrote reviews for *AllMusic*, the book, *Blues for Dummies* (YUP). Liner notes galore (Rhino, MCA, Motown, etc.) for everyone from Al Jolson to Slim Harpo. He had a twenty-two-year column "The Vinyl Junkie" in *Goldmine Magazine*, a million other articles for various publications, a radio show, managed to wander into movies, and produced other artists. His SINGING prowess? HA. How did he find the TIME for all this, AND play a million jobs, AND write songs, AND record?

Ask folks who knew him. Ask Stephen Thomas Erlewine (check him out on <u>All Music</u>).Crikey, go listen to Bobby Dylan's radio show, and HE will tell ya. Okay, so it's in that scary voice of his.

Cub and I were shuckin' in the same circuit for years (lucky ME). He and his wife Lady J. opened their home for my mess of a slobby crew when passing through Portland, Maine. Only met you once, Jeannie, but would like to know you, and right now...I'd like to THANK YOU for sharing your man with us.

I never enjoy staying at someone's house when I'm on the move, kind of preferring more privacy. I know what you're thinking, but road living with band mates IS like being alone. They may as well be part of the furniture. Tune them in...tune them out. Staying with Cub was like being alone TOO. It felt comfortable. Holy cow, he could yak away at ya like no one else. Didn't care if you fell ASLEEP...he'd keep on going.

OH my...I once stayed at the Koda abode after falling down a long dark flight of stairs (at some hole in the wall we were playing), and darnit, badly sprained BOTH ankles. YEAHHH...gave me plenty of TIME to pick that patient man's ENORMOUS musical brain and comb through his ENORMOUS music collection. Wonder if I took the big tumble on purpose?

The Cubmaster LIVE? LIVE? I wish every one of you could have witnessed the spectacle. Those who did can enlighten you. He'd lay you out flat. He'd bulldoze and BANG you DOWN. He'd make you fairly DRIP with the sweat of DEFEAT. Go ahead. TRY getting' up off the barroom floor after a Cub Koda show.

HELLO, R & R HALL OF FAME? ANYBODY HOME? WELL, THAT'S UNDER

DEBATE. Y'ALL HAVE SOME SNOOKERS ON YOUR LIST THERE. THINK WE HADN'T NOTICED? HEY, DO YOU THINK THERE'S ALL THAT MANY BIG TALENTS WHO HAD AN IMPACT AND SELFLESSLY CARRIED THE TORCH? SPREAD THE WORD LOUD, FAR AND WIDE? DO YOU KNOW WHAT HE DID FOR THE WORLD OF MUSIC? WHAT HE DID FOR US?

CUB KODA WAS THE VOICE OF A WARRIOR.

A WARRIOR FOR AMERICAN MUSIC.

HE CONSIDERED IT HIS JOB. HIS ONLY JOB.

INDUCT HIM.

WELCOME HIM TO *YOUR* JOB.

Thank you for your time.

LISTEN UP, SNOBS AND CRITICS…you'd darn well better understand EXACTLY what you're hearing or seeing in order to make any knowledgeable judgment. Furthermore, **I don't think one should expect any art form to stay within ANY line that's been drawn in the sand by ANYONE.** THAT'S why snobs are insidious.

Here's Nevard's rules then:

If it MOVES you, and you don't know why, and you're not a musician, that's GREAT. YOU'RE great. I love Vermeer's paintings, but I can look at one till I'm BLIND, and I'll NEVER understand the broadness of his vision, the usage of camera obscura. (Who knows how the heck THAT works?) How did he pull off that stupefying chiaroscuro...the intensity of incoming daylight? I'm not well versed. I'm NOT a master painter. Maybe I'd be even MORE impressed if I knew. Maybe less. IT DOESN'T MAT-TER. I don't NEED to see.

I would not in any case, ever PRESUME a piece of art is LOUSY, if I DO NOT understand it. I don't care WHO you are though, if you've SLAMMED IT before you UNDERSTAND it, that's NOT GREAT.

DO NOT Spurn it before you Learn it, Bloody it before you Study it,

Flame it when you can't explain it, Blow it before you Know it,

Burn it before you EARN it.

If any of these describe YOU, then you're a snob. You don't have to LOVE it, but you'd better not critique it, or I'll be on your doorstep ready to smack you upside your head.

We don't all have to have the same TASTE, for gosh sake. There's music that's not at the top of my favorites list, and I KNOW it's good stuff. I wouldn't SLAM them, and I'm not a complete dolt. I don't expect everyone to have an affinity for everything, but geez, can you snobs at least appreciate things YOU are not doing?

The third and last species of snob is the Music PURIST. They are stalking about in abundance to make SURE you're not FOR THE LOVE OF GOD, mixing any musical styles together. WHAT are you THINKING? YOU are going straight to HELL, you bad and disrespectful mixer you.

You're just not bluesy enough, or folksy enough, or punky enough, or jazzy enough, or metal enough, blue grassy enough, rock enough, for THEM.

I find these folks to be wildly hysterical. If you happen to be one of them, gosh, I have nothing to say to you except...nope, there IS nothing to be said to these folks.

I'm veering off the subject of snobbery now. NOW I'm doing my business rant. THE BIG MONEY MACHINES. It's a load of YOU KNOW WHAT. I don't know about you all, but I'm downright tired of seeing good artists hustle to make a living. Why do they need to tour till they drop? Most of us love to do it, but a break from the grueling pace might be nice.

I've spoken of a few gifted bands and instrumentalists in these pages. There are hundreds I didn't mention, but I'm thinking about them right now. You bet I am. Life could have been less of a constant hustle for these bands. How many T-shirts can you sell? Do you know sometimes the hustle takes away from what they're put on earth to do?

I'm talking about the artistic hustle as well. The struggle to retain what you, and what you SOUND like when you're ON such and such a label? Y'all know what a fight THAT can be?

I don't believe the bands I'm thinking about during this quite unattractive rant of mine were looking for unbelievable wealth or God-like celebrity status. They were doing what they did in an extraordinary way, with a great deal of love, pride, and integrity. Their passions were in the right place.

I do think they were disgusted to hear support given to non-artists, or mediocre ones, year after year, and decade after decade.

They would have appreciated the exposure to a wider audience, and recognition of their rare contributions to the world of music. I know they would have liked credit being given where it was due, namely to THEM, dammit. And as I said, their lives could have been less of a struggle. I think the struggle shortened the life of my friend Jeff, and it still makes me sad and angry.

The American public has its mouth gaping wide open to swallow anything you pour in, and they're more than able to digest good music. Don't you TELL me JACK, that "the powers that be" couldn't have given these bands a hand up, given them the air time, and made it happen. They certainly have no trouble making it happen for pure unadulterated crap.

OF COURSE THEY COULD HAVE. And don't ANY of you DARE believe anything different.

We have no trouble pouring out mediocre corporate PAP, SO WHY CAN'T WE GIVE THEM SOME GOOD STUFF? Why do we feel the need to aim for the lowest common denominator?

THE A&R PEOPLE ARE NOT THE BREED THEY USED TO BE. THERE ARE NO JOHN HAMMOND SR. GUYS LEFT. John JUNIOR is out there, but he's playin' with the REST of us.

I could give you chapter after chapter on the A&R people alone. You'll never know how many times I heard lines like these from that special breed.

"You're great. If we could just change…" "I REALLY LOVE WHAT YOU DO, but I don't know where you would FIT IN." "Want some coke? No? Personally I LOVE you, but you're not middle of the road enough to…" "I admire your music, but what STYLE would you call it?"

"PERSONALLY, I'm DIGGING it, man, but you're CONTROVERSIAL for TODAY'S audience."

"I love your music, but it wouldn't fit in with radio's format." "WOW. I mean it. WOW, today's music isn't READY for you." "Sooo, if you're NICE to me…" I'm sorry? NICE to you? I'm not CORDIAL enough? No, I KNOW what you MEAN, you creep, i'm just playing dumb. I'm playing as dumb as you'd like to think I AM. That last example was the most disgusting. Do you think this doesn't still go on? Think again.

The other remarks were typical. Controversial? NAAAH. They just didn't sound like anything that was in the top forty at the time. That's controversial?

Middle of the road? I'm not moved by, nor do I WANT to be in the MIDDLE of the ROAD, you moron. WHY? Because, my friend, if I were IN the middle of the ROAD, I wouldn't have the NERVE to call myself a MUSICIAN. I'd be WALLPAPER music.

The world of music isn't ready for you, you're not recordable, you wouldn't fit the format—every one of them, are repeating the same belief. What they're saying and what I heard most often, was, **we just can't put a label on you. What ARE you?** What did I hear most often? **"I can't figure out WHAT STYLE YOUR MUSIC IS."**

Did I say the words half witted imbeciles before? Oh good. Let's say it together, shall we? HALF WITTED IMBECILES. Why don't we add COWARDLY to it?

I'm fairly sure the bands I've been talking about heard similar things. There's no doubt in my mind. (*NOTE 2017- The music biz has changed quite a bit since I wrote this…but much remains the same.)

Sometimes bands like this will be sucked into a deal that can potentially bring them more security, but then they find themselves crammed into a hole they don't want to be in. The attempt to homogenize the sound of a band never works. It is always a needless bleeding of their inherent power. It's painful and diminishing for the artist. A LOT of us find ourselves stuck in a deal we can't get out of. I know. I've been there.

Musicians who recognize all the different people, attitudes, and situations I've been describing, might agree with some or all of my personal assessments.

Most have been publicly quiet and polite about these subjects.

They have NOT for the most part been uncivilized enough to squawk loudly. Some may not agree with anything I've written, who knows? Some may agree, but are afraid of displaying what might be interpreted as a "sour grapes" attitude.

HONESTLY, I don't have bitterness concerning my own experiences…well, except toward one or two malevolent people. All in all, the years I've spent practicing my craft have been an ecstatic adventure. The experiences I've been given are an unparalleled GIFT.

I DO feel strongly about the treatment received by those I admire, and so, I'm yelling it out for THEM. I don't give a darn WHAT the industry thinks of me, if they THINK at all, and I'm sure they're not thinking about ME. I'd also like to tell people starting out—

ABOVE ALL, IF YOUR WORK IS GOOD, CLING LIKE THE DEVIL TO THE INTEGRITY OF IT, NO MATTER WHAT ANYONE SAYS. DO NOT BE SWAYED FROM YOUR VISION, NO MATTER WHAT THE COST.

Oh...I forgot I have a good snob story. I had a boyfriend (not telling which one) who displayed quite an unappealing amount of snobbery.

When asked if he'd like to go with me to a performance of Mozart's Requiem, his startling reply was, "I don't want to go hear that faggy stuff."

"Excuse me, did you just call Mozart FAGGY? Did you? I'm pretty certain you're not referring to any personal leanings he may have had. I don't think you're THAT kind of a bigot are you? No, I think you're talking

2

about his music, and I distinctly heard you call it FAGGY. Are you saying Wolfgang MOZART is lacking a sort of hetero heftiness? That he's a LIGHTWEIGHT? That he's in fact not quite as HEFTY as ...oh, let's see now... YOU might be?

"I'm having a tough time believing this. I'm pretty sure ...I mean from all accounts Amadeus was a fairly lusty, audacious kind of a guy, not exactly TIMID, and that's identifiable in his music. Maybe I'm wrong (except I'm NOT) I'm thinkin' if he were here today, he'd have the power to blow us ALL to blazes and back with the crook of ONE Mozarty FINGER.

"I think I can assure you, his prolific outpourings have got more bollocks than your musical endeavors could ever HOPE to have. Or mine. I don't CARE if he had that goofy laugh in the movie. What were YOU doing at the age of eight? Were you pretty much sitting and drooling on yourself, like I was, OR were you writing an entire SYMPHONY? YOU wanna go up against HIM, smarty?"

I don't know about you all, but every time I hear something like "Eine Kleine Nachtmusik" I have to stop it a million times. HOLY SHIT did I just HEAR that? Did you hear that? Oh god, that's brilliant. Have to hear that again. And again.

So I couldn't bring myself to leave out the obvious inequity and discrimination that's present in the modern music business. I didn't even dig into the REAMS of dirty dealings, and stealings that go on and I've only dealt with the last thirty years or so. Stealing? YES. OF COURSE.

Almost every musician I know has been stolen from at one time or another. I won't speak of big stealings, but I'll give you a small tidbit from my own book of wrongdoings.

I turned an old revved up song into a ballad. It was altered in a distinct way from the original. It was to be on a product due for release in the near future, and was "for the moment" parked on a "pre-production" tape. A wise guy from a competing label sent it to a "friend" and thought HE should do it. It was released in a flash, and became a nice big hit for the friend. You couldn't escape the darn thing. There it was big as life, with every single note and vocal nuance in place, done by a guy with a heap of respect in the industry.

Did he know what he was doing? Grow UP, people...you BETCHA he did. HE didn't care. Why did "someone" send the arrangement he knew was not yet copyrighted to that A&R slime? We never know these things.

Stupidity? A favor called in? That's an itsy bitsy stealing. I won't give you big ones I know about. Oh OK…here's just one. No names though. I can think of a song that had a HUGE amount of airplay fifteen years ago, and it was MORE than obvious—gosh, I can point to the song that was lifted COMPLETELY intact, INCLUDING the VOCAL. Lord have mercy, only some different lyrics. Lifted from an exceptional band that had been shucking around the circuit forever and a day, working their tooshies off. A band with songwriting that is QUITE recognizable. Hey, fellow musicians, I'm not talking about the "dust my broom" lick.

Oh sure, you don't have to tell me… We ALL get bits and pieces, from everywhere, and everyone, but I'm talking about the ENTIRE thing. I've heard plenty of attempts at copying this band's sound, but no one's ever quite caught it.

You couldn't MISS this atrocity. At least I couldn't. Personally, I was dumbfounded and sickened for that ripped off band. Do you think this "artist" could have at least tweaked it a little bit? You're not thinking YES, are you?

I hadn't planned on mentioning things like this. It's a last minute addition for those of you starting down the music trail. I want you to KNOW this sort of thing goes on regularly. Did you believe only our rock and roll pioneers were raped? NOT SO.

If you'd like to wade into our pool, GET USED TO IT, and learn to TOSS IT OFF YOUR BACK like a pinch of salt. Toss it off with a laugh, and keep going. Now that I've mentioned the pioneers of American music, I'd like to inform you—the abuse THEY dealt with would make the two things I just relayed seem like TRIFLES. It was brutal for a lot of them. Here is the lesson to be learned from this unavoidable fact:

Some of these great pioneers are still alive, standing proudly amongst us, teaching us, and practicing their miracles with GLEEFUL countenances. (*Note – In 2017, there are only a couple left.In the last two years, a large amount of them left us.) It is the enthusiastic and joyful faces of those GREATS that are urging me toward one more musical thought. It is the MOST important one. It's going out to those who think music is their calling.

I want younger musicians to know what you are facing. I want you to hear the fun, not so fun, the beautiful, and the hideous. If I'd had someone to give ME the real lowdown, it would not have deterred me for a second, and If YOU truly have that devotion blazing away, it won't deter YOU either. You have to know this. Some of you need to be told where the passion and drive comes from, and the ONLY reason to be doing it.

MOST of us don't get big hits. **MOST** of us don't get the mega bucks. **MOST** of us are not household names. **MANY** of us can make a pretty good living.

I'll tell you what else we can do. I'm talking here about folks who can WIPE the stage with most anything that would be considered "IN."

Not all great musicians pass up elaborate stage shows.

There is nevertheless, a colossal number of offensively BAD and "manufactured" pop music to be had. Lots of times, it's hiding behind 500 outfits per show, backup dancers, choreography, pyrotechnics, stage sets and other trappings.

Guess WHAT? Copious amounts of us could do our simple THING, and leave the stage with these so-called musicians whimpering, bleeding, and agape. We can do it without props. I sure as hell can do it with my hands tied in KNOTS behind someone else's back, and there are countless others. COUNTLESS. Large numbers of them are more talented than I and there is no END to the amount of virtuosos who possess more than I could ever hope to. Quite frankly, NONE of us CARE.

The one thing you MUST have is a compulsion to keep on learning and growing. God, I've been at it for years, and haven't learned a tenth of what

I'd like to learn. Even geniuses don't EVER feel as if they know half enough. Even musicians who have been at it for twenty or forty more years than I.

YOU NEED TO BE HUNGRY FOR IT.
ALWAYS.

I've said it in as many ways as I could possibly SAY it throughout this book. If you don't have this unquenchable desire to make music, you're doing it for the WRONG reasons. Let me tell you why.

Every one of us that is worth a darn and has been in it long enough can tell you this. We have all been through professional heartbreak and betrayal. Betrayal visited upon us by people we've loved and trusted. People we thought had our backs.

I'm not talking about a lousy night, or an audience that hates us, or a critic slamming us to hell. Those are things we get USED TO, and they generally roll right off our backs. Just a little sting, and often amusing.

No, I'm talking about true disloyalty that can shake us to the very bottom of our boots. Our jobs are not like punching a time clock, or a nine-to-five thing. What we have invested is our inner selves. Our hearts. It can be hard for us to slough it off. It's not just a paycheck to us. ALL of us in this business have been hurt like that. At least once. AT LEAST. No one gets by unscathed…at least no one I'VE ever met.

We can pick ourselves up and continue in spite of it. Just like those pioneers I described to you. Sometimes we'll get burned out and take a vacation, but eventually we start having a thirsty jonesin' and we'll come back in one form or another.

If you're doing it for the wrong reasons, and surround yourself with drivel instead of music, and if you're not willing to listen, and learn, you'll get hit too, but you're not gettin' back up, Buckaroo. Do you know WHY? It is because you've invested your life in something that is smoke and mirrors. You probably think music begins and ends with you, and you don't have the need to learn. You're not happy playing for the bartender. Or your pet. Or no one.

So why can people that are infused with music keep getting up?

DON'T YOU KNOW YET?

It's the Music.

It's the soul mates in music we meet along the way.

It's the love of it that we share with them.

It's the ones that instruct us.

It's the circle that always takes us back to

The Music.

Like the learning that never stops.

Like a lover you never stop yearning for.

Like the Music.

If you're not thirsty to learn at the feet of those who have given us their sublime outpourings, and you don't want to absorb all the music there is and HAS been in this world, from a soda commercial to a grand opera, then don't you DARE call yourself a musician. I mean it. Get the FUCK out of our way.

If you don't understand some of it, delve DEEPER, and if you're not WILLING, then please don't take up the space. Please don't be a music snob. PLEASE.

Are you mistakenly thinking I'm Miss "I love every piece of music I hear"? No, I'm far from that. Did you read the darn term paper I just wrote about judging ANYONE'S art?

There's plenty of music out there I detest, but I'll let you in on something. If I detest it, you'd better believe I understand every single note and move in it, and I know WHY it's crap. I've earned the right. OK, OK…you're aware of my ignorance regarding WHO is doing things, but I sure do know WHAT I'm listening to. Stop laughing.

If you haven't studied, delved, and learned or if you are a music snob, you HAVE NOT earned the right. Until YOU know, just keep your mouths shut. I mean it.

Am I being too harsh? Probably. I'm not really a harsh type, but I feel strongly about this.

By the way, there are a lot of knowledgeable journalists who are cognizant of the sounds they hear, and are capable of conducting intelligent interviews. On the other side of the spectrum, there are a heap of writers who have been given the "music/arts" beat for their local rag.

They're usually very nice, but don't know Lennie Bernstein from Alex Chilton. I'd just like to BEG those nice, well-meaning people. Start listening. Edumacate yerselves…you might enjoy it.

Don't expect musicians to be playing any kind of "style" in particular. The best musicians, the most inspiring, will ingest a conflicting mixture of musical food…as much as they can fit in their hungry mouths, chew on it for decades, and then spill it all over you in a yummy, yummy way.

I think I can speak for a very large number of us when I declare—we have not appreciated the seemingly endless line of questioners over the years that have made our teeth grind when faced with the inescapable "What kind of music DO you play? What style would you say you perform?" These questions must be really funny to people who DO stick to one type, or those who are not AWARE of the different genres inherent in their music…but as for the rest of us…

Please do NOT let the proceeding question ever leave your lips again.

"AND JUST HOW WOULD YOU DESCRIBE YOUR MUSIC?"

Why? WHY? Well, if it's the ten thousandth time we've been asked, you'll extrude unwanted violent thoughts from us.

I was always too polite to say it, but believe me what many of us are thinking is, "HOW would I describe my music? I don't know. How would YOU describe your ass?" This list is for YOU too.

Start listening. Listen to:

Charlie Parker, Love, Paul Geremia, The Kinks, The Weavers, Bunky and Jake, Ornette Coleman, Kurt Weil, Bach, Ella Fitzgerald, Roy Buchanan, Screamin' Jay Hawkins, Rogers and Hammerstein, The Dictators, Mel Torme, Jimi Hendrix, EVERYONE from Stax, Sister Rosetta Tharpe who's like Tampa Red in a skirt. Listen to HIM too.

Listen to The Band, Black Sabbath, Link Chamberland, Link Wray, The Missing Link, Mozart, The Who, Dinah Washington, Muddy Waters, Tom Jones, Rocket from the Tombs, Colin Linden, The Yardbirds, Wagner,The Temptations, Louis Armstrong, Georgie Fame, Johnny Cash, Jimmy Page, Thelonious Monk, MC5, B.B.King, Vernard Johnson, Fats Waller, The Stones, Frank Sinatra, Rachmaninoff, Buddy Guy, The Crystals, Don Covay, NRBQ, Julie London, Guitar Slim, Howlin' Wolf, Mose Allison, The Fleshtones, Buddie Holly, Sun Ra, Beethoven, The Charlatans, James Burton, Stacey Phillips, The Ramones,Herby Hancock, Motorhead, Verdi, Jelly

Roll Morton, The Stooges, Wanda Jackson, The Poodle Boys, Little Rich-
ard, Miles Davis, The Dictators,Willie Dixon, Nina Simone, The Righteous
Brothers, Solomon Burke, Chopin, Etta James, Junior Collins, The Cramps,
Dizzie Gillespie, Roy Buchanan, Lambert Hendrix and Ross, Bob Wills,
Otis Redding, Charlie Parker, Kurt Weil, George Gershwin, The Beatles,
Memphis Slim and Charles Ives.

AFTER YOU'RE DONE WITH THOSE, CALL
ME FOR THE NEXT FIVE THOUSAND.

Upon reading the cheeky and "shoot from the hip" opinions I just
hurled your way (goodness, could I have spit out a more mutinous rant?)
I'm ready for something frivolous. How 'bout you? I know, that was some
rough reading there, soooo…

Are you ready for the MOST absurd attempt to climb the unwilling Mt.
Vardzie? I don't usually play with the heads of drunks, and very rarely get
mean, but I do NOT suffer fools gladly.

This kid's unstoppable and determined pursuit of what he obviously was
not going to accomplish set my once in a while fresh mouth in motion, and
the poor thing just couldn't seem to STOP himself. He was like a
FREIGHT train comin' at me, I tell ya.

What did Mose write? "Your mind is on vacation and your mouth is
workin' overtime."

Uh oh…that could be ME.

I must have been in my mid thirties. This time I remember where we
were playing. It was in Stowe, Vermont. This kid was what…twelve? I never could grasp why the BABIES would be nippin' at one's heels, and often
couldn't resist asking, "Did Mommy drop you off here? Shall I call and tell
her you're ready to go home? Because I know I look younger than I am,
and I'm sorry to be the bearer of bad news, but I think maybe I could BE
your mommy. Get a move on there, little boy."

Sometimes this speech didn't slow them down, which was the case in
this story.

We're packing up, and I'm having a soda at the bar with Boo, the best
waitress, and most wonderful girl I ever DID know, and Eddie Izzo. They
mean nothing to you, but I adore them.

This kid approaches me with the bravado of a thoroughly liquored up fella and proclaims to one and all…

"Nevard, I have to fuck you."

"OK, thanks, kid. Stop that PUBLIC potty mouth. You're not old enough to indulge."

"But, Nevard, I been watching you a long time, and I have to fuck you."

"Alrighty, THANKS for watching. As for the other thing…you're in no shape to fly SOLO. Just stop it."

"Ahhhhh, come ON. Can't stand it. I HAVE TO fuck you!!"

Now, he's starting to repeat this over and over, and loudly enough to wake the dead…Boo and Eddie, a few other stragglers, and the band are beginning to think this is hilarious, but I just want a little peace, and my patience is running out. One more time he repeats it, and slooowly I turn…step by step…

"Nevard…NEVARD… I HAVE ta fuck you!!"

"EXCUSE ME, let me just get this STRAIGHT. Aside from the bad public POTTY mouth, that you are altogether too young to be spouting, you're saying…let me get this crystal clear…you actually **HAVE** TO? I'm sorry, is there a **CITY ORDINANCE** here in Stowe that says I am not allowed to LEAVE TOWN until I KNOW someone IN THE BIBLICAL SENSE? I can't pass the town border without first SCREWING one of the fine citizens of Stowe, Vermont?"

"Yup."

(Now I'm so annoyed, **I'M** getting potty mouth.) "Well, if that's the case then, I feel compelled to sadly tell you I have played here a NUMBER of times, and not ONCE did I lay down with, roll in the hay with, fondle, share carnal knowledge with, LICK, SUCK, or **FUCK** ONE PERSON in this fair city before I blithely crossed the Stowe line. Not a **ONE**.

So I'm pretty sure I am breaking the law here, and I am evidently a repeat offender. Boo, Eddie, would you care to make a citizen's arrest?"

The two of them are almost rolling now.

"Naaah… I won't tell. Come ON, Nevard, I SWEAR **it won't take long.**"

"Won't TAKE long? Did you just proudly say, **IT WON'T TAKE LONG**? So then, you're not the SIXTY-minute man. You'd be the SIX SECOND man. Now I'm feeling an almost irresistible pull in your direction….wow. I'M impressed. YOU impressed there, Boo?"

"YEAH. HAVE TO. Come on, NEVARD, I promise, you won't feel a THING."

LORD HAVE MERCY. Do I have this right? "Did you just …in an unprecedented and truly seductive manner promise me… I WON'T FEEL A THING? Not a THING? NOTHING? HOLY CRAP. You're SMOOTH. You sure do know how to talk to girls, because now, you've got me goin' in a way I've never GONE. GO ahead, and just reel me in NOW."

"Yeah, **yeah,**" he responds with a grin. (Is this kid really buying this? Is this not a cautionary tale to warn you all not to drink beyond your tolerance level?)

My final words to him: "Do you realize, you **SMART** ASS, that if it WON'T TAKE LONG, and I WON'T FEEL A THING, **you could have HAD me** at least **TEN times** while we were standing here, without me BEING the WISER?" With that, I walked off, and behind me I could hear the unmistakable sound of him hitting the floor. "IT WON'T TAKE LONG, and YOU WON'T FEEL A THING, Nevard" became another often repeated band saying. We all have them.

THINGS THAT WOULD
PUZZLE MANY MUSICIANS
WHY?
HOW THE HELL DO I KNOW?

WEDDINGS

I'm sorry I can't keep it in. I'm feeling the need to delve into the subject of the horrible wedding SHOWER tradition. You can't escape this when you're a female, and if a relative or friend is sweet enough to give you a party, how can you possibly beg off? You cannot, and so you've got to suck it up, cheerfully spit up all the poise you can muster, and trot out large amounts of ooohs and ahhhs, while opening gift boxes containing rather thrilling items.

"Oh goodness, thanks so much for the towels. Thank you kindly… I love a nice garlic press."

Many showers include games more suited to eight-year-olds than adults. Not so appealing. Very "in the nursery" nightmarish. Here's my question.

WHY don't the GUYS have to participate in this sort of thing? Why can't THEY sit and eat tiny sandwiches and open the pastel-colored boxes?

Okay, okay, it's not about the shower. Not really. Here's the real issue. I've never felt good about the "ahh, ya poor slob" for the guys, versus the "oh you lucky, lucky girl!" attitude. Something's not right here. It seems kind of mean.

I don't enjoy weddings much. They are overblown, decadent, creepy, never-ending, greedy-like affairs that people are inclined to spend insane amounts of money on. Gosh, I know girls who have spent ten thousand dollars on a wedding dress, and many pay at least a thousand smackaroos.

Am I the crazy one here? Will you be wearing this item beyond the ONE day? That's just the goofy dress. The whole wedding is an event evidently worthy of re-mortgaging your HOUSE.

HAIR

The subject of hair reminds me… I have NEVER had my nails done. Why? I'm positive

It is because I am aware that I do possess opposable THUMBS, and am able to do my own damn nails, and if I'm in the mood I can slap on polish. Sorry. Let me try this again.

HAIR

I have not had my hair cut by anyone but myself since I was nine and a half years old. This seems to be a simply astonishing and foolhardy accomplishment to every single one of my girlfriends. What they find even more unbelievable is the fact that I started cutting my FATHER'S hair at the age of ten. Why would he have trusted the scissor-wielding ten-year-old Vardzie, they'd like to know.

I don't know either. He seemed to place a downright irrational amount of trust in me when I was a kid. Many of them knew him, however, and they did have to admit—he looked nothing less than DAPPER at all times…including his tresses.

As far as my OWN hair—I had acquired a fierce and irrational fear of salons, or any haircutting establishment when I received a haircut that resembled one of those horrid "bowl" cuts they used to give little boys. You know, much akin to the photos of John John Kennedy when he was a toddler.

"WHERE did my soft long HAIR go, Mommy??"

WHERE THE LIVING HELL IS MY HAIR?

When I espied all of my hair on that linoleum floor, looking forlorn, lying there every which way, and suddenly disconnected from me, it felt like my very soul had been torn out.

I vowed never to step into an establishment like that again. Even my stubborn little Mississippi Mamma couldn't budge me.

My girlfriends already think I'm nuts for not having my hair done (to me this means mangled), so I might as well confess all.

I don't like makeup. It makes my face feel dirty. I mean it. The most you can get me to wear is a little eye shadow and liner. MAYBE something under the eyes if I only got two hours of sleep. MAYBE once a year, mascara. I don't care for mascara either. If you're a man, go ahead and put some on. What's it feel like? SEE? And for gosh sake, it just ends up running down your face anyway.

NO face makeup though. None of that stuff that covers your face. I also won't tweeze my eyebrows so they look like skinny clown brows.

I refused to put makeup on for photos needed for the dam Record company. The photographer was not a happy man. I positively rejected his notion of turning my FACE into an unrecognizable rock 'n' roll girl mask. He was not amused.

I advised him that if he dared to pull some of those repellant air brushing techniques out of his little bag of tricks—thereby making a person's skin look distinctly PLASTIC—I'd sic my quite large and drunken bass player on him. He became even less happy and amused.

I guess the photos were acceptable because he seemed a bit calmer after he got the proof sheets. Disaster averted. Most people can't stand photos of themselves. YUP, I'm in that club. If you're NOT, then you're most likely a narcicisstic ASS.

BAD WORDS

Until I was around seven years old, I actually thought the name MARION was Jesus's middle name. Thought his entire name was Jesus Marion Joseph.

What was I talking about? Oh yes…WORDS. I've been told that my vocabulary grows exponentially in accordance with the mood I'm in. The madder I am, the bigger the words. The unbecoming over usage of cuss words came from the boys. In the band I mean. Someone wrote THIS exchange down… "Listen you freaking pusillanimous little thief. I'm sick of y'all trying to extort a gigantic amount of dead presidents. Ya think I'm devoid of any muthafuckin' THINKING process, you unconscionable mo fo? I KNOW unequivocally …you're saying shit with a mouthful.

"I did not SAY you are a piece of shit, although I'm confident of your inherent fucking crappiness. I am trying to convey that you are saying NOTHING, and you are SAYING it, with a big MOUTHFUL of nothing. Well…SHIT to be exact."

BAD WORDS - 2ND ATTEMPT

The following is what I MEANT to bring to your attention six thousand paragraphs ago. The continued mispronunciation of this word is a knife in my heart that I live with each and every day. I'm talking about the word NUCLEAR.

There has not been ONE president of these United States that has pronounced this word correctly since Gerald Ford uttered it. I AIN'T JOSHING YA. '

The word is (OK, work with me people) **NEW – CLEE – ER.**

The word is NOT NUKE **– YU – LER.** It just is NOT.

I find it positively embarrassing for the leader of the FREE WORLD to not be able to utter this word correctly.

Why do they keep changing words? They could be perfectly fine for ages and ages, and all of a sudden, the familiar word is a whole new thing. WHY? And who STARTS it?

When did **doughnuts** become **donuts**? So wrong.

When did **humour** become **humor**? Wrong too.

When did **catsup** become **ketchup**? REALLY wrong.

I need to get over it, and move on, don't I?

THE EVER CHANGING PEOPLE

You know these folks. They are the ones who drape themselves all over you on Monday, as if you're a piece of fly paper. They couldn't be more friendly and cordial. They couldn't be more concerned about you, or more attentive. They love you, love you, love you.

Come TUESDAY, however, it appears they've made a TERRIBLE mistake, because NOW, they can't seem to remember WHO you are, and are offended by the very presence of you. No, no...on Tuesday you deserve all the snottiness they can muster up for you. IF they don't simply ignore you altogether, that is.

HERE ME NOW, you psychos from the underworld. Yes, YOU, you evil minions of the dark place, with the 666's etched into your bad tempered/good tempered scalps (oh WE know it's there). Just PICK A WAY TO BE, and BE IT, will you? So we'll know what to expect from you? We're begging you now. Be nasty, or be nice. No more of the see-saw thing. We're much too busy to have to worry about taking your confounded temperatures every day or so. Please...let's have some consistency here. That's all we're asking.

FOOD WORTH DYING FOR

I wish I could tell you why I fuss over these pointless things, but I'm passing them along to you so you can take up priceless brain space to ponder them as well.

Do you all have any idea how many foods there are in the world that I'm fairly sure had to be discovered by way of people dropping dead?

Let us start with the unprepossessing little Castor Oil product. The one that NO-ONE wants to ingest. My father told me in his day, they'd give a spoonful to every child at least once a day.

The sticky part of this informational blip is this. The leaves of the Castor plant are very large and harmless. The Castor BEAN, however, (the seed of the plant) is DEADLY. And I do mean deadly.

The lethal dose for an adult is merely four to six ingested seeds. So um...how many truckloads of folks perished while they were inventing a way to extract the oil from the seed? The oil nobody wants anyway? This is the same oil that Mussolini used to torture prisoners (and countless children right here in the USA).

OK, get THIS. My mamma used to GROW the castor plant right in our back yard.

"Honey, aren't the leaves wonderful looking?"

"Yes, they sure are, Mamma…and by the way, Dad, you might want to run out and get that nice blouse Mommy saw. No, I mean NOW."

Let's move on to the scrumptious qualities of the Cassava, or Tapioca plant. The root contains a gazillion milligrams of cyanide, and a few bites can kill a COW.

There is a process by which they extrude the cyanide in order to make the darn stuff edible, involving cooking, squeezing, and multitudes of mysterious ministrations.

The FLOUR they end up with (OH BOY) is what's used to make TAP-IOCA.

How many people bought the farm for TAPIOCA PUDDING? Do we care that deeply about tapioca pudding? Good LORD, what an embarrassing way to go.

"Yes, I'm afraid we lost Miriam in an unfortunate tapioca accident."

Now, there's an end product that's worth slipping off the raft for.

Those babies are just two of the thousands of food items that have felled armies of folks in the discovery of them.

OH, I DO wonder about cottage cheese. Who invented it, and how did they decide WHEN it was finished?

CONVERSATIONS IN THE VAN
AND
MORE LIFE ON THE ROAD

I've racked up an awful lot of miles through the years, and altogether have had…let's see…four drummers, four bass players, four guitarists, and two horn players. And I don't know how many vans or busses. Usually mine, sometimes other's. Every band has at least ONE nightmarish and potentially deadly van or bus story. Here's one of mine.

I remember one particular van that blew up in the middle of NO-WHERE in Maine. It occurred at about four in the morning. I think I was the first to notice something was terribly amiss.

"Hey, you know what? I'm seeing flames out the window. Looks like it's coming from the rear wheel. THAT can't be good, can it?"

With that we pulled over, and indeed a rear wheel DID have flames pouring out of it. It's amazing what you'll grab up in unthinking moments like these. I, for instance, did NOT grab my bag, with wallet, ID, etc., nor did I reach for the 1935 solid Bakelite Electro Rickenbacker slide—that bad boy had pickups that HOWLED.

No, what I took from the van just before it blew up was something more precious. I took a hardboiled egg.

As soon as we made our hasty exit, every single window in the van exploded. Unbelievably, there was no real damage to instruments or equipment. A little charring on some cases, but that's all.

People who didn't make their livings on the road would usually view my life as one long musical and glamorously hedonistic stroll through the park. YES, making music is the only thing I ever wanted to do, and the only thing I knew HOW to do, or COULD do. I'd had a couple of other short-lived jobs before I started full time.

The most outrageous one? I was a store detective for approximately three months. I'm picturing me right now, running hell bent down Bridgeport, Connecticut streets after huge guys with television sets in their big hammy hands. When times were extremely tough or slow, my girlfriend Evita would let me come and clean her house. I occasionally gave piano lessons, but found I didn't have much patience for that. "Let's try that one again, sweetie. NO? What do you MEAN, NO?" That's pretty much it, except for my nightmarish foray into the corporate world when I was really hungry and things were falling apart. I had a couple of unthinkable jobs then. Thankfully fairly short-lived. But that comes much, much later.

No, my non-travelling friends didn't quite get the picture of life off stage.

My girlfriend Robin queried: "Isn't it lots of fun travelling with a bunch of cutie guys and seeing all those places?"

"Yeah, I GUESS... Really, it depends on what your idea of FUN is, and I have a feeling it's not the same as MY idea of fun, and I DO miss female companionship lots, although musicians ARE kind of girly in some ways."

"I'd like to come along sometime and see what it's like"

"Sure, come on along. I DARE ya."

"Well, what's it like?"

"You want the lowdown first, or the high points?"

"OK, I'll bite. Give me the lowdown first."

"Alrighty then... Would you dig getting up every night in the middle of the night—and by the middle of the night, I mean about eight a.m.—and stumbling half asleep to the bathroom, and every single time your rear end falls in the toilet bowl?"

"Ewww... every night?"

"Pretty much. That's NOTHING. I'm just starting you off slowly here, so your head won't fill up too quickly and start to leak unattractively. That bathroom inconvenience is just a fact of everyday life, if you're in that stage of sharing hotel rooms. Want me to go on?

"How about your bass player telling you he's going home for the night with a girl, and he thinks she's got a cop boyfriend, but supposedly he's out of town, and you say 'well, bud, it's your funeral, but I do love ya, so please be careful, and be back here by two on the button tomorrow, or I won't love ya anymore.' THEN, you get the call at about seven in the morning. Your beloved band mate is cowering in a phone booth, because the cop boyfriend DID come home unexpectedly, waving a gun about (a Magnum and I don't mean Tom Selleck's) and could you please come get him NOW, before the cop boyfriend finds him?

"Now, you've got to pick him up, and on the way pray like the dickens that your bud isn't lying in a pool of blood, and the cop guy isn't there waiting to shoot you too. Meanwhile unwanted guilty thoughts are popping up: 'Where the HECK am I going to find a bass player for tonight's job in Gonesville, Maryland? Do they HAVE bass players in Gonesville, Maryland?' Ahhh, it's all fun and games till somebody gets their eye poked out, right? "

"Get OUT."

"Who could make this up? You go ask any band. We all have the stories. THOUSANDS of them. Ahhh, I've got a pretty one that was repeated a number of times. It's the charming story about any club owner that resists paying you at the end of the night. Did you say WHAT do you DO? Well, you have to fetch your drummer who's packin' a little heat. Now don't get all squeamish on me, Susan. It's a fact of life. He's NEEDED.

"He has to enter the club owner's office, open his jacket a tad, and in a supremely PLEASANT tone of voice, inform the owner that he really DOES want to pay the band. He then has to count the bills, exit the office, and yell out to the rest of us,

'We'd best slam it into HIGH GEAR, guys. I think I've just worn out our welcome.' We need to MOVE it, and get out of town before the owner's reinforcements appear."

"OK, how about this one? You wake up in the middle of the night (you know what time THAT is now, right?) and find some big time monkey business going on in the next bed, with somebody your drummer picked up, and like a car wreck, you have to stare for a while, mostly because you're still half asleep, and frankly you have to ADMIRE your drummer's moves for a moment. Then race out the door because any more sleep is out of the question now, and you don't want to be lusting after your own drummer, do you? DARN…too late for that.

"You have to hightail it to the room next door, the contents of THAT room being the rest of your sleeping band. The trick is to awaken at least one of them, AND a roadie. Or TWO (NOT an easy task to accomplish), get one of them to roll out of bed to open the door, and then do some pleading.

"Come on, make some room here. Just move over. Come on…PLEASE? OK, can I have just a bit more than the TWO inches of bed? Geez, I'm SO tired. No, you CANNOT go in the other room and watch. Oh I don't care. Do what you want."

"Are you SERIOUS?" Robin asks.

"Of course I'm serious. You know how many times we've driven at least a hundred and fifty miles to find the club has burned down? No, I'm NOT making this up. Club gone. No club. Big pile of ashes. OK, maybe a window sticking up. It's happened at least once to EVERY band I've ever known. Go ahead and test it out. Ask any band. It's happened THREE times to me, and since the first time, I CALL the night before we're to appear."

"Hmm…there are so MANY. Your drummer—no, different drummer than the last one—this one is Bam Bam Tanski…GREAT rock drummer, and a wee bit underage when he began his time with me. He breaks his collarbone, and the only immediate replacement available is a guy who says:

"You mean I have to play three sets, EVERY night?"

"No, not EVERY night, but some of them."

"But I don't know that many songs."

"You do NOW, Buster. Take these tapes."

"I don't think I can PLAY that long."

"Really? Remind me never to sleep with you, OK?"

"You do this all the time?"

"We do what is required."

"Well, how many songs do YOU know?"

"At least enough to do fifteen sets back to back, and then wing another five or ten maybe OR enough to do about ten solid SHOWS back to back, and enough to wing some more."

"You kiddin?"

"Course I'm not KIDDING. What's WRONG with you? Are you supposed to be a musician?" (Note: this guy was from the "seven bands a night" circuit, so he knew twenty songs…tops.)

"Here's a band mate the rest of us couldn't take our EYES off of when we happened to look out the window one night, in some hotel or other, and caught sight of him getting very busy in the back of a car. We knew it was wrong, but we couldn't stop LOOKING.

"OK, we have to walk away. WALK AWAY. One, two, three… Nope, I'm still frozen. This is a spectacle. Yeah, yeah, I'm disgusted with us. What's WRONG with us? This isn't nice. All right, let's all turn around at once. One, two, three….woahhhhhh look at THAT, will ya? No, we have to stop this. I mean it."

We finally did tear ourselves away. WHAT, were we eight years OLD? How seamy could we GET? This is what can happen when bored musicians are touring. I'm not sure if we got much worse than THAT. OK, we most likely DID, but believe me; WE were on the tame side, compared to some of our contemporaries."

"Does that sort of thing happen a lot?"

"Listen, girlfriend, do you think it's easy to have any kind of relationship with ANYONE when you lead a life like this? This is one of the sacrifices you make to do what you love.

You really don't meet people on the road. Well, you DO meet lots of people, some very NICE people, but as far as romance goes, you get lots of offers for quick fun, but you don't often meet anyone you'd actually want to be WITH. And even if they COULD be somebody you might "click" with, you don't really have the time to find out. You're packed up and out the door to the next job.

The people you'd really want to be with are not always, but often, too nice or shy to approach you anyway. They wouldn't want to intrude, so many don't even try. As for me, I'm much too shy to approach my SHADOW, never mind a stranger, contrary to what I may seem like up on that stage.

If you're fortunate enough to meet someone on your travels, where the heck would this lead? They have THEIR life in THEIR town, and they don't particularly want that to be disturbed, so where are YOU fittin' in there? There you are, the goofy musician with your crazy band, and you're always talking about things that sound like another language.

OK, let's say you meet someone in or near the actual town you live in, or someone from your travels that would MOVE to your town. How many folks want to hang with your lifestyle? Are they going to wait around for you while you're away pretty much most of the time? Do they even like the hours you keep? Think they'll be up at three in the morning to chat with ya?

It takes a certain sort of person to want to put up with that, and even amongst them, there are lots that'll just go CHEAT on you, or lose interest while having you away so much. It happens eventually. It happens more often than not. The guys have a better chance of finding someone who will put up with the "away" thing. Maybe women do better with that sort of thing...I don't know.

Just how many GUYS do you think there are out there who will stay with a girl that's away? Take it from me, not so many. There are NOT too many of those guys hanging around, and the ones that are, won't be very happy about it.

I have to tell you, girlfriend, I don't know about others, but I get BORED with someone who doesn't speak music. You know, I have plenty of friends who aren't musical in the least, but to have that kind of relationship with them...oh boy. It's such a part of my fabric...don't think I could do it. I once went out with a guy for a good TEN MINUTES, and he was NICE, but he couldn't tell the difference between The Monotones and Motorhead, for gosh sake. I tried to SHOW him stuff, but he couldn't HEAR it. He didn't appreciate the glory of it all. I think you get to the age of thirty or so, and you don't WANT to be teaching. This is why, girlfriend, I've ended up with not exactly great relationships. As do a very large number of musicians.

IT IS THE PRICE YOU PAY, unless you're EXTREMELY LUCKY.

"You never met anyone you wanted to get down with?"

"Sure, I did. But I keep tellin' ya...I was mostly not free to do so."

"Oh. Were you happy with what you had at home?"

"Not really. I wasn't. Thanks...now I'm getting morose."

"Sorry...I didn't know. But you STILL love your life?"

"Sigh. Of COURSE. I CHOSE it. Anyway, those were a few of the crazy OFFstage things that are free-falling off the top of my head."

Add blizzards and ice storms, wrong bookings, bad situations of all sorts that band members need to be rescued from, equipment or instrument malfunctions, vehicle wrecks, booking fiascos, thefts...

Would you like a smack of reality? Yeah? Here you go. A band member of yours has a substance problem. A bad one. This is not an uncommon scenario. Your band member is a great player. What do you do?

You hope they'll clean up eventually, but don't hold your breath, and there's always going to be drama involved, because their LIFE is dripping with drama, and they're in YOUR life so much, it's going to invariably spill right into your lap—and the laps of the rest of your band mates.

There will be crazy, crazy behavior and attitude too. You can bet on that. They can be nasty to you, or to other band members, or both. They can also be a joy, but if they're heading downhill, the joy part shows up less and less.

You'll at last be forced to make the tough decision to let them go. They may begin to interfere with the music, the logistics of your business, or they can start making your other band members' lives hell. I remember one particular guy I worked with for years. He was sometimes in OK shape, but often not.

I only asked that he keep it together on stage, and try not to bring chaos to the band's offstage life together. It worked for a long time, but he wasn't exactly an easy guy to live with (I'm stating this very mildly here), and he began to decline. In the long run, his erratic behavior developed into a less than tolerable thing to deal with, and his playing became unacceptable. You can't put up with sloppy playing, darnit, and I knew it was time.

The notorious "last straw" came one night, just two hours before a show. He had a tantrum—probably over a MIC CHORD or something equally pointless—and refused to go ON, like he was a 1920s Hollywood DIVA. Off he stormed. He crossed the line you NEVER cross.

Did we do the show? What do YOU think? You don't EVER miss the show. I don't care if you have to get up there and read from a power drill manual.

The next day, I had to make the call and fire him. It was hard, and of course him being someone I loved dearly, I worried. What the HELL would he do now? He knew though. He knew it was time for him to go, and was accepting of it.

I had good reason to worry. His descent into the seamy side was rapid. He had to do the usual things for his habit, which had spread to more expensive substances. Stealing, dealing, pimping, selling his OWN services on the street. It was about as degrading and desperate as you can get.

Thankfully, he did clean up, and we started working together again. The whacky thing is that some of the behavior I thought had been due to his addiction was in fact a deep rooted part of his SOBER personality. The drugs had been for the most part HIDING it for years and it would just peek out now and again.

When he was high, he was USUALLY sort of docile and amenable. We'd pick him up, throw him in the van, and then we'd just POUR him onstage. Now he was belligerent. MOST of the time. Oh, there were still a few fun moments to be had with him, but his capacity for lightheartedness was greatly curtailed. EVERY little thing was a sign to him that the world was about to end…and didn't everyone else GET this? Armageddon. AR-MAGEDDON! NOW, he had a hair-trigger temper that was rampant.

The other band members, people who had never worked with him before, were ITCHING to kick his butt every DAY. I finally blurted at him, "I loved you a LOT more when you were high. Almost comatose? Even BETTER. Now yer a schmuck." This is something you don't want to say to a junkie.

Finally, he did it AGAIN. Yup, he did it sober. At least this time it was a day before a job, not two hours before one. "I'm not going ON." Oh CRAP, here we go again.

We had to fill his seat mighty quickly. You know how many times I've had to do that? Not TOO bad if it's a drummer. Oh, they may miss some stops here and there and whatnot, but it wouldn't be apparent to most audiences. It's a bit worse if it's the bass player, because then you're dealing with CHANGES being missed, so you've got to curtail more sophisticated arrangements until they can be learned. A GUITAR player though. A guitar player in a power trio? Oh boy, there's a nightmare waiting to happen.

I once had to replace TWO players (including guitar), AND a vehicle, AND a P.A. system within one WEEK. Somehow, it got DONE. There's some fun for you. What I just described to you is another one of those" It's happened to everyone" things.

"You want me to try to think of some more?"

"Please no. I'm late for an appointment…ummmm SOMEWHERE. I SWEAR. Bye."

Need to find another victim. GOOD. My girlfriend Dawn has asked me, "Vardzie, what do you talk about in transit, or offstage? All those hours together, driving, and after shows?"

Ahhh, now we're into the FUN part of our lives….

"We talk about music, music, a new song one of us wrote, old songs to do, bang out parts, THEME music from old TV shows, movies, commercials, music we love OR hate, cartoons, books, we WANT sex, want sex NOW, Vardzie's music lessons which are actually sex ANYWAY.

"We talk about the meaning of life, how our personal lives suck, things to make us feel BETTER about our sucky personal lives, politics, more old

TV. I once had an entire band that LOVED soap operas. It took me weeks to realize they weren't gossiping about real people.

"We argue about where to stop for dinner, tell each other war stories like the ones I'm telling you. For musicians, this is like sharing ghost folklore around a campfire. There's stream of consciousness talk to keep the driver awake, and six degrees to Tuli Kupferberg, MORE music, if we don't have sex soon we'll DIE, and music."

"Are you maniacs? Do you like this? How much music can you talk?"

"MANIACS? We seem pretty normal to each other. There's NO LIMIT to the amount of music we can talk."

"God that sounds boring. How much SEX could you possibly talk?"

"ALMOST limitless. We're pretty, uhh. You want to hear a typical one, I mean besides describing every excruciating detail of the last experience any one of us just had…unfortunately usually not MINE?"

"I'm not sure."

"Well now, Friday once brought up a downright incredulous accomplishment."

"On a FRIDAY?"

"That's the drummer. Friday Soloman. GREAT drummer. He can fly with ANYTHING. This is quite a few years ago. He piped up to inform us he'd heard about a sports guy who claimed to have slept with 20,000 women. Right away, I've got questions. I reckon Friday has just said the guy merely had SEX 20,000 times during the 25 years of his career, so I said:

'That's ASTOUNDING! Hats off to YOU, sports man. I don't think I'd have the sheer STAMINA. Wow, you're a busy man, YOU are. That's commendable. Boy, there's a record for us all to shoot for, although gosh, he must have worn OUT some poor women. 20,000 times?'

'Vardz….Vardzie….NEVARD!!'

'WHAT?'

'He didn't just mean DOING it 20,000 times. It was 20,000 DIFFERENT WOMEN.'

"Stunned silence from my corner for a good minute. Silence in the whole vehicle. We're trying to absorb this audacious claim. I can't take it anymore."

'NO. It just can't BE. CAN it? Twenty thousand DIFFERENT women? Is this possible? Mind you, I'm not making a moral judgment here, I suppose EVERYONE has to have their own mission in life, and that's a pretty dumb one, but OK.

'I've got the calculator. 20,000 women, within 25 years. He started this when he was fifteen, you said? Well, the first few years had to be just ONE woman per day. How many women could there have been in his town? He had to slow down that LAST year, so let's figure just the one woman a day for the last year too. This is boggling.

'So, we've ended up with 883 DIFFERENT women EVERY year, for 21 years. Oh come ON. This means that Mr. Busy Man has to do approximately two and a half DIFFERENT women EVERY SINGLE DAY. So, I guess, maybe two one day, and three another, with NO days off. Every DAY for twenty-one YEARS?

'Where the heck is he FINDING them? Oh, it's doable on the road, but when he's at home? Won't he run out over the twenty-one-year period?" What if he's SICK? He's got to make it up. Uh oh, have to do SEVEN different gals today. I missed FIVE this week. Gotta make the quota.'

'Here's a thought. What if he LIKES one (although you'd think after the first TEN THOUSAND, things would get a little blurry there)? Nope, sorry, I'd love to go again, but...NO CAN DO. NO REPEATS ALLOWED. I've got a tight schedule here. Have to make my quota.'

'Hey, Vardz, guess what else? One of his teammates said he'd SING while getting down to business.'

'SING? Who could be SINGING while...I mean wouldn't you run out of breath? Well, I guess if you're Dizzie doing that circular breathing thing...but oh my! How did he KEEP TRACK, and why 20,000? What's wrong with say...EIGHTEEN THOUSAND, FIVE HUNDRED? Wouldn't that be a respectable enough number?'

"That's a typical sex discussion for us in the van, Dawn. Anywhere else, for that matter."

"What is six degrees of whatever?"

"Oh that's a Nevard torture game. You know... 'Hey, Vardz, I slept with a girl, that slept with your ex, that slept with a girl, that slept with a guy that slept with a girl that slept with TULI KUPFERBERG. So, YOU, Vardzie girl, have done it with...yes, that's right, YOU have screwed Tuli Kupferberg by proxy."

'Ahh no, PLEASE don't make me do it with Tuli. I'm sure he's a very nice man, but (cringing now) I'd rather not do it with the guy who wrote

Caca Rocka. Really. Thanks. My retinas are BURNING. It may take YEARS of therapy to get this one out of my head.'

"Yeah, they do that one with any number of people. People who would make me wonder why I was BORN."

"Who's Tuli Kupferberg?"

"Oh for gosh sake. He's a founding member of the Fugs. You know, Ed Sanders, sometimes Allen Ginsberg, once in awhile Danny Kortchmar on guitar. The beat guys. Influenced Velvet Underground and others. "I saw the best minds of my generation ROCK"...instead of gosh, girl, you know...Ginsberg's most famous...ahhh forget it. My fave Fugs title was this one:

"In The Middle Of Their First Recording Session The Fugs Sign The Worst Record Contract Since Leadbelly." Now THERE'S a stellar song title for you.

"How come you talk about TV so much?"

"Sorry. LOVE the old TV. We'd usually arrive home just in time to see some of these magical re-runs and then we'd argue about them. *Dr. Kildare* or *Ben Casey*? I make a good argument for Ben. His deadpan face alone is worth watching. He had the ham factor of Joe Dallesandro, and about as much depth." "Who? WHO?" "Never mind, girl."

"Let's see... *Twilight Zone* or *Night Gallery*? OR *Alfred Hitchcock*? Now we're into TV AND movies."

"HITCH! Gosh, the first director to use MUSIC to drive the vision. Ever heard anything like that shower sound in *Psycho*? Everyone started taking BATHS after that. OH, his ground breaking point of view shots, and the ZOOM! The ZOOM shots! The Alfred CAMEOS! OHH. Most of us LOVE Jerry. Lewis, I mean. We could never understand why folks make fun of him. BRILLIANT writer, director... and not appreciated in his own country. Why did they have to do a REMAKE of *The Nutty Professor*? Why mess with perfection? How come Europeans "GET" our good stuff lots more than WE do?"

"You do KNOW, don't you, Dawn...he was the FIRST director to use video on a film set? WHY? So he could see what was happening IMMEDIATELY. Didn't' have to wait for film to be developed. Boy, that's right up there with Desi's usage of multi cameras for the first time on TV, don't you THINK? Or Orson Welles' first ever view of a CEILING!

Yeah…the band would talk a lot about the bad remakes. *FATHER OF THE BRIDE*! Who could surpass Spencer TRACY? Dawn, am I boring you?"

"This is the most boring thing I've ever heard."

"REALLY? This subject can go on for hours with us. Days. YEARS even. You're not even hearing the very TIP of the iceberg. I mean really now, don't you ponder these things? "

"NO, and I don't think anyone ELSE does either."

"Wait. WAIT! Do not TOUCH this TV dial!"

"Sigh…OK, OK."

"REALLY? Boy, I hadn't even STARTED the TV stuff. There's *Jack Benny, Burns and Allen*, and *Ozzie and Harriet* who had the added attraction of music. Oh…GOD…once a pal of Cub's (KODA, Dawn…remember? I TOLD you about him). So, Cub's friend said I just LOVE Ricky Nelson, and Cub said…at a very young age…REALLY? I just love his GUITAR player. Know who that WAS, Dawn? It was James Burton. Whadya MEAN…who's that? Come ON. OH fer crikey SAKE. Never mind."

"*The Beverly Hillbillies* had a LOT of music. Goodness, they had The Enemys and The Standells who were also on *The Munsters* TOO. I don't think they played "Dirty Water" on either show. Lester and Earl, played the theme, and there was the unmistakable fingering of Les Paul in the soundtracks. Roy Clark was on a few times…who else? Chet Atkins? No I think he was on Johnny Cash. Hey, don't you love that album *Chester and Lester*?"

"I almost forgot the Andy Griffith music! The DILLARDS! THE KENTUCKY COLONELS! GOSH, Howard Morris was on that show. Director, writer AND the crazy character."

"Vardzie?"

"Then there's *Shindig, Hullabaloo, Smothers Brothers, Glen Campbell, Perry Mason, Dragnet, Adam 12, The Rookies, The Rifleman, Zorro*! *Peter Gunn, Steve Allen, Gleason, Sid Caesar, The MILLIONAIRE*! Remember *What's My Line*, with Bennet Cerf, Dorothy Kilgallen, and was it Oscar Levant? NO, he was a guest. They had to guess who HE was."

"Vardzie, you're REALLY bothering me now"

"Wait, have you ever seen clips of Oscar Levant on the Jack Paar show? They'd haul him out of the Bellevue psych ward, stuff him in a limo, and bring him to the studio. He was really SOMETHING, girl. Did you know

Oscar Levant was scared to death of LEMONS? I saw one clip…Jack asked him what he did for exercise. Do you know what he said? No?

'I stumble, and then fall into a coma.' Poor Oscar. Sixty cups of coffee and four packs of cigarettes a day. There was NO ONE like him though. Razor sharp guy. Just brilliant."

"Vardzie, WHO'S Oscar Levant?"

"Come on. Come ON. He was George Gershwin's favorite pianist. THAT'S who he was. LORD. He worked with Copland and Toscanini. I think he was a Tanglewood regular, oh, and he was in lots of old movies. FUNNY. His most famous quote was aimed at Gershwin, who believed he was the best thing since toilet paper, and of course he WAS. It went something like: 'So, George, if you had it to do all over, would you fall in love with yourself again?' Oscar was known for his sharp tongue. Mamma and Dad saw him once. When the audience yelled for an encore, he gave them the finger and walked off. PRE Miles.

"That reminds me, do you remember the radio guy who once said, 'And now a song from George Gershwin, with lyrics by his lovely wife Ira'?"

"NEVARD?"

"Yeah?"

"I have absolutely no clue who or what you're talking about. You're putting me to sleep. I have to go now"

WHAT? George GERSHWIN? Get out! IRA was his BROTHER…not his WIFE, for crikey sake. This is sad. I guess there IS no one to talk about this stuff with. I'll talk to myself. Geez, didn't even get to cartoons, or Abbot and Costello, or….never mind.

HUH. They ask the questions, but they don't want the answers.

"Hi Denisee, I spoke with Dawn yesterday. The subject we're on now is how a band fills up the off stage hours, and what in the world we talk about. Anything YOU'D like to ask?"

"Yeah, Dawn told me about the boring TV stuff, and said everything else sounded sick. She wouldn't step foot in your world for all the tea at the bottom of Boston Harbor. Hey, do you have any INTERESTING stories? What about OTHER bands you played with?"

"Gosh, we didn't really get to play much with other bands a HUGE amount. Unless it was festival sorts of concert things. When would we have had time? There were some musicians or bands we'd team up with, and put together tours with them. THAT was usually fun. Cub Koda, Sleepy La

Beef, Ed Vadas and the Fabulous Heavyweights. Remind me to tell you sometime about HIM...GOD, he'd blow your MIND. OHHH, girl, I've got one. You want to hear?"

"OK. It had better be good."

"Oh it's GOOD alrighty. Your head is going to spin off your NECK. For a while we'd sometimes tour with a solo act that was a New England legend. We'd happily share jobs—divide the night between our two shows, at a number of crazy clubs. His name was (and still is) Sweet Pie. Pie for short."

"Pie was a crazy musician. Although his abilities in that direction were in some ways limited by KEYS he was able to play in, he COULD perform an impressive and key banging rendition of some fantastic traditional "boogie woogie" on any set of eighty-eights. HUH? Oh...that's a PIANO, Denisee. A piano has eighty-eight keys."

"His singing style was that of an old time blues shouter, and I must say...when in the mood, Pie could let go with a poignancy that was unexpectedly moving. And THAT talent WAS unexpected because...well, because a couple of things sometimes LOOMED above any musicality he possessed."

"Number ONE: he was a burlesque-like comedian, and he worked blue. Well...that means he was considerably filthy. Actually, he was filthy beyond my 'filth' threshold, which isn't all THAT low. But WITHIN that aspect, was a flowing line of social commentary that was searingly astute. Pie was the Lenny Bruce of the music world in those days. He was also a good artist, lugging around an easel to every job, and he'd draw wonderfully executed caricatures as he stalked about the stage (smoking a pipe) between songs."

"Here's number TWO...and boy, you couldn't miss it. HE WAS NAKED. And I do mean, completely and utterly NEKKID when he could get away with it...and sometimes when he could not. He was arrested any number of times."

"WHAAAAAT? Are you making this up?"

"No, ma'am, I am NOT. He performed without a LICK of clothing on. If need be, he'd slap on a loin cloth (has anyone worn one of those since the sixteenth century?) or cover up in accordance with any given location he'd be appearing in. OR he would acknowledge any holiday that was looming. Sooo, you might see a scallop shell hanging from his waist near the shoreline, or a skull and crossbones covering him on a Halloween eve.

"Go ahead and ASK, girl. Did Sweet Pie limit the showings of his birthday-suited self to JOBS? No. That would be a big old NO. He waltzed amongst the heedless masses nearly naked each and every day. I knew him for YEARS, and never ONCE saw him in a pair of pants."

"One weekend we were playing together in a great club in Newport, Rhode Island. It was the middle of winter, and I always thought the off-season times were the BEST times to play in that touristy area. That's when the music hungry locals came out in droves. They came to listen, so it was a lot more fun than playing for a gaggle of sloppy drunk kids who were there after a day at the beach, looking to hook up. This is true for a slew of vacation areas. Not ALL, but many.

"The name of this club in Newport was Harpo's, and we were all staying in rooms above the club. It was a beautiful old building with a 1920s gangster history. There were secret doors and passageways, two-way mirrors—an interesting place to explore.

On a Saturday morning, following our Friday night show, I was sleeping the sleep of a spent musician, when there came a knock at my door."

'Hey, bubble butt. NEVARD...has your Venus-like body arisen from your bed yet?' (Pie is a crazy and articulate man.)

'That YOU, Pie? Nooo...I'm still sleeping.'

'Well get UP then, kitty cat. I need to visit the local Kmart, wherever THAT may be located, for a mini shopping spree. There are a few items I'd like to pick up. Might be up for a bit of lunch after that. Would you care to set forth and accompany me on this journey? Vardzie? NEVARD? Have you fallen back into your slumbering state?'

"I hadn't responded in a timely manner, due to my head being covered by a heavy sweater I was hastily pulling over it. Believe you me, as soon as my sleepy brain had registered and absorbed the word Kmart, and then connected THAT word with the name Sweet Pie, I moved faster than a speeding meth freak. Did Pie just ask if I'd like to run to Kmart with him? K. MART? Why YES...yes indeedy, I sure WOULD!"

"How come?"

"Oh GOSH, Denisee, THINK about it. Would YOU want to miss a once in a lifetime (I'm positive) opportunity to lay eyes on (I'm positive) the celebratory inaugural MOMENT a naked guy walks through the front door of Kmart? We're talking about KMART here—the mecca of suburban BLANDNESS. What're you brain dead? Who'd want to miss THAT sight?"

"I GUESS."

"You're guessing right. I flew out my door, and just as expected, was met with the familiar sight of my pal Pie wearing nothing but a pair of sheepskin boots and a loin cloth, which by the way, resembled a G STRING. His tooshie was on full display at all times. I forgot to tell you that. Oh yes, and the pipe was hanging out of his mouth. Ho, Ho, HO, Santa, his is going to be a merry scene."

"I stayed behind him. Wanted to get a good view of the reactions to be seen on the countenances of all those Kmart goers. Innocent shoppers who would shortly have their unwary eyes filled with the climactic FESTIVAL that was Pie. NOT all-American apple pie. NOPE. They were going to get SWEET PIE in his state of nekkid grandeur. Eye yi yi."

"So what happened?"

"He looked like MOSES PARTING THE SEA. That's what he looked like. And the shoppers in Kmart? THEY looked like they'd been hit by a METEOR. I still can't understand why he wasn't escorted out of the joint, but he simply lollygagged about the place, shopping away. WOW. I've got to add...in some quaint, childlike way, Pie was unaware of the effect he HAD on people, and SURPRISED when confronted."

"Yeah, that IS unbelievable. Now I wish I'd been there. But, Vardz, if the 'filth' thing was too much for you, why did you hang around with this guy?"

"Denise. The filth was only a small part of Pie. He was an engaging and smart man, his unique take on the world was interesting. He was enjoyable and FUN to be with, and Sweet Pie was a loyal, openhanded friend who'd BE there for you. No questions asked. There are a multitude of his friends who benefited from his good nature, and we all loved him."

"There is a curious ending to this one. Sometime during the late-eighties, Sweet Pie disappeared. Dropped off the face of the earth, without contacting even his closest friends. We were worried to death for YEARS, because he was involved with a few shady deals, and we were convinced he'd been MURDERED. Years later, maybe 2002, I received a call from a student in Boston. He was an independent filmmaker, and told me he was working on a documentary about…guess who? PIE. He asked me if I'd mind doing an interview, as he was aware of my close friendship with Pie."

"You could have knocked me over with a feather. No one had heard a PEEP from him during all those years. Kind of made me angry. WHY didn't he TELL anyone he was OK?? How did this KID know who Sweet Pie was, anyway? How in the world did he know who I was? I discovered Pie has been residing in Arizona, is STILL naked, and owns a bookstore. Now he's an Arizona legend. Who KNEW? And the filmmaker Boston kid? Well, HE has disappeared now."

"If you'd like to hear some brain twisting Sweet Pie, I think you can still order his recordings from the ESP label. ESP is great. They've got some interesting offerings. Charlie Parker, Sun Ra, Randy Burns, William Burroughs, although I can't imagine what HE recorded…"

"That was an OK story, Vardz."

"So then…all is forgiven, and I can gab about old TV again?"

"NO."

"I give up. No more TV. We didn't just talk TV. It was mostly music. THE MUSIC, girl! Don't you love Irving Berlin? He married a girl whose folks said, 'You want IRVING? He can't even play the white keys. What's WRONG with him?' Gosh, he was prolific.

"A WWII movie had 'Oh How I Hate to Get Up in the Morning' in it. Some grip guy on the set said, 'JESUS, glad the guy who WROTE this ain't here to get a load of THIS schlemiel SLAUGHTERING his tune.' He didn't know it WAS little Irving singing. Did you ask what he WROTE? What DIDN'T he write? 'Remember,' 'Always,' 'What'll I Do,' 'Blue Skies' were some of the most achingly haunting songs. Irving had a bit of the Cantor in his songs. The luscious minors, joltingly hopping to the major…beautiful. There's a million. What about 'How Deep Is The Ocean'? 'Easter Parade'? Picture Ella and Satchmo doing 'Cheek to Cheek.' 'Puttin' on the Ritz.'

"You should to hear those Belgium De Cauter boys do Irving's 'Without My Walking Stick.' They SWING it, baby, got that Django Gypsy guitar going, and Waso doing rhythm guitar…banging, I mean BANGING on that thang, till you wanna just grab that kid and KISS his FACE off. What sort of guitar do those guys like? Castellucias? I dunno.

Damm, I just went on YouTube, and there it is all right. The version I remember." What ELSE did sweet Irving Berlin write? 'WHITE

CHRISTMAS' and 'GOD BLESS AMERICA.' What more do you want from the guy?"

"NEVARD. I'm falling asleep. You're on your own."

Well, there you have it. There IS no reason for choosing the artists I've spoken about here. Am I a huge fan of the Fugs? No, I haven't heard them in YEARS, but they had some fascinating aspects. Random music things fall out of our heads. Are you getting it? THAT was a random sampling of how we talk. There's scads of music I may enjoy a LOT more, but we talk about it ALL. If you find rambling music talk a bore then you shouldn't become a musician. I don't know if other bands like the old TV, but mine always did, and I know a NUMBER of bands that include it in their late night ramblings. I didn't even include the LIMITLESS amount of rock, blues, jazz, and all the rest. There's a HUNDRED years of it to discuss. I can't even THINK about the volume from earlier centuries.

THERE'S SO MUCH GOOD MUSIC. Too little time, so much music.

I suppose I get a little worked up about these things.

THERE'S SOMETHING I AM COMPELLED TO SAY...

Europeans relish our music more than we Americans do. America's black musicians, our Jazz greats made an exodus to Europe when they weren't given the time of day and were banned from performing in segregated venues in their OWN country, and that could have something to do with this phenomenon.

What kind of music? Blues, Jazz, Rock, Gospel, and every brother, sister, and cousin of it.

Yeah, yeah, purists...I know this music has roots in Africa and Eastern Europe. Everything is derivative. I don't have to tell you that do I? BUT...

MAKE NO MISTAKE... THIS IS OUR MUSIC.

THE MUSIC OF AMERICA. BORN OF STRIFE, CARRIED ON WITH JOY, AND TOO MUCH UNSUNG LABOR.

I could write another book on that subject alone. There ARE books dealing with just that. What is wrong with this picture? We are stupid, clichéd ugly Americans. Why do we not have more gratitude for the TREASURE that came out of our own? Go check out a Dutch blog: keepswingingblogspot.com. They're so nuts for our music they're excited about a BEER called Thelonious Brew. It has NOTHING to do with the MUSICIAN, but the NAME sends their carrots for a whirl.

If you stroll down a street in France, and start talking about our music, most will know. *Ahhh oui, les blues, les jazz.* They have a thirst for our Rock pioneers as well. Why is this sadly lacking in our own country?

Go ahead and try it in average-town USA. Go right ahead and mention Art Blakey. You'll be met with blank stares for the most part.

From Louis, to Buddy, to those Adderly brothers…Cannonball and Bowling Ball (just kidding). From Fats Waller to Sun Ra, from Robert Johnson to B.B., to The Bird, to Link, to Sister Rosetta

Tharpe the TRUE mother of Rock, to Ella. **SHAME ON US. THIS MAY WELL BE ONE OF OUR LARGEST CONTRIBUTIONS TO THE WORLD.**

In only small ways have we been able to keep it alive. This miracle should be more accessible; it should be in every school child's lexicon HERE. Oh sure, we have the odd PBS special with the Marsalis brothers, and if you're in an urban or artsy area you can find a few clubs, but it's not in schools, except for organizations like the Smithsonian's Jazz Heritage initiative, OJI, TMIJ, or small blues programs.

OUR MUSICAL HERITAGE is not part of the curriculum. All arts are beginning to be cut out. NO history is being served well. I know a guy who has never heard of Winston Churchill (in spite of the fact that every infant resembles him)

This sort of historical knowledge and gratefulness is what separates us as a civilization from BRUSSEL SPROUTS.

The Canadians have done a better job of subsidizing their art community. And might I add…those Canuks are mighty peeved at our strange idea that we're part of North America, and they are not. We are not instilling in our young 'uns the knowledge and love of what SHOUD be **precious** to us.

"Hi Denisee, it's me again. I just finished a boring lecture. I need more questions."

"CRAP. I thought I was going to have a good day. You said it was lonely on the road sometimes, right? What about that?"

"I guess you want to know HOW lonely, right? The answer is, pretty bad sometimes. I'd look out and see people having fun and cuddling, and yeah, I'd long for someone to hold, to feel like somebody's baby. My band would try to make it better:

'I swear, Vardzie, if I weren't your band boy, I'd do ya till yer head popped off. Yup, you'd be mine, if you weren't the boss.'

'Thanks, that does bring me a degree of comfort. Thanks for trying, but considering the fact that you'd screw any object that isn't nailed DOWN, I have to consider the source, yes?'

"Humor would usually snap me out of it. They'd make me laugh after we had auditioned someone atrociously BAD.

'OK, Vardzie, the bad news is that guy can't play his way out of his own bathroom. The GOOD news is...NOW you can SCREW him! How's THAT?'

'Well, great news, I guess, but if he can't PLAY, what makes ya think he'd be...GOSH, even amongst those who CAN swing it, you'd be hard pressed to find...'

"My friend Bob told me last week, that the best thing I ever said to him was: **"Just 'cause you got a flame, it don't mean you can COOK."** He told me he's been repeating it for years. I have no recollection at ALL of saying this, and who knows where I got it."

"AUDITIONING new players was always a nightmare. Would you like the scoop on that? Most of the time, I like to audition people in my living room. I used to have a full P.A. in the basement, but I like to hear them low first. THEN I can tell what they are capable of. Bands that play for a living, and experienced musicians, do NOT have a need to plug in all the time. Some of the best creative activity is done unplugged, or softly.

"REHEARSALS? WHY? We'd work enough...it wasn't truly needed. We would work on NEW songs in hotel rooms, dressing rooms, or in the bus. Are you getting the picture? The drummer bangs on pads or a table, and the guitar and bass would be sometimes plugged in, sometimes not, everything going at low volume. Singing without amplification is good, especially if there are harmonies."

"Other instruments? I still want to hear it low first. There's nothing to get in the way of putting your heads together and hearing each other. Just bare bones. Effects? They can be added later. I don't know how other bands feel about this. It might just be a personal preference I've got."

"When an auditioning musician walks into my living room, sits right down, and says, 'YEAH…let's DO it,' this usually tells me I'm looking at a musician.

"If I run into folks that HAVE to plug in to audition, and are UPSET if they can't, it tells me TWO things. First, this is someone who doesn't play out much. This is someone who gets a THRILL out of volume, and probably not a seasoned musician. The second thing it says about the person is THIS is someone who thinks volume will cover a lack of proficiency. They think it'll hide their lack of knowledge or experience."

I have advice for those of you that feel the need to always plug in. If you can't swing it soft, then you can't ROCK it plugged in.

"You can usually see these folks coming from a mile away. Sometimes, I'd just get them the heck out.

'PLUG IN? Gee, I'm sorry I thought you knew. We're a completely acoustic band now. Yeah, we don't even use mics.'

'Whaddya MEAN? I saw you last month. You were LOUD.'

'Well, we've had a change of heart. We're anti-electronic now. We think the electronic waves give you brain damage. As you can SEE, I'm already a little dumb here. I don't know, we may become an entire air BAND. So sorry.'

Then there were the dinner arguments…"

"I didn't know. What does a band argue about when it comes to dinner?"

"THAT subject could begin at breakfast. One band member would want pizza in New Hampshire and has to be reminded: we're no longer in New Haven, or New York, and you might find TARRAGON or SAGE on your Pizza (at least in those days, you would). There's no Sally's here, OK? NO VINNIE'S. OK chump…take a good gander at the gal who's going to be making your pizza. See that peasant dress? See the tambourine she's carrying? Smell the patchouli? You're getting' ZUCCHINI and CARROTS on your pizza. You want that on the pizza? NO, you DON"T. On your PASTA…YES. On the PIZZA? OH LORD…it'll be WATERY…and have cinnamon swimming around on it. You want good sauce and scamotz. Maybe meatballs or something. NOT ZUCCHINI. GOD.

"OR, someone wants seafood in Vermont. That would be a landlocked state you're looking at, buddy, and the chances of finding good seafood are slim. Can't you wait till we're in Boston next week? How about MAINE? ALRIGHTY…DO NOT order the Philadelphia Pretzel in Rhode Island. OR in DC. Don't get the Philly Cheesesteak either…unless you find yourself standing in front of Geno's at four in the morning. And please do not order up a pastrami sandwich in any town but NYC. Does the name Katz ring a bell? GOOD. Have we got this all straight?

"I had a lineup for a while that loved raw seafood so much, someone wanted to book us for a party, but didn't have the dough to pay us. The answer was of course NO, until my band heard this: 'We're going to have all the raw clams you can eat.' The answer quickly turned into 'OH YEAH, we're THERE.'

"One pal from this lineup, a sax player, contracted hepatitis once from eating raw oysters in a truly dumpy joint in Philly. Did this stop him? HECK no. He just said, 'I'll never eat raw seafood again in a place that can't afford to be sued.'

"I just love him. Mark Dark. The most disgusting food any band member ate? I'm thinking about this because it's something Mark would run into surprisingly often. TRIPE. TRIPE subs."

"Dawn said something about your music lessons in the boy's bus. What are those?" "Music lessons that are sex anyway. Those were fun for me. Not so fun for the band members they were aimed at. Boy, what a patient bunch of mates…stuck in that vehicle with me. They couldn't ESCAPE. I'd rant on for HOURS, and they'd take it with good-natured spirit, and umm, now that I'm thinking on it, they'd LAUGH now and again. Not I. NO, I was DEADLY serious."

> *"Art isn't something you marry, i*
> *t's something you rape."*
> *—Edgar Degas*

DYNAMICS and RHYTHM are my battle cries. These are MY theories about music, and truly, they apply to LIFE as well. Your theories could be different. Mine are right though. Let's start with dynamics.

There are three types of dynamics within a musical unit. The three types are the dynamics of a singular instrumentalist within a song, the dynamics of a complete piece of music (or song), and the dynamics of the entire performance. We'll start with the instrumentalists.

Have you noticed an abundance of modern vocalists seem to be endowed with a tendency to sing the entire scale within one measure? Loads of people love this, but I find it to be more than bothersome. When I come across that *Idol* show on TV, I find myself yelling at the darn thing, as if they can hear me.

"Hey. HEY, YOU. You don't gotta show EVERYTHING you got throughout the entire thing. Did you attend the YNGWIE MALMSTEEN SCHOOL of vocalization? Can you please hold the ONE NOTE for a SECOND? I'm begging you. WHERE is the melody? A good scat is nice, but I can't even recognize this SONG. Would you have informed OTIS that he needed more notes??"

This deplorable tendency is displayed in instrument players too. Guitar "slingers" are notably guilty of this crime against humanity. Notice I mentioned Yngwie before? He'd be a guitar player, he would. Here's the wrong thinking that goes along with this common attribute."

"How many notes can I fit into ONE bar? Can I show EVERY lick I own in THREE seconds? Have to show them NOW."

My van music talks would usually contain something like this:

"You betcha, you guitar MONSTER you. You SHOW 'em. Can you PLEASE stop showing them all of it in the first few MOMENTS, though? WHY? You wanna know WHY? Cause then you'll have NOTHING LEFT to show them AFTER THAT, you eejit. What will they have to look forward to? Not to mention the fact that you're screwing up the BUILD of the entire SONG."

Are you noticing the word BUILD in the above dynamics rant? Do you know why I'm using that word? It's due to the fact that music is like sex, and most importantly, music IS sex.

I'd rant away at the offending player…

"At some point, you're going to become a technician, and no longer a musician. You understand that? Do you think greeting a girl, maybe shaking hands with her is the climax? WHAT are you not getting? If you can't get THIS, then there ain't any satisfaction going on in YOUR bed."

Annnnd BACK to the lecture we must return. "DYNAMICS, dammit. I SAID DYNAMICS. Let it BUILD. Give them a little, and make them BEG for it. You can show them SOME of what you've got. You can give them a little. Do it really GOOD. They'll be WANTING it.

And THEN, you can SLOW it down for a while. WHY? WHY? You don't want to numb them out, do ya? Oh lord have mercy. Why the pause, he's asking.

'Cause THEN after that LITTLE taste you gave them, they'll be wanting it MORE. They'll most likely be uncontrollably SLOBBERING all over themselves. You see? THEN, you can finish them off. Give it to them without MERCY. Give it ALL to 'em. They'll be lying on the floor like dishrags. Men, women, ALL of them. Don't you WANT them to have that fun? Wouldn't YOU want that kind of excitement?

Don't be afraid to slow it down, OK? Go ahead and let one note ring for ten minutes. God, it's a basic move. You don't have THAT trick on you? Learn when and where to put the notes. DYNAMICS. I'm not just talking about notes here; I'm talking about VOLUME, and PACE too. Good golly Mr. Molly…it's like sex. What's not to GET?"

Gosh, I do believe the best "note hold" I ever witnessed was executed by Mr. Buddy Guy. Fer the love of all guitar gods there ever were, he up and twanged the one note (OK, granted…it was a harmonic one), set his guitar on a stool, (YES…of COURSE it was almost against the grill cloth of his amp) then toodled off for a bathroom break. This took a good five minutes. When he emerged from THERE, he moseyed up to the bar for a refill, and THEN slooooowly made his way back to the stage. The darn note was STILL ringin' out. I can recognize feedback when I run into it, but it's impressive in spite of that knowledge.

THAT is a description of the BUILD. The same thing applies to the whole SONG, and to the entire PERFORMANCE. Are you listening up, budding musicians? Just go ahead and ask anybody that's good. You've got no idea how many people don't get it, and most likely never will.

The other night on the phone, my friend Bob (the one who agreed all music IS sex, as is every other art form) told me he went through a short period of time doing the bad "show everything you know now" thing. It surprised me, because when WE were playing together, he didn't DO that. But we figured since that was twenty years ago, he probably didn't have enough under his belt yet to bury a crowd within five seconds. He thinks it's a real guitar player affliction. Like a pissing contest.

Bob says that for a little while, he'd do a job and notice people weren't listening. One night, he just relaxed, and went with the flow, the beat, and didn't CARE about WHAT he was showing them, and he noticed, all of a sudden he had a rapt audience. When he was driving home, he figured it out. DYNAMICS. BUILD. Bob says the best advice he ever got was this: "You gotta play for the girls." WOW! THAT'S **IT,** BOB.

"Where does that leave YOU, Vardz?"

"Oh yeah. No WONDER I get attacked in the girls' room."

I DO sling on a guitar myself. I'm a pretty good rhythm player. Kind of like Elvis. I'll play harp too, and I'm so good, I'm better than Bobby Dylan!

Never mind. You don't get it. Dylan is NOT a good harp player. Not good. You can be pretty darn bad, and still surpass old Bob. At least I can BEND a little, but I'm still basically pathetic. You wouldn't be calling me the second coming of Little Walter. Did you like the dynamics and build rant? Are you ready for the rhythm section rant?

"I don't know if I can take it. That one was draining."

"GOOD. That means I did a good build for you. Here goes, toots. To me, a band is DEFINED by their rhythm section. I may have said this before. It bears repeating. Usually the problem lies with the drummer. Usually."

My rhythm rant would sound like this:

OK, darling, I have to tell you this. You need to start pushing the beat. PUSHING IT. What do I mean? Well, first you've got to start getting a bit looser there. Let the wrists be pliable. They're not at that point, an extension of your arms. UNSTIFFEN THE WRISTS. They've got their own thing going, so let them have it. Are you afraid of looking too girly or something? LET THE WRISTS GO.

Please, drummer boy. Please stop playing on TOP of the BEAT, play a WHISPER behind it. No, not WAY behind like a bad lounge singer. Play it an almost undetectable amount behind the beat, so only WE know. GET IT? NOT ON TOP OF THE BEAT. NOT EVER. Play BEHIND it, THEREBY making true the old adage "IN THE POCKET." Please make note of this fact. NOBODY has ever described a swingin', rockin' band as being ON any damn pocket, OK?

Did you ask WHY? First of all, you've got to leave a little room for your BASS PLAYER to get in the sandbox WITH YOU. You're not the ONLY one in the RHYTHM SECTION, and here's the THING, my man.

When you play RIGHT BEHIND the beat, you can DRIVE it for us. PUSH US. We NEED that from you.

Usually the rest of the band likes the drum rant, and they egg me on to new heights of descriptive blabbering. "That's RIGHT, sister. You TELL it like it is. THAT's what we need. Get DOWN with it, girl." Which would make me laugh and ON I'd GO.

"ARE you HEARING ME? We NEED you to DRIVE it. We need to FEEL IT.

I'm BEGGING you. GET BEHIND US, AND DRIVE IT.

DRIVE IT HARD.

I **SAID**, DRIVE IT SO DAMN HARD, OUR FUN PARTS FALL INTO OUR SHOES.

DRIVE . IT."

I wonder how many times I just said drive it? By the way, I'd like to address YOU Mr. Piano or Keyboard Player. YOU are in the rhythm section TOO. YES, YOU ARE. You go on and get in there too, and help to drive. Do you know how many of them know how to do this? Not all that many. Just a few. Do you know how many piano players there are who have NO sense of rhythm? Good God. The keyboard is simply EIGHTY EIGHT DRUMS!

Music done right is like—how many times do I have to SAY it?

Hey, you know what I don't get? Musicians who can't harmonize. You'd be surprised how many can't.

"OK, get off MY note darnit. Find YOUR third, or fifth, or whatever. No, NOT a fifth of Jack Daniels, you moron."

"You know what Denisee? If I sing a song a cappella (it means singing without accompaniment, Denise), or just sing it in my head, I can hear every note of the chord that it's embedded in. I can hear it, and if you ask me to, I can sing each note in the chord for ya, or pick it out on the piano. I never thought this was a rare or mysterious ability…in fact, I thought ALL musicians heard things that way. I found out recently, they do NOT all hear it. Don't you think that's odd?

AFTER the shows?

"Oh, we'd zone out, talk, eat, do music, whatever. Do you want a specific night, or a regular general one? I'll give you one of each.

"Here's a specific one. The very last time I smoked pot, and by that time I only smoked it once a year, was right after a job. We went back to wherever the club put us up that night, and turned on the TV. Someone lit up a joint, and for some reason I wanted a hit. It was pretty idiotic of me. Every year when I'd take two tokes, I'd think *'Oh yeeeeaaahhh. NOW I remember why I don't like this.'*

"I took two hits of the joint, and we all sat around the TV, staring at it in a pot haze. A movie started up. I think it took a good twenty minutes for one of us to get up the nerve to say: 'Am I really messed up? Am I hallucinating? I'm getting REALLY freaked out. Is it just ME, or is EVERYONE in this movie a LITTLE PERSON?'

"We had all been thinking the same thing, but nobody wanted to SAY it. Every one of us figured we were so GONE, we had LOST our MINDS. The funny thing IS, the movie DID have only little people in it, AND little Shetland ponies too. It was a movie called *The Terror of Tiny Town* from the late thirties. It was a western MUSICAL, populated with ONLY little people. Are you picturing this Denisee? We thought we'd gone CRAZY."

"God, I love little people. Almost hired a GREAT little person guitar player once. He was such a HAM. He'd show up to sit in and LEAN up against me when he'd take a solo, and the women would SQUEAL. LOVED him. He decided to go into his Dad's business though. Boy that would have been some lineup there. The bass player at six feet eight, and me (big whacky looking difference there), and then the little person guitar guy (not too much difference between me and the little guy). Wow, what a visual delight THAT would have been. Ahhh well.

"A regular night? That would usually look something like this.

"We'd go back to that evening's digs, which would be anywhere from luxurious with a fridge full of gourmet delights, and a hot tub, to an average hotel, to a less than average motel, to the club owner's or waiter's house, to…you don't even want to KNOW what we were faced with in the early days.

"A typical night would involve going over a new song maybe, talking about music, or about anything…like old TV shows. If there's something open, we get a bite. No one likes to stuff themselves before a show. It makes you too logy. If nothing's open, we pull out the traveling food stash that one or all of us has, and a lot of times we play poker.

"So, picture this. We're starting to play Low Hole, our bass player is tottering around naked as usual, and I'm making a fluffer nutter sandwich with the last remaining bit of fluffer stuff at the bottom of the jar. My naked and lovely (I told you, 6'8") bass player leans over the table, laughing, and DROOLS in my fluffer nutter sandwich before I have a chance to put it together. "I haven't had a bite all day, so I'm darned hungry, and amongst many groans from the rest of the band, I close the darn sandwich and start eating it ANYWAY. We play poker till we start passing out, and call it a night.

"WANNA COME ALONG? Boy, that bass guy of mine drooled a lot. His NOSE was always running TOO. Usually on me. Because we were always a band that mingled a lot when we played, sometimes he'd drool or nose-run in my MOUTH. By the time we left the stage, I was soaked in his special bass playing fluids. Like a nice rum cake. Considering the vast amount of him I absorbed, I SHOULD have a much greater proficiency on bass now."

"That was a usual night for you?"

"Yeah, that was a fairly precise description."

Hey, you want to hear one of the three best pickup lines before you hang up on me?"

"Why not? If I lived through THIS stuff, I might as well hear it."

"Allrighty, I'm forking over one of the three greatest pick-up lines ever tossed at me. I swear.

"As I stated about fifty pages ago, sometimes a dressing room will deter eejits. Not always. They'll wander on back, with the confidence of Wally Cox packing an Uzi. Lots of times, there are club goers lurking about after the club is closed. Often they're friends of the waiters/waitresses/bouncers, whomever. Often they're fans, and they're usually a delight. I never felt put upon, as some musicians do. I've always appreciated the HELL out of them. Why wouldn't I? Some folks don't, and I don't get it.

'Hi there, Nevard, I'd like to say I thoroughly enjoyed your band this evening.' (HEY, this one is COURTEOUS! There's something you don't see every day!)

'I would very much like to take you home with me tonight. I promise I'll show you a great time, and tomorrow morning, I will take you out to chop some wood. Wouldn't that be fun?'

'Did you just say CHOP WOOD?'

'Why yes, I did. And perhaps after that—'

'Let's just stop right there, shall we? Right at the outset here, let me assure you—the answer is a resounding NO. I don't think I've EVER had an offer QUITE like this, however, and…just let me think on this idea for a moment, will you? Okey dokey, young man, here are my thoughts for what they're worth…and I **do** think you need a serious talkin' to. I am a female, yes?'

'Yes, you are, Nevard, a nice one. There's no denying that, and I am very observant.'

'Don't get smart with me, fella, I'm trying to do you a favor. OK, we know I'm a female. We also know I'm dressed in a frilly way, yes? And yet, somehow you've deduced—or maybe you have NOT deduced, in which case, you'd be even MORE of a dolt than I'm thinking—in any case, you have assumed I don't mind physical labor. You are correct in this assumption. Being a farm girl's kid, I'm no stranger to working the land, and do enjoy it. I can muck out stalls if need be, and could INDEED take an axe to wood, though I don't think I'd last more than a minute at that particular activity.'

'Oh, well, then that's a GOOD thing.'

'NO, it is NOT. There is not a woman in the WORLD that is going to IN ANY WAY relish this proposal of what YOU think will be a satisfying first encounter. Know WHY? Because, during any first encounter between two people, they will undoubtedly be on their very best behavior.

'If your idea of "best" behavior is to show a woman an unforgettable evening of unparalleled erotic bliss, and then awaken her out of a cozy sleep early the next morning in order to have her CHOP SOME GODFOR-SAKEN WOOD for ya, then I've got a little bad news for you, Bucky. She is going to think, *if this is what he requires of me right at the start, what pray tell will he expect of me if he gets comfy with me? Will I be plowing the fields without the mule? Will I be ultimately giving birth in said field? Just a quick push, and on with the plow-ing?* DO YOU GET WHAT I'M SAYING?'

'I THINK so, Nevard.'

'That's good. That's very good. Because, please believe me, someday, you will throw that line out to the wrong girl, and you may THINK your darned idea is a SWELL one, because perhaps she's wearing a plaid LOG-GING JACKET. But she is STILL a woman. And she's a woman who, when she hears your sweet line, is going to BEAT the LIVING CRAP out of you.'

"This speech of mine was met with a stunned silence. Sure hope he took my suggestion."

THE JUDGE

You may find it awfully strange to find so much writing about my folks within a book that is mostly about music. Yet THIS is where I gained the courage to face a lifestyle that was NEVER SET IN STONE. In a career like music, you have to learn how to stand in the trenches.

EVERYTHING ABOUT MY UPBRIGING GAVE ME THE NERVE TO BE COURAGEOUS IN MY FIELD. TO POSSESS A DESIRE TO NEVER STOP LEARNING, TO NEVER LOSE A SENSE OF WONDER. TO NEVER BE JADED ABOUT ANYTHING.

In MANY ways, it was a wonderful life. I had an easier time than many, so I was blessed and luckier than hell. My unusual parents were the reason that I was able to bring forth the gumption to work in a large amount of places, where the audiences were EXPECTING to be served a musical menu of things they heard every day on A.M. radio, and became sometimes RABID when faced with music as foreign sounding as MY friendly yet ornery band. And was able to make a decent living DOING this, without needing to join the weekend "five bands a night" crowd.

YOU SIMPLY CANNOT MISS IT. THE WAY I WAS RAISED CONTRIBUTED TO A DEVOTION TO SOMETHING THAT WAS AT TIMES A HELLISH WAY TO MAKE A LIVING. MY FOLKS WERE NOT AFRAID TO SPEAK ABOUT ANYTHING, AND YES, OF COURSE THIS WAS AN ARTISTIC INFLUENCE. I DOUBT IF MANY PEOPLE HAD THIS KIND OF FEARLESS SENSE OF UNFALTERING HONESTY IN THEIR HOMES. CERTAINLY NOT WITH PARENTS OF THAT GENERATION. ARE YOU KIDDIN' ME? IT'S WHY PEOPLE THINK I'M FREAKISH. THEY STAYED YOUNG UNTIL THEY LEFT THIS EARTH.

I have regaled you with stories about my daddy and mamma, and lord knows they were an exhilarating couple to be around.

This is who my father really was. He was Judge Aram Hagop Tellalian Jr. He was an influential man in his community, and he played a large part in our country's history as well as the history of our allied countries.

He didn't start out as the "Judge" of course.

He was born of two Armenian refugees, who fled the town of Adana during a massacre by the Turkish Ottoman Empire, in 1909, and saw most of their family slaughtered

The largest part of the Armenian Genocide, often referred to as "The First Holocaust of the Twentieth Century," spanned from 1915 to 1923. It actually began at least as early as 1909, so the one and a half million Armenians, and five hundred and fifty thousand Greeks and Assyrians that are assumed were murdered, is a very low number. Killings, torture, mass burnings, and gassings occurred in twenty-five concentration camps. They were marched into the desert and left to die, and children were dumped off boats to drown at sea. Armenian women were raped, and then literally crucified. My grandma saw most of her family hanging in their town square, minus many limbs. The world turned its head away as this widespread "religious cleansing" took place, and to this day, the United Nations has not been able to persuade the Turkish government to admit to this atrocity. Two decades later, Adolph Hitler cited the Armenian Genocide as a precedent for his OWN slaughter of the Jews. On the eve of the Holocaust, he said, "Kill without mercy. Who, after all, speaks today of the annihilation of the Armenians?"

My father's brother Bob and his wife Jean are gone now. A sad loss. Uncle Bob had insisted on meeting Jeremy, and so up to Connecticut we went. He loved him, and Jeremy was thrilled to visit the Aram H. Tellalian building.

Born in 1913, my pops was bright and eager to learn. He was fascinated by America's constitution and wanted desperately to become a lawyer. He put himself through both Yale undergraduate and Yale law school by working in factories and whatever odd jobs he could wrangle. He took the trolley to New Haven every day, beginning college at the age of sixteen.

He started serving his community at a young age, because he wanted to be a PART of things…to give and HELP.

During World War II, he was recruited by the O.S.S. (Office of Strategic Services), and became a spy. They were interested in him not only due to his education, but because he spoke Armenian, Turkish, and French. He proudly served under Wild Bill Donovan. My father once in a while told me enthralling things about being a spy, and covert operations. He knew how to kill someone with a newspaper, and so…NOW I KNOW. Don't

MESS with me when the Sunday Times is present. He described to me a little device that looked like a pack of cigarettes. If you were aiming to kill someone in a crowd, you'd open the "cigarette" pack, and press it against you to shoot the bullet out. Who knows HOW many ways he had been taught how to kill.

The training I imagine was intense and he remembered making his way down long tunnels completely in the dark, hanging from a pole, moving hand over hand, and suddenly told to DROP. If trainees didn't drop on command, THEY were dropped from "spy school."

They were taught how to withstand torture, and tested over and over to determine if they'd give up their false identities under any duress. Many trainees were dropped along the way.

I was told about the ways in which they could easily detect someone from the "other side." One thing I remember...they'd ask a suspect to sing the National Anthem. THEN, they'd ask for the second verse. If the suspect KNEW the second verse, chances were THAT was the enemy. Yes, he DID carry L pills, in case of capture.

After the war, my father served as general counsel on the Nuremberg Trials. Amongst other duties relating to international law, he accumulated most of the visual evidence against the Nazi war criminals. Many people who were touched by that horror in some way don't speak of it often, but Pops never hesitated in telling this cautionary tale. He told it because he never wanted ANY of us to forget.

I think the experience cost him in some ways. It must have felt as though he were living his own family's past yet again. He combed through these inhumanities day after day, month after month, year after year, building and building cases against these perpetrators, and briefing his BUTT off.

It was not required of him, but he sat across tables from monsters such as Hermann Goering, the man who was second only to Hitler. He scrutinized Hitler's deputy Rudolph Hess. My father wanted to SEE the evil, to recognize it, to absorb the lessons to be learned from the purveyors of the largest mass murder the world had seen.

I can remember asking him why he did it. He told me, "Love, I NEEDED TO LOOK INTO THEIR EYES, TO SEE WHAT THE FUTURE OF MANKIND COULD HAVE BEEN."

He got a close gander at Alfred Rosenberg and his racial theories, with Ribbentrop, the Nazi minister of Foreign Affairs, Wilhelm Frick, author of the Nuremberg Race Laws, and many other equally horrific…monsters. He set up that courtroom himself, simply to make sure that NO ONE would MISS THE SIGHT OF BULLDOZERS PUSHING MOUNTAINS OF CORPSES INTO DITCHES.

I think it DID cost him dearly (not as much as those who were slammed in those camps of course) but it also taught him empathy, and a humility that was radiant and touched everyone he met, no matter how briefly.

People thought it was a sort of charisma he had, and he surely carried not a small amount of presence, but that wasn't all it was.

I knew it was an immediate and intense caring. It was a deep interest in every single person he encountered…from the busboy clearing off his table, to the most important U.N. dignitary he may have dealt with.

He was changed forever by having to delve so deeply into that world of cruelty. My daddy could feel the tender human in everyone. He knew just how fragile that was, and constantly stretched those arms out wide, to lovingly envelop those he could reach.

After the war, Daddy opened a law practice with his brother Bob, and became Trumbull, Easton, and Monroe Connecticut's first Probate Judge, holding that office from 1959 to 1979. It was an elected office, and after the first term he had become so beloved, he was endorsed by both parties.

Oh he was immensely befitting for ANY occasion when called upon…and he usually WAS called upon, but the Judge was one of the wittiest men I've known. He wasn't too shy to display his impudence in board meetings, or any other place.

"The U.S. Treasury Department has submitted a proposal to simplify and improve the generation-skipping transfer tax - and to be able to pay more taxes of a gift than the gift

itself. **Small wonder that all and sundry shovel so hard to find the pony!" Thank you kindly…**

Oh LORD what a crazy man. I think he spent half his life making speeches and receiving honors. The other half was spent on the phone, writing letters, or in Court.

"I have introduced you to the ingenious device of financing a lawyer to fight against you in a consent proceeding, which didn't sound very consensual."

There's not room enough in this to include even a smidgen of the massive amounts of outpourings the Judge put forth in speeches. I have samplings from scribbled notes. Do you all have any IDEA how utterly BORING Probate Law is? Not when the Judge spoke. Here's part of a speech below about Probate proceedings. He made it sound like a FESTIVAL.

"You intrepid explorers on the uncertain seas of Probate Law have been piloted through the fearsome currents of judicial exposure to punishment by governmental grievance boards, ethics commissions and similar medieval-type inquisitional bodies for alleged amatory misconduct. Remedies of "recusal" and "remittal of disqualification" are available on forms.

All relevant evidence is admissible unless excluded by an enumerated exception, and hearsay is inadmissible unless made admissible by an enumerated exception!' Translated into easy language this means that in Probational Proceedings, Hearsay is the best evidence, especially from a dead man.

We may dissolve corporations by probate decree—or, horror of horrors, apply Greek law re: Usufructory and Naked Interest ownership. If you think that's sexy, you should hear my dissertation ..."

Daddy recognized a kindred spirit in my sweetheart Jeff. He would have seen it in Jeremy as well. They were very much alike. They all HAD it. What they had, is that once in a blue moon combination of brilliance, inherent sweetness, an endless capacity for nonsense, and a like-minded determination in chasing and pointing out prejudice, injustice and hypocracy wherever they'd find it. They had that need to touch others—giving natures acquired through hellish conflict. They NEVER gave up; failures didn't matter. KEEP GOING. Because defeat is OUT OF THE QUESTION.

They dealt with adversity in the same fashion, with strength, laughter (of the dark humour ilk), and rarely did I see them lose that inherent OPTIMISM.

I seem to be thinking about all three when I speak of any. Maybe it is the grief of losing them that's still raw. Jeremy and Jeff WERE extremely daddy-like with me. If a woman has a wonderful father, she will be forever looking for a partner that resembles him.

When I was in the company of my parents, not ONE DAY passed without my father doting on my mother. Admiring her, chasing her. Daddy's brother Bob behaved the same way. Cousin Beth and I spoke of the "doting" factor in them. Cousin Beth commented, "God…my dad gives Mom such admiring attention. Do they MAKE men like that anymore?"

"I don't know Bethie. I met a couple. There MUST be others. I hope."

I came to understand my father and Jeff loved each other's company. If Jeff and I made for an odd couple, then he and Daddy would have been viewed as a downright shocking and improbable meeting of minds.

There is something I've learned—old and tender souls come packaged in different forms.

Funny the way life goes in circles isn't it? During the War, Daddy met Helen Keller, and then as a judge, probated her will. It was beautiful. It read like poetry. He was honored to have known her.

Who else did Daddy know? The list is endless, and impressive. I could start with Dwight D. Eisenhower and move along from there, but my father wasn't impressed with names, he was impressed by what he found in eyes, and how much they cared about things WORTH caring about. He taught ME to look into eyes.

Throughout his life, he never stopped helping. He said during an interview

"Service is a great honor. It's a sense of gratitude."

Daddy was FILLED with an unlimited number of words. He passed this love of language on to me, but MY vocabulary isn't HALF as voluminous as the Judge's. He never used a thesaurus, and neither do I. The Judge DID spend half his time on the phone. When he got home from his office, he'd have a dinner break. He'd then be on the phone until midnight, and beyond. He did this every night, unless there were visitors. Plenty of troubled people showed up at the DOOR. Why was he on the darn phone so much?

He was on the phone to help those in need, to give wise counsel (whether it be legal or personal), to comfort, to plan and help support a thousand charitable causes in need, to help fight for those who were unable to help themselves, to keep any lonely person company, and to boost the morale of everyone he could STUFF into the calls. It did NOT matter if they were friends, neighbors, clients, or strangers.

Yes, I said strangers. TONS of them. I need to repeat this. IT DID NOT MATTER. Strangers reached out statewide, often other states, and sometimes other countries.

My parents did not have an unlisted number. You could freely look him up, and call. He NEVER turned ANYONE away. Ever. When folks had a problem, they would confer with friends, and eventually they would be advised to "Call Judge Tellalian."

Strangers who called with trepidation were gently put at ease. I had countless pals over the years who would call him for any trouble they might be in the middle of, and he would spend hours with them.

The Judge didn't judge. There were DUI's, paternity suits, kids with problems who wanted to confide (he NEVER told their parents), divorces, abortion advice before it was legal, drug busts, girlfriends having trouble with boyfriends or husbands, and everything else dealing with life.

It mattered to him not a bit. If they needed help or a shoulder to cry on, so be it. He gave everyone the same time, the same care. After he gave them his time, he'd FOLLOW UP and call THEM to see how they were doing.

There were no real problems to him. Everything was solvable, nothing was too horrible or tough to handle. He'd find a way for them ALL.

I'd hear him say repeatedly, "No, no trouble at all. It will be OK. You'll see. This is NOTHING. It's NOT the end of the world! We'll figure out a way, and you're going to be all right. I promise."

To the Judge, nothing WAS too big, or too much trouble, or the end of the world, because he had SEEN real trouble, and had more than a glimpse at what COULD HAVE BEEN THE END OF THE WORLD. This man, was in charge of affidavits from places like Auschwitz. That's REAL trouble.

If during those calls (or any other time) he found iniquity, or injustice, or someone being abused, or taken advantage of by an entity or a person, he would MOVE FAST. FAST. There would be a flurry of calls, and his naturally booming voice would develop a resonance that was overpowering. He wasn't afraid of ANYONE OR ANYTHING.

He was not afraid to take a stand. He was not afraid to take a side. He was not afraid to call someone on their crap, and was not afraid to do his damndest to reverse a wrong. He'd try with all his might, and would NOT give up. I saw him do it countless times. My father did NOT CARE what **PRICE** "standing up for what is right" could extract from his professional life. He was fearless. I can tell you about a small one…well, not small for the folks involved, but not one of his larger battles. Those, I won't talk about.

There was a man who had lived in our town for many years with his wife and school- aged children. He was a hard worker, gave to the community, and was well liked.

Before settling in our town, he was in the military, and accepted a ride while on leave one weekend. He was raped, and he pulled out his knife to defend himself. He then did time for manslaughter. When released, he came to our town and started a life.

Years later, an ambitious young reporter at a local paper dug up his past, and the newspaper did the unthinkable. They PRINTED it.

This man's CHILDREN went to school and learned about their daddy's past. He was ruined. Who did he give a frantic call to? He called my father...a stranger.

Within SECONDS of this call, the Judge was on the phone with the editor of the paper. Then he called the publisher. AND THEN he called the reporter. He blasted the HELL out of them. I remember hearing words like "CHICKENSHIT" coming out of his mouth. I heard Daddy spew the following with a force that must have slayed the listener.

"YOU are the kind of COWARD who would, with no COMPUNCTION OR REMONSTRANCE, DROP A BOMB IN A CROWDED ROOM, and THEN casually ask if everyone is ALL RIGHT, you FUCKING BOHUNK.

"YOU SELFISH, SELF SERVING... Don't you DARE hand me that CONTRITE CRAP. I will SHOW you what ANGUISH IS. You, with your IMPERCEPTIVE MIGHTY PEN, have DESTROYED an ENTIRE FAMILY.

"You PROUDLY demolished THEIR LIVES. And NOW, I hope you are AWARE, NOW YOU HAVE **ME** TO ANSWER TO."

Lord, that is where I got the big word/potty mouth that pours out when I'm angry.

Well, the damage had been done. Daddy helped the family relocate, and made sure they were not hurt again. What my courageous Daddy had done in the name of honor was a dangerous thing for a politician to do. It could have caused him irreparable damage. To force members of the press to assume the damn position, and answer to their inexcusable actions, was not a safe thing for any human who desired to be voted into ANY old office, to be doing.

It wasn't usually too late when my Daddy stepped in to help.

His decency was carried into his professional dealings as a lawyer and a Judge. He wasn't inhibited by anything. Justice HAD to be served, and he fought in a way that made his adversaries feel GOOD. I don't know how he accomplished it, but even criminals loved him,

Earlier, I mentioned playing Mob-owned clubs. I had warned the owner, but when he saw my Dad stroll into his joint he said, "JEEESUS…the JUDGE is really your FATHER? He's a good man. Not on my side, but I love him."

I had jury duty one year, and was brought down to the courtroom with a group for Voir Dire. The trial concerned a "connected" guy, who had allegedly murdered someone, and stuffed him in a refrigerator. Lovely. I recognized the defense attorney. Then I looked at the accused and he looked at ME. We looked for a long while, and finally it dawned on me…he was a bouncer in a club I'd played. Damn. The prosecutor, the judge, the defense, and the accused KILLER were all staring at me after roll call. They herded us all into a room, and before you could say O.J., a guard proclaimed, "Nevard Tellalian, you are excused."

I don't know why I told that story, except I was called for jury duty every two years, but they didn't want me there.

I once lived in a neighborhood that started to go downhill, and one night after there were bullets flying in my driveway, I called the folks. Daddy said, "Not to worry. GOSH, they weren't shooting at YOU, were they sweetie?" I also mentioned the dead guy they'd found in the front yard across the street the week before, and the other shooting through a neighbor's living room. My dad calmly said, "Hmm, time to move, hey?"

A call to my folks long after midnight would be answered with details like this: "HI SWEETIE! Mommy and I were just out back. We're trying to see what is EATING the Rhodies.

Margo, are your jammie bottoms as soaked as mine are? Can we put them in the dryer? WHAT'S in there now? Well Jesus Marion Joseph, Mommy, when will they be done? Margo, I think this flashlight needs new batteries. Did you notice it was fading out there? OH…I have to call…of course NOW, dammit."

They found enjoyment and fascination everywhere. The lesson they taught me?

BE HUNGRY.

During the last few years of his life, there was a restaurant on the bottom floor of Dad's office building. My ninety-two-year-old daddy was TICKLED that he had a key to the back door of the place, so he could enter from the lobby instead of going outside.

I'm picturing Daddy and Uncle Bob at the little door, trying to put the key in. By then Daddy's hands shook. "Bob, BOB, the damned key doesn't…all right, you try it." After fifteen minutes of fumbling, they would gain entrance, and IN they would LURCH, with the biggest BEAMING smiles you ever did see. A PRIVATE entrance to the SANDWICH SHOP! What could be more thrilling?

HUNGER. HUNGER FOR EXPERIENCES LARGE AND SMALL.

When the folks traveled, I would receive letters like this:

"One wondered—upon reaching one's little home away from home—where to hang one's pajamas, or washed hose, or similar unmentionables, except on doorknobs (from which they invariably slipped off). And, surprise upon surprise—the distance from the bathtub upon emerging in a state of drippage, to the nearest bath towel on a rack, is 7 feet 9 inches, a span not to be speedily traversed.

"Not to mention the state-of-the-art computerized air conditioning system controlled by the telephone—requiring resetting every half-hour on the hour. I almost forgot—how COULD I?—the eye shattering hits you without warning as soon as you open the bathroom door—cyclopic, magnified 100 times mirror, with the surgeon's light! It's most dangerous for anyone over 23... a physiognomic encounter, causing the most permanent traumatic shock that one could ever confront. The epidermal lines create a Dorian Grey syndrome!"

The day my daddy died was one of the four most sorrowful times in my life. Another two came with the loss Jeff and Mamma. Now I'm still mourning the loss of Jeremy. They were my instructors. They showed me how to love.

My father had always wanted a New Orleans send off. He wanted Satchmo to be marching down State Street, Bridgeport, playing the good stuff.

I'm sorry, Daddy, it was February, and Pop was already gone but I set up a celebration that ROCKED. No wake. We're not a wake kind of family.

The church was more than horrified, to tell the truth. "You're going to have WHAT music? Shouldn't it be more dignified. After all, he was a JUDGE. He had an impressive history that calls for a solemnity befitting…he would want the sort of respect…blah, blah…"

NO. NO HE WOULD NOT. He DOES not. HE POSSESSED NOT

ONE PRETENTIOUS BONE IN HIS BODY. THE JUDGE WANTS LAUGHTER AND LOVE.

I set up good music he'd want, and called Fred Vigorito, the BEST trumpet player in the U.S.A. Daddy got his favorites. Mozart's "Alleluia," "In the Garden," "St. Louis Blues," and the "St. James Infirmary" were some of them.

I called Ray Baldwin, the First Selectman in Trumbull, and John Klein, CEO of Peoples Bank, two he had mentored who I knew had the gift of gab. "Please come and talk for Daddy. I can't without crying. There will be too many people there. Make Daddy laugh. I want you to CELEBRATE what he really was. Please."

So many emails, and letters came in, it was difficult to handle. They came from everywhere. There was one from the folks who sat and waited for chemo with him. They said he gave them comfort, hope, and laughs. He was the only thing that kept them going…made them happy to be alive.

Daddy got the party he wanted. Funny, everyone who spoke remembered the Judge's pet names for them.

The Hon. Ray Baldwin then got up and said, "I don't know where I stand in the hierarchy between Your Worship and El Presidente, but he called me Your Excellency. Now, today belongs to Aram and his memory.

"I first met Aram when I was a young patrolman on the Trumbull Police Department. Aram loved big cars and he loved to drive them fast, so it was inevitable that our paths crossed one summer night in 1972 on Main Street. When I approached his car he greeted me in his usual gregarious fashion, and within a very short time, without his knowing it, he had not only talked me out of a ticket, but had made me his friend.

"From that day on Aram took me under his wing, and when I graduated law school it was Aram who insisted that he be allowed to sponsor me for admittance to the Bar. Aram was not just a proficient lawyer and respected Judge; he was a teacher and a counselor. He loved schooling, if you were willing to listen and learn.

"I would often call for advice, and he never once put me off or said he was too busy to help. When I would join him for lunch, it was a treat for me and anyone else who joined to listen to Aram hold court and regale us with stories. He was an encyclopedia of information and possessed one of the sharpest intellects of any man I've ever known."

Wonderful Ray Baldwin, once said of Pops with a chuckle, "He's one of the few Republicans I'd honor."

Daddy mentored more people than he ever realized. He'd do it without KNOWING. He did it by being himself. He did it for hundreds. I'm having trouble writing this. I'm having trouble keeping the tears in, because this sweet, sweet man is gone.

While I was still working at that bank, I sat next to a guy named Vernon. He did well within the organization. One evening after work, I followed Vern, my girlfriend, and a few others to the Holiday Inn to hang for a while. I didn't often join them, but I'm glad I went that night.

We began to discuss heroes, and the fact that there weren't too many left in the world. Vernon said, "I have a hero. You know who MY hero is?"

"Who, Vern?"

"My hero is YOUR FATHER, Nevard."

"What? What are you talking about?"

"Vardz, I used to work as a security guard at the building your father's office is in. I sat there at that desk in the lobby every morning, and NO ONE EVER said a word to me. Not even good morning. It was as if I didn't exist. Only ONE PERSON spoke to me. He came in whistling every day with a smile, and every single morning he came over to talk with me."

"Yes…of course he did, Vern, and he was whistling 'Country Gardens.' I'll bet he asked questions."

"God, QUESTIONS? He wanted to know every single THING about me, and he'd ask every single DAY. Vardzie, he encouraged, and encouraged, and pushed me. I started taking classes, and he pushed some more. He pushed me out of that chair and into a career. Never gave up on me. He loved and cared, when no one ELSE cared or even noticed. THAT'S A HERO."

Thank you, darling Vern. Thank you.

Wonderful writer Donald Eng, who is now the editor of the *Trumbull Times*, wrote something amazing about Daddy after that "Celebration." Here it is, in part:

That was one of the most remarkable memorials I have ever been to," said First Selectman Ray Baldwin following Friday's service. "When I got back to the office afterwards, I was motivated to start thinking about what music I want playing at my funeral."

EVERY LEGACY HAS TO START SOMEWHERE.

In a eulogy for Judge Aram Tellalian, People's Bank CEO John Klein asked how to properly memorialize such an extraordinary life.

And so it was Monday night of this week when I sat down to write, and I felt very much like John Klein. When someone has lived 93 years, summing up his life's accomplishments in about 700 words is a challenge.

I am not the world's fastest writer, but the piece about Tellalian took me quite a bit longer than usual. There was a very good reason, too—my thoughts kept interfering with my fingers.

I read Tellalian's obituary several times, and each time I was amazed at just how deeply he was involved in the community.

The list of his accomplishments went on and on. WWII Army major with the OSS; legal counsel at the Nuremberg Trials. Those two achievements alone provide plenty of material to fill a book. Yet, the obituary went on.

When did this man sleep?

The list continued: vice president of the YMCA, chairman of the Boys Club, and believe me, much more.

I put down Tellalian's obituary and wondered what mine would look like.

I came up with:

- Once got third place in a subcategory of a regional newspaper writing contest.

- Had a dog named Daisy.

Note : I have that huge list of accomplishments. It is two pages long. I didn't include it, because I'm SURE you'd be thinking..."WHAT. Is she kiddin' us? Who the Hell could have done this much? NAAAAHHH...THIS must be a big ol' lie. If you'd truly like to read it, I'd be happy to send it to you. Just send me your e-mail.

JEFF AND NEVARD PART II

I was told this story should be relayed, as an implication of this man's true nature I guess, but it was MY final decision to write it… good and bad. When I think of Jeff, lines from *Hamlet* come to me, the most obvious one being—

> *"This above all…to thine own self be true."*
> *—HAMLET*

So I'm including them.

This is someone who left a considerable and lasting imprint in my life. He knew what drove me, grasped my very core, and I had never been so naked in front of another human being.

> *"You would play upon me; you would seem to know my stops; you would pluck out the heart of my mystery; you would sound me from my lowest note to the top of my compass; 'Sblood, do you think I am easier to be played on than a pipe? Call me what instrument you will, though you can fret me, you cannot play upon me."*
> *—HAMLET*

But he could. He could play me… and could have damaged me beyond repair with the knowledge of that. He didn't.

I'd like to ask a favor from those who knew Jeff. If you're reading this, please if you will, excuse me for not KNOWING what parts of his life are common knowledge now. I've stepped lightly on subjects I'm not certain Jeff would want known.

If you knew him well, PLEASE don't contact me in order to perhaps unwittingly tell me things about this man which might hurt me. I was NOT in the LOOP, and was purposely kept out of it.

He would NOT appreciate it, wherever he might be lurking, and would in fact be angry, just as he would not have wanted to know about any part of MY life that may have hurt him.

I'm sure you can understand this. I still can't bear to see or read much about Jeff. I visited a couple of sites, but couldn't delve in. I spied a photo, and the obvious signs of his illness blindsided me. He never wanted me to see it. I couldn't watch a DVD of the band when it was played. I was able to read one thing, and even that was too much.

Were we exclusive? I'm not telling you whether I was, and I have no idea if he was. Neither of us wanted to know.

I CAN tell you, we were both extremely jealous and possessive in that respect. I would have been crushed if I had known he was messing with anyone else, so did not let myself think about it. Jeff would sometimes obsess late at night. "Babygirl…am I the only one? **Am I**? No…I don't want to know, all right? Ever, ever, ever. Am I though? Nobody else is TOUCHING you, right?" He was as terrified as I. We only wanted to know what we had. We were in a safe place, and hid in each other.

We weren't very brave. But we were not stupid.

I don't THINK I'll offend anyone with the telling of this loving story, and if you're someone who knows who he is, I'm finally OK with it, but I can't bring myself to name him. I don't want people unfamiliar with him going off and googling this guy. Some won't like him. I can't bear the thought of anyone not liking this man, because he deserved admiration.

And admire him I did. I adored Jeff. He was like a tower of playing cards that was perpetually in danger of keeling over. He was awkward in an endearing and touching way. He was NOT an easy person though…could be hard as nails in certain ways. Jeff was infinitely patient most of the time, but he would bite back with a VENGANCE when he felt pushed, hurt, or frustrated.

We were very much alike and seemed to share one nature between us. How could two people from polar opposite upbringings and worlds resemble each other so fundamentally?

Traits that were normal for us, was a pronounced connection; Jeff thought we'd been separated at birth.

"O day and night, but this is wondrous strange!"
—HAMLET

We each possessed an enduring stubbornness, were IMMOVABLY loyal, and demanded the same from others. If we didn't get it, the door would be SHUT and never opened again.

Both of us could be easily confused, and bewilderingly naive, but annoyingly analytical, wanting EVERY detail. We were strangely blind in some ways, but intuitive in others, and we repeated things. Over and over.

We were physically and emotionally affectionate seemingly beyond the laws of nature. Jeff had a limitless ability to love, and was doting.

We were both notoriously clumsy (I've been known to wrap FOAM around table legs so I won't hurt myself), but slap us on a stage, and we could seem graceful as hell (didn't know this about HIM at the time).

The two of us were engulfed in music, wanted to keep the CRAP at bay. In spite of innate insecurity, and paralyzing self-consciousness, we were outrageously bold, and could roam the earth with an audacious swagger.

Both of us knew how to hide crippling shyness when needed. Did I say insecure? Yes. HOWEVER, **neither of us wavered or cowered regarding what we knew was right. PERIOD. We didn't give a Flying FUCK WHAT people thought of us. We accepted who and what we were**. Sometimes, however, we cared TOO much what people thought of us (although NEVER admitting it), and due to our obsessive tendencies, we'd wrung the life out of issues that gnawed at us. "Why the FUCK can't we get airplay, when there's so much SHIT going out, babygirl?" A while ago, I was told about the toughest obsession for Jeff.

Too softhearted, easily hurt in spite of our bravado, suspicious to the point of paranoia, but overly trusting, and sappily sentimental were traits we shared, along with anger that was hard to express. It would spill from our otherwise kind natures at the darndest times. When feeling cornered and scared, we'd act out like two-year-olds.

Both of us had a highly developed sense of the absurd. God, Jeff was priceless, oh so FUNNY, and bright. Sometimes quiet holding was all we wanted.

I think the most compulsory trait we shared was a profound and deeply rooted need for unconditional love. It was an endless search…never feeling the devotion we craved (at least not in the exacting way we WANTED it)…and so it DROVE us. Just about consumed us. My need was at last filled by Jeff's fervent attention, and he said I was able to finally quiet the screaming demand in him as well. I sure hope so. Until recently, I was afraid I'd been more the "taker" and hadn't given back nearly enough.

The reverse and almost perverse side of this trait was confusing and vexing. Attributes that were fine and dandy in friends were NOT what we wanted in a lover. Dumb, yeah? Neither of us had ANY sort of long-term patience with really easygoing people, OR glomming types of folks, and eventually viewed them as doormats. We'd THINK we wanted what they offered up, but I'm afraid we'd lose respect, ultimately fall into an attitude of permanent irritation, and would PUSH at them until they couldn't STAND us anymore.

How do I know this? We talked about it a lot. What a conundrum, yes? Jeff and I were most likely the witch's brew we'd been waiting for. I guess we were both aberrations (gosh, I HOPE not), but no other guy I'd been with seemed to understand me. HE thought my expectations were perfectly natural, and with the excitement of a damn PUPPY, he forked it right OVER. AND wagged his tail for me. Always. THANK YOU.

I'm more than positive the above descriptions will be tedious for some. I'm hoping it will shed some light for those who cared deeply about Jeff. I hope you might be able to have a better understanding of his behavior, and can forgive the conflicting signals that came out.

Can I somehow describe what this man meant to me? Can I bear to tell you what I saw that broke my heart?

If some of this becomes a bit too steamy for you…it can't be avoided.

I wouldn't be ABLE to escape this dominant part of our relationship. It describes the way we conducted ourselves with each other and the constant push and pull we exercised. It was by far one of the most powerful ways we communicated.

One story would make Jeff so darn happy, I can hear that laughter ringing out. He'd REALLY want a couple of people to read it, and would be spittin' mad they're no longer with us. His opinion would be, "Crap. I wanted to rub his nose in it." Not very nice on Jeff's part, but he'd want it anyway. If you knew him, you'll see it, and for the rest of you it will just be a funny story.

Was Jeff a good lover? He'd want me to tell you the way in which he shaped the essence of what HE wanted our relationship to be.

I may have been pretty heavy-handed with Jeff during our first encounter, but I quickly became simply a willing participant in his design.

I DON'T know why he didn't run from my "hackles raised" attitude the evening we met. Loads of guys would have. He **didn't** run though. He raced head-on, aimed his dauntless self right AT me, and proceeded to forcefully turn me on my head.

It is a stunning testament to his unbelievably strong will, and his ability to face STRAIGHT ON what might have been intimidating to a less determined man.

It was a pretty good clue to what he in FACT was made of, and I'd realize in the future that he was the bravest person I have ever known, and I'd like YOU to know…

There are significant things to be LEARNED from this man, and from the way he lived his life.

I realized during our initial get-together, he was less experienced than one would guess. I had a glimpse of this when we met, and assumed he was used to being pandered to. It confounded ME, because I'm pretty sure he'd been with ten thousand compared to my paltry ten. The first time he came to my home, I had to almost SIT on him so I could file down his fingernails.

"All RIGHTY, Jeff, those nails are altogether TOO long. What are you, a girl? You don't need those unless you're SEGOVIA, and even THEN, you need long nails on just the ONE hand. Love your hands. Whaddya mean why? They need it 'cause I'm NOT getting scratched up like a big old POLE CAT is on me."

The things I saw in his eyes were true. Staggeringly and almost frighteningly true. He was a one-minute study, and then there was no stopping him.

What might have been submerged in him began to fly out in a breathtaking, overpowering way. He sure as HELL blew me out of the water.

Jeff became the most aggressive and barbarically playful creature on earth.

> **"Though I am not splenitive and rash,**
> **Yet have something in me dangerous"**
> **—HAMLET**

He was violent (I don't mean abusive, OK?), outrageously smutty, and sometimes demanded complete surrender; often wanted ME to order and push him around, and sometimes, LORD sometimes he was gut wrenchingly sweet. Jeff could be tender as anything, with achingly soft words of love, and adoring inquiries. "Ya like that? You my sweet babygirl?"

In short, Jeff could damn well DANCE. He understood the profound dynamics between two people. Good lord, to Jeff, the dancing was a never-ending discovery.

I'd say a good half of our time together was ruled by an overwhelming need to erotically OWN each other. Ridiculous, wasn't it?

Our behavior was absurd. When I'd pick him up at the train station, the taxis in the line behind us would start honking, because we couldn't stop kissing. No, I'm wrong…HIS behavior was infinitely more absurd than MINE.

Once in a while we'd stop for a bite, and as soon as we were seated, good GOD, Jeff used those impossibly long legs of his to push his knees forcefully between my legs. Wrenched them apart, he did, and before I knew it, one or both of his hands would move in…and he'd MESS with me. BUSY. Busy with an evil smile. Everything looked perfectly calm on TOP of the table, but I'd be pleading.

"Ohhh, don't DO this, Jeff."

"YEAH? Whatcha gonna do? Wanna make a scene? Announce it?"

By the time the waitress made an appearance, I'd invariably be almost PANTING (despite my protestations…weak ones I must admit), and by golly Jeff would casually ask, "So…can you come back? I think my gurl needs a couple more minutes to, uhhh…decide her future."

"Ohhhhhhhhhh, Jeeeffffff…this isn't right…"

" NAAAAAH. Let's go finish ya UP, babygirl." Whereupon I'd find myself pushed into the bathroom, the door slammed and locked, and Jeff would put me on the SINK. With authority. All I can say is thank

GOODNESS the entrance to that bathroom was not visible from the dining room. No one saw us go in or come out of the LADIES room together.

Once we arrived at my place, making it all the way in was a challenge. We'd head up the stairs, start playing, and couldn't quite reach the door. About the only place we visited was a health club. Late at night the indoor and outdoor pools, locker room, showers, steam room (how did we breathe?) and the whirlpool were basely baptized. Why were we never caught?

Jeff had a THING for putting me on any counter or table he encountered, partly I guess, because of our difference in height. Damn...as soon as he'd step into the kitchen he'd march over to the table and sweep EVERYTHING off with his arms, not giving a darn what might be broken in the process.

I didn't care WHAT he threw off that table in a fury. Being forcibly pinned to a table top is something NONE of us should miss in life. If we moved to the basement, he'd get bossy, and PULL me to the laundry counter. Well, it certainly IS riveting to have someone banging the BREATH out of you, while you're face-to-face and he's standing there with a dangerous look in his eyes.

If we left the house (not often) I could SEE him eye every surface with unmistakable interest.

"GEEZ, cut that OUT, Jeff. You can NOT FUCK me on my dry cleaner's COUNTER."

"Yeah, but uhh, LOOK...look where it comes UP to on me."

"We're in PUBLIC, Jeff. Why don't we make a MOVIE?"

"Yeah...OK...why DON'T we

"STOP it, Jeff."

> *"Lady, shall I lie in your lap?*
> *No, my lord.*
> *I meant my head upon your lap.*
> *Aye, my lord.*
> *Do you think I meant country matters?*
> *I think nothing, my lord.*
> *'Tis a fair thought indeed to lie*
> *between maids' legs."*

—HAMLET

Jeff had an affinity for playing while I slept, and I'd be regularly awakened during the night to find his head resting on my legs, perfectly still, and contemplating.

"Whatcha doing there, champ?"

"Just looking."

"OK. Enjoy. I THINK."

An hour or two later, I'd feel a little gentle probing...and there he'd be.

"Still looking, huh? You got anything interesting to report?"

"Nope."

"Don't get a neck ache, all right?" And I'd drift back to sleep.

"Then you live about her waist, or in the middle of her favours?"
—HAMLET

MORE time would go by, and by golly, he'd STILL be there, not having moved an inch, except now my legs would be falling asleep.

"I hate to spoil your fun, Jeff, but I think I need to MOVE, or lose the use of my legs. Stop LOOKING and get to PLAYING with what you're LOOKING at."

"That's a SMART suggestion, babygirl."

"You're so very welcome, Jeff."

I'd wake up with his head on my tummy, "looking and touching," or his head next to mine, and he'd be stroking my face.

I was startled once by a feeling of something cold between my legs, and there was Jeff, with a stick of butter he'd gotten from the fridge.

"What in the WORLD... What are you DOING, Jeff?"

"Butterin' ya UP."

"OK...God you're really SOMETHING. You going to clean up that mess?"

"Yup, all right. Oh yeahhh, right when I'm done doing..."

I took a degree of relentless crudeness I wouldn't have taken from anyone else, but somehow, coming out of him, it was delicious, and surprisingly sweet. Because Jeff was sweet. Jeff and I were insomniacs. He, more than I.

> *"If it be now tis not to come*
> *If it be not to come it will be now*
> *If it be not now yet it will come,*
> *THE READINESS IS ALL"*
> *—HAMLET*

We'd rock each other to sleep to silence the turmoil in our heads. Sometimes I'd sing or read aloud if he was having a bad night. It served to quiet his frenzied thinking machine, and he'd be able to nod off.

More than occasionally it would be a futile endeavor.

> *"Take up your weapon, Buttons OFF"*
> *—HAMLET*

"I'm wide awake now, babygirl. Too much to DO. Too much…too much…too much." He'd sit up, and those legs of his would swing over the side of the bed—and I'd know he was going to keep ME up.

"Come here to me, right here in front of me." No mumbling came out of Jeff when he was after a little sugar.

"FUCK, yer EARS workin', ya bitch? I SAID…come HERE. Fuck. So I gotta MAKE YA?"

"Yup."

"Oh yeah? GOOOOOD. Get OVER here…that's right. Get on your knees ya little CUNT, and deal with THIS."

"Yes, SIR. You sure I can deal with THAT?"

"Yep. You sure CAN. You know HOW. And you WILL. Like right NOW. Sooo, how much ya WANNIT?"

And it would start. Ferocious, devilish, and loveable he was. Don't know HOW he managed to combine those attributes.

"Babygirl, can I be your, um, little whippin' boy tomorrow? Give me the orders? Yep…get all kinda mad and use the big words, all right? I mean you give the orders good."

"Sure. Big words. OK. You better be scared to wake UP, you little pischer. You're IN for it. I MEAN it." I'd start to get comfy and sleepy. "Jeff? I love you."

And as I'd begin to go under, all warm and wrapped, Jeff up against me, kissing my head, his arm draped over and holding my tummy I'd hear a soft whisper in my ear.

"I love you even more."

Oh crikey…I'll never get the last word.

We constantly said "I love you more" to each other. It's been almost ten years now since I last heard that phrase march out of Jeff's mouth. NOW, I see it in catalogs, on pillows, on jewelry…EVERYWHERE. And NOW I can't bear to see it.

I don't know where Jeff found the sheer fortitude for these constant romps. He was ill much of the time, but he wore ME out. It's how we were together.

What else did we do besides paw at each other? MUSIC. Movies, fun TV, games… Mostly music. Ever hear Vince Edwards sing "Stormy Weather"? OHHHHH, something not to be MISSED. Jeff and I would sing it the Vince way. Other than that, just being together was the largest thing we craved, and we didn't get enough.

We did go to the symphony one night. I leaned over and said the thing I always say at the symphony: "How many strings there, Jeff? How many? You see a tuner? Ahh, ya sissy rock boys." He laughed through the entire program.

I'd pick up Jeff at the Bridgeport train station. He'd call when he got in, because he'd never make the train he MEANT to catch. It's a good thing the station was five minutes from my house. Jeff could get into trouble anywhere.

Took him so darn long to pack things. Sometimes he'd go to a phone booth and call me in the middle of it. "Babygirl, should I bring…?"

"Jeff. JEFF, you're not going on safari. We have STORES in Connecticut."

"I know, I know, I know….so umm, should I bring…"

Oh, he was a troublesome THANG all right.

What the hell…I'M troublesome too. When I pack to go ANYWHERE, a constant thing for YEARS, I'd freak out if I forgot, oh…say my toothbrush. As if my darn TOOTHBRUSH were the only one left on the PLANET. That's right. Nope. This is the LAST ONE. I'm TELLING you.

I was ALSO compelled to clean EVERY hotel room my band and I stayed in. COMPELLED. Do you know how many hotel rooms there

WERE over the years? I COULD NOT leave without making every bed. I couldn't get in the vehicle without cleaning the bathrooms, the ashtrays, picking up all the trash.

The band would logically point out, "Nevard. VARDZIE. The maids are going to strip the freaking beds you just made and clean the room AN-YWAY. Why do you always need to DO this? Get in the damn BOY BUS, girl, wouldja?"

This was eminently SANE thinking on their parts, and I was more than aware of that inescapable fact, but I had to do it. I had to. I drove them to distraction. Lord have mercy on Jeff and me, and any poor schmucks who had to deal with us regularly.

I began to keep stockpiles of "Jeff" things at my house (clothes, meds, and vitamins) so he wouldn't NEED to pack, but he'd STILL call in the middle of it.

Jeff told me he drove everyone around him nuts. He felt horrible about it.

It didn't bother me. I thought anything he did was pretty delightful. I'd just watch him do his thing.

I didn't have to live with him, but I knew what a pain in the butt he could be, and how ornery when frustrated, and I'm positive quite inconven-ient to say the least, but the REAL BURDEN was carried by Jeff. Did peo-ple know how much of a burden? Some might have. His head was never quiet for him (one of the reasons HE was quiet), so any added clutter was downright painful.

Did anyone imagine the fortitude and determination it took for Jeff to go about a regular DAY, never mind deal with schedules, details, and con-current tasks that needed to be dealt with, and were ALWAYS present in his life?

I'm not even including the creative outpourings he accomplished, or the act of getting on a stage and PERFORMING every other minute, or the million things he didn't HAVE to do, but did because he cared.

Did they know what chaos went on in that genius head of his?

Yeah…that's what I said. He was a genius. Let me say it again loud….

**He was a GENIUS—
that's what he damn well WAS.**

He told me what he went through as a kid, and later. No one could figure out WHAT he was, but he sure as the dickens HAD the last vengeful LAUGH.

Oddly, Jeff was at first a little unnerved by the billion books on my shelves. "CHRIST, have you READ …oh maaan….I can't be with YOU." WAS HE NUTS?

What did I learn from HIM? He was a GREAT music historian and knew his stuff. He was conversant about the ecology, and stunningly knowledgeable about a great many things. This man couldn't peel a carrot to save his LIFE, but he took the paltry bit of savings I'd managed to accumulate and managed to quadruple it within a short time. He then repeated this COUNTLESS times over the space of a few years, and finally doubled it for me. Jeff had a facile mind, and his conceptual powers were limitless. His artistic powers were too. We painted together. He was GOOD, but would always rip up whatever he did, because he was such a perfectionist.

The REAL truth is THIS. Jeff was MILES and MILES smarter than I'll EVER be. I'm just a plodding little bookworm. But JEFF? Oh, he was BREATHLESSLY brilliant, in more ways than most folks probably ever knew.

I think people couldn't see the immense scope of him, the prodigious breadth of his talents, because LITTLE things would confound him. Does that sound familiar? Like maybe the brain of a genius?

He'd dumb himself down now and then. More than anything else, Jeff loved to be with people, and liked them to feel comfortable with him. He genuinely DID. He told me, but I knew anyway. Sometimes his shyness took over, and he simply couldn't FACE people, but he never stopped trying. I've already told you where Jeff acquired the desire to touch other souls. It came from the struggles. That glorious man was in pain…every single day.

He'd say something that would FLASH by me. Then, he'd GRIN and patiently WAIT for the HOUR it would take for me to GET it. I was stupefied when Jeff told me that my father didn't make him feel "stupid." Jeff was just as smart as Daddy, and the Judge had a HUGE intellect.

By the time I met Jeff, by whatever means, he said he was less driven…at least outwardly, and a bit more in control of the bedlam.

He confided that he was tormented by some because of his offbeat behavior. I know it hurt him an awful lot. He was unwilling to address it with them, which I'm sure didn't help matters. I presume Jeff felt comfortable being open with me about this, due to my own eccentricities.

Please know, not everyone in his life was abusive. There were caring people he was very close to, but there were also people he believed to be friends, who dropped him as he became more ill. He became too much of a bother. Heartbreaking.

Jeff told me he often distanced himself from people. Once in a great while, he'd say how wounded and bewildered he felt, when even those he loved seemed to turn on him.

I was not told much about the personal lives of his band, but the few things Jeff passed on weren't pleasant. I don't mean substances. Musicians deal with it. You participate, or you don't, and most have seen comrades destroyed. We helplessly look on, until they either clean up or die. Jeff was pretty sober by the time we met, but he'd had his battles. We all had.

No, what Jeff described to me was anarchy. Degrading relationships and betrayals were on the menu. My take on any such scene is "people live the way they want to live, and I'm just happy I ain't living it with them." Judging from the few spotty stories he DID relay, I think I can surmise that life around mutating personalities couldn't have made for a restful ride.

This is why the attitude that Jeff lived with was sad. He could NOT govern these things. SO, I've got to ask… WHAT IS WRONG WITH PEOPLE?

Are YOUR pain in the derriere idiosyncrasies superior to another's? Does it give you a license and passport to behave without a moral compass? I don't GIVE a flying monkey's BUTT how long it took him to do WHATEVER, OK?

I know, again, I didn't live with him, so I was not that put upon. Could I have handled a day-to-day Jeff? The answer is yes. Just as I would for any loved one. I put up with a harrowing degree of horror from someone that made Jeff's anxiety driven behaviour feel like the singing NUN'S. He was kindhearted. Deeply.

I could usually snap him out of it by redirection. "You know, Jeff, you're such an unmitigated ass right now, it's a good thing you're in possession of something fun in your pants; otherwise your mean little butt would be curbside."

"Yeah, yeah. I'm so fuckin tired of…ya know what YOU are… WHAT? Whaja SAY?"

"You heard me. Your nasty little self is still sitting here because, lucky for you,

you're MORE than AMPLY STUFFED."

Looking a little disquieted, he'd inquire, "Huh? Oh. Is that, uh, what you LIKE about me? Yeah? GOOD! FUCK. Is IT THAT…"

"Shush. I must say, you being such a jerk and all, right at this moment what's in your pants is undoubtedly your ONLY REDEEMING QUALITY."

Rest, Rest, perturbed sprit!
—HAMLET

He taught me a lot of music, and I taught him. Let's see now, what music did we listen to? Only a musician would be interested. We loved the '60s, the last and most prolific era for good radio music. We considered later offerings to be in the "lost age of rock and roll" catalog, at least concerning radio music.

We loved things that would most likely surprise folks. We'd sing the entire Burt Bacharach songbook, Tom Jones, I'd sing to him Irving Berlin, Rogers and Hammerstein, (Jeff wanted to do "I'm just a boy who can't say no"). I could go on for pages and pages.

We had all the same favorites. Both of us loved the harder stuff, but we had some leanings that differed. Someone who knew the sound of both our bands would find this pretty odd. Jeff was more of a Motown boy, and I was a Stax girl. Funny, he liked the smoother sounds, and I loved the rougher Stax repertoire. I was Screamin' Jay, and Jeff was Marvin Gaye, but **we dug ANYTHING that wasn't BULLSHIT.** It didn't matter. As long as it was real, and not kissing somebody's ASS. "Oh BABY, come here. Check THAT out. LISTEN…That's GREAT. SHIT." I loved his collection of old obscure stuff, and he loved mine.

All God's children should love to hear
everybody's collection of whacky cool old
obscure stuff.

Jeff's passion for music was firmly planted in the right place. It lived in every nook and cranny of him. Did we talk about the BIZ? Not a lot. We didn't want to waste time. He gave me wise advice, and we both hated most of what was on the radio.

The BIGGEST thing we hated was the repugnant fact that some deserving artists were pigeonholed into a tiny BOX they couldn't escape (as happened in HIS case). Or else the very same BIG DONKEY BRAINED BUFFOONS wanted to pigeonhole other deserving artists SOMEWHERE, but couldn't seem to figure out WHERE to pigeonhole those that didn't WANT to be pigeonholed ANYWAY (which was my scenario). Twenty years later, things haven't changed.

Jeff used to play the old Pearl drum kit in my basement (it had a mother of toilet seat finish), and I'd plug my old Gretch into an old Fender Super Reverb. I'm here to tell you, Jeff wasn't a bad drummer. Would you doubt me? I know what's good. He liked to mess with my old solid body electric stand up bass, and I'd figure out things on piano.

I thought he was a great songwriter, and he thought I was better (he was wrong). God, what a voice Jeff had. He could make things DRIP with soul. I remember a couple of old songs he made downright LUSCIOUS. The original versions couldn't have come close.

Did Jeff ever write anything about us? Sure. Did I write about him? Sure. Did we work on stuff together? Sure. Nobody's business. EVER. PERIOD.

> *He hath, my lord, of late made many tenders*
> *Of his affection to me.*
> *—HAMLET*

Jeff couldn't stop trying to take care of me. About four years after we met, I finally had to take a disgusting job, and it drove him out of his MIND.

"A BANK? A FUCKIN' BANK? Ahhh…what're ya gonna do THERE?"

"I don't know. It's just two days a week and I need the insurance."

"Maybe I could like put ya on the payroll…ummm…for insurance. FUCK, I don't want you ta be working in a BANK, NEVARD. You CRAZY? You're a MUSICIAN. You're not…I mean, you're not BUILT for anything else. Maybe, can you kinda LET me help ya OUT? Would you? Baby girl, you're so stubborn, so stubborn, STUBBORN."

"JEFF. On a payroll? You NUTS? You can't even CALL me from… STOP it. REALLY. I DO NOT WANT HELP. NOT TAKIN' IT. OK?"

"So can I pay for DINNER?" "Yes."

Curiously, and for a long time, Jeff kept asking if I was "wanting" to marry him.

"WHAT? NO. **No.**"

"Why don't ya, uhhh, WANT to get married? Any girl I was EVER with wanted to get married."

"Well, I don't rightly know what THEIR problem was, but I don't NEED to marry you. It wouldn't mean anything. Is it weird for you that I DON'T want to? Is it insulting? I just want YOU. Gosh, do we have a problem here?

"Huh."

"What do you mean, HUH? OK, what's bugging you? What IS it, baby? Are you SCARED to death I might WANT to marry you? OR are YOU hankering' to marry ME? What's UP, pussycat?"

"I wanna have a baby with you."

"WHAT? You WHAT, Jeff? Oh, I'm sorry. I didn't mean to sound so GEEZ… I didn't know you had this on your mind. Why didn't you TELL me?"

"Thought you'd laugh at me."

"Why would I LAUGH at you? I thought… OK, what's going on here? Do you want me off the PILL, JEFF? Is that what you want?"

"YEAH. That sounds good. If THAT doesn't work, we could getcha all turkey basted up, or we could adopt, right? I don't CARE, babygirl. I just wanna have it with YOU. Do YOU?"

"Boy, you can sure throw a curve. I couldn't for years, you know, being away, so it was of out of the question for me. I could NOW. I don't KNOW. We have to really think about this. Just how long have you been keeping this in?"

"I , I, um, always wanted one of my own, so…YOU know… I met you and I kinda knew you were the one I wanted to have it with."

"What? You mean you wanted to right away?"

"Yeah. Like the minute I met ya."

These two issues would simmer for a long time…right up to the end.

> ***"The flash and outbreak of a fiery mind,***
> ***A savageness in unreclaimed blood"***
> ***— HAMLET***

Sweet Jeff and I had only one real fight. It wasn't exactly a fight, but something that freaked…

Jeff and I were lying in bed one day, talking away, and we were discussing politics.

We didn't always have the same outlook on things, but it didn't bother us. On this particular day, Jeff started talking about the last presidential election that had occurred. He asked me who I'd voted for in the Democratic primary.

"I didn't vote for anybody, Jeff. I couldn't vote in that primary."

"Oh yeah…OK yeah. You're an Independent."

"No, I'm a Republican."

I don't think I've ever witnessed a person moving that fast. Just a blur of frenzied action. Jeff sprang to his feet like he'd been shot out of a jack in the box, from a lying down position, WHIPPED the sheet off the bed, and had it WRAPPED around himself before you could say reactionary. He stood by the side of the bed, and started spewing.

"You're a REPUBLICAN? YOU'RE A FUCKING REPUBLICAN? A MUTHAFUCKIN' REPUBLI… WHAT THE FUCKIN'… HOW THE …"

Holy Cow…he was SPITTING. Literally spitting MAD. I didn't know WHAT to do. Now HE'S all covered up, because it's suddenly apparent he wouldn't want to be caught naked in front of a REPUBLICAN, and there I am now, the NAKED REPUBLICAN being SPIT at by the furious Jeff.

"Jeff…JEFF…what are you DOING? Jeff, it's ME. All I said was—"

"REPUBLICANS ARE FUCKING ASSHOLES. HOW CAN YOU BE A FUCKIN'…"

Now I'm trying to cover up, because I'm the ONLY naked one in the room…with the frothing at the mouth guy I love, who doesn't RECOGNIZE me. He's scaring me, and… Is he going to get violent? The room is spinning.

"Oh GOD, Jeff, it's just ME here. Please. I'm still ME. I'm SORRY I'm a Republican. It's ME. What did I DO?" I burst into tears. Jeff seems to snap out of it, and remembering who I am, he starts to wind down a little.

"Oh shit. What'd I do? Oh FUCK. I'm sorry, babygirl." He lies down next to me, and starts rocking me, while I'm hiccupping away.

"I'm sorry, I'm sorry, baby. Don't cry, come on, all right? Shit, I made you cry. I made you CRY. I love you. **Jesus Christ I LOVE A FUCKIN' REPUBLICAN.** I'm sorry… won't say it again. Shit, babygirl"

"But it's ME, Jeff, I'm still the same…*hiccup*. I'm not the **nooge**. I mean….I dig HIM, but I don't like shooting animals…*hiccup*…ok, PEOPLE maybe, but I believe in a lot of the same things you do…*hiccup*. Now you hate me. *Hiccup*. You want me to not be a Re…*hiccup*…I'll go and…"

"No, no. I'm sorry. Fuck I'm so sorry. WHY? Why the hell are you a Republican? I mean you're so liberal. I'm STUPIFIED. FUCKIN' STUPEFIED. WHY?"

"Well, it began with daddy Jeff, he's a Republican. You know, running for judge and all…and I wanted to vote for him in the primary."

"The JUDGE is a…I mean he's a Republican? And uh…crap. I fucking can't believe it. Most amazing guy I ever… What the FUCK?"

"JEFF. I wouldn't say we're liberal OR conservative. We're just not STOOPID. Jeff, YOU of all people, YOU don't judge like that. It matters to you that much? How I'm registered? You want me to change it? I don't care if I vote in primaries or not."

"Course not. I'm kinda bein' a jerk." He's smooching to make it better now. Actually, Jeff may have CALLED himself a Liberal..... but truly? He was quite a bit more conservative than he could ever admit out loud. It really WAS adorable.

"Jeff…Martin Luther King was a Republican. Nobody likes to admit it, but…"

"Yup. No talkin'. No talking. Enough. I'm in love with a Republican. SHIT."

I think Jeff's preconceived world took a little bit of a tumble that day.

I didn't know why he had such an explosive reaction. Most of my friends can't believe I'm a Republican, but it's never made a difference to them really. And if it did, or

does make a difference, guess what? I do not view them as friends.

A few hours after we've made up, Jeff starts laughing. I mean LAUGH-ING. NOW he's getting a big KICK out of his Republican girl.

Not only that, Jeff is now strangely and HUGELY turned ON by the Republican thing. Laughing, and laughing, and repeating, "I'm FUCKIN' a REPUBLICAN."

"Uhh. Yes you are, Jeff. You sure are. I think that's quite apparent. Seems to be a good thing for ya there."

"Know what? I think I know a REPUBLICAN that needs a little LES-SON. Yeah. I need ta **FUCK** the livin' **CRAP** out of a REPUBLICAN. NOW. Come HERE. I'm gonna GIVE it to ya like you NEVER…"

Frankly, I thought this was pretty captivating. At least for a while I did. Jeff would go do a slew of dates, come back, and the Republican thing would seem to be ALL stirred up in him.

"Know what? I got sumthin' real BIG in my PANTS…and um …I put it aside just fer a fuckin' Republican. Wanna SUCK it?"

Oh lord…the Republican thing. How adorable is Jeff. Can't BELIEVE him. You BET I want to play.

"Hmmm. That's interesting, Jeff, I believe I DO wanna suck it be-cause…don't know if you're aware of this, but I happen to BE a fuckin' Republican, and this MORNING, I was thinking, I SHOULD be made to do something naughty with something BIG today. NOW I know it's seem-ingly in those eminently LIBERAL PANTS of yours. If you would do so, please, PLEASE deliver that to my door for me. I'm confident I do know what to DO with that. I'm gonna DO what a Republican does BEST. By the way, how's your Liberal TONGUE feeling? Thank you, Jeff. This has been a public service announcement."

"You gonna beg me for it?"

"Oh YEAH, I am. Can't wait. Right on my knees I'll be beggin for ya. Soon as you finish your whimperin' fer ME. I'm going to SEE what you can do for the LITTLEST Republican, you bleeding heart little **FUCK**. Come on and GET the bad REPUBLICAN, and make her do what you WANT."

"OH JEEEEsus. On my way. Two thirty."

"Think you can get outta the phone booth with the big thing in yer pants, Clark Kent?"

You know what? You don't run into that kind of fun every day.

The "Republican" thing went on for quite a spell, but after a while I started to feel funny about it.

"Hey, Jeff? Do you still dig ME, or do you just like the Republican thing??"

"WHAT? Are you CRAZY?"

"Well, I'm beginning to feel a little…well, invisible in a way. I mean I DO like…but... I don't know. Maybe I'm not ME to you anymore."

"ARE YOU KIDDIN? **NEVARD**." (Jeff always called me Nevard when he was serious. Never DID call me Vardzie).

We did not often visit the possessiveness felt toward each other, but I recall this conversation. Jeff was vainly trying to convince me that I was IT for him. I was skeptical, and not buying it:

"Nevard TELLALIAN, YOU do it for me. Never been so excited about ANYBODY. Don't you KNOW that? Haven't I TOLD you? YA can't tell?"

"Yeah, yeah…you have."

"Ya don't believe me."

"Well…not really. It's nice you want to make me feel that way, Jeff…but geez, you're all over the map. JEFF, I've spent HALF my LIFE smack dab in the BOY BUS, and after a while they forget I'm a female, so they start showing their piggy selves. I have to BLEND to get along in a world that's sort of misogynistic. I have to bite my tongue, and love the more human part of them in spite of it, or I wouldn't survive. I'm not BLIND…you think I don't know?"

"Ahh...babygirl. You think ya know. You THINK so, but you don't know my life. Look, I ...I need to do things TOO, ya know?"

"No. I don't. HOW would I know?" This was the only time Jeff really spoke about band living. He said he often felt as though he was from another world too.

"A lotta times I don't fit either, right? Like, um, I'll start shit and laugh, but you know. Fuck. I try blending TOO. It doesn't usually work. I mean, EVERYBODY THINKS I'M FUCKIN' REAL WEIRD, Nevard. It's hard. I just shut up when I can't....ahh FUCK. Yer not getting it."

He said there were people in his life who felt sorry for his seeming inability to hold on to a relationship, but that he'd been looking for somebody he would "fit" with since he was a kid. Since he was a KID??

Jeff always described us as being "funky" together. I thought that was a MILD way of putting it since he was capable of an astonishing amount of wanton ...well, you know. Oh he was a wicked thing, and pulled it out of me as well.

He told me something staggering: he had been PRACTICING the kind of behavior we displayed together in his HEAD, since he was TEN years old. The dialogue he spoke, were SCRIPTS he ran over and over and over, since he was a child. He was constantly looking to let his true self out and feel comfortable with it.

It made SOME sense to me. I was almost as obsessive in some ways...but since he was TEN? Jeff confided to me that he wouldn't dare GO there with women who were obviously not going to appreciate his conduct. When he'd find someone who WASN'T put off by his innate style, he suddenly didn't LIKE it anymore.

Part of his explanation of this phenomenon was, "You know how we're funky with us, right? So listen. I ALWAYS had it in my head and, um... I mean I studied fer years in my head, ya know? And so, here you are. OK?"

"OK, I guess."

"I just wanted what we are. I mean, OK, if I'd be with somebody that, you know, wouldn't dig it, I'd get fuckin' bored. And uh... if I actually could meet somebody like WE are, then I'd DO it for 'em. So ya'd think I'd like it, but it always made me feel kinda funny. All of a sudden, I... I'm...not interested. You know what I mean? Ya see?"

"I'm hearing you Jeff. You're talking a LOT."

"Yeah. So I wasn't stimulated. I felt real crappy. I mean nobody knew, but ummm…I'd get bored. You ASKED how long it took me ta get bored, yeah? I'm tryin' to TELL ya.

FUCK. NEVARD, I always thought somethin' was really wrong with me in that department. I was always thinking—isn't there SOMEBODY out there I'm gonna FIT with? Ever? Well, WE fit… I mean it's the whole package. We got the whole package, babygirl."

"Jeff, did you ever TELL anybody this? I mean what you were LOOK-ING for?"

"Naaah. Too weird."

Right after Jeff's stunning confession, I reminded him of the notes I'd always gotten and the crude come-ons. I told him they'd sometimes make me cry. No one understood why. I WANTED that from SOMEONE, but not from THOSE people, or anyone else I'd been with. They made me feel creepy. So WHY, I asked Jeff, did I feel right with HIM?

I've already told you…what I'd always craved, I found in HIM. Who knows what it is that ANY two people find in each other that would set off this sort of combustion?

After MY stunning confession, we silently stared at each other for a good half hour, accompanied by one "wow," and one "holy shit."

I doubt anyone KNEW what the heck he was looking for, except for re-lief from an old obsession. The last part of our talk that day was this…

"OK…you believe me NOW, Nevard?"

"Oh sure, about what you LIKE, but other than that…"

"FUCK. Why do you think I kinda grabbed you up real fast? You think I didn't see… You think I'M STUPID? Like I don't know what's after YOU?"

"Well, I'M not OUT there at the moment, but I've told you, what's al-ways after me. Babies, idiots, glomming scenesters, or all three in one."

"Yeah. That's RIGHT. Whaddya think is after ME?"

"How the hell do I know? I've never even seen YOU. You're one up on me there." (Oh damn…why are we headed here? NEVER wanted to face this.)

"There isn't anyone but YOU, Nevard. Never will be. You think I'm, ummm, some kinda big womanizer, huh?"

"You probably are. I try not to think about it."

"That's what you think though. Yeah, good, you just keep thinkin' that."

"That's what you WANT me to think?"

"YEAH." Now, Jeff is laughing.

I'm beginning to tear up, hoping he won't see.

"Hey. HEY, BABYGIRL…we're gonna be OK. I have to say it again? IT'S YOU. The Republican thing's just a bonus. It's the extra BONUS ROUND, baby girl. NO. NO. It's like the extra BONER."

"So what if I were to join the D.A.R.? That would REALLY get you going, huh?"

"D.A.R.? Like those upright, uptight lay-DEES? YEAH. You get yourself to a MEETING; I'll come FUCK you right on the, uhhh, BUFFET TABLE. That would be MORE than satisfying."

"Uh huh. I figured as much. So, how would it strike you if I up and MARRY ----------- for you? You could do the living DAYLIGHTS out of MRS. --------------. You'd self-IMPLODE."

"Yeah, I could GO for that. Do I know somebody that, uh, knows ------ -------- ? All right, if we can get **YOU** IN there, then I COULD GET IT in **YOU**."

"Very good. OK, Jeff. I'm going all out for you now. I'm joining a nice friendly white supremacy group. Geez…then you can FUCK the ENTIRE ARYAN NATION."

"Wow, WOW…uhhhh…no, I'm LOSING it now. Too much. TOO much. Little bit over the line. Nope. Nope. Can't bring myself to. Naa. Yer just MY PERSONAL Republican (laughing). I love you, ya little…"

"So happy I can be of service. I love you more, Jeff."

"Naaaah. I DO."

This is getting stupidly long, and I know why. Eventually, I'm going to have to write about the end. I've been dreading it. I think it's time now. Jeff was right. The whole package. We had to let it go, but …

> ***There's a divinity that shapes our ends,***
> ***Rough-hew them how we will.***
> ***—HAMLET***

I don't think I'm betraying Jeff by talking about the illness he didn't want known, but anyone familiar with him at ALL would have to know this by now.

I've been told that Jeff was battling his illness for about seven years. It can't be. I knew he was ill when I met him. It was obvious he was battling something serious, and I'm not sure, but I think he must have been for quite a while. He NEVER spoke about it, but the signs were there. Larger than life. Jeff seemed to have NO immune system, or possessed a severely compromised one. He caught every bug making the rounds. He couldn't fight anything off.

Maybe this was due in part to medicines he was taking. I'm picking at straws here. He left things at my house. I saw not only a huge array of vitamins, teas, etc.—but also prescriptions that looked serious.

He had healing problems. His skin told the story…bruising, rashes, and swelling, things that appeared and wouldn't go away. His feet were often a mess, he had trouble walking, balancing. Exhaustion, sore throats, night sweats…. GOD, this was a YOUNG guy…under forty when I first met him.

> *He took me by the wrist and held me hard;*
> *Then goes he to the length of all his arm….*
> *He rais'd a sigh so piteous and profound*
> *As it did seem to shatter all his bulk*
> *—HAMLET*

Jeff had considerable physical strength in SOME ways, but he was profoundly fragile in others. Although his dazzling ability to wear me out didn't diminish, the physical logistics slowly changed as he became more ill. After a couple of years, we stopped in the middle of my staircase, because he couldn't WALK all the way up without stopping for a spell, but he'd STILL take advantage of the intermission to mess with me. Unbelievable.

His always-desirous proclivity to slam me upon any table or counter became, as time went on, a way for Jeff to have fun that was less stressful for his slowly diminishing agility. He had something to LEAN on.

Jeff's health started heading downhill. I could see, feel, and sense the decline of that inspiring vibrancy. It was shattering to see. It might be, since I wasn't with him all the time, I had a clear view of the difference a little time made.

This man was a GIVER, and could never say no. He gave to the band, and he ALWAYS appreciated his fans. No matter what it entailed, because that's why he was there. For his fans and for the music. It's what he lived for. He gave to them, he gave to his community, he gave to struggling musicians, he gave to a huge amount of causes, and he was always gracious. And it cost him. I think it shortened his life.

The play's the thing.
—HAMLET

I once heard a friend make a comment about Jeff's band. She didn't know I'd been involved with him. "I used to LOVE the Blanks, but they didn't get along, and so it ruined their viability for me. What kind of integrity is that? It makes it all a sham, doesn't it?"

NO, IT DOES NOT. Her thinking was entirely and PRECISELY, ASS BACKWARDS.

Yes, I knew that Jeff wasn't always on good terms with all the members of his band. Not speaking to this or that one (I didn't know he'd barely spoken to one for years), and of course the rest of the band had "not getting along" times betwixt and between them too. It may have gotten to a "we ALL hate each other" point. Who knows? I didn't have details, and they don't matter.

What matters is this: The play's the **thing**. The music's the **thing**. The art's the **thing**. The search for an AIDS vaccine's the **thing**.

Whatever endeavor might inexorably entwine any group together, if they have a DESIRE for what they have created, then the TASK itself, is worth WHATEVER it takes to keep proclaiming it, even if the price is dear.

It is THAT DESIRE—the willingness to endure for the sake of that creation, which separates the **yahoos** from the dedicated.

Chaos off stage and perfection on. THAT'S not a sham. THAT'S ARTISTRY. It's a profound recognition of the whole being greater than its parts.

It didn't matter HOW they were or were not getting along. Once on a stage, and practicing what they'd given birth to, that "getting the job done" challenge was all that existed.

There are not that many truly revolutionary moments in any art. This band was INDISPUTABLY one of them. No ifs, ands, or buts. And the countless musicians they inspired can attest to that fact. When you are a part of something that truthful, you don't stop doing it. You just DON'T.

AND THAT, MY FRIENDS, **IS** INTEGRITY.
Jeff would have done it for NOTHING. He knew what they had.

> *"If you ask me what I came to do in this world, I, as an artist will answer: I AM HERE TO LIVE OUT LOUD."*
> *—Emile Zola*

There IS no band that doesn't have a degree of inner turmoil—one member wants to take things over THERE, another wants to add a zither. Egos clash, you're SICK of living in each other's pockets, WHO'S really the boss here, hey, I had MY eye on that one—you can expect it.

I might not have been as huge a road rat as some, but I think I can safely conclude, that having climbed, and sometimes crawled on stages almost 2,000 times (often not in the vicinity of home), I'm reasonably sure I'd be considered as good a source as any for "band living" info.

In Jeff's case, the endurance it took for him to travel and perform was at times dangerous for him. It was rough to see him going, when he had NO BUSINESS doing it.

The most wretched part is that Jeff was pushed, mocked, and made fun of by some. He was bullied into going when he was NOT up to it, and at times accused of exaggerating his condition.

I know there were people who were cruel. He DID let that out, and it made him feel lonely. But he still wouldn't tell me what was up.

I can't honestly say that it was completely the fault of those who were unfeeling; after all, Jeff didn't TELL anyone how ill he was. He did his damnedest to hide it. Did people have no EYES though? No SENSE?

I knew what he looked and sounded like when he was sick. He couldn't hide it from me over the phone either. His tone, words he could barely speak, the exhaustion was obvious. I'd hear it, and know what an effort it was going to be for him to just SING and STAND. I begged him to cut back. There had to be others that tried. He didn't want to let them down. He had a will of IRON. Damn him. I was so afraid for him.

**Jeff NEVER gave up. EVER. If it was important to him, or something he knew might be important to OTHERS…
he SOLDIERED ON.**

He did it with grit, and a kind of backbone you don't often see in ANYONE. He did it with a smile and a laugh. He did it with an outward OPTIMISM that wouldn't be dampened. He did it trying not to rain on anyone else's parade. I'm not saying he could always pull it off. He couldn't. But he NEVER stopped TRYING.

NEVER.

A break from this sadness is needed. Still can't face the rest.

Jeff called me from the road sometimes, the calls invariably (invariably because, well, Jeff was JEFF) began to turn into love fests. When his calls began to head in the direction of merrymaking, Jeff stopped caring what time it was on MY end of the phone, because he could only call …well, you'll see.

The first time he executed one of these delicate procedures, he woke me up.

"Babygirl. Babygirl? It's uhhh Jeff. (As if I wouldn't recognize him.) I'm missing you like CANDY. Like fuckin' CANDY. Can't fuckin' sleep. I'm thinking' bout… when's the last time I had some babygirl REFRESH-MENT?"

"I miss you too. Damn. Jeff, you know what time it is here?"

"Woke yoo up, DID I? Sorry. No. No…I'm NOT. Love you sleepy. You're fuckin' SWEET when you're sleepy. Like candy."

Now I'm laughing. "OK, what's with the CANDY thing, Jeff? THAT'S new."

"I've been thinking what I wanna DO ta you, when I see ya. I can't fucking STAND it. Let's do it…let's fuckin' do it NOW. I got it planned OUT."

"Planned out?" Ohhhh boy.

"I've got it ALL figured out. I'm going to tell you what you're in for next time I…"

"Jeff…JEFF…are we doing PHONE SEX? I've never DONE that."

"Me EITHER. It's gonna be GREAT, right? All right, let's DO it."

"I'm game…though I don't know if I can do this without laughing. Wait. WAIT. JEFF. Where the heck ARE you?"

"Uhh, what difference does…you mean the name of the fuckin' town?"

"Not the TOWN. I mean, you must be in the LOBBY PHONE BOOTH, Jeff; you don't call from your ROOM. You're in the LOBBY? Oh God, don't tell me you're in the STREET."

"Naaah naah. I'm in the lobby. Why?"

"WELL, uhh…Jeff the LOBBY would be PUBLIC. You want to have PHONE SEX in PUBLIC? IN THE LOBBY? Of a HOTEL?"

"Yeah, it's OK. Nobody's here. It's LATE. ALL PLANNED out, baby-girl. I came down five times tonight. I've been thinking for …ohhh, I don't know, few days, few days, few weeks, few weeks, few months."

"God, I love you. You're CRAZY. HOW are you going to…are you supposed to ask what I'm wearing?"

"No, YOU are. All right, I'm IN the booth, and I've got a…a shirt on my lap. NOBODY's gonna see. Yeah, what ARE ya wearing?"

"My blue nightie."

"Oh yeah? The one with…uhh, the ruffleeee bottom, or the one…AHHH FUCK. Just **pull** IT the **FUCK** UP. PULL UP THE NIGHTIE, NEVARD. I'm NEEDIN' TA FUCK you NOW. JUST CUT THE CRAP, I don't have all DAY, ya little CUNT. I can almost TASTE ya….so SHUT the FUCK UP, and start getting BUSY, cause your MAN'S gonna talk trash, till you… Oh FUCK, the shirt fell off."

God, it was funny…but he called me Nevard, so he meant business.

OHHHH…I'm not laughing NOW…because he's starting to give off some pretty intense heat… think I'd better just HEEL. WOAH.

"Nightie is OFF, Jeff. OFF."

"Yeah. Good girl." And it started.

His voice was so delicious; he could have read me the back of a Quaker Oats box and gotten the same response.

This is the very ecstasy of love.

—HAMLET

"HOLY CRAP, JEFF. I think you missed your CALLING. YOU'RE JUST…you could maybe have a SIDE career there."

"Yeah? REALLY? You liked it, babygirl? So…uhhh I was GOOD?"

"GOOD? GOOD? Jeff, I might not need to actually SEE you ever again."

"Ummm…no, no…don't want it being THAT good. FUCK, I miss, you know, all the kissin' an' shit, babygirl. So, next time, YOU'RE talking. Taaaaa –MARROW, TAMORROW"

"I hate that song. How long did you plan your hot talking, ANNIE?"

"Ah, a few weeks. TOOOMORROW—same bat time, same bat place."

"You get a couple WEEKS, and I get only a DAY? WHY? Not FAIR."

"BECAUSE, you're uhhh better at the WORDS. Yer the Wordsmith. Babygirl…sing me a song? 'I'll Be Home for Christmas'?"

"OK."

"Love that. In my dreams, ya know. You're in my dreams, babygirl. I love you…love you in my dreams."

"Me too. In every dream."

SILENCE. I'm not hearing Jeff's last words and the click. What's wrong here?

"Uhhhh, JEFF? Are you still THERE?"

"Yeah."

"Ummm…Jeff…did you maybe, uhhh, plan getting IN the phone booth and FORGET to plan getting OUT of the PHONE BOOTH?"

"**Yup**."

Jeff wouldn't tell me how sick he was, even when he was aware that I knew. He'd never acknowledge it. A few years later, my father did the same damn thing. He wouldn't tell about the chemo OR the PORT in his chest. "Oh, just for my heart." He wouldn't tell my mother, his darling of SIXTY years.

Jeff comported himself in an identical way. I've never seen anything like it. I had to bring Jeff to my family doctor once. He was a wonderful man.

When Doc finished with Jeff's problem, an infection that wasn't healing, we thought if Doc could fit me in, I should get some yearly exam stuff done.

Jeff was oddly EAGER for me to see Doc that day, and he had no problem marching himself right IN there with me. He just muscled his way in.

"Where do you think you're going, Jeff?"

"I'm going wit choo. I'll be comin' with you-oo oo oo, oo oo oo...and you'll be with me too-oo oo oo, oo oo oo. Let's go and look!"

Oh THIS is going to be PEACHY. Jeff's following me and singing his version of the "Indian Love Call." Let's keep in mind, Doc was also my gynecologist. The kind of old fashioned doctor that didn't know bout no privacy practices. If someone came in with you, he didn't care if it was a STRANGER you'd pulled in off the street, he'd discuss things with them as if you weren't even THERE. In fact he would almost let them HELP with the exam. I don't think you could imagine how this THRILLED Jeff.

"So, everything looking great there, Doc? Verrrry good. Uh HUH."

GEEZ, do you think Jeff could maybe keep his HEAD out of the way? I was getting a little annoyed. And THEN Doc starts in with the thing he'd invariably discuss with me EVERY year—my smallness, and what this would mean in terms of child bearing. Oh geez.

"Yeah, she's kinda little there, huh, Doc? OK, that's real nice fer, uhhh, for ME, but, ya know, my girl can't WALK when I'm going home. Soo...maybe it's a little too much for her. You got any suggestions?"

HOLY CRAP. No, they are NOT talking about this together. This is MORTIFYING. And I'm looking at Jeff's serious and completely engrossed face and just want to SMACK him one.

"Well, Jeff, my suggestion would be some more lubrication, which should cut down on undue friction that may be irritating to..."

"MORE? Really? Yeah? I don't think... like you know...between her and THEN we've got my SPIT factor so... I really...you know, I kinda think we got more than enough happening THERE."

Doc is plainly not disturbed by Jeff's questions, but by now, I'm lying there with my hand over my eyes, and I'm shaking with the laughing I'm trying to keep in, because Jeff is so very EARNEST in his questioning, and there I am with my feet in the STIRRUPS. Ohhhh, how did I know this was going to be a doozy? A DOOZY.

"AHH, SPIT. Yes, yes... Then you should get something water soluble so it will mix with SPIT in a way that won't..."

"Yeah, OK, get it. We're gonna be SWIMMING. We can DROWN…gonna be fuckin' swimming. Oh sorry, Doc. All right, so we should get the KY, and…"

GEEZ, I CAN'T TAKE ANYMORE. THIS IS SURREALISTIC. IS SALVADORE DALI IN THE HOUSE? THE DALAI LAMA? Some Dali's here. WHO'S HERE?

"No, I wouldn't use KY. It IS water soluble, but it is also…"

Doc suggests a different product, and Jeff says, "Huh. Huh. OK, Doc. So, uhh that stuff wouldn't, you know, TASTE real funny, would it?"

HOLY CRAP. NOW I THINK WE'RE BEYOND THE SURREALISM, and quickly MOVING RIGHT INTO A DADA SCENARIO. IS MARCEL DUCHAMPS HERE? IS HE THE ONE WITH THE FUR COVERED TOILET SEAT? IS HE HERE? WILL THIS EVER END?????

Doc, bless his heart, begins to DRAW one of his famous illustrations. OF MY INSIDES. And the two of them have their heads together over it.

"Now, Jeff, Nevard is very small boned, and so not only is…blah blah…so as you can observe, here is the beginning of her cervix, and her ovaries are right about HERE…I can easily…blah blah…. Now if you can see how narrow her hip bones…blah blah… I do think she would need a Cesarean section in order to…"

"Oh yeaaaa. Huh. I can seeee, Doc. There's not much room there to…oh FUCK. Sorry. Ya think I'm BANGIN' into her? I could be um INJURING her? CRAP."

"Oh no. I don't think so, Jeff. I wouldn't be concerned. You would both know if you were doing any actual DAMAGE because there would be a GREAT deal of discomfort, and to…"

"Yeah, oh good…OK, OK…. So you kind of think the C SECTION would be necessary, the way to go, if, ummm…"

I simply remained SILENT at this point, because I could have easily wandered OUT of there, and they wouldn't have known. BLAH BLAH

But break, my heart, for I must hold my tongue
—HAMLET

As we were leaving the doctor's office, I looked at Jeff. He was limping a little, but doing it in a BOUNCY way. I don't know if Jeff was able to whistle, but if he was, I think he would have been at that moment. Limping, bouncing, and whistling, with that radiant smile on his face. The smile I loved. The smile that was so sweet and beautiful it would rip your heart open.

We got in the car, and Jeff was still grinning away as if he'd just been to the carnival.

"You wanna go pick up some of, you know, that STUFF? Ya know, that C Section. We could do that, right? Are you up for it?"

It was at that moment I burst into tears.

"What the FUCK? What's the matter, babygirl? NEVARD?"

"Nothing, Jeff." Sniffle. "I just love you."

"Well yeah, COURSE ya do. Is that making you CRY? I belong tooo YOU ooh ooh ohh… What's WRONG? I made you cry? Babygirl, don't make me all fuckin' weepy now. FUCK. Oooh, your NOSE is red. You hate the red NOSE. I like the red nose. Ahhhh, come here, Nevard. No crying. Don't know what's gotten INTA you. Ya fuckin' REPUBLI- CANS…lookit whatcha did to babygirl…"

Oh, Jeff… I knew what had gotten into me. I looked at you that day, and my heart started to ache. It was becoming more difficult to hide, each time I saw you. And every minute became more precious.

I looked at you that day, and you were so happy, and I knew—had always known—you just wanted to have a happy normal life, just make the love, make the music, cuddle up with someone that adored you, and maybe that baby you wanted so badly.

I looked at your smiling face, Jeff, and I knew I couldn't make it happen for you. DAMMIT. I wanted you to have that. Whatever you wanted. What you deserved. And it just wasn't going to HAPPEN. Ever. You were getting sicker, and my heart was shattering. I felt RAGE and helplessness. I hated whatever the HELL made this happen to you. Why couldn't it have been me? Go ahead, DAMMIT…I'll take it. Just please let it leave him. Leave him alone. Please.

A few days after the appointment, Doc called me. He was, after all, a family friend as well as our doctor.

"I think your friend, Jeff, has serious trouble. What I saw should not pose a health risk for someone in his age bracket. He seems to have neuropathy starting. Not a condition normally seen in someone that young, and

I'd be inclined to think it is a secondary syndrome that indicates…well…it could be a number of things. Is he seeing doctors? Is he being treated?"

My "learned in the cradle" desire to shelter loved ones, caused me a great deal of agony when I faced Jeff's illness, and my father's. NEITHER of them understood my NEED to know, to help and comfort, and BE there with them. THEIR protectiveness clashed with MINE.

I can tell you, with unquestioning certainty…

Jeff KNEW that he was going to leave this earth a lot sooner than he should have. He knew it when I met him, and felt it without a DOUBT within a few years.

He did not often LET himself articulate the fact of his own mortality. For the most part he would not, and COULD NOT face it.

But he knew. In his heart of hearts, he knew.…

During the last year and a half of our attachment, more things began to slip out of him. They became louder as time went on.

I saw him shed tears only a few times at my house, and during our very last phone calls. I'm sorry. This is getting harder. Here's more Jeff fun.

When Jeff would visit, if it was a work day, I'd call in sick. A few times, I had to go in for a few hours, and Jeff was left to his own devices. Hmmm. The first time this happened, I gave him an 800 number in case he felt the need to call. OHH, he CALLED all right, and they thought he was a customer. Rhonda took his call, something I'm sure she'll never forget.

"Is, uhhh, Nevard there?"

"May I have your account number?"

"Whaa? PLEASE, I WOULD LIKE TO SPEAK WITH Nevard."

"ALL right, sir. Do you have your Social Security number?"

"My SOCIAL SECURITY NUMBER? OK, uhhh, I was very POLITE. I JUST wanna talk to NEVARD. WHAT the FUCK's that gotta do with my fucking SOCIAL? Just tell her JEFF called." SLAM.

Yeah…THAT'S my guy. You go GET 'em, JUNIOR.

Rhonda advised me that swearing Jeff had called, and when I got back to him, he was flustered. "My SOCIAL SECURITY. What the…?" I had to explain they were trying to pull up his account. They thought he was a customer.

"OH. Uh, maybe you better tell that girl sorry. Whatcha want fer DINNER?"

I didn't realize what he was doing while I was out. He went through EVERY SINGLE closet, drawer, nook and cranny at home. He did it a few times. And what did Jeff DO during those rummage fests? He left little NOTES. Left them everywhere. I found notes for years.

"This is a nice cleaning product, babygirl."

"Don't like the SOCK COLOR. All WRONG for you."

"GREAT spatuuuulllaaa. I love you."

"Is this coat kind of scratchy? Because it's wool, and your skin's sensitive."

"How come you never wear this for ME, Nevard?"

"When you going to FUCK me? I need a TIME. "

"This soap smells good. Can we use it, or is it for special company? Am I special company?"

"Ohhhh, did you write this? Real good. Real good. When are you going to finish it? You need to finish it."

"I need to LICK you. Where ARE you? My tongue's ready. OK...NOW?"

"Have you read this book, babygirl? Because I think it might be too disturbing for you. No disturbing…love you."

"Could you organize this drawer a little? This is messy, messy, messy."

"How come you need so many screwdrivers? I don't screw you enough?"

"I love you, love you, love you, love you. Nice shirt."

HUNDREDS OF THEM.

I asked him, "Jeff, aren't you ASHAMED of yourself, going through every single thing of mine?"

His reply was, **"Huh? Whaaaaat? No. I enjoy it."**

Darnit, thought it would be diverting, but it made the tears come. Can I ever face this?

Please help me.

Put it off. Stave it off a little longer.

Once, Jeff demanded one of the MOST appalling "fun" plans I'd heard. Here goes. Hope you don't cringe. He'd be hoping you DO cringe.

"Babygirl, whatcha been doin' today?"

"I was just out working in the garden."

"In the garden? The GARDEN, right? Yeah, pretty hot out today."

"I guess so. It IS pretty."

(Oh my…I could SAY it to you I think, but I just can't write this one down. Sorry, Jeff. I know it would thrill you to pieces. OK…here's the gist of it).

"WHAAAAAATTTTTT? Jeff, when are you coming? I SEE where this one's heading. I REALLY don't think I want to—"

"HEY LOOK. I don't give a FUCK what YOU want, BITCH. It's what **I** want."

"Yes, you do."

"Yes, I do **WHAT**?"

"Yes, you DO give a fuck what I want."

"Yeahhhh, I know. I know I DO. But uhhh…I've been PLANNIN'."

"Ohhh boy. The planning. This one's disgusting. Most times you're both ADORABLE and disgusting, Jeff—quite fetching actually—but NOW, you're just disgusting."

"FUCK you. No adorable. I'm NOT fuckin' **ADORABLE** today. I'm settin' a MOOD."

"OK, I GET it, Jeff. Usually you're BEARABLE and disgusting. That better?"

"Yep. I'm disgusting. You're the fuckin' wordsmith. I'm the licker. Let's get our ROLES straight. And uhhh…ya got some rope? Never mind. I'll find…"

(Skipping more salacious talk here. Sorry…too much again)

"You think so, Jeff? Think you're going to get your way?"

"Oh, I don't THINK. I KNOW. Get USED TO IT, ya little CUNT. I don't want your BACKTALK EITHER, OK? "

"Allrighty then, Jeff. Although I don't know—"

"I said no BACKTALK. You're GETTIN it. And yer gettin' it fuckin' SLOW…an' I BETTER not hear…I'm gonna get yoo in LINE. In MY fuckin' LINE. Mmm…I love you, babygirl."

HERE'S what I'm trying to convey to you. I LOVE you, babygirl? At the end of a rapacious RANT? I tried to keep the giggles in. DARNIT, in spite of his outrageous rant—that precious part of him was STILL in the mix. It always WAS. Just couldn't help himself. Who in the world wouldn't love this man?

Jeff always said "we're gonna be ok" or "everything's gonna be all right, babygirl." He said it a lot. I mean A LOT. I asked my friend Claudia if a lot of Jeff's songs contained phrases like that. She said yes, they sure did. I had a feeling they would have.

It's crazy, but my collection of his recordings never **did** grow after I met Jeff. There were some CDs later, but I think the guy that had moved in bought them. I couldn't listen to Jeff's voice, and I'd ask him to turn it down.

There must be a lot I've never heard. Sometimes things in progress, but not end results. I know he didn't want me to SEE him, and I guess he didn't want me to HEAR him either. It's more than strange. He always wanted to hear ME.

Jeff liked to show up with treats. Little ones. Tea, a hair clip…things like that. He'd remember and celebrate not only lovely things but the most RI-DICULOUS as well.

"So, I gotcha like a little something, babygirl. Remember? All right, a YEAR ago THIS WEEK? It was the FIRST time I stuck my tongue up yer NOSE. SHIT. Ya told me if I ever did THAT again, ya'd SNAP me like a FUCKING TWIG. Yup. Now THERE'S somethin' ta CELEBRATE. Dontcha THINK so?"

He began to fret about my future. He couldn't keep it at bay. One night he presented me with something insane.

"What the heck?"

"But WHAT, babygirl? Don't say it, don't say it, all right? I just shopped, OK?"

"I'm sorry. No, I HAVE to. I can't let you…have you taken leave of your senses? This is… holy CRAP. It's a ten THOUSAND bucks, lovely thing."

"How do YOU know?"

"Because this is an antique, sweetie. I'd say late nineteenth century. Art Nouveau…Pre Deco, and English? Jeff, this is beautiful, but you're CRA-ZY. I can't KEEP this JEFF. You can't just throw away… You NEED that dough."

"No, I don't."

"Well, what if you DO in the FUTURE? This is altogether too MUCH, Jeff."

"Yeah I know. I want you to have it, NEVARD. I want you safe."

"What're you talking about…safe?"

"YOU might NEED it. ALL RIGHT? What if I get hit by a truck or somethin' like that?"

"Then I'll just have to sell the FUCKING Pre REVOLUTIONARY FREAKIN' TALLBOY in the KITCHEN that I keep the GARBAGE BAGS in, WON'T I?"

"WHAA?"

"JEFF. I have antiques. Years ago, it was like shopping at Goodwill." (Jeff touched the tallboy a lot after that…he loved its age.) "You take this back, and get me something LITTLE. I CAN'T keep this, honey. Wouldn't be right."

"Naahh…. I NEED ta make sure you're OK. Babygirl…can't we get married? OK? Then you'd, um, be protected. SHIT. I wanna do it. You're always askin' the questions. OK, if we got married, you'd be PROTECT-ED. You know…by LAW and, um, I mean nobody uhh would dare con-test…"

"JESUS, you're scaring me. Are you talking about your WILL? HUH? You're not going anywhere for a long, long time. Not if I can help it you're not. NO."

This was the first time Jeff addressed his mortality out loud. HE was facing it, being utterly heroic. For me. I was the coward who was afraid to look.

"Ahhh…baby, anything could happen, you know. I'm not sayin' it IS. I just wanna make sure. Yup, always, um, makin' you cry. I'm FUCKING GOOD."

Darnit, I didn't want him to see me cry. I've already started to let him down, and he's holding me, comforting me. This isn't the WAY.

"I DON'T WANT your money, Jeff. I'm hustling now, but I'm TELL-ING you, I might be MORE SET than YOU. You can stop fussing. Just STOP it."

"Yeah? Then I gotta marry YOU, so ya know, so I'M set. HEY, baby-girl, stop cryin'. Does the Judge know you're struggling? Sooo, um, how SET you gonna BE?"

"Oh geez… I don't like the folks OR you to see when I'm struggling and the answer is…pretty set. You want to marry ME to be more set? You got it. Any time. I don't want yours, that's for your family, and whomever. OK?"

"You ARE family, baby girl. OK? Don't think I'm not gonna CHECK on that SET thing…cause I AM."

"I'm sure you will. No doubt in my mind. Oh for goodness sake, Jeff, YOU helped me to BE set. Have you no recollection of that?"'

"I want some sugar. Fork it OVER."

True to form, Jeff pretended to take it back, and hid it in a drawer, with the usual note. "It's pretty. Just like you. I love you, babygirl."

I've never shown it.

> **During the entire time I was seeing this man, he carried on his seemingly frail shoulders inexorably mounting physical horrors. A seemingly endless nightmare that felt unstoppable and made him frightened.**

> **He carried it alone.**

> **He carried it with a degree of silence, strength, and bravery that was mind boggling, because he didn't want it to change the people around him.**

> **That unflagging degree of confidence and faith.**

> **That astonishing and absolute certainty he never failed to express… "Everything's gonna be all right."**

> **That CHANT, like a magical mantra, repeated until there was a possibility it might just come true.**

> **That outward posture of fellowship, cheer and interest, worn like the cloak of a champion.**

> **Like the champion he WAS.**

He didn't wear rose colored glasses for nuthin'.

Jeff was a complex man, and constantly at war with himself. His true nature was that of a generous soul, but he could act out selfishly. He talked about it once, and felt guilty. I think his lifelong struggles, even though he accomplished things that brought him a degree of self-worth, that EVERY SINGLE DAY fight left him with a never-ending mourning. It left him with a deep desire to have some things, dammit, SOMETHING for HIMSELF.

He gave away, with a great deal of effort, almost everything that was in him. Or, it was taken from him. Once in a while, he had a greedy compulsion to grab on, and who could blame him? I sure as heck couldn't bear to see him denied anything, because the love I gave WAS the love I got.

I went out one day, and returned to find Jeff sitting in a chair listening to a recording of mine he had found. I could hear the song "Stay With Me" coming out of the speakers. Tears were streaming down his face. Oh God...Oh God.

I dropped what I was carrying, and fell to the floor, my head in his lap. "What is it, what is it, what's wrong?"

"Oh, babygirl...I never in my life heard, um, I mean, I can't do that. FUCK. Your innards laid out. No shame. No shame. I'm lucky. I mean to ever HEAR that. People can't do that. They CAN'T. You even know? I want people to HEAR it, and I never told. I can't, all right? I'm a FUCKING BASTARD. I'm so fucking SELFISH, and you never deserved it, babygirl."

"What's WRONG with you? I KNOW you love what I do. I respect your opinion, Jeff, so it feels sweet to me. I don't CARE who you didn't tell. It wouldn't have MATTERED."

"SWEET? It's not FUCKING SWEEEET, NEVARD. You're NAKED AND RIGHTEOUS. It's ya know, it's DEVOTION. You sing truth. I should've helped, like, get it OUT. What's that SHIT on there behind ya?"

"Jeff. I never played this for you because I hate the SHIT behind me. JEFF. STOP THIS. You wouldn't have been able to HELP me more than I was ALREADY helped. Would have made NO difference. NONE. Just STOP it, you schmo."

"I'm MORE than a fucking idiot. You know how I feel? You REALLY know? FUCK. You always WILL be, always WILL be. I'm stupid. How much TIME did I waste on...so much time. I could have had you. We could've had each other. I'm gonna lose you, Nevard. All right? I mean, I don't wanna do it … I'm gonna lose you…"

"YES, you're an idiot, and NO, you're not losing me."

I had no idea what some of it meant. The "wasted time" he'd alluded to before, but like all the other vagaries he uttered…I didn't know until now.

"I think we're gonna run out, ya know? SHIT…outta time. It'll be OK. We'll be all right? Let's have the baby, all right? We'll be together more, and, um, are we having swordfish tonight? You gotta sing me that song, babygirl. Sing me really good."

AND I CAN'T AVOID IT ANYMORE with my Jeff stories.

After that day, Jeff continued to be amorous as ever, but something changed in his eyes. There was wistfulness, sadness, fright, unbearable tenderness, a yearning, and a need to feel every second. Time for us was running out.

> *O help him, you sweet heavens!*
> *Oh heavenly powers, restore him!*
> *—HAMLET*

After that day, I knew, just as surely as he did. We were beginning to unravel.

After that day, our declarations of love poured from us faster and faster.

After that day, he held me tighter than he ever had—and began to slowly push me away.

Just as Jeff had prescribed from the beginning what our relationship would be, he determined the end of it with resolve and strength. I could only oblige, and follow his wishes.

I don't know when Jeff received the diagnosis of the damnable beast that was to take him. Take that glorious man. Maybe the illness I'd witnessed in those first few years was a mild version of it. Perhaps it was a precursor. I've no idea.

The dream that had meant so much to Jeff was the first thing he loosened his grip on. He'd been flying on the baby idea forever, and the only man I'd ever considered it with, was Jeff.

Yes. I should have. Yes. He wanted it so badly, and Jeff would have been the most wonderful and loving daddy.

I still carry a lot of guilt. I wavered, and maybe I shouldn't have. One night, lying in bed, holding each other, just as we would be with the letting go of everything over the course of that year, he sighed, and said, "Nevard, we can't have the baby. I want to… Oh FUCK. I wanna have it with you."

"Why can't we, Jeff? Because of your reprehensible potty mouth?" Sometimes I'd try to keep things light, so these things wouldn't press even harder on our hearts. It didn't help.

"Naaah. I just don't think, uhhh, I don't think it would be fair to ya. I mean, you know…I'm away so much. Everything would fall on you."

"Are you sure, sweetie? Because if you want it, you got it, Toyota. I mean it, Jeff, I'm down with ya. I could handle it."

"No, I don't think we better… FUCK. I wanna see a little girl, just like my babygirl. I love you so much. I love ya so fuckin' much. So much."

Jeff's face was snuggled up to my back, and I could feel his tears.

Oh God, I'm sorry, Jeff. I think though, by then he knew he didn't want me to be there to see what was in store for him. I believe he'd already made that decision, and had set it stubbornly in stone, so he was right…how would it have worked? Send me the baby, but don't YOU come over?

Doubt thou the stars are fire;
Doubt that the sun doth move;
Doubt the truth to be a liar;
But never doubt I love.
—HAMLET

"Nevard, you really love me? I mean…uhhh it's really ME you love, right? There hasn't been anybody else yer lovin' like ME, has there?"

"WHAT? Who the FUCK do you THINK I've been? ARE you FUCKIN' BLIND, JEFF? What's WRONG with you? You REALLY think I've been forking over the same kind of lovin' to somebody else

TOO? WHAT…I'm feeling the SAME WAY… about …oh I don't know…maybe a few MORE all this time? I wouldn't be ABLE to give…oh shut UP, Jeff."

"Well, you know….you know… I just…"

"NO. I DON'T KNOW. What are you THINKING? Do you wanna know how MUCH I LOVE you, YOU PLANK HEADED SON OF A BITCH? What do you think I WOULDN'T do for you?"

"OK, babygirl. I'm sorry."

"You BETTER be SORRY, or I'll kick your SORRY ASS round the CORNER. I would TAKE the BULLET for you, Jeff. NO hesitation. THAT'S how much. You GET it now?"

Jeff went off. He began to yell at me, with an anger and determination I had never seen before. I'd never heard him like this.

"No, NO. **NO**. I'm not **LETTIN' YOU** TAKE ANY BULLET. That's **MY** JOB, and you're **NOT** gonna stand in the WAY of **THAT**. Do **YOU** get **ME** now, NEVARD? **You fuckin' GET me? YOU'RE MY BABY. DON'T TAKE THAT AWAY FROM ME. DON'T YOU DARE TRY TO TAKE IT. I'M NOT GONNA HAVE IT"**

We were defining our end. No. I'm wrong. JEFF was defining it…resolute and strong- minded. Exactly and as tenaciously as he'd governed the beginning.

So DID I ever mother Jeff? NO. NO, I did NOT. It sure wasn't an easy task. It was difficult NOT TO mother him. He sure as heck needed it.

I'd fret over him when he wasn't looking though. I did it when he was asleep. I'd feel his face, his body, put my head on his chest and listen to his heart. And I'd cry. He caught me just a couple of times.

"Babygirl…what's wrong?"

"Nothing. Just a bad dream."

"Awww, baby. Just a dream, just a dream." And the sheltering arms would go around me.

The rest is silence.
—HAMLET

Having trouble finishing this. No more trouble than Jeff and I had though.

I haven't been on the beach for weeks. I've been writing this…but Jeff and I had often dreamed of coming here. He yearned to BE at NASA to hear the thunder, see the ground moving, to see the fiery lift off, and the separation. He wanted to meet an astronaut and ask questions.

> **When sorrows come, they come not single spies,**
> **But in battalions.**
> **—HAMLET**

Jeff would have loved it here, would have loved the night and the phosphorescent fishes to be held in your hand for a moment. The warm salty water under the stars. The grief is coming on strong, as it has been these last few weeks.

The last two times we were together, I could see his illness showing in a more tangible way. I can't summon the fortitude I would need to describe our last hours together. Hours that seemed to span a moment, but needed to stretch to infinity. They were filled with love and wonder. They were filled with horror, and a thirst that would never be quenched again.

We spoke on the phone regularly; even visited "Jeff's phone merriment." His phone calls became slowly less regular, and oh…I questioned. What is happening? What is going ON? I don't care—please tell me. Please. Let me come. I received only riddles. Always declarations of love, and wanting…always promises of "beating" his problems. Never telling me what the problems WERE, but asking, and asking…did I still want him? Could he come be with me when things were OK? Yes. Yes. YES Jeff. YES.

> **I must be cruel, only to be kind;**
> **Thus bad begins and worse remains behind.**
> **—HAMLET**

Jeff sounded tired one day. After a bit he said, "I don't want you to be alone. Don't want that for you. Don't wanna know…"

He couldn't finish the sentence.

"Jeff…are you cutting me loose? Have you found someone else? What? JESUS…WHAT?"

"NO. NO, NEVARD. There's never GONNA be. FUCK. Oh FUCK. I LOVE YOU."

Click.

Be thou assur'd, if words be made of breath,
And breath of life, I have no life to breathe
What thou hast said to me.
—HAMLET

I had already started having the dreams by then, and they intruded more and more often. Dreams of Jeff hurting. I just can't write everything we told each other during phone calls…precious words I still have.

He'd want me to write this part.

"You OK, babygirl? You're, like, not alone?"

"Yes, Jeff. Yes. I'm…"

"I don't wanna FUCKING HEAR. Don't let me HEAR. Need to know. Know you're not alone."

"Are YOU, Jeff? Please, don't shut me out. DAMN you. You're stubborn."

"NEVARD. Babygirl. I want ya ta HEAR me. You listening?"

"Yes, darling…I'm listening."

"I'm taking the bullet. You remember? REMEMBER? I always KNEW. I'M TAKIN' THE FUCKING BULLET HERE. It's what I WANT. WHAT I NEED. I NEED TA LEAVE IT PERFECT. I need it, Nevard. NO asking…please. **Just give this to me if ya still love me.**"

I spoke with Jeff twice more after that day. He wanted to know if I'd seen photos of him. I could tell, he didn't want me to. His voice had fear in it.

"You seen, um, any pictures of me around?"

"No. Why? You been up to no good, Jeff? Huh?"

"Naah. Um, yup, up ta no good. No good."

He wanted me to sing to him.

"Babygirl, sing me the Christmas song, ya know…I like that one."

After I did, he said, "Yeah…I'll be with you, babygirl. You're in my dreams. We'll have Christmas together? Always wanted that. Can ya sing that one about how I'm gonna love youuuuu? Ya know the one?"

"Come Rain Or Come Shine?"

"That's the one. You, um... ya DO love me, the way nobody else could. I love you good enough, Nevard? HAVE I? Tell me, babygirl."

And I told him. I told him again, and again. And I don't know how I sang or spoke at all, with the tears running.

The very last time I heard his voice, was…god, I don't know quite how long before he was taken. It was a call filled with pain and longing, but also filled to overflowing with the final and loving things Jeff wanted to tell me. And what I needed to tell him. I'm going to tell you some. Part of it his loved ones will want to know.

"Babygirl, sing me that song. I love that song. You know, bein' in your room."

In my room, I can see you late at night,

In my room, I can feel you hold me tight,

Tell me how can this be true?

I'm safe from everything but you,

In my room.

"I can see you real clear when it's late, when it's really quiet, I see ya. I don't wanna be safe from you, OK? Maybe everything else. Yup, everything else, all the other stuff, an' everythin' else. I feel ya right in me. I feel you. Alright? So, um…yer really here with me, right?"

"Yes, Jeff, I'm there. Never leaving you. Never."

If thou didst ever hold me in thy heart,
Absent thee from felicity awhile,
And in this harsh world, draw thy breath in pain,
To tell my story.
—HAMLET

"Nevard. I need fer you to know. Ya have ta know now. NEVARD, ya hear me, all right? Alright?"

"Yes, baby, I'm here."

"You TOOK somethin' away from me, Nevard. YA TOOK SOMETHIN', NEVARD."

"Oh no…please, no. I'm sorry, Jeff, I'm so sorry. I didn't mean to hurt you, ever hurt you. I'm sorry, sorry, forgive me. I never… I just wanted to love you."

"No, Nevard, NO. NO. Ya didn't take like anything GOOD, ahh FUCK. Didn't MEAN that, OK? Ya took somethin' BAD. NEVARD…I'm tryin' ta THANK you. YOU. YA TOOK A REAL BAD **THING AWAY**. I never woulda been, um, RID of it if I never met YOU. I had YOU, babygirl, an' ya helped me. I could get it outta…oh FUCK. Ya don't know. Too crazy. Too scared to tell about you. Sometimes, ya know…I won't, um, see real clear. You don't know, babygirl. I wanted to. So much, so much, so much…I kept it. Why? Why couldn't we have it years ago? Why? Why…I keep askin', but there's no answer. No right answer. You can go make it right, babygirl. OK?"

"Jeff, did I help get rid of some of the noise in you? What are you scared to tell me? Can you tell me? I'll be OK with anything you need to …God, you've been the biggest joy. Did you know? You KNOW that, Jeff."

"Yeah, me too… I always wanted to tell. Couldn't fuckin' do it. Wanna be with you all the time. I told ya that. We didn't get ta the finish line."

"Tell what, Jeff? Is it my stupid singing again? I never cared for a second. No more stressing, OK?"

Sigh. "Someday. Someday, maybe yer gonna KNOW, babygirl. Wouldja sing me the Irving song? You, umm, give it yer BEST…'cause ya can."

I'll be loving you, always. With a love that's true, always

Days may not be fair, always.

That's when I'll be there, always

Not for just an hour,

Not for just a day
Not for just a year….But ALWAYS.

**"Always. Always. Always, my babygirl. You
understand? NEVARD? Always.**

"With my last breath. Always."

**"NEVARD…BEYOND my last breath.
ALWAYS."**

Those were Jeff's last words to me. The dreams came faster. Sometimes
I was so scared. I had no way to get in touch. I didn't try. He didn't want
me to.

A few years before I heard his beloved voice for the last time, I had finally gone to see Jeff's band. With trepidation…I went.

I could barely look at him, knowing he wouldn't want me to. I'm sorry,
Jeff. I wanted to finally know that part of you. Jeff kept looking in my direction. I was terrified that he knew I was there. He seemed distracted and
disturbed. I hope not. I stayed there only a short while.

Funny, I described Jeff's stature a few times, and he surely WAS loom-
ingly tall. You know what though? His height seemed greater than it was.

Jeff LOOKED even taller than he truly WAS, because he had a presence that was enormous. He seemed like a mountain. When I finally saw
him on a stage, that one time, I realized I had been right. Jeff WAS a
FORCE. He was spectacular and intimidating as hell. Do you think that's
why he never wanted me to see?

Could I have wiped the stage with Jeff? NO. Never. God. That's why he
was treated badly.

The day he died, I woke up silently screaming, and stayed in my bed, in
and out of a feverish sleep.

Now cracks a noble heart.
And will he not come again?
And will he not come again?
No, no, he is dead;
He never will come again.
…He is gone, he is gone.
And we cast away moan.
—HAMLET

The next day I went to that damned bank. It was my birthday. A guy I worked with said to me as casually as if he were commenting on my skirt, "HEY, guess what? Know who just died? Jeff Blank. You know…from the Blanks."

I was paralyzed. Couldn't move, and then I felt my head drop down.

"Wow, Vardz, what's wrong? WOW, you must have been a big fan, huh?"

"Yeah. That's right. I was a big fan."

I stood up and walked out. I can't remember anything but the pain.

To die…to sleep, No more…
And by a sleep to say we end. The heartache, and
the thousand natural shocks…That flesh is heir to…
—HAMLET

Two years later, I was driving on the Merritt Parkway, and a song came on. A song Jeff and I used to slow dance to. Me on a chair, Jeff holding me… a favorite of ours. He had recorded it. I had to pull over to the side of the road, and I may have sat there for hours. The memories started flooding, and I stuffed them down. Stuffed them down.

Three years after that, I was packing up my Connecticut home to come to Florida. In my closet was a pair of boots I hadn't worn for years. As I held them over the trash bag, a little slip of paper fell out of one.

"Too pointy. Too pointy, too pointy, pointy, pointy, pointy, babygirl. Not good for babygirl's feet." I sat on the floor and wept. I rubbed the scrap of paper against my face, until it melted with my tears. Can't I hold him just one more time? Just one more time.

Was he the perfect love? Of course he was, because you see, Jeff WROTE it.

He wrote it like a perfect love story.

He wrote it like *Romeo and Juliet.*

Complete with the warring factions, the secrets, the sneaking, the constant yearning, and ending with the final tragedy.

I pushed away the grief for years. I had abandoned Jeff, and left him for another, when he needed help. I had become the musician's nightmare.

I felt disgraceful, and filled with self-hatred for so long, I didn't see the truth. Maybe because I just didn't KNOW all the pieces of the puzzle.

The TRUTH is, Jeff didn't want me to see him shattered. And as selfish as that may seem, I don't think he would have been able to bear the alternative. No. not selfish. He didn't want that for ME. Didn't want me to suffer because of HIS suffering.

He HAD to remain the creation he'd carefully sculpted.

Some of the guilt is gone, but it still hurts to have been pushed away. What the HELL kind of a thing is THAT to leave a girl? Life isn't THAT perfect, DAMN you, Jeff.

Always leave them wanting more.

THAT'S the way.

Jeff knew when to leave the stage.

THESE ARE THE THINGS JEFF WOULD LIKE YOU TO HEAR, AND FINALLY KNOW.

He did NOT want anyone to pity him… but he knew they did. All the Jeff stories were for those who cared about him, felt sorrow for him, and wished he could have found what he was looking for. I did not give these stories lightly, and they were not easy to part with.

DOESN'T MATTER. I OWE HIM. I OWE HIM MORE THAN THIS.

What Jeff gave to ME was immeasurable, and if that moment is all I am meant to have, so be it.

He'd want you to know NOW, he DID find it. We both did.

I'd like for those who truly loved Jeff to be aware of this.

Turns out…he was NOT hopeless in "that department." I know what most of his puzzlements were now. I know now what that particular obsessive torture was.

The one Jeff said I'd "taken from him." Please take comfort in the elimination of that.

He'd WANT YOU TO KNOW…he was able to own what he'd always wanted. I may not be what you would have had in mind for him. I'm not that darn special, but he created the exact relationship he needed so badly.

Deliberately, and willfully…he became what he'd always wanted to be for a girl.

Not a schoolboy.

Not a kid.

Not someone to be mothered.

He created the man he desired to be for a woman.

He showed me what he wanted me to see.

I sure as hell loved the view.

We didn't get to have it for long, but it was a ferocious, urgent, and desperate loving. The nature of it was unrestrained…almost beyond reason…because almost at the beginning we knew time for us was limited.

It went by so swiftly, it makes an improbable love story, to say the least, but we grabbed as much as we could hold, and embraced it so hard it was sewn into our flesh.

There was an enraged anguish in us, for the loss of past and future time, but within that drowning sorrow, was an overwhelming gratefulness. A gratefulness that is STILL difficult to feel…but it is there. Perhaps buried in grief, but there.

No matter how fleeting, we were given something NEITHER of us thought we'd ever get during our lifetimes. Be happy knowing this. Be happy for him.

Please. I don't know your names, but I know Jeff loved you so very much, and was thankful for YOUR love. He told me this, and would like for me to TELL you. And I knew, just as surely as Jeff did…he would NOT have been able to carry on without your help…without your devotion and your love.

He was a man, take him for all in all,
I shall not look upon his like again HAMLET

Even if you never knew Jeff had lived, I've been saying it, but I'll say it again.

LEARN FROM HIM. HE HAD SOMETHING RARE TO TEACH US.

COURAGE. COURAGE. MORE COURAGE THAN I'VE EVER SEEN

NOT FOR JUST AN HOUR, NOT FOR JUST A DAY, NOT FOR JUST A YEAR,

BUT ALWAYS. DO YOU UNDERSTAND? IT TOOK IMMENSE COURAGE TO GET THROUGH EACH AND EVERY DAY OF HIS ENTIRE LIFE.

No matter WHAT obstacle was cruelly slammed IN HIS FACE—he FORCED HIS WAY over, AND CONQUERED every one of them.

OVER, AND OVER, AND OVER

IT DIDN'T MATTER HOW FRIGHTENING IT GOT, or what anyone thought, or how many times the terrors came. HE DEALT WITH IT. With laughter and camaraderie, and showed never-ending optimism as often as he was able.

HE WAS FRAIL, BUT HIS STRENGTH WAS ENORMOUS, AND SO WAS HIS LOVE.

Through it all, he NEVER stopped giving... NEVER stopped being generous with his time, his encouragement, kindness and love.

HE INVENTED HIMSELF, AND THEN REINVENTED himself, to fit whatever came his way.

Over and over.

Christ...he even reinvented himself for ME. Why? Because he WANTED TO.

**THERE WAS
ONE MORE THING
HE HAD.**

HE HAD GRACE.

HEY! I'VE BEEN KICKED OUT OF BETTER JOINTS THAN THIS

You all know by now…I was unceremoniously booted from the Brownies. Still haven't recovered from the humiliation. The Brownie troop was the first place I was ejected from.

I do think I may have mentioned in passing that I once caused a riot in a college gymnasium. I must admit I didn't REALLY start it, but I love to say I did. Don't you think it has a dashing ring to it? I wish I could put it on a resume somewhere. What college WAS it though? Was it U Conn? It was somewhere in Connecticut. If anyone remembers, will you let me know? Was it in Willamantic?

The gym was filled with jocks. Armies of them. They covered half the room, and they were stereotypically plastered, sloshed, drunk, and full of machismo. They were already emitting sports type of hoots, arm wrestling, pushing and punching each other to compare their muscles before the band started.

The other half of the room was filled with non-jock specimens. How did I KNOW? They had NECKS for goodness sake. They were NOT mixing together. Jocks to the left and non-jocks to the right.

The most dangerous aspect of this spectacle was an inconvenient fact. There were not nearly enough females hanging about to keep them interested. I'm talkin' maybe TWENTY to their FIVE HUNDRED. Inconvenient for ME I mean, because there I was …a female, and I was not hiding or blending into the crowd.

No siree. I was conspicuously perched atop a stage, more than five feet off the floor, and visible from every corner of the vast room. Are y'all getting the picture, and looking into the future that was going to be mine that night? Yes, I think you ARE. I'm referring to the wolf pack.

The belligerence they began to display was in direct proportion to the acceleration of their drunken states. Why, oh why, I asked myself, do they have to build these gym stages so high up? This one is higher than any big rock club I've EVER been in. GEEZ, don't they have any GIRLS attending this institution of no learning?

I tried to be as quiet as possible, and didn't move an inch. OHHH, but I knew. I KNEW what was in store for me. Eventually those football (or whatever sport they'd gotten into college with) boys were going to get tired of looking for females to give them the sugar they thought they were DUE.

They were going to get weary of the hunt for babes at eye level. Their scurvy and by now hostile attention was going to focus straight up at me. YUP. I was a perfect target on exhibition for them. I had put myself on DISPLAY, and was brazenly standing on that stage way up there, JUST for them. I was in short, ASKING for it. Who did I think I was, standing up there?

It started with the expected wolf pack heckling. You know the kind I mean...hey, baby, why dontcha take it off for us...you got some nice...hey, you suck. You wanna suck ...blah, blah. I've never been able to understand what kind of response idiots like this would expect to get in return for their efforts. Did they think they'd be hearing an eager "WOW, thank you, I'm taking it off NOW. WOWIE, yes, I DO wanna..." Naaaah...I'm sure they weren't capable of any thought beyond that of an amoeba.

OK now...that is what was emanating from the jock side of the room. The OTHER side of the room, filled with non-jocks, began to shout out their own declarations...as if it would STOP the brick-brained guys. "Hey, shut up, I wanna hear this song. Hey, you asswipes, why dontcha leave her alone?"

Valiant attempt, boys. By the way, where were the security people? Did they have any? The band and I couldn't get off the stage if things got out of hand, which they DID. We would have stepped right into them, so we were stuck.

Pretty soon, the muscle boys were grabbing at me, or trying to get up on that stage, and they were yelling. Don't know WHAT they were yelling, but it couldn't have been pretty.

I was able to get only one warning out. Something like..."Get the hell off here NOW, or I'll kick you're ASSES" before I had to get busy literally kicking them off. I was wearing boots. I must have kicked some heads in, but they kept coming. WHERE THE HELL IS SECURITY? The rest of the band? Don't ask. Pretty soon, I was using my mike stand as a ramming thing, and I've never used a tripod bottom stand. Oh boy.

Before you could say 'melee,' the OTHER side of the room—the non-jock boys were trying to pull them back, and fists were flying. That's when it really started. Tables, chairs, bodies, and who knows what all else became airborne, and I was STILL stuck on that stage. BEAUTIFUL.

I guess eventually some campus task force, and the local police came in to break it up. And it WAS a full-blown riot. Are you asking what the up-shot of this fun-filled night would be?

Your pal Vardz became notorious on the college circuit and was banned from every college job in the United States for years. Yes indeedy, banned from a source of many nicely paid jobs. The colleges had lots of dough to spread around in those days.

There were articles in their college paper, the local paper, and ten years later I ran into someone teaching at that school. They were STILL talking about it.

What could one do? I can't recall the name of that dumb organization that rated bands and other performers for colleges. They had conventions every year too. I'm talking trash about them because I was treated unfairly. I'm sure there were nice people involved.

Oh yeaaaaahhh....I was listed in their book all right. And it WASN'T nice. I became KNOWN as someone who **REGULARLY** INCITED RI-OTS. I didn't feel guilty about the incident. HELL no, I hadn't done a thing, but I did feel hurt by the unfairness of it all. I was young, in my early twenties, and didn't know much about the world. The thing I REALLY felt badly about was the loss of much-needed income, but within a few months I didn't miss it.

After a year passed, it became mildly amusing, after a few years it was downright uproarious, and NOW, I proudly claim bragging rights.

A club owner once claimed I started a riot in his joint years later, but he had a bit too much stuff stuffed up his nose, and I don't believe it. He had powder all over his face. Lord.

Why do I keep calling myself your pal? By the time I'm done, you might not want me to BE your pal.

I was thrown out of The MacDuffie School for Girls, in Springfield, Massachusetts. Yes, I was. I was kicked out of school for "Suspicion of smoking marijuana, and encouraging radical behavior amongst the student body." I hated it there. This fine institution was filled with snooty, bigoted, rich, brainless and spoiled Muffies, and a headmaster who had no idea what was happening in the world beyond his finishing school.

Sorry, I'm generalizing again. Not everyone there was like that, but the atmosphere was rife with a class-consciousness that was foreign to me, and provided a view that I did not like.

They had no proof of any pot consumption (although I HAD begun to indulge), and that "encouraging radical behavior" thing was pulled out of the air. It didn't exist. NO idea what they were referring to. While the headmaster had me in his office throwing me out of his school, there was a lightning storm, and the lights went out. THEN, he was aiming a glaring FLASHLIGHT in my eyes and throwing me out of his school.

The truth? I was a perfectly polite kid. I had manners that could not be faulted. I did, however, ask questions. LOTS of questions. I asked them in classes. The teachers did not like it a bit. I suppose learning was not included in the curriculum. Did this booting out bother me? NOPE. Here's the funny postscript. For years I received requests for alumni DONATIONS from them. HEY, McDuffie! I'LL HAVE THAT CHECK IN THE MAIL FOR YA POSTHASTE. PROMISE.

I was thrown out of summer camp. (How many paragraphs do you think I can start with "I was thrown out"?) A fancy French, girl's camp in Ferrisburg, Vermont. That darned lake was FREEZING. I have to admit...I did NOT like it there. I was thrown out for two reasons, the first being my proclivity to hang with the stable hand kids and muck out stalls rather than follow my fellow campers. They were more interesting. That's what Mommy and Daddy were told anyway, but it wasn't the real reason.

Actually, I wasn't thrown out. I was invited to NOT return. This invitation was given to my folks by the owner of the camp. NO...sorry, he was married to the camp owner's daughter, who was a lovely woman. He was in charge though, and he was a sleazy man.

He kept a full-grown PUMA in a tiny cage in his private cottage. The poor thing could barely turn around in it, and he fed that piteous and beautiful animal by pushing meat into the cage with a stick. I know, because he brought me in the cottage to SEE his recent acquisition, and was proud of it. I, on the other hand, was heartbroken to see that wild creature hopelessly moving in circles, enclosed in that tomb. I still can't get the terrible sight out of my head.

I'm not afraid of him, the S.O.B. His name was Claude. I was asked to not darken the doorway of that camp again because he did not want me around. WHY? One night after an often and boringly repeated campfire event, he messed with me.

He leaned over to kiss me goodnight. I guess I started being stupid at a young age, because not suspecting a thing, I smooched back. I was blind-sided by his damned hands on my bottom, and everywhere else he could reach. I pushed him away, looked at him, and RAN. I was nine years old and had been molested by a thirty- or-so-year-old sumabitch. I don't think a nine-year-old needs to be felt up by a thirty- something-year-old, do YOU?

There was no emotional scarring attached to the incident, but most like-ly there would have been if my parents hadn't provided a healthy upbring-ing. I was MAD though, and told my folks what had happened when we got home. They wanted to KILL him, but what could we do?

You know what? Seeing that poor caged PUMA was the real horror.

The school I attended after the girl's school in Springfield, Massachu-setts, was located in New Hope, Pennsylvania, and I was almost thrown out of THAT one too. There, I WAS caught smoking pot, but gracious, I don't think there was a living BEING that didn't smoke pot in that place. I re-member smoking pot with my math teacher.

NOO, not YOU, Kenny, ANOTHER one.

I started school early, so I was a little younger than the rest. Never told anyone—at that age you're wanting to be OLDER—but I was about four-teen when I showed up. I remember HITCHHIKING (sometimes alone) to Manhattan every weekend, and going to the Fillmore. We'd always get in free—somebody was a bouncer or something. After shows, we'd follow anybody hanging about to ANY party. Why am I not dead? I also remem-ber New York Hell's Angels parties in art galleries at that age, and going to a fancy party in somebody's penthouse, and I'll be darned…the butler was passing around joints piled on a silver tray.

My punishment for being caught doing the weed thing was to move off campus and stay at this wonderful woman's house. She didn't care what the heck I did, so I don't know how that fared as a punishment.

Nice little happy hippy school, and I did like it. WHEW…a school I wasn't thrown out of. There's an accomplishment.

BLOOD ON THE BARROOM FLOOR or
CLUBS? DID ANYONE SAY CLUBS?

Woo hoo, now we're heading into riotous territory. Why don't we all sit quietly and have a moment of silence. Let us give thanks for each and every agent who had a moment of insanity and recklessly thought it would be a grand idea to book dates for me.

That was nice of you all. They're probably grateful for your kind consideration. I wonder how many agents there have been over the years? Oh, those poor creatures.

My manager's contributions to the booking process were usually confined to opening spots. Some of these were nice pairings with bands who attracted the kind of audience that would like ours. Some were most definitely NOT.

Every band does openings, or warm-ups, or whatever you'd like to call them. I don't know why, but when I see a band's "resume" it bugs me if they list all the folks they've warmed up for. I have had agents attempt this with my info, and it turns me off.

Why do my fellow musicians bother with this? Just cut it OUT. We've ALL got a big ol' list of them. Does anybody CARE? I sure don't. I don't even care who I opened for MYSELF, and can't remember half of them, so I'm assuming you readers would find it mind numbingly boring as well. I am not going to name them. If you're inexplicably fascinated, give me a buzz, and I'll fork it over.

Oh yeah, and stop saying you "shared the stage" with a gazillion people. You didn't "share" the stage with the Beatles, OK? You may have opened for the Beatles, or you could have been "on the bill" (another doofy saying) with the Beatles. Did I "share" the stage with Duke Ellington? No, I didn't share a SANDWICH with him.

The list of people I've "shared" the stage with is a little shorter than the "opening" list. If yours is not, then you ARE the Beatles. If you'd like my list of "sharing," you'll have to call me for that one too. IT DOESN'T MATTER PEOPLE.

As far as I'm concerned, the only vaguely interesting thing contained in any "warm-up" story is the sometimes painful but usually funny "UH OH, **BIG** MISTAKE" pairings that invariably happen. I wish bands would put THOSE on their little bio sheets, and provide us with a few laughs.

There are other "warm-up" war stories that don't involve the bad pairing boo boos, like the one my friend Claude recalled. She can remember the member of a band she was opening for being unduly snooty to her before a show.

After the show, it was another story altogether. The unfriendly band member CAME ON to her with the same RELISH he'd shown in giving out the snotty demeanor. SNOTTY had miraculously turned to SMUTTY. Are you sure you want to be a girl on the road?

The hilarity of warming up is this. Someone always wants you to open for bands that possess audiences that would HATE YOU. I was offered loads of opening spots for bands with names like "DEATH, DEATH PAINFUL BLOODY DEATH AND I'M GONNA DECAPITATE YOU RIGHT HERE AT MY SHOW."

When faced with an opening like that, I would of course ask the obvious and intelligent question. Huh. OK, WHY?

If you're a musician, you already know the answer. The dumb ol' answer you'll get each and every time.

"It will be great EXPOSURE for you."

"Uh huh. Exposure to WHAT exactly? People that want to KILL me?"

"I'm telling you…EXPOSURE."

"Huh. Exposure. Exposure. OK, besides the bloodthirsty crowd feeling the compulsory need to annihilate my BUTT, precisely WHO would be attending the DECAPITATE show? The show that by the way is being held in BUM Fuck New Hampshire. Will John Hammond Senior be strolling in? How about ol' Ahmet? Will he be there? Cause soon as he spots that Armenian name of mine—NEVARD—HE'S going to want to decapitate me TOO."

They'd once in a while convince me to take part in one of these scientific musical experiments, and by golly I'll be darned, on the rarest of occasions, the "Death by Decapitation" crowd would go APE for me. Usually, they'd want to kill me though.

I opened for a popular hometown Southern rock band regularly for a while. Their crowd despised me. THEY, however, were big fans of mine, and on their off nights would trot out to see me with their honeys. They'd even take nights off to come see me. They were a wonderful bunch of folks, so I'd go DO the hellacious warm-ups for them. AHH, what the heck, I can take it. I'd get off stage, and go directly to their dressing room to report on the crowd and hang a while, and the conversation always went like this:

"How are they tonight, Vardzie?"

"Are you kidding me? They're not merely warmed up, they're downright HOT for ya now. Let's see. I caught only three big gobs of spit in the face tonight, but I DID manage to land a spit back on ONE of them, although mine wasn't big and icky like HIS was. Yup; all in all, a rousingly successful evening I think."

"You GO, Vardz. You just GIVE IT TO EM."

"That's what I'm here for."

Does life GET more fun than this?

I'm tired of the warm-ups. I was tired of them when I DID them. Weren't we talking about the "to be pitied" agents who did bookings for me? OHHH, that's GOBS more entertaining. They would get mystifying phone calls from club owners the day after I appeared in their clubs. Here are a few that I can nail down for you.

I was booked into a blues club. This club didn't want to hear ANYTHING but pure blues. NO MIXING allowed. I agreed to perform nuttin' but the blues, and DID. The next day, the booking agent received a call.

"That Nevard was here last night, and I don't think she performed the blues in a way that was REVERENT enough." Uh oh, that word again.

I called the club owner myself. I called him greedily. Gosh, how can you pass up a chance to rib the heck out of a snob?

"Hello, Mr. Blues? This is Nevard. Yes, that's right. I'm the Nevard that stepped into your sacred milieu of blues last evening. I was happy to be there, Mr. Blues, and had a good time. Your patrons seemed to have a jolly time as well.

"My understanding is that you are not entirely happy with my IRREVERENT handling of the delicate pieces of music I performed for them. May I with respect ask a few questions, Mr. Blues? I'd like to know where I might have gone wrong in my interpretation of the BLUES.

"You see, I've always thought this was a living art form, and not a dead reconstituted one. You know…just add water, and WOW, here's Pinetop. I

just need to ask. Did you in fact KNOW any of the performers that originally practiced this art form? I'd like to fill you in on what you could have
expected if one of THOSE revered musicians were in your club last night.

"I'm assuming you'd have been in HEAVEN if good old Guitar Slim
showed up instead of ME, yes? Do you THINK, Mr. Blues, you could have
HANDLED Mr. Slim? Are you quite sure you would have liked his lime
green hair and matching lime green-suited self CAREENING through your
FRONT PLATE GLASS WINDOW? Huh. I see.

"Would you, Mr. Blues, have enjoyed a little Robert Johnson poisoning
going on in your establishment? Ahh…a bit TOO reverent, perhaps? Well,
we don't know if that's true so how about some of those always exciting
Leadbelly STABBINGS happening in your fine establishment? Yes, SIR,
busy with the KNIFE, he was, and a Blues LEGEND.

"I'm picturing Howlin' Wolf right now, Mr. Blues. Yes. He was certainly
one of the blues greats, wouldn't you agree? Yes, I would TOO. And I am
picturing him accurately, and WITHOUT QUESTION as he WAS, Mr.
Blues. I am picturing him as he was the last time I saw him alive.

"Oh, YES, he was wonderful, but I don't believe HE would have been
appropriate for your BLUES club, sir. I am picturing him in all his Howlin'
Wolf glory. Yes all three hundred pounds of heavenly JOY in those over-
alls, with his hand in the trouser part of them, RUBBIN' HIMSELF like
crazy. OH YEAH he was.

"Ahhh, he WAS an inspiring sight, and WHILE he was TOUCHING
himself in a decidedly not so innocent way, his TONGUE was sticking out
and SLURPING at EVERY WOMAN in sight. EVERY SINGLE ONE.
His intent could NOT have been misinterpreted. NO SIR, Mr. Blues. I'd
just like to say, IF you'd like to make a NON-prejudicial comparison, I
WOULD BE FREAKIN MARGARET THATCHER compared to those
boys. No bodies through your window, no fatal stabbings, and a mere
TEENSY bit of the always fun, inappropriate touching of myself."

There's nothing more fun to play with than a purist snob.

Another "snob" booking guy story just entered my full brain.

For some unknown reason my bands and I went over like gangbusters
in Punk type of clubs. I didn't play very much that would resemble it, and I
didn't look AT ALL like I would belong in that scene, but they dug me, and
I dug them, in the usual places like CBGBs, the Rat (although that wasn't a

punk only club), clubs in Philly, Providence, etc., and a couple of places close to home.

When I'd play them, I'd hop on a table, and the club-goers would grab hold of my ankles for dear life. In some places, they'd hold signs up that said "you are my goddess" (what did THAT mean?), and there would be multi-pierced spikey heads of guys, lying on the front of the stage, attempting to look up my skirt. Funny stuff.

That reminds me…why are musicians always described as "somebody meets somebody else"? In my later band line-ups, I was often described as "James Brown meets the Sex Pistols." Sorry, but what does it MEAN? Frankly I don't believe funky James would have particularly enjoyed the Sex Pistols.

OK…the "snobby booking guy" story. Here goes. There was a punk/new wave sort of club I played regularly, and we always had a great time there. The dough was good too…IF we put our OWN person on the door. After having performed in this place for a few years, I got a call from an agent.

"Vardz, Stoopid club has a new guy doing the booking, and he doesn't want your band in there, because…OK…get THIS…you're "professional musicians.""

HUH? OK…uhhh…HUH? Did I make the call to THIS eejit myself? Ohhhh, you gotta love yourself a nice "MUSIC TERRORIST," so I made the call.

"Hi there, you new booker of Stoopid, I just wanted to touch base with you, and make SURE I've got the facts. I must have sustained too much hearing loss after all these years. I THINK I heard something along the lines of…well, that I'm not welcomed in club Stoopid because my band and I put food on our tables by performing music in a professional capacity. WHY didn't I wear the earplugs? I KNOW I couldn't have heard correctly, because that makes no SENSE. Are you THERE, new booker guy?"

"Yes, I'm here, Nevard, and you heard correctly. I'd like for club Stoopid to be an exclusive venue for New Wave bands. Our bands should be experimental in nature, and not professionals."

"OK and YOU are in a band that plays your Stoopid club, yes? Course you do. And you are being compensated for BOOKING the club, yes? Course you are. AND, you're putting more bands per night on the stage now, yes? OF COURSE you are. I'm getting the picture.

"Alrighty then, just so you're aware I'm here to tell you…**I am the UNDERTOW OF THE NEW WAVE, SPARKY**, and why are you saying PROFESSIONAL like it's a DIRTY WORD? Could it be due to the undeniable fact that you're too much of a COWARD to get out there in the trenches with me, pal?

"Are you under the mistaken impression that there is more HONOR in staying cocooned in your teensy world of crap, rather than DARE to put yourself out there? You don't even know enough SONGS to DO a full show, never mind an entire NIGHT. Listen UP. I spend five and sometimes six nights a week shucking from here to eternity, playing music that a good MAJORITY have NEVER heard the likes of. Oh sure there are places where my crowd is present, but there are tons of joints too, where they have NO IDEA what the hell I'm doing, and lots of them don't WANT to hear it.

"I HAVE TO **SHOVE IT**, SOMETIMES NOT SO GENTLY, DOWN THEIR GULLETS AND IN THEIR FACES. I'VE LEARNED TO DO IT SO THEY'RE NOT AWARE OF THE SHOVING.

"Eventually a lot of them learn to appreciate what is not familiar to their ears. Eventually a lot of them don't. It's a lot of work, baby, and a lot of abuse is dished out in the process. I don't think YOU'D be able to TAKE IT. NOT EVEN FOR A NIGHT. YOU would end up curled in a FETAL POSITION in the corner of some godforsaken dressing room.

"**WANNA GET IN THE TRENCHES WITH ME, YOU PISSANT?** WANNA GET ENOUGH GUMPTION TO MAKE YOUR LIVING AT IT? **WANNA GO WHERE YOU'RE TOO SCARED TO GO, YOU SNOB? CAN YOU DO IT YEAR AFTER YEAR?**

"Wake up and face north, Porky, **I'M THE ONE THAT'S DOING THE EXPERIMENTING. NOT YOU.**

"You, ya little pischer, are surrounded by your little pals, and until you can tell me you spent the night playing your music in some strip mall disco club that thinks you and your band are freaks, and you're able to BLOW THEIR HEADS INTO OUTER SPACE in spite of it, you can go to HELL. Thanks for listening, dear. That was more than satisfying. I almost need a cigarette. You're not the only one of your ilk. Do me a favor and PASS IT ON."

Gee, that one was fun…like sliding down a swishy slide. Turns out the guy above set off aggressive tendencies in scads of people. I found out the other day an old band mate of mine had a nasty encounter with the snob when he was playing with someone else. The booker of Club Stoopid made them SO mad, they set fire to his sleeves one night on the street outside the club. I can't tell you how delightful I found this news. Still laughing here. Sure. YOU know who you are.

That does it for the snobs. The calls agents received après a Nevard appearance, were I think anxiety producing for them.

"It's me, Jack Ruby, owner of the Grassy Knoll Club. That freakin' NEVARD took her CLOTHES OFF here last night. Naa, I wasn't here. That's what they're TELLIN' me."

NOW it's time for the panicked agent to give me a call, and read me the riot act.

"VARDZ. Whatcha DOIN? YA TOOK YER CLOTHES OFF? NE-VARD?"

"Took my clothes off? Don't be silly...I wouldn't take my clothes....uh, uh ....well...ummmm."

"OK. WHAT THE HELL DID YOU DO?"

"Wellll, there was a girl in the crowd. She screamed her admiration for the dress I happened to be wearing last night, so I asked her to come closer to the stage. You know, so I could SEE her. And as fate would have it, SHE was wearing a dress too."

"Crap. I have a sinking feeling. THEN WHAT, Nevard?"

"Nothing REALLY. She looked to be about my size, so I thought...wow, if she really likes my darn dress THAT much, I'll just give it to her. So I said 'I like your dress too...wanna switch?'"

"Sigh. You switched, huh? On stage. ON THE STAGE. WHAT THE...?"

"Gosh, I had on a full slip under the dress. A FULL SLIP, fer crikey sake. A SLIP I wear as a DRESS sometimes. It LOOKS like a dress. Sooooo, I took off took off my dress, threw it to her, and she in turn threw HER dress on stage. I slipped HER dress right over my head. I like it. Want to see it? It's black, and has little pink flowers ..."

"JEEEESUS. You tryin' to RUIN ME? Do you want ANY jobs?"

"Why would I want to ruin you? I'd never do something to HURT you. God, the slip I had on went BELOW my knees.

"Lord, my slip was infinitely more reserved than the outfits worn by most of the girls in the crowd. THEY had on short shorts, and BRA tops.

GEEZ. NOTHING was showing. WHAT THE HECK is the problem HERE? And the club owner wasn't even THERE. I'll bet he was given a completely wasted version of the entire two minutes. It was INNOCENT, I tell ya, and I'd do it AGAIN. What a nice way for girls to recycle dresses, wouldn't you agree?"

"You're gonna be the DEATH of me."

Honestly, I never saw a thing wrong with this, and DID repeat it a few times. We all got a kick out of it. It was always a field day for both the girls involved, and for me. We were having a SHOPPING spree on stage.

I always wear a slip under my dress, or a half slip under a skirt. I have a habit of scrunching my skirt with my hands when I'm singing. Who knows why? It's like playing with your hair when you're thinking hard about something. If I lift the skirt UP, there has to be something under it. My girl Claude says I lifted HER skirt on stage once. Hmmm. Well, what could she DO? Her hands were busy playing bass.

"I don't want Nevard in my club again. She was rolling around the floor with someone in a WHEELCHAIR. We couldn't believe it."

"She was WHAT?"

Dear me, the agent on the other end of this call was MAD at me, and I still can't make sense of it.

"Vardzie, did you SIT in the lap of someone in a wheelchair, and roll around on the floor? DID YOU?"

"Umm, why YES. Yes, I DID. WHY?"

"The club owner is upset, and never wants you in there again. As a patron, OR with your band, and said he was disgusted."

Did I make the return call for this one myself? You can bet your LIFE on it. I was so darn mad, I couldn't SEE straight. This was not a small OR a humungous club, but a semi large one. I could have apologized, crawled in an unseemly way, and kept that club on the list. It wasn't too far from home, we didn't have to load in or out, and they paid well. Did I apologize? HELL NO.

"Good afternoon, Mr. Bigot? This is Nevard speaking. How ARE you today? Good to hear, Mr. Bigot. I've just finished an unduly unpleasant discussion with my agent. From what I can gather, Mr. Bigot, you are of the opinion that any physical contact with a disabled patron is an unappetizing sight to you. I believe you used the word 'disgusting.' My band has spent many nights in your club and I think you'd agree we always pack your damn joint, Mr. Bigot. We pack it with a fun-loving respectful crowd, who by the way, drink gallons and gallons of your overpriced, watered-down booze every time we come calling.

"Let me point out the obvious. Unless the crowd I draw is a destructive one, Mr. Bigot, the ONLY thing you have to listen to or CARE about is the ringing of your CASH REGISTER.

"Secondly, Mr. Bigot, one of our fans is a disabled man. He uses a wheelchair. Do you have a problem welcoming disabled people to your exclusive bar, Mr. Bigot? Ah, that's mighty magnanimous of you, and I'm relieved to hear it. How do you suppose a man in a wheelchair DANCES with someone? I'd love to tell you, since you're glaringly ignorant of the physical details involved.

"When that music-loving man in the wheelchair DANCES, someone sits in his lap, and they roll around the floor with a heap of enjoyment. That SOMEONE dancing with him is often from the audience, and sometimes, Mr. BIGOT, it is ME.

"I'm thinking you're a big JERK. My guess is you don't think that man had the RIGHT to dance any way he could, and in FACT, thought it was an offensive sight. The man in the wheelchair would like to HEAR your true opinion. Oh yes he would. Would you care to know why? He, sir, happens to be a lawyer. He is in FACT a lawyer who specializes in discrimination cases.

"We BOTH know who the disgusting person IS here, Mr. Bigot…that would be YOU. I wouldn't step foot in your place again if it was covered in chocolate, and ready to drip itself into my MOUTH. Do you have any doubts about what I'd like for you to DO with your club? Didn't think so."

"Nevard played last night, and she was PROFOUND. Right on stage. I don't want you to book her in here anymore."

"I'm sorry…she was WHAT? Oh NO…was she trying to discuss Dialectical Materialism with the crowd again? I keep telling her, and telling her, but she never listens. I'll give her a ring."

"Hey, Nevard, you're never gonna believe this. Just got a call from the guy that owns….oh…where did you play last night? Oh. Well, he told me you were profound. Yeah that's what he said. You can't go back there 'cause you're PROFOUND. You think he meant PROFANE? Hahahahaha. What did you SAY?"

That was an agent with a great sense of humor, as I'm sure you can tell. I told him the truth. I told him the all too often occurring story of a belligerent drunk, that wouldn't leave me alone. He wouldn't let me BE offstage, and finally started coming AT me on stage. I had informed the bartender, the doorman, the owner, and anyone else I thought might be in a position to do something with this guy. I warned them "He's getting out of hand, and I'm being as non-combative as I can possibly BE. I'm avoiding HIM, avoiding eye contact, and I'm avoiding his obnoxious and filthy heckling. Do you get me? I'm NOT answering back, and he is STILL gunning for me."

They did nothing. He finally made a desperate lurch for me while I was on stage. I knew it was going to turn to violence sooner rather than later, so I let him have it in the most commanding voice I could muster. I said it loudly, and on mike. "ONE MORE **STEP,** PAL, AND I'M COMING DOWN THERE TO KICK YOUR **FUCKIN' ASS**. BACK OFF **NOW**."

Who's yo mamma? Who's more PROFOUND than me?

I am covering the "groping wars" in another chapter, but I haven't touched on this subject. Was there a lot of violence to be had in clubs? I know you're asking, and the answer, is NATURALLY. You are working in establishments that most often sell booze. If you're presuming a female musician will not have as many violent war stories to tell, you'd be wrong. They may have more.

You are not as likely to run into these forced participations in a larger club. A big venue protects the artist in a few ways, the most obvious being something you're already aware of. The audience doesn't SEE you unless you're on the stage, due to a (usually) separate bathroom for the band, so you're not wandering amongst the crowd.

Security in a large club is more efficient. There will be a visible abundance of big burly giants hanging about, and there is always a stage. A HIGH stage. This "high stage" didn't protect me in that college riot, but there was no security around until the place was a war zone, and so the local Mounties were called in.

A smaller club is not chock full of security types. Maybe they've got a bouncer/door man, or a few bartenders with moxie, but you'd better not count on THAT. There is no end of smaller and tiny clubs with stages, but they are lower in height, can be invaded with the greatest of ease, and no more help than a club with NO stage.

A small club involves bathroom sharing with the audience, and visits to the bar, so you're all over the joint. YOU, my friend, are UP FOR GRABS!

You may have a roadie or a pal who will fetch a drink, but there's NO avoiding the bathroom. I've covered bathroom attacks elsewhere. They aren't HALF as scary or as frequent as events ON THE WAY to the bathroom.

Stories like the "Nevard is PROFOUND" one are plentiful. I can't possibly tell you how many times I've had to turn my heavy mike stand sideways, hold it like a barbell, and PUSH or BASH a combat-ready stage crasher off the stage (or lack of stage).

The stage equipment these ardent or angry and sloshed people are capable of demolishing is ALWAYS a more critical concern to me than my own physical safety. At least on stage it is.

The intentions of these unruly folks can be hostile drunkenness aimed at a female who's got the NERVE to be on a stage. It can start with lust-filled heckling or physical grabbing, and veer into a desire to annihilate you. I've had PUNCHES coming at me. I'm not kidding. If it comes while I'm on stage, the mike stand serves me well. I have no idea what kind of injuries I may have inflicted through the years.

I ALWAYS try to warn the club staff. Usually they give back the familiar "AWWW, he's not REALLY like that" story. "He's a NICE guy when he's sober." My response to this?

"I'm sorry, but it seems he really IS like that, and he's not sober NOW, so how will this help me? It's gonna get physical soon, and if he hurts ME, God help you. If I HAVE TO defend myself, I'm TELLING you NOW, I will not ANSWER to a THING."

Do they throw these guys out, or even cut them off at the bar? Not frequently enough. Here's a call to an agent for you:

"So, Nevard PUNCHED my good friend drunkenschmuck last night. She broke his fuckin' NOSE. What are you gonna do about THAT?"

"Nothing. I'm going to do nothing about it. Nevard is not a violent person with a hair trigger temper. If she had to PUNCH someone, I'm sure there was a reason."

This was the only time I have EVER punched another human being. I've been cornered before, but drunks are clumsy, and tend to be slow, so a good shove with my hand covering a face can do the trick if I see a hit coming. The agent called me and queried, "What HAPPENED?"

"Geez, I'm sorry. Wait…no I'm NOT. I think my HAND may be broken. I don't CARE what happened to that stinker's nose. HE had me in a CORNER. When I saw that arm go back, and that fist headed toward MY face, I WENT for it. Broke his nose, did I? GOOD."

Was I "barred" from that club? Yes.

Can it be dangerous BETWEEN band members on stage? Yup. I've been bashed thousands of times by guitar and bass headstocks, especially when I was working with the almost seven-foot-tall bass player. My teeth were chipped on a regular basis. Yes, yes…the same droolly nose-running guy I told you about earlier. Boy, there's some litigious goings on. I'm calling my lawyer today.

A good barroom brawl can be a side-splitting thing to view if it is not in your vicinity. If it's in your FACE? No.

I have to tell you though, when I was talking to my friend Claude the other night, and we were trading "girl on stage" horror stories, she told me about an extremely rough biker bar she was playing in one night, and when a guy came toward the stage with a dollar bill in his hand, her head started spinning. "Oh DAMMM, is he going to try to stick that down my strappy T-shirt?"

You can imagine the possible sequence of events that were going through her brain—pushing the guy away, his biker friends throwing punches, or meeting the band in the parking lot later—none of it was pretty.

She was surprised and relieved when he smilingly stuck the bill in the headstock of her bass. WHEW. A great number of them did the same thing that evening. Sometimes when you THINK you're in trouble, you're NOT.

I can remember playing biker bars as well, and they were always respectful. ALWAYS. They were overly protective, and my biggest fear was not of THEM, but of the damage they could inflict on a non-biker that might try to mess with me, or the band. They'd hire us for parties in the summertime, and if memory serves me well, that big biker magazine (was it called *Biker*?) wanted to do a feature on the girl they thought was the reincarnation of "Janis." My manager put the kibosh on that one.

My favorite club owner call came in to an agent in the following way.

"I was out of town yesterday, but Nevard played. I'm in here trying to pay bills today, and already, I got TWO guys calling me and they want to know who cut their HAIR last night. I can't tell if they're happy or not. My wait staff says NEVARD gave haircuts. ON STAGE. What the…"

"Haircuts, huh? Well, Vardz is, um…a woman of many talents. Is there a problem with it? Were they BAD haircuts?"

"I don't KNOW. I don't know WHAT the hell they were. I thought they did strictly music. I've never heard anything like this before. I better not get complaints."

"Uhhh, Vardzie? Did you by any chance give a HAIRCUT or two last night WHILE YOU WERE PLAYING?" "Yeah, I DID. Gee, that's what I call living it up…music AND haircutting. Hey, how did YOU know? Were you there? You didn't say hi?"

"No. The owner called me. I hope you know what you're doing. He's saying they'd better not get complaints. How did you DO it? I'm assuming your victims were drunk. They couldn't remember where they got the haircuts. Oh God…why do I even KNOW you?"

"Cause you're a smart, smart guy, THAT'S why. Well, I'm sure they were three sheets to the wind; otherwise would YOU let someone give you a haircut on a stage?

"I always have the haircutting shears with me, in case somebody in the band wants a trim, so…oh I don't know…I was in the mood, and grabbed a towel from the hotel. I found a chair, stuck it on the stage, and asked if there might be someone in need of a haircut. Lo and behold, I got a number of requests, but there was only time for two. You can't spend the entire SHOW cutting hair, you know.

"They came on up, sat down, and after I draped the towel over their shoulders I just ran between the microphone and their hair till I finished. What a BLAST. Did I do a badie?"

Sigh. Pause. Sigh. "I GUESS not. I HOPE not. This is the first time HAIRCUTS ON STAGE has ever come up. OK? You are NUTS. You're going to wear me OUT, Vardz."

Well, I liked it. Did it on occasional nights, and only got one complaint. I took too much off the length in the back. It was a guy. Never DID get a complaint from a girl. OHHHHH, you SISSY boys.

Since we're in the clubs, I'll add this. Someone asked about the smallest and largest audiences I've played for. I thought It was a useless question, I mean EVERY musician knows the answer to that one. But then I realized—you, the reader may not BE a musician, so here's the answer.

The smallest audience? A bartender. No, I'm wrong…the bartender went back to the kitchen, so that would be NOBODY. Do you think this was just one time? If you DO, you're definitely not a musician.

The largest audience? That question is more difficult. I'm not good at numbers that way. The biggest crowds were at outdoor jobs. There were plenty of them. I don't know…forty or fifty thousand? Don't know. I can tell you my FAVORITE outdoor one though. It must have been a huge one, because the stage was WAY up. A girl toward the front yelled out "I LOVE you, Nevard" a number of times, before she flung off her dress, and threw it at my feet. Unlike the girls I'd done the trading dresses thing with, THIS girl was stark NAKED underneath her attire. Her boyfriend, husband, or whatever he was did NOT look pleased. I was pleased. I thought:

"OK then. So THIS is how Tom Jones feels. Kinda COOL. YAAY TOM!"

SEX, DRUGS AND ROCK AND ROLL
OOPS, SORRY. ROCK AND ROLL IS COVERED
ELSEWHERE

I'm reasonably positive this chapter has to be included in the book. It's expected, and I aim to please. Really there was and IS a heap full of sex and drugs available in the world of music. Sex? Because, as my friend Bob screamed to me over the phone last night, Rock and Roll **IS** sex. **ALL** music is sex. Bob's assessment is correct. You sick of that statement yet? I could add more, and I will do so later.

Drugs? That would be another YES, my friends. Why do so many musicians either dabble in, or become inexorably trapped by the siren call of drugs or drink (which in case you aren't aware…is a drug TOO)?

Maybe because drugs are offered to us regularly (at least they used to be) and we spend most of our time WORKING in bars, so booze is constantly surrounding us, and this COULD be the biggest reason.

Maybe it is because our minds are rarely quiet, even when we're not actively practicing our craft.

There is an INFINITE amount of things for us to explore. An overactive mind is the natural state of most musicians.

Some musicians are not able to compartmentalize, or never learned how to force the brain to let go a bit, so they seek relief by self-medicating. Most of us feel relentless compulsions regarding our craft, and the act of creating as much, as we love it, can be draining.

Some artists are more autobiographical than others. Some are more ANGUISHED than others. Think about all those Pulitzer Prize-winning writers.

What I'm trying to convey to you is this: to a lot of musicians, or artists in ANY medium, the constant digging and dredging from our own

SELVES can be tiresome, and the usage of things readily available, like drugs, or drink, can provide a restful escape.

We THINK this escape or vacation will allow a refueling to occur. It sure CAN, but some artists rely on it more and more frequently, until finally it stops serving its purpose and THEN some are left with the painful monkey on their backs. I'm talkin' bout Mrs. Jones. GET IT?

When we PERFORM music for an audience, we are striving to give them the same thing WE get out of it. We want them to feel the things WE feel when we listen.

Sometimes it's an easy sharing that feels effortless, and sometimes it's not, but usually, when we're doing it right, playing the music spins us straight up into a frenzied stratosphere that's difficult to return from.

When we hop off that stage, there it is…the "always around" drugs and/or booze that can help pull us back to earth. OR, there are stimulants that can keep that "stage buzz" GOING if we're in a party mood. Not all of us feel the need, and tons of us that DO, can indulge with no lasting ill effect. Like any population, many can dabble away, and not transform into junkies. I was one of those lucky people.

There's one MORE reason drugs are so prevalent in the world of music. MOST of us, as kids, did not fit into the general population surrounding us.

At the very LEAST, I'd say ninety percent of us were considered a bit odd, and a good eighty percent of us were viewed as downright freakish, or geeky.

Most of us had interests that were not considered popular. It depends on where we lived, and how our families perceived our "leanings" as well.

Not all of us were fortunate enough to be brought up in an artsy, or urban community, where music was looked upon favorably, and in many families our interest in music was met with disdain. This wasn't the case in my house, but my relatives thought I was crazy. Tons of us grew up in places where the music we craved wasn't available to us.

Sooo, there you have it. Musicians are BORN with a yearning for something IN us that will NOT be ignored, and the drive to go after it, no matter WHAT social consequences go down.

We could be stuck in a town with no pity, in a school where we feel like outsiders, and in a family that thinks we're NUTS.

Our art becomes an act of rebellion, which fuels us even more, because good art IS an act of rebellion in some respects.

When we grow into our talents, and feel comfortable in our own skins, we begin to "come into our own." THAT is when we begin to suddenly be viewed as cool, or hot, or whatever.

DRUGS? PERFECT. It dulls the growing pains of musicians that feel uneasy in a world they can't quite fit into, AND it's an act of rebellion. What could be a better combo?

I can GUARANTEE you THIS. **ALL of us retain at least some of that childhood attitude. The attitude that says, in no uncertain terms:**

> ## "FUCK YOU, and DAMN THE TORPEDOS. Love me, or LEAVE me, you TASTELESS BUFFOON. Come here and TRY to push over the LIGHTWEIGHT MUSICIAN. Come ON an' GET it, because WE PUSH BACK with a force that'll knock your ASS into the next STATE."

In my case, it takes a lot to bring it out, but it's there.

It's in ALL of us.

It's in the nicest and the kindest of us. EVERY SINGLE ONE OF US.

You'll have to trust me on this one.

What about MY drugging days? Not all that much to tell. I started smoking pot at the age of thirteen, and began taking "shrooms" or acid at fourteen. By the time I was finished with high school, I was bored with psychedelics, and indulged in pot rarely.

For some reason, pot began to bring on feelings of paranoia. I'd say something simple like "hello" and think, "OK, who's laughing at me? What did I say? I just said HELLO. How come everybody's looking at me?"

What drugs did I dabble in when I was travelling around with my band? Well, I never WAS a good drinker. One shot, and I'm gone. GONE. People regularly think I'm either drunk or under the influence of SOME-

THING or other when I'm on a stage. Nothing could be further from the truth.

I DID slug down a shot of whisky before leaping on stage approximately five times during twenty-something years. Those nights became kind of legendary within my various bands, because after a shot, I think I can FLY. I have no recollection of the stage antics that ensued on those nights. I guess it must have been hugely entertaining for the BAND, because they'd snicker for months and would try to get me to imbibe again.

ONE time I snorted some coke before going onstage, and it scared the hell out of me, because I couldn't feel my throat. "Uh oh…this can't be a good thing," I thought.

Other than those few exceptions I am ALWAYS completely SOBER on stage, and as I said, a huge amount of folks think I'm SNOOKERED. This has always puzzled me. STILL can't figure it out.

What happened after hours? Or many hours before a show? Let's see…I DO remember a roadie who for a while had a ton of morphine tablets to pass around. After a week of seeing the rest of my band ingest the little blue pills, I tried one. Wowie. All I can think of to describe the effect is Felix Unger singing "Happy, and peppy, and bursting with love," which is what I started singing when I got off. I took the little blue jobs for a couple weeks, and one morning when I woke up WANTING one, I thought it was time to stop, so I did.

I tried blow once, and didn't like it. Smoked opium twice, and couldn't understand the attraction. Did some ludes, and all I can say is "Bendy knees. Bendy knees." Once, I let someone shoot me up with coke, and it felt so good, I figured that wasn't something I should EVER do again, so I never did. That's about the extent of MY dabbling, except for coke, and I didn't take a whole lot of that either. Coke was the biggest thing around.

When I first started out in the club circuit, coke was the popular drug of choice, and readily available. When I say readily available, I don't mean it was simply available on a purchasing level. I'm saying you couldn't ESCAPE it. The stuff was everywhere. I could have taken a BATH in coke if I so desired, and if you were a musician, it was offered up to you in staggering amounts. At almost EVERY job.

Everyone wanted to give it to musicians, before, DURING, and after shows. When you trotted off to get paid, the club owner's office usually had over an ounce laid out in neat big lines on their desk, and a straw would be shoved into your hand. "Hey, where's the rest of the band? Tell 'em to come on back." This would often happen before the show too.

Legions of fans came at you with little spoons outstretched in the vicinity of your nose. If you took a snort in one nostril, the spoon would quickly be filled for the other side of your nose. Then they'd repeat. There'd be thirty more behind THEM. They'd come at you in the dressing room (with the spoons, or just plop down at a table and lay out line after line), and they'd come at you in the bathroom if there wasn't a separate one for the band.

They'd appear outside the club, inside the club, and sometimes they'd even come at you on stage. It wasn't only fans, it was offered up by everyone. Who's everyone? Waiters, waitresses, other musicians, patrons, owners, promoters, record people (oh, the A&R guys were notorious for showering you with it), agents, managers, journalists, other musicians on the same bill, or not on the same bill, photographers, your relatives, YOU NAME IT.

How often did I indulge? I'd always say "No, thanks" before a performance, because it's BAD for your vocal chords. After hours, I'd do it occasionally, maybe a few times a month. Usually I'd indulge if we had a particularly long drive ahead of us, or if the club gang was an especially gregarious group of funsters.

I must have done it at least once in high school. I have no real memory of it, but I can CLEARLY envision the first time I snorted a heap o' powder off a club owner's desk.

The effect was this. I immediately wanted to accomplish only two things. I WANTED TO SMOKE A CIGARETTE, AND I WANTED TO VACUUM. Smoke and vacuum. Yup, that's what I wanted. I hopped into our van, and said to one and all:

"Who's got a fag? I need one."

"Vardz, you're not smoking."

"I don't care. I need a smoke. I need it now. DAMMM. This van could use a good cleaning. Do we have one of those hand vacs, and some paper towels? Maybe some Windex? I can't STAND it. Gimme a cig. SOMEBODY."

"Oh God! It's Vardzie on coke. THIS is gonna be a FUNNY ride, guys."

"Whaddya mean? I'm OK, here."

We took off…on our way to wherever we were on our way to that night, and I was FULL of energy, but frustrated there was no vacuum around. All of a sudden I noticed something.

"Hey, guys, are any of you feeling, uh, amorous? Because I'm REALLY feeling it. I think I'd be willing to bed down with the Horse With No NAME right about now. OK, kidding…no horsie. Not a good vision for the head, not Katherine the Great here. Ya think that story is TRUE? Naah…can't be. I don't imagine anybody could WANT… I'm TELLIN' ya though. Am I the only one here?"

"Vardz, we're all feelin' it. It's what the stuff does to you."

"Ohhhh. NOW I get it. No wonder it's so popular. Hmmm. I'm feeling TINGLY in my girl parts. But a little NUMB. Yeahhhh…I'm definitely beginning to feel ENTIRELY numb. Still itchin' to get busy, but numb. Well then. Aha. Now I'm confused. WHAT GOOD would this DO YOU, if you're NUMB? Do you guys have the numb fun parts TOO?"

"Yup."

"Oh thank goodness. Well, what a nice feeling of CAMARADERIE then. Sailing down 95 with my mates at four in the morning, and all our fun parts numb together. Boy, you can't beat that, can you? I love you guys. Geez, this van's dirty."

"Hey, Vardz?"

"What?"

"I'm not numb."

"Now why'd you have to go and SPOIL it? Big showoff."

"Sorry."

"I don't feel so good now. My head hurts."

That's what would happen when I'd do coke. The buzz would last for MAYBE an hour, and then I'd get a headache, so I couldn't understand why this was such a desirable drug. I could take it or leave it. And did leave it, a while before the fad disappeared.

I haven't experienced recreational drugs in twenty years. I know, I know…pretty pedestrian. I have lived through other people's struggles with addiction. Some of them were very close to me, some considered family. DT's, convulsions, band mates shooting up in my bathroom, near overdoses, needing to fire a band member, junkie traits, like lying, stealing, manipulative emotional abuse, etc.

I've lived with it at home, and can't begin to describe the endless pain that goes hand in hand with it. Thank goodness my own limited drug taking did not grab me up and into clutches of a nightmare. It could have gone the other way.

LET'S JUST CHEER UP, SHALL WE? I know YOU'RE going to cheer up considerably, because I'm about to delve right into the sex part of the rock and roll equation. Not ME though, no cheering up for ME here, because my personal "touring" sex stories are limited in number, and I'm a LOT more sorry about it than YOU are.

The only loose frolic you'd be remotely interested in is a romp in which I play the part of a complete FOOL. I'm going make the sacrifice for you though.

I was able to indulge in a couple more "road" tumbles, but there's nothing interesting attached to them. And I do mean nothing.

I guess this is finally the place to put what I've called elsewhere the "I'm a reeealllyyy big name, so of COURSE you want me" syndrome. I always thought for many of them it was only force of habit.

"Hi there. I'm (so and so). I liked your show."

"Thank you very much."

Sometimes I'd be thinking "Who? Damn...I think I'm supposed to know who this is."

Often, the person would introduce himself, and then just STAND there looking at me. If I DID know who they'd be, I'm afraid my expectations were a bit too high. Like perchance they were looking to CONVERSE with me or something. GOLLY, bud, I didn't approach YOU (I never approach ANYONE I don't know), so is it too farfetched for me to be thinking you're wanting verbal contact? Am I missing the secret "big name club" hand signals? What do you WANT? HUH?

You most likely have no idea, how utterly BORING and fairly empty-headed some people you'd think would be fascinating actually ARE. Not ALL, just some, and I'd be thinking:

"OK...I have nothing to say to you. For the love of Yahweh, can't you simply walk away? Please. I have things to do. GEEZ, I sure wish I didn't have to meet you. I could have kept on thinking you're maybe intriguing or sumthin'. EVEN BETTER, I could have remained unaware of your presence here altogether." Most of these people were NOT musicians. No, we usually have plenty of things to natter about with each other.

This scenario never played out that way with females. Women are more social, and not upset if you don't recognize them. They will TELL you who the heck they are, and start chatting away in a friendly manner. THANK YOU.

Back to the "betcha you WANT me" guys. My guess is, some of these men made passes because they thought they were EXPECTED to come on to virtually every girl they met, especially if they had a "player" reputation. Who knows? They might have been lacking in any interesting qualities besides their specific area of expertise, or they used the pick-up as a standby. OH hell...I shouldn't judge. Maybe some were just shy, like me.

Regularly, the plainly NOT shy guys toted around an amount of arrogance that would knock over an elephant. I suppose they thought every girl would be eminently flattered.

This "off handed" verbal grope fell on me more than a few times and it was NOT flattering. It felt demeaning, and sad. I've related the most startling one, but usually it would go like this, about ten minutes after "Hi there."

"So, uh, you want to...(Take me home? Come to my hotel? Your van? Screw me in your dressing room?)"

I always replied politely, "No, but thanks for inviting me to the party, sport."

There are only a couple of times I can think of that I've been in fact duly AMAZED by a man's attention. We're all human after all...and It IS flattering to be zeroed in on by a legendary personage you think the WORLD of. And that statement will lead us nicely into my MOST awkward romp.

I guess I just have to come out and say it. I slept with an icon. When I say icon, I mean ICON. In all likelihood, there are three people in the world who wouldn't recognize him. No, I am NOT going to tell you who this is.

I don't mind telling you who he was WITH the day I met him. He was someone who came out to see the band often, and HIS name was Terry Southern. Ninety-nine point nine percent of you won't know who Terry was, and I described him earlier. You can't contact HIM to find out, because he's gone. Nice try though.

I'll call this "icon" Sam Patrick. He was quite delightful. The icon attribute he carried with him was beyond his control, and he couldn't have gotten away from it if his life depended on it. He didn't seem burdened by his vast prominence as some are; he was used to it, and cheerful about it.

I wasn't cowed by that aspect when I met him. He wasn't full of himself, so you'd easily forget. We had a lot to talk about, and Sam was a screaming joy to be around.

When he asked for my number, the thought of being intimate with him didn't cross my mind. He was outrageously flirtatious with me, but Sam was someone who slept with super model types, so why would he want to sleep with unglamorous me? Maybe I'm just thick as a plank. OK, I AM. In any case, I forked over my number, looking forward to nice phone chatting, or meeting up somewhere.

We DID have phone visiting. But along came a day…he was on his way from somewhere to New York City and asked, "Are you off 95?"

"Yes. Right off 95."

"Are you going to be around later? Can I come over? I'll pick up some takeout."

"Sure! I have those clips I was telling you about, and that unreleased Otis thing. Remember? Before he was killed. Yeah, I KNOW you want to hear it."

Sam did his own driving (I THINK he did), so "stopping by" didn't surprise me.

I felt comfortable around Sam, until the moment he took his first step into my HOUSE. Maybe the icon fact didn't hit me before, because I'd been around him in a neutral place. I don't know for crikey sake, but as soon as he was in my home, it barreled into me like a TANKER. Somehow, my brain was incapable of computing or absorbing his BEING.

My head took a header. It was taking an undesired direction.

"HOLY SHIT. SAM PATRICK is in my KITCHEN. How did that happen? I don't think he BELONGS in my kitchen. He belongs on a magazine cover. Sure. He looks fine THERE, but now he's THREE DIMENSIONAL, and in my KITCHEN. This doesn't look right at ALL."

That awkward moment (for ME of course) reminded me of an experience I had when I was about five years old. My folks and I were having dinner one early Sunday evening at Sardi's Restaurant. There we were, in a booth under those famous old caricatures, and right across the way, in another booth, was Ed Sullivan. He must have been noshing away before his weekly and live Sunday show.

I stared, and stared, until finally my Mommy couldn't stand it anymore, and said, "HONEY, why don't you go over to Mr. Sullivan, and ask for his autograph. Here, I'll give you a piece of paper."

I violently shook my head NO. I must have done it fifty times.

I did not WANT Mr. Sullivan's autograph. I did not want to get anywhere NEAR Mr. Sullivan. I was scared to DEATH of Mr. Sullivan. I'd been staring at him, because at that age, I thought EVERY PERSON I saw on our TV set LIVED INSIDE the TV SET! They couldn't be walking around OUTSIDE the TV set like WE did. They weren't REAL.

That is the feeling I was suddenly engulfed in when Sam Patrick casually walked into my kitchen. It wasn't HIS fault, and he didn't know about the terror in my head.

I gave him a hug, hoping that if I touched him I'd get over the awful feeling. Maybe he'd turn back into the regular Sam guy.

HE was perfectly comfy and wandering about, talking away, getting drinking glasses out of the cabinet, peering in my fridge and sorting through condiments, asking me to put that tape on, while I stood there partially paralyzed, and agape.

It took a good hour, but I settled down. Not totally, but just about. He was such a goof, the otherworldly thing went away. We were sitting on my couch, stuffing our faces with Chinese takeout, with the TV on.

OK, much better now, and then, suddenly he was ON me. Fairly pinned to the couch. HOLY COW. Back to square one.

"Nevard, I wanna tumble around with you right now. You wanna?"

HUH? HOW CAN THIS BE? There's no glamour girl here. What's he want with ME?

Why was I unaware of his intentions? ALL my friends say I miss the obvious signs.

Did Sam possess the thing in his eyes that I look for? I have positively NO IDEA. I was much too uncomfortable to check it OUT. He could have had a completely blank stare. I doubt it though.

Was I attracted to Sam? Yes, but in an academic way, as if he were a poster on my wall. He HAD been a poster on my wall. Was I flattered? God YES, who WOULDN'T be?

"Um, Uh, YEAH, Sam, absolutely," was my answer to his question.

We won't go into details of the act, but my thinking machine shot into overdrive. My head sort of went completely askew, and I truthfully couldn't get past Sam being Sam. He couldn't make a MOVE without my screwy thoughts running amok.

OK, I'm being kissed, and very nicely I must say. OK, I think I can handle...uh oh, my top is being taken off. UH OH, evidently CAN'T handle... I can't be NAKED in front of him...HOLY...SAM PATRICK is taking his PANTS OFF. I don't think I'm supposed to SEE this. Where's my camera? OK, that's a tawdry thought. I'm so SORRY that crossed my mind. I have to call my girlfriend because I'm LOOKING at...and damn, now he's TOUCHING...oh this allll wrong feeling. HOLY CRAP, I think...no, no, no, no... WHO could be relaxed DOING this with him? Exactly who would be UNAWARE or unaffected by... GOD, he'd have to find an eight-year-old...OH NO, am I in bed with a pedophile?

Sam rang me up a while after our visit and said something like, "Hi, darling, I'm going to be in the area. Wanna get together? Had a great time the LAST time I was there."

"OK, why don't you, uhhhhhhhhhhhhhhhhh."

He noticed my hesitancy and asked what was wrong. So I TOLD him. Lord have mercy, I actually told him. I told him that while I loved his company, being intimate with him flustered me. He wanted to know WHY, and what was I TALKING about, and so I let him in on the bashful and muddled thinking.

Sam thought it was a RIOT.

"I think you can stop laughing at me now. Didn't you notice the 'deer caught in the headlights' look on my face?"

"No, I didn't see ANYTHING like that. It was FUN. How could you have been so scared? It's just ME, Nevard."

"Really. Huh. I don't rightly know how it could have been... well, maybe it WAS. How would I know? I WASN'T THERE. You really didn't SEE the look on my face? Huh. Maybe it's the look you see on EVERYBODY'S face. I mean you're just YOU to YOURSELF, Sam, but don't you KNOW? How could you not know? You may as well be the POPE."

guess nobody had said these things OUT LOUD before, so he was getting even more of a kick out of my embarrassment. Nice.

"Well, was I really good TOO? HEY, so did you call your girlfriends?"

"Are you NUTS, Sam? Of COURSE I called my girlfriends. TWO of them. What're you THINKING? You don't do it with the POPE and not call your girlfriend. But I was LOOKING ON like I was at a parade. I was having the scary OUT OF BODY experience. What're you not getting here, Mr. "on my wall during my formative years'?"

"Hahahahahahahah. Soooo, what did you tell your girlfriends? I WONDER. Who would scare ME? HAHAhahahaha."

"What did I tell my GIRLFRIENDS? I see Paris, I see France, I see SAM PATRICK'S UNDERPANTS!"

"I don't WEAR underpants, love."

"Yeah, whatever. OK, who would YOU be intimidated by? Mother Theresa? No, you're bigger than her. I know, not such a lusty air, but who knows what's lurking. WOW, there aren't many women with your kind of—AH HA, I know who. Queen Elizabeth. She's got that twinkle going, AND she's every bit as scary as YOU. The Queen of England. THE QUEEN MUM, Sam. Are you down with it? Are you picturing?"

"I don't know…yeah, she's… I THINK maybe I could. YEAH, I could do the Queen."

"Very sporting of you, Sam. IN YOUR HEAD you could, but picture THIS. You're in a room with her and she leans in for a polite kiss, and then she gets steamy. I'll bet you're OK so far, but NOW, think about her being in your HOUSE. The Queen of ENGLAND standing in your bedroom, unbuttoning her blouse, stepping out of her skirt, and now Sam, right in front of you, she's NAKED. The QUEEN, Sam. Can you get busy with her?"

"I'm trying to see it, Vardz, just a minute. Uhhhhh, No. NO! She would scare the CRAP out of me, especially if she had that HAT on. I get it. I get it, but the QUEEN is MUCH bigger than ME."

"NO. She's NOT, Sam. SHE IS NOT."

I saw Sam once in a while, until either I or both of us were in a relationship, and we kept in touch, but I haven't spoken to him in a long, long time. If he read this, he'd recognize himself in a second, and I can hear the laughing from here. Were we in love? No, just pals… but what an incredible guy. Did I ever get comfortable? Not REALLY.

Wasn't that humiliating? You're welcome.

My girlfriends say I have appalling taste in men. When they point out a man that's attractive in THEIR opinion, which is frankly always a guy MOST people would find gorgeous, I never SEE it.

"Vardzie, CHECK out that GUY! Isn't he a BABE?"

"No."

"NO? How can you SAY that? Look at that butt of his. God, he's so BUFF."

"Don't get the butt thing, girl. Never notice the butt. They could have a butt the size of Kansas, or NO butt. It makes no difference to me."

"OK, but look at the REST of him. This guy works OUT. Look at the muscles, and his chest."

"Yeah whatever. It does nothing for me. I don't care if men to have NO muscle tone whatsoever. Ya know what's weird, Dawn? I've always been a JOCK magnet, and I couldn't be more disinterested. I'm referring to the no neck type. Do I LOOK like a jockette here? What do they want with ME? You can't HUG them. They're not pliable or skwooshy good feeling. Feels like you're holding a BUILDING."

"There's something wrong with you, Vardzie."

"So I've been told."

"So what if they're really skinny or fat?"

"Don't care. Has no bearing on whether I'll be attracted. Not crazy about the blond population in general. They just look UNFINISHED to me, like they need a bit more cooking time. Isn't that dumb? I wouldn't rule them out either though. NOPE."

"What in the world DO you like?"

"Do you really want to know? I look at their eyes. There has to be something IN there. Just THAT would do it. JUST THAT. I like faces. They don't have to be pretty. I'd PREFER not pretty. Interesting would be good. I like hands. Mostly it's the eyes though."

"That's IT?"

"OH HELL NO. After eyes, you can just move right along down, and unzip those pants for me. That's all I'm interested in. Physically speaking, I mean. Love what's in the pants. I'm endlessly excited and fascinated."

"ENDLESSLY excited? What's WRONG with you? How about being in working condition? You're a freak of nature, you know that?"

"Working condition? Well, I guess at least fifty percent of the time would be nice. OK, some people think I'm a freak of nature, but guess what…I think I'm RIGHT, and they're terribly WRONG. "

"Here's what's bizarre to ME. Do you know how many females tell me they're not all that infatuated with what's in the pants? They'll visit, if it's expected, but they don't want to live there, and can happily survive without getting too close. This doesn't seem NATURAL to me. There are male counterparts of that too, I've heard, but I'd find them just as stupid, and they wouldn't last three seconds with me. Why wouldn't you be endlessly fascinated with the fun parts YOU don't HAVE? Nature intended for us to be excited, don't you THINK?"

"Yeah, right. I can't BELIEVE you." You don't care what their body looks like, except you'd prefer not buff, don't think blonds are finished, like faces, and hands, but even THOSE things wouldn't make a difference. It's just eyes, and what's in their pants. Do I have it right?"

"YUP."

OH I'm very VISUAL. Something males often say to women, when they're rudely looking over the shoulders of whomever they're hanging with. Sorry to be the bearer of bad news, but I'LL want to unzip and stare…at least seven times a day, and will get hotter than hot, from that…will ultimately need to touch.

Other physical details ultimately don't MATTER. At least not to me. Let me be blunt. If they can't do the DANCE, who cares? Why do you think I look in eyes? It's about attitude. Desire. Dynamics. It's like MUSIC, dontcha GET it?

IF they've got what I'm looking for in their eyes…THEN…they are almost unbearably beautiful to me. My daddy taught me how to look into eyes. He also taught me this…Don't EVER trust anyone that's never been shaken up. EV-ER.

Now you know why my girlfriends think I'm weird. Maybe you do as well. I DO think it's more than strange that so many women don't adore the guy fun parts. Do you think there isn't a MALE behavior out there that's just as disturbing? Think again. There's something MORE than alarming going on.

I can think of EIGHT women I know (right off the top of my head), who have either LEFT men, or are THINKING of leaving them, or have started looking elsewhere, because these so called men are now addicted to porn. Some of these women are quite young (as are some of the ones not moved by guy parts), and their MEN are young too. We're not talking about people that are lacking energy.

They're not TOUCHING their women. At all. That's a huge percentage. I'm counting only women I'm close to, and they confide things of this nature. I'll bet there are legions amongst my casual girlfriends.

Last year, I was felled by some bug or other, so I turned on daytime TV. Boy, THAT'S some bad stuff, but I came upon not one but FOUR talk shows that had females of all ages complaining about the SAME thing.

THEY were disgusted, and their guys didn't get it. Every one of them had the same smart-aleck retort, delivered it in a smug manner. "It's just images. It's not real. It's not like I cheat on you."

I've got some info to pass along to men like that, and it may be illuminating or painful for them. There are millions of women who are more than capable of indulging in faceless sex with no meaning attached to the act. There ARE women entwined in cultural constrictions, but those beliefs are EQUALLY as foolish as the antiquated outlook confidently put forth by the porn addicted men who don't touch their women.

I know I could run out every day, lasso me a guy, and have a quick toss without a backward glance. Just physical gratification I wouldn't think twice about. I wouldn't DO it, but I sure as heck could. All women can, and more and more ARE, because nothing is happening at home.

Would our prevailing societal beliefs consider this cheating? You bet they would, but how would this be different from the behavior of the guys I'm talking about? Just the brief physical contact? That's it?

There are men who'd like to continue buying the old fallacy that says women need an emotional attachment to enjoy sex. IT IS NOT TRUE and almost every woman reading this will stand up and applaud the audacity I've shown in declaring it.

I have one friend, whose man got lost in porn and would only touch her if she initiated. She was so angry, she just stopped, and so he didn't touch her for six months. Huh? Ya can't chase your girl? Are there ANY men left?

WHAT is going ON here? Is this the sexual version of Columbine? Is interfacing with a living person too bothersome? How have people become so detached from other humans? Is everything just an image now, and we're so NUMB toward our fellow human beings they have become unreal?

Killing isn't real, passion isn't real, world hunger isn't real, suffering isn't real, pleasure isn't real, compassion isn't real, betrayal isn't real, integrity and loyalty aren't real, hurt isn't real, LIFE ISN'T REAL? This is FRIGHTENING to me.

Did Marshall McLuhan have it right after all? Is the media really the message? Here are some things HE warned us about:

"Once we have surrendered our senses and nervous systems to the private manipulation of those who would try to benefit from taking a lease on our eyes and ears and nerves, we don't really have any rights left. Leasing our eyes and ears and nerves to commercial interests is like handing over the common speech to a private corporation, or like giving the earth's atmosphere to a company as a monopoly."

"Visual space, is the space of detachment. Audile - tactile space, is the space of involvement."

"Madison Avenue is a very powerful aggression against private consciousness. A demand that you **yield your private consciousness to public manipulation."**

"All media exist to invest our lives with artificial perceptions and arbitrary values. When our characters are extended by any medium, we become changed in a fundamental way."

What Marshall McLuhan had to say is enduring, and it holds true for the written and visual worlds. They are "extensions" of our human senses, bodies and minds. There can only be disaster arising from unawareness of the causalities and effects inherent in our technologies.

Our TRUE selves are now a memory.

There are STILL some valiant fighters in the media world who will point out the BULL, with FEARLESS insight and bravery, but their numbers are growing smaller and smaller.

Why don't you check out Burt Kearns's blog (and book) *Tabloid Baby*? Go DO IT. At first glance, you'll see plenty of comedic lampooning. A kind of burlesque commentary including an unlimited amount of "scenesters" who seem to be taking over our society. People who live and die like brats. Sadly, many of them are serving as guides and road maps for our country's youth. There ARE truths to be gleaned from Burt's entertaining mockery of these behemoths of self-entitlement and unthinking lifestyles. You'd have to be fairly brainless to miss it. There are a lot of other funny things there too.

You must look closer though, because darling Burt is one of a "Seldom SEEN now" breed. Just like my daddy always did, he seeks out answers and is NOT shy in pointing out the misdoings of those with no conscience. He's NOT too scared to APPLAUD greatness when he sees it, no matter HOW unpopular it may be at the moment.

Are there any more like him? Yes…thankfully a few.

WE NEED THEM. WE NEED TO SUPPORT THEM, SO THEY WON'T DISAPPEAR.

Boy, I sure wish Burt had some music capabilities. I could do another "hall of fame" rant. Maybe he plays a kazoo. (ACTUALLY, since I wrote this, I learned…Burt plays BASS. WHO TAUGHT HIM? DAVID HULL…the lucky beast.)

Take heed, folks. We are going to lose each other, and when all is said and done, what else do we have? What else matters?

The hearse doesn't stop at the bank.

Here is my favorite McLuhan quote.

"Mud sometimes gives the illusion of depth."

VARDZIE IN THE CORPORATE WORLD

AM I SUFFERING FROM
STOCKHOLM SYNDROME?

Oh goodness, this is going to be a nightmarish romp. The ability to make a living doing the only thing I knew HOW to do came to an abrupt halt one day. I guess I could have hustled into some musical situations that would have paid the bills, but they weren't situations I was dying to join forces with. So, having just been through the mill personally and professionally, maybe it was time to take a breather.

I took part-time jobs in the "real" world (a world I knew precisely NOTHING about), so I'd be able to put together some music endeavors without the fear of being expelled from home and hearth.

The first job I acquired was in a Telemarketing company. Can you picture it? It took up only two evenings a week, and amongst other absurd aspects of this job was a disconcerting thing. It was an OK place, and donated part of their proceeds to deserving places. I was actually OK with it. The other big surprise...people who toiled in this joint, were boisterously CRAZY and immensely entertaining.

They'd give you a stack of people to call and you'd dial away, all over the country. The most ridiculous one I ran into was a man I rang up, named Richard Dick. Good LORD, what sadistic parents would give their child this wretched name? Geez his name is Dick Dick. OH NO. My heart went out to the poor thing, and yet, I was struggling to keep the laughter in. Other unfortunate names began to enter my overactive mind. Peter O'Toole. OH my. Dick Butkus. DICK BUTT KISS. Why would people do this to a child? Can you imagine their school experiences?

This reminded me of my dad, who knew a man that had proudly put on his license plate, a combination of HIS name, and that of his wife's. It came out ANAL. As soon as my pops saw it, he asked the distinguished gentleman, "Um, Al, do you REALIZE your car is saying ANAL?" In those days the word anal was not paired with the word retentive.

"Of course, Judge. Why, is there something wrong with it?"

"Is there something WRONG with it? AL. AL, your CAR is driving around town screaming ANAL."

"Oh, Judge, NO ONE thinks like that."

"Are you KIDDING, AL? EVERYONE thinks like that."

So I strengthened my resolve to NOT laugh when I called to ask if Mr. Dick was in. Ohhh GOD…did you just HEAR what THAT sounded like?? OK…dialing, ring ring. "Hello, may I please speak with Mr. Dick?" Oh…good…made it.

I then heard something that will live in my brain until I'm stricken with dementia, and even THEN, I don't think I'll be rid of the courteous Midwestern voice of that woman.

"Sure, dear, did you want big Dick, or little Dick?"

DID SHE JUST SAY…I THINK SHE SAID…OHHHHHH.

My first thought was that I'd have to CHOOSE, wouldn't I? WHAT do I SAY? Do I say…well, if I've got a choice, I'll take…?

My second thought was inescapable. Not ONLY was Dick Dick SENIOR stuck with this name, they UNBELIEVABLY passed this tragedy right along to their SON. And did they in fact CALL him LITTLE DICK? WELL, why not just go ahead and scar him for LIFE. I'll bet they say it in front of the WORLD, because this woman, this friendly woman is obviously UNAWARE that there is ANYTHING unseemly or funny about this name.

What am I laughing at? I'll bet there are countless people in countless offices who are laughing at MY name. Nevard Tellalian.

Once the marketing firm's home office realized there was a pack o' moolah to be made off sales, they cut the commission. So I up an' quit.

I did music pick-up work for quite a while, aided by the windfall left over from the phone job, and then hit bottom again. By then I HAD another lineup I'd put together. But…

I arrived; well, not arrived…it was more like a screaming belly flop down a thorny slope. The unavoidable crash unceremoniously plunging me into a netherworld that was populated with denizens who spoke in a foreign tongue.

Sounds nice, yes? I don't mean to be dramatic, but for a musician a job in a BANK is not unlike a "Right to Life" person working at Planned Parenthood, or a drunk joining the Mormon Tabernacle Choir, or…you get the picture.

This job only took up a couple days a week as well, so it wouldn't get in the way of music, but STILL. The job was in the Credit Card division in the corporate headquarters. It was a Connecticut-only bank, but the credit card they had was national and in the U.K.

I'd rarely had DEALINGS with banks, never mind the ludicrous idea of working in one. If you knew me, you'd have a rough time picturing me there. Trust me, I didn't blend. Oh, I can clean up when necessary, but staying the course for any length of time was not easy. Eventually the corporate mask starts going askew, and all hell breaks loose. It was a freaky experience though, and not lacking in gobs of laughable moments.

Unbelievably, there was trouble on the first day. I'd dressed myself primly, in a conservative skirt and blouse, my Rasta hair was lassoed and pinned to the top of my head. I entered the huge grey lobby and stepped into one of the grey elevators, along with five grey "elder statesmen" suited men, sporting crisp red power ties.

One of the grey men pressed the top button, so they were headed for the corporate suite. I was headed for the lowly eleventh floor, but when we reached the third floor, in walked a younger guy, who wasn't as grey as my other elevator companions.

I felt a little conspicuous, when he began to study me with considerable interest. As the elevator slowly climbed, he stared more intently, and finally blurted, "Hey, aren't you Nevard?"

"Uh. Yes. Yes, I am."

He POINTED at me, turned to the older grey suits, and with enthusiasm, he commenced to EDUMACATE 'EM about WHO was sharing their elevator.

"You know who that IS? It's NEVARD. She's a rock star, man. You ever SEEN her? I've seen her a BUNCH. It's AWESOME, man. Oh YEAH. One night she took a BIG SWIG of BEER and SPRAYED it ALL over the CROWD. AWESOME MAN, you GOTTA go see her."

Oh NO. NO. The grey suits began backing away, and it wasn't an easy maneuver to pull off in an ELEVATOR. Oh come ON, did they think I was hiding a cold Bud so I could reenact the spitting trick? In the bank elevator? I gave them a comforting smile and stumbled off when it hit my floor.

The most troubling thing about this would be? I mean besides the usage of the word awesome? The description the kid gave them wasn't TRUE. I would never spit beer into ANY audience. I don't DRINK on stage. I rarely drink offstage.

If it was a sweaty hot summer night, I WOULD take a slug from my WATER bottle and spray THAT around. The crowd has to be pretty rowdy to inspire that kind of fun; it would have to be a crowd I'd feel comfortable STAGE DIVING into. I might be an absolute dunce now and again, but I DO know an audience, and wouldn't deal out anything they're not ready for. Spitting beer would offend my sense of tidiness.

I'm not telling you I'm lacking outrageous leanings. If a club is set up right, I'll exuberantly climb onto the bar, and WALK the darn thing, kicking drinks off it as I go, but I'm careful and usually manage to kick empty glasses with maybe some ice sitting in them. I'll even DRAPE myself on a bar if I'm in the mood, like it's a grand piano in a 1930s movie. J.C. Dobbs in Philly was a good "bar walking" club, and so was the old Lone Star in New York. Maybe THAT's where this kid saw me playing with beer. If a stage had a balcony hanging over it, I'd wear a washable outfit, and let the balcony dwellers try to pour their beers into my mouth. That's some BIG fun. A little MESSY but FUN.

My pal, lil' Jen Bee, says she'll never forget her first day working there. Ahh I'll let HER tell it....

"Nevard...you must include the part where you 'sensed' a fellow weird-o was in your midst. (YOU BET, Jen girl...Let your freak flag FLY!!)

The background: The bank offered several "co-branded" credit cards including, the NRA and the Uncommon Clout branded cards. Revenue was split between the bank and the co-branded entities. Best as I recall, Uncommon Clout was an organization that used their co-branded card profit to donate toward LGBQT causes.

The scene: Jen's first week at work.

"Nevard, a person I'd never met before, stops at my desk, lowers her body, puts her face near mine and whisper-growls, 'Wait till the NRA people find out about the Uncommon Clout people!' Then...leaves."

"You know...I DO remember doing that, Jen. And sure enough, threatening calls began to pour in."

Well, they plopped me on the phone, to answer credit card queries, but THAT didn't last long, because I'd give away the store.

"Oh…you were out of the country (you were in the hospital, etc.) when your statement came? I'm taking off the late fee right NOW, OK?"

"So you PAID your balance in full, and you've got finance charges left over, huh? You paid eight thou…and we want another five bucks? Nope, I'm refunding it. I think you've spent enough money with us. Hey, if you're passing through Bridgeport, stop by. I'll take you to lunch. I bet Citibank won't take you to lunch. It's been lovely talking to you."

The most absurd calls I took during this brief time were worth the price of admission. A man who was an authorized user on his girlfriend's card called and begged me to increase the card's credit line. I gently advised the request would have to come from the card owner, namely his girlfriend, and asked if she could give me a buzz. Oh NO, he informed me, he was travelling, conducting TOP SECRET business for the FBI, and was an undercover agent.

As he blabbered on, I studied the account and saw the extensive list of charges, including hotels, restaurants, and OK, BUDDY, I'm seeing ESCORT services. Yup, he was doing some important undercover work all right.

My helpful attitude made a quick getaway, and I not so gently told him, "Oh YEAH, John, and may I use your name in the pejorative sense? I can SEE you're working your little heart out there, because I know BERMUDA is a notorious HOTBED of dangerous COVERT activity. THANK GOD you're over there, and making sure nothing compromises our national security. I'll be giving your girl a call to let her know how much you're willing to SUFFER for the good ol' USA. YOU are a DILIGENT and DEDICATED man, you are. Boy, she's going to be PROUD. Thanks for calling, John."

I hung up with the smarmy boyfriend, called his girlfriend, and gave her the skinny. I also passed on to her the wisdom of my father. "Cut up the card NOW, girl, and throw his nervy ass to the curb. He's just NO DAMNED GOOD. Call me if you need a shoulder to cry on, OK?"

The most truly staggering event I saw while toiling in this place was the number of employees who tried to commit fraud.

OK, WORK WITH me, people. If your heart's desire is to make some unlawful financial gains at your workplace, I'd heartily suggest you don't try to pull it off at a BANK. KNOW WHY?

HERE"S WHY. A bank's ONLY PRODUCT is MONEY, so THAT would be the product they're watching like hawks. KABBISH? Aye yi yi. If you'd like to rip off your employer, then go to work for a soft drink company. THEY'RE busy watching their secret recipe.

I can't BELIEVE how many took a crack at stealing. Every ONE of them was quickly caught. Every single one. I have countless stories of employees trying to remove balances from relatives' accounts, or their OWN, running up balances on corporate cards at gambling joints, raising credit lines—the list is endless. There was even a guy who got onto MY computer when I ran to the bathroom for a minute, and did things to his family's accounts. Computer footprints don't lie though. HE was caught as well, and I was interviewed at LENGTH in a secret basement room, and in the lofty legal department, while they were in the process of pinning this deed to his stupid butt.

The weirdest crook I met at the bank belonged to the infamous Nigerian Gang, a worldwide network of criminals. He had infiltrated the bank (it's what they DO, folks) and sat right next to me. Nice guy. How the heck would you know? His modus operandi was a favorite of his gang members. He'd change the address on a credit card, send a new card to a P.O. drop box, and change the address back to the correct one. Before the customer received their next statement, the card had been charged up to the hilt. I don't know how many accounts he successfully compromised, but they hauled him out in handcuffs one day, while he was lightheartedly saying "bye bye" to me. I was to witness the handcuff show on several occasions.

My general approach to customers didn't sit well with the bank. I didn't care how many calls I was expected to take per hour, and I did NOT like seeing customers ripped off. It especially turned my stomach if they were elderly or folks they'd suckered into overextending themselves.

They didn't fire me, darnit. I became a systems tester. I know LESS than nothing about computers, but being the lowest common denominator I possessed the makings of a GREAT tester.

They used an inspiring amount of double-talk to describe what I did. It was worded the way all corporations say things. SMOKE and MIRRORS is the name of the game. Here's just a small portion of it...

"Gather requirements and write detailed business analysis for users and program-mers. Provide development supervision, and work with programmers to construct accepted applications.

Serve as departmental liaison between the Cr. Card Operation's staff and the Infor-mation Technology Division.

Specialize in problem assessment, documentation and prioritization for the Business Unit. Write and edit technical documents for multiple projects, including status reports and client communications."

My findings in the corporate world are these. It is a world populated with a large contingency of arrogant kowtowing minions. It's like high school, but worse. Lots worse.

Personally (and maybe you've got a different take on this), I feel kindly towards most people lacking brain power, and friendly towards the simply ignorant. It's not usually their fault. I'm able to put up with a certain amount of arrogant behavior, but there had better also be some BIG spec-tacular quality they're toting around, because it's tedious to deal with those specimens. It is the unholy pairing of snotty AND dumb that gets to me. The corporate world is STUFFED with people like that. There were some fascinating, affectionate, and loyal humans I met up with, but they were rare creatures.

I was eventually moved to the operations area of the Credit Card busi-ness. For quite a while, I continued to sit in the call center, in order to pro-vide the system support they needed, which most of the time resulted in a phone call to the programmers who would hear me spewing words like "What a piece o' CRAP. Come on down and FIX this thing, because SA-TAN is beginning to reveal a holographic image of himself on their com-puter screens."

Strangely, my father was on the board of directors of this bank, but the ones hiring me did NOT know, and I never told them. He attended the shareholder's yearly meeting, and they anticipated his irreverent speeches.

Eventually, the CEO of the Credit Card division (soon to be CEO of the whole joint), wandered into my area, saw my name, and put two and two together. "For God's sake, are you Aram's daughter?"

"Yes, sir, I sure am."

His name was John Klein, and I know he looked up to my dad, as a mentor. They were cut of the same cloth. I admired John, and in the future he displayed the same love and courage that I'd seen in my Pops and my friend Jeff AND Jeremy.

The first time I met "the man" he showed up to see how the computer conversion from 16 to 32 bit was going. I was testing, and timing, and in came John.

After the introductions, he said, "I'm so GLAD you're here Nevard, because I think YOU'RE the one to ask. What are we GAINING from this conversion to 32 bit?"

Let's ask me a pertinent question. Did I know the answer to John's inquiry? Did I even know what a BIT was? No. HELL no. I was more than capable of pointing out DEFECTS to the IT people, and would ask them to "make that magic happen, y'all," but I wasn't aware of how they DID that, and not particularly interested.

So when John Klein asked for my expert explanation of the "bits," I confidently replied, "Huh. WHAT ARE WE GAINING?? It's a good thing you've come to ME, because I can TELL you PRECISELY what we're gaining. You SEE, John, we HAD 16 bits. NOW we have 32. Are you WITH me? ARE YOU WITH ME SO FAR? Good.

"We have DOUBLE the bit now. YES! I'm SAYING we are in proud possession of DOUBLE, TWICE, TWO TIMES the amount of BIT. Not SIXTEEN, no SIR…now we've got THIRTY-TWO! I hope I've cleared that up for you. Thanks for letting me work in your company."

The dazed look that came across John Klein's face was pretty. "DEAR LORD, Aram's daughter is an IMBICILE. She's got to be missing a few toys out of her toy box. Twice the 16 bit? Is she unbalanced?" That exchange with John became a Klein family legend. Sure was fun for ME.

I worked two days a week, arriving at eight thirty in the morning and leaving around eleven thirty at night. As I did my work, I could hear around me the voices of the hundred or so customer service people speaking to customers. Some of them did it in a demeaning way, and some were nasty. Some were fine, but many were NOT.

Finally, I was so irritated by the sound, I marched into the V.P.'s office and said, "Look here, Mr. Customer Service leader, do you know what your employees SOUND like out there? Why haven't they received training in the art of SPEAKING to people? They sound like NAZIS. If I were a customer I'd close my card faster than you can say RETENTION, and from where I'm sitting I can HEAR them doing just that. The reps you've thrown willy-nilly on those phones are PERFORMERS, and their AUDI-ENCE is not exactly getting stellar treatment out there.

"Tell you what. I'll write a SEMINAR, on dealing with customers. I'll do it in my SPARE TIME. I'll do it for the hourly NOTHING I'm being paid, so you won't have to SEND them to a class at the Marriott, and pay THOUSANDS per student. I'll do it because I can't STAND to hear the SLAUGHTERING of your customers anymore. HOW'S THAT grab you?"

WHY did I volunteer? WHY? What prompted such a rash offer? I wrote a six-hour seminar so these people could be taught how to speak without alienating customers.

Soon after I wrote it, I was asked to GIVE the darn seminar, so I did that TOO, and after I'd done a couple of them, figured…let someone ELSE do this crap…not ME.

A woman who was the head of some department evidently didn't like the fact that I had done this seminar. (OK, I'm sick of that word now.)

I wasn't the least bit interested in this person's department, and the seminar thing was a one off, but darling John Klein, kept insisting that I should be interviewed for a JOB with this person, and so I finally gave in.

Oh mercy, THAT was a bloodbath, and I don't mean mine.

As I entered a room, I found this woman reading papers. She rudely ignored me for a spell and then proceeded to tell me that I was MORE than unfit to take on the job she was interviewing me for.

She began by stating that I wore socks. I wasn't wearing them that day, but she did not LIKE socks. She then asked WHO had authorized my darned seminar, and when I told her, she was clearly peeved.

THEN, she smugly announced that while she thought my laugh was agreeable, she found it to be quite inappropriate sounding, and furthermore if I were dreaming of joining her exclusive group, I would need a great deal of "smoothing" out, and she added another little gem of character assassination. She had overheard me chatting with someone, and announced that she was not really GOOD at small talk, and did not believe in it, but she WAS offering me a ninety-day trial period for this job.

By the time she had finished her unsavory speech, I was seeing red amongst other colors wave before my eyes. What did I do? I let her HAVE it

"Pardon me, MS. Gloria Jerk, I need to answer your SEEMINGLY helpful commentary on my sense of style, character AND my sense of cultural refinement.

"It is more than strange to find myself using the word 'helpful' to describe the un-asked for trouncing you boorishly voiced for my edification, but let's give you the customary benefit of doubt, SHALL WE?

"If you WILL, MS. Jerk, allow me to give you an explanation concerning the presence of my offending SOCKS. I have a FOOT DEFORMITY that calls for cushioning between my feet and shoes. (That was a big ol' lie, but this was FUN.) I COULD with very little prompting REPORT your comments to our Human Resources Department. Those comments were pointedly aimed in a malicious way toward the congenital deformity of an employee…namely, MINE.

"I'd like to point out, Ms. Jerk, that YOU should not be allowed to serve on the fashion police brigade, given your rather recherché hairdo, which is unattractively accompanied by the sight of at least two inches of terribly neglected roots, and I'm going to go right ahead and add the following. That fucking dumb SCARF you're wearing is unduly unbecoming.

"If I heard you correctly, madam, and I believe I DID, you more than clearly criticized the SOUND of my laugh. I do not THINK I am of an age that would allow an easy transformation of the actual TIMBRE of my LAUGH. To expect such a vocal change would be too much to ask of anyone, and I find it to be an impolite request. As a matter of fact, why don't I give voice to MY opinion of a physical trait that would be more than impossible for YOU to change? I'm talking about the bottom of your lower limbs, which seem to be lacking ANKLES, thereby conjuring up a bovine image.

"Moving painfully along, please DO let me address your last two comments. I do not need SMOOTHING out, Ms. Jerk. I am perhaps the SMOOTHEST character the likes of YOU will EVER encounter. I am capable of, and on occasion, DO comfortably hang about with people holding high positions in our government, and some folks who have contributed widely to this country's (and often the WORLD'S) knowledge and expertise in vital areas. Given your obsessive fear of SMALL TALK, I'm afraid YOUR limited social capabilities would fall short if you were faced with the sparkling and erudite conversation of accomplished and eminently NICE people. It would take them but a MINUTE to see YOUR true colors...that of a STUPID and blindly BIGOTED woman, and speaking of SMALL TALK, Ms. Whatever the CRAP your name is. I'm talkin' bout YOU, the woman who would find any witty repartee to be a WASTE OF TIME."

NATIONS have been built on small talk.

CIVILIZATIONS were built on small talk.

CURES for DISEASE are sometimes brought to fruition through small talk. OUR COUNTRY'S DARING REVOLUTION, and our CHERISHED DEMOCRATIC FREEDOM was built on a strong foundation of small talk, and SHOOTING THE SHIT.

This is how people touch each other. This is how they exchange ideas.

"Why don't you indulge your small-minded self in some fun readings from the indisputably eminent mind of Ben Franklin? THERE was a man who was FOND of small talk, and engaged in it EVERY chance he GOT. Ever heard of HIM?

"Please do let me add one more thing. I DO not WANT to be smoothed over. I'd prefer to remain as I am, and YOU can take a firm hold of that ninety-day WHATEVER the FUCK it is, and SHOVE IT SIDE-WAYS. **HARD**. It's been a pleasure meeting with you."

A few days later, I got a call from a laughing John Klein. He had obviously heard about the wayward interview, but I'm certain he wouldn't have heard my uncensored responses. He STILL tried to talk me into taking that job. God, he was an endearing man.

"Why didn't you TAKE the ninety-day offer? You're a gambler, right?"

"Yeah, you're right, I AM, but that woman did NOT like me. I don't like to go where I'm not wanted, but the REAL reason is this."

"What, Nevard?"

"I DO NOT AUDITION."

He giggled like crazy.

Shortly after that daffy thang, I was approached by a woman named Sally. She asked me if I liked gospel music.

"LOVE that music, Sally. Don't dig the new stuff though. I like OLD gospel music."

"Oh yes, this is traditional gospel. My church in Brooklyn is having a gospel concert this Friday. I'd love for you to come."

I didn't have the use of a car that week, but Sally was insistent and said she'd have her friends stop by to pick me up.

Along came Friday evening, and as promised an SUV pulled up. I hopped in, and met the kind folks who were giving me a lift to the "concert." They WERE very nice.

Shortly after we arrived at the auditorium (Sally had said CHURCH), we took our seats, and the THING commenced. I used the word THING because this was NOT a concert…it was a full-blown revival meeting, and the MUSIC? THE MUSIC? Well, I would never have called it gospel. I'd call Sister Rosetta Tharpe or Vernard Johnson gospel. This stuff was the MUZAC of gospel. You betcha. It was the modern corporate gospel I had told Sally I was most definitely NOT interested in.

I'm not going to go into every gory detail…just a few highlights. Let me say that within a half hour, SALLY was standing next to me, and talking in tongues. Soon, she was shaking, and shortly after THAT, she was clutching ME in her sweaty little embrace. YUP. Sweatin', clutchin', and shakin' she was, and every few moments, she'd scream in my ear, "TALK TO JESUS, NEVARD. TALK TO JESUS!"

"Talk to Jesus, Sally? Talk to Jesus? Let me just give that a GO, OK?"

"That's right, TALK TO JESUS, NEVARD."

"Oh yeah, Sally, I'm talkin'." *HEY, JESUS! WHAT'S WITH THE BAD TOP FORTY GOSPEL CRAP HERE?*

Sally clearly cannot hear the dialogue I'm having with Jesus, and she's egging me on like I'm a possible runner up at the Preakness.

"THAT'S RIGHT, TALK TO JESUS, NEVARD."

"Oh, some more, huh, Sally? Okey dokey." *UH, JESUS, I'VE BEEN KIDNAPPED, AND I HAVE NO CAR. WHATCHA GONNA DO*

*BOUT THAT? CAN YA GET SALLY THE HELL OFF ME? I'M
SOAKING WET HERE.*

Did my night out with the rollers start to wind down after my talks with
Jesus? No, NO. Sally wants to march me up to the STAGE, so I can get in
on the vigorous pushing-you-to-the-floor-with-the-hand-on-your-forehead
thing. Hopefully after THAT move, I'd be speaking in tongues just like
HER.

Sally was enthusiastically pulling at me, but I planted my feet firmly on
the floor, until her sweaty hands let go. I'd like to think it was the last conversation with Jesus that finally did it.

*HEY JESUS, I'M TELLIN' YA. BETTER GET THIS SALLY OFF
ME NOW, OR I'M HEADING UP TO THAT STAGE, HOPPIN' UP
THERE, AND DECLARING TO ONE AND ALL—I'M ONE OF SA-
TAN'S CHILDREN. YOU THINK MY VOICE AIN'T LOUD
ENOUGH? TRY ME!*

The torment finally ended. The Sally thing was pretty entertaining for a
while, but I was getting a headache from the music. Sally thankfully took
off for a moment, and I sat to wait for the folks I'd arrived with to start
moving toward the door.

Still sopping wet from my satisfying evening being doused with Sally
sweat, I looked up to see her coming back. She had the preacher with her.
The preacher approached me, told me how GLAD they were to have me
there (what…all five HUNDRED of them?), and wasn't it GRAND to
meet me after hearing ALL ABOUT me. OK, am I hallucinating now? Did
the good reverend just tell me he'd HEARD about me?

Afterward I politely grilled Sally. "Uhh, SALLY. WHY does your
preacher know anything about me?"

"I thought you'd be a good CANDIDATE, Nevard, for—"

"HEY, SALLY. I'm not your HEATHEN for the night, baby. NO
SIR."

That's some scary stuff. I'm surprised they didn't dump me off a bridge
on 95 on the way home.

CONFORMITY IS THE LAST BASTION
OF MEDIOCRITY

I tried like the DEVIL to get FIRED from that infernal place. I was moved to the Operations floor and had two testing helpers, Chuck and Tony, who were a riot and a much-needed distraction for me. I was so BORED and sick of the place, I began to act in ways that were outrageous simply to amuse myself.

With Chuck and Tony egging me on, I was ready to SHAKE IT UP.

Tony began to twice daily play a recording of the song "Dancing Queen." He played it nice and loud, and it could be heard throughout the entire floor. "Dancing Queen" is not a song I'm particularly fond of, oh what the hey…I could hardly bear to hear a second of the thing, but I quickly learned to LOVE it.

As soon as I heard the opening strains of this tune, I'd abruptly rise from my desk and move into the aisle. I would point at someone, and yell, "I'd like to dedicate this dance to YOU, Merelice Camporiale!"

I made my way down the aisle…sloooowly…some zany dance moves began to work their evil way out of me. Wiggling away, I'd do the goofy cat eyes, a little shimmy and shake, and at some point someone would push a desk chair into the aisle.

AHHH, here comes a fake faint into the chair, and soon, my legs be kickin' high up in the air, and rolling fast in the ergonomically correct vehicle. NOW, I'm reaching the end of the aisle, LEAPING from the chair…KICKIN' it down the aisle, and some devilish and FRENZIED dancing is goin' on y'all… with the hair flinging around in circles, a foot thrown on the top of someone's desk…just CRAZY dancing.

The entire time, Chuck and Tony were standing behind me doing identical boy dancer moves. They were GOOD. I'd finally reach that rolling chair in the middle of the floor, and collapse in it. Chuck is running at me with a silver lamé James Brown-like cape, draping it over my shoulders (a la J.B, of course), leading me back to my desk, and sittin' my butt down. You KNOW what comes next. You BETCHA. Right in the middle of that grey-walled hell, in a room the size of a football field. Filled to the brim… with pale, bored desk dwellers. FLING off that cape, GET the JB feet moving, and, dance like the devil is chasing me, till the song ends.

Tony thanked the crowd (folks sitting at their desks, or peering out of their grey cubes), asked them to tip their waitresses on the way out, and instructed them to "please drive carefully." All the goofy showbizzy clichés. "Thanks for coming. We'll be at GIGGLES in Newark this weekend.

HEY…we ain't the warm-up baby, we're a Giggles HEADLINER. Please don't miss our matinee today at one. Two shows a day, ladies and gentlemen, TWO SHOWS a DAY! BACK BY POPULAR DEMAND! YOU CAN"T STOP US."

I don't think the bank had ever seen anything more ridiculous. EVER.

Sometimes we'd get complaints…music's too loud…not appropriate… Did this stop US? NOPE. TWO SHOWS A DAY. After a while, people from other floors began to hear of our un-bank-like misbehavior, and the three of us began to get whispering calls. "What time's the show today?" or "Would you dedicate a dance to so and so?"

Eventually they came from all over the building, bank people and security people, the Connecticut Bar Association housed in the building: sneaking down staircases and standing in doorways. They'd fit themselves in wherever they could, hoping their bosses wouldn't catch them, and then they'd run INTO their bosses who had come to see.

During that time I was forced to attend meetings. A LIMITLESS amount of meetings. My shins still have the scars from the kicks I'd receive under the conference room tables, because often I wasn't able to keep the snickers from coming out of my mouth.

The first time I heard the phrase "I think we can find a more elegant solution" I "accidently" dropped my notebook under the table, so I could dive under there, and hide my giggling. ELEGANT? That would be describing dinner at the Four Seasons, not a business procedure.

The little V.P. that uttered THIS gem HAD to be under the influence of a psychedelic substance. He smugly said, "We are running out of time for this. Let's just go after the low-hanging fruit." My pen spontaneously flew out of my hand, and I burst into laughter that was so violent, I fell out of my chair and under the desk again. LOW-HANGING FRUIT? Come HERE, because I don't think there's any low hanging NOTHIN' on you.

Why did EVERYONE used the phrase "let's take this offline," even when we weren't ON any line ANYWHERE.

WHERE do they get this tripe, and how do they utter it with such seriousness? The amount of corporate lingo that was repeated, over and over was so delicious to me, I started an email that was passed between my girlfriends. Actually Robin started it with her first laughing email to me. I wanted to freeze these yummy tidbits so they'd never die. Like Trigger. My girls stepped up to the plate in a spectacular fashion. Here are our contributions to posterity:

From: <Nevard.Tellalian@rbsnb.com> *Here's a little something we've been doing, to preserve the ever invasive, always banal (and usually hilarious), corporate lingo. If you have any to add, please do feel free to update our catalogue of shame!! Let's keep this tradition of trash ALIVE!!!*

Very, very, very truly yours,

Vardzie

First entry... Robin

Yes, we need someone who can think outside the box so our core business project can launch successfully. Let's dialogue onsite, shall we? Hahahaha.

Second Entry...Nevard Tellalian

Gee, I don't know if I could step up to the plate on that one, as my plate is full, and I think a more elegant solution would be to go after the low hanging fruit before we move the goal posts on this slippery slope, and put this issue to bed.

IN ADDITION, if we can leverage resources, and push the envelope...in effect, become proactive, and not reactive with a result driven game plan, we can find a strategic fit with a value added enterprise.

AND if this client -focused paradigm can actually empower employees to go the extra mile, we can then touch base with our knowledge base and fast track ourselves into a win-win situation.

FINALLY, I'd like to think this would be the benchmark of a hardball mindset, serve to effectively display our robust suite of products, push the envelope, and force a knock-on effect so that we may revisit the big picture in a no blame environment... lest we find ourselves out of the loop, and virtually kudo-less.

From: <Nevard.Tellalian@rbsnb.com>

Here are the latest entries into our growing anthology of Corpspeak....and might I say how very proud of you I am...so proud, that I am starting to capitalize properly.

Third Entry......Robin

Hahahahaha – well done but I like the acronyms best...

I submitted a Scoping Doc along with my OMR to SAM. Yeah...I was approved...now all I need to do is write the ORD, submit a BAR, wait till WAM, approve the RSD, have a lot of meetings with a BA reviewing the BRD, submit a BIRR to InfoSec, submit an IA to UAT, manage the PP, talk to the PMO just in case, and get approval from the EMC. Easy...

From: <Nevard.Tellalian@rbsnb.com>

The startling and cavalier way our Kings English has been mangled has long been cleverly concealed under the veritable rock of "the man" for which you and I work (big wheel keep on turnin').

I salute you, oh plucky writers....your inimitable bravery shines like a beacon that illuminates this path we wearily tread...glory glory halleluiah,

HERE ARE NEW ADDITIONS...AND I'M CALLING THE LIBRARY OF CONGRESS TODAY.......

Fourth Entry.....Denise Jacob

What you are telling me is the current customer facing solution that is maintained by our business partner is not as intuitive and user friendly as the organization would encourage. In an effort to gain market share, a sexier, provocative user friendly solution will have to be implemented if we want the organization to succeed and have ultimate speed to market with our outstanding goods and services.

In an effort to make the customer smile, whilst speaking with one voice as an organization – we will implement a simple "out of the box" , "plug and play" intuitive and interactive business solution that will enable us to gain share of wallet, increase the bottom line and create a stellar, best in class, benchmarking solution that will surely wow our employees, customers and business partners, henceforth – we will take this to the next level, be a benchmark for other organizations and blaze a path of excellence within the industry.

Fifth Entry....Jennifer Banks

I simply don't have the bandwidth for that

Sixth Entry....Merelice Camporiale

GLOBAL PENETRATION!

Meetings were a challenge for me. I had an un-corporate tendency to call these creatures on their crap and a complete disregard for their place within the hierarchy of this outfit. This unstoppable tendency elicited admiration from some, fear and loathing from others, and affection in a few.

The Credit Card was bought by the Royal Bank of Scotland, and suddenly, from across the pond, little Scots were swimming to our shores by the dozens. We were used to having U.K. folks about, because we'd had a card there for years, but this was a new group. Still, the stupefying dullness of the whole scene began to change something within. This is not the kind of work that feeds the soul.

Whenever one of those Scottish Executive V.P. boys would call to ask me questions about any project I might be working on, I'd pointedly ignore their requests. Considering...that many of them lived in London, I asked

THEM things like, "Soo, what is the origin of that saying 'and Bob's yer uncle'? Where does that come from? Hey, don't you love the Henry Root letters? I love 'em. Do you read Saki? Um, is Ralph Richardson still living? LOVE Dickens like the dickens. Oh yeah, WODEHOUSE...um, would you come to my desk later and do a nice Jeeves for me?"

Sometimes I'd go into a long musical riff when they'd call. This would REALLY get them going. "Do you know Pete Best? He's my hero. I've got an altar set up in my living room. Do you think his wife slaps him upside his head every morning? Is that club, um, you know, The Speakeasy. Is it still there on Margaret Street in London? Know what? We gave you ALL our good stuff way back when. We sent over all the good blues, and rock and roll we had. I'd like to thank you for sending us the Beatles in return. Great gift. Oh yeah, the Stones, the Kinks, the Yardbirds and all. Thank you very much. You STOLE our Jimi though. What's THAT? Not very cricket of you, mate.

"We had a nice exchange going for a while, but then you had to go and BLOW it. I mean, I dig YOU, but I think we've ALL about had it with that Andrew Lloyd Webber. Ah bollocks, he just wrote the ONE song. OK, maybe TWO. They've all got the same chord pattern. God, we gave you GERSHWIN, and you sent us HIM? You think you could take him back? We're a little tired of him. Nice chatting with you. Bye now."

These poor men would finally hang up, and I wonder how long it took them to realize they never DID get an answer to their question.

One can only wonder why they kept me on.

There was an email circulating with a game. I can't remember...you'd put in the first and last letter of your last name, or something and it would spit out your porn name. Silly really, but I immediately sent an email to the most pompous and tedious Senior V.P. I could think of. It said, "I thought you might be interested. Your porn name is apparently The Aryan FUCK Toy."

Why didn't they can my insidious rear for these rebellious actions? We had a systems conversion—don't know what THAT means—I only know...nope, sorry...I didn't know ANYTHING. I agonizingly DROWNED in their darn conversion, worked seven days a week to map their old front end to their NEW front end. What that's all about? Dunno... but it was a big ol' bummer. Y'all can go ask some IT Nazi if interested.

Well…I converted, and mapped. The new system was NOT looking as if it was good to go on the eve of the "LAUNCH" date. Not nearly ready for "LIFT OFF."

DARNIT….WHY DO THESE PEOPLE SPEAK AS IF THEY'RE ASTRONAUTS? JUST HOW SELF-IMPORTANT CAN THEY GET IN THE CORPORATE ARENA?

Oh. Was I telling you something? YEEEESSSS…another pitiful attempt on my part to get fired. And a great attempt it WAS. The big kahoona came to my lowly grey desk at about midnight to inquire if the new whatever the heck it was would be ready for "LIFT OFF" the next morning, and were we set to "PULL THE SWITCH" (geez, as if the space race lingo isn't un-attractive enough, there were allusions of uncomfortable electrocutions).

When "the man" unsuspectingly posed these questions, guess who of COURSE could not stop her mouth from pouring forth the truth? The truth that NO big kahoona ever wants to hear.

"Are we READY? READY, DID YOU SAY? TO PULL THE SWITCH, AL? ARE WE? So glad you asked. The answer is HELL NO, PAL.

Your I.T. department's been sleeping at their desks, and sneaking off to bars, and calling me drunk from said bars to come and sing tunes with them. Guess what, AL? WE'RE FUCKED. Yes indeed, you heard me. Your proudest moment tomorrow morning will be when your little pet pro-ject …you know AL, the one you didn't want to spend any dough on? Oh yeah, AL.

"YOUR BABY'S GONNA SHIT THE BED ALL RIGHT. Can I say it again? WE'RE FUCKED ALBERT…and I DO mean in the Biblical sense. You may as well assume the position NOW. I'll DO THE SAME…OK?"

Why they kept me on? I DUNNO.

I finally stood up one day, in the middle of that vast grey mass of desks, and very loudly broadcasted the following statement.

"HELLO, BANK PEOPLE, LISTEN UP. I
HAVE AN ANNOUNCEMENT. I'D LIKE
YOU ALL TO COME TO YOUR SENSES. WE
ARE NOT PERFORMING BRAIN SURGERY
HERE. WE ARE NOT SAVING LIVES. WE
ARE NOT CONTRIBUTING A THING TO
ANYTHING. WHO AMONGST US IS
TAKING ANY OF THIS CRAP SERIOUSLY?
WE ARE TEENSY WEENSY PEONS,
WORKING FOR A COMPANY WHOSE ONLY
PRODUCT IS MONEY. I FOR ONE AM
DULY EMBARRASSED FOR THE ENTIRE
SAD COLLECTION OF US."

That was my last stand in corporate America.

I LOVED JOHN KLEIN. HE WAS A GOOD
MAN. HE DIED FROM EXACTLY THE
SAME THING THAT JEEREMY DIED
FROM.

MARGO WALLACE TELLALIAN
THE LESSON

The lesson I've been going on and on about and sneaking into every chapter of this book came in large part from my mamma and daddy. It was Mamma who finally and perfectly crystallized it for me after we lost Daddy. I'd always known it, felt it, and understood it, but my mother's verification came out of her in such a guileless, simple manner, it took my breath away. She seemed surprised that I even had a need to clarify these things. This subject had ALWAYS been clear to her. It felt like I was one of her famous banana pies and she had finally popped me in the fridge to solidify. I'd like to tell you about Margo.

Margaret Wallace was born in Bogue Chitto, Mississippi, and brought up in Macomb, the oldest of thirteen children. Her folks, Onie and Parshall Wallace were both of Scottish descent, and were farmers. Their home was tiny, and living was primitive. Their main crop was cotton. Margo looked after all the younger children. By all accounts the Wallace babies were a handful. They were brought up the old Southern way. Elders were ALWAYS sir or ma'am, and they were strict Baptists.

Margo always spoke of their life as "slow and deliberate" due to the energy-sucking heat and humidity in which they performed never-ending physical labor. It was a more innocent time, and fun was found in church, or at the creek, or quilting, or burying potatoes to cook in the ground. Music. They always had music.

This was a **farm** girl. She loved the land, and knew more about nature than you could shake a stick at. Some of her stories were everyday things to her, but horrifying to me. I can hear her now. "If we had those good RED squirrels here in Connecticut, I could make y'all a NICE squirrel pie." Or "Well, it's EASY to wring a chicken's neck honey—it's all in the wrist." And she'd display the exact SNAP needed to do the job.

Mamma was a little girl with curiosity that could not be fulfilled within her surroundings. She had a longing that was STRONG to see more of the world, so she ran up north, to Washington DC during WWII. It must have taken a whole lot of bravery. In those days girls simply didn't DO that. She was expected to marry a guy in her little town, and settle the heck DOWN, but lil' Margo Wallace was a rebel.

She got herself up to D.C., and got a job with the Provost Marshall's office in the Pentagon.

The fateful meeting with Aram Tellalian occurred during this period, and ohhhh LORD, Daddy told me Margo was a wicked and wild girl on WHEELS. Mommy didn't KNOW her suitor Aram was a spy. She found out AFTER the war.

She moved on to NYC, at some point during this time, and lived near Washington Square. Their stories of the jazz clubs they frequented and the parties they had were what LEGENDS are made of.

The Mississippi Queen was a VORACIOUS reader, and passed this love along to me. The most painful punishment she ever gave me was the day she wouldn't allow me to go to a BOOK fair.

Mommy was a horticulturist, an environmentalist, and an artist who was decades ahead her time.

Our home was always teeming with Mamma's artistry. Her learning and experimenting NEVER stopped. SFSDF

She'd make arrangements from all the plants in her gardens, not only for us—she brought them to Nursing homes, and anywhere else she thought needed brightening up. They'd often be brought with some of her Southern cooking.

What she loved more than anything was working the land. She covered every inch of soil she could get a hold of with glorious plantings. Not only her own, but the entire TOWN'S land. The amount of plantings she did on roadsides and around EVERY public building was breathtaking. I know there were a heap of folks who moved there due to the bountiful landscaping installed by Margo. She even recreated one of her rock gardens in a public park.

It was dangerous to drive around town with Mamma. She'd see some flowers she'd planted in a street MEDIAN and stop to do some weeding. Oh, you went WITH her, and weeded away in the middle of the street, or wherever she saw something that needed attention. She didn't care if you were wearing a ball gown—if you were gonna HANG with Margo, you'd darn well to do your PART with Margo.

When Daddy died, the light went straight out of my darling mamma's eyes. HER light had left her, and I knew in my heart she was lost to me too. From that very moment of his passing.

They called each other Mommy and Daddy not because they had children. They used these names because she was his little girl, and he was her little fella. They would always be that to each other.

About a week after we lost him, Mamma felt like she was getting an infection, so off we went to the urologist. I said, "You know, Mamma, we should both go to see Doc. Shouldn't you be paying him a visit soon?"

Her inconceivable response?

"Oh no, honey, there's no need to. I haven't had sex in three months."

"I'm sorry, Mommy…did I hear that right? THREE MONTHS?"

"Well sure, honey. You know Daddy wasn't feeling too well."

"Three MONTHS, Mommy? THREE MONTHS? Not FEELING WELL? Mamma, Daddy was getting that radiation every day, and Chemo…and…ARE YOU SURE?"

"Well of course I'm sure, Vardzie. Daddy and I never stopped RO-MANCING. What's the MATTER, honey?"

"HOLY…ARE YOU FU…OH. MY. GOD."

"You stop that cussing, honey."

"Yes, Mommy."

My daddy died at the age of NINETY-THREE, and Mommy was EIGHTY-something. Daddy worked until two months before he died, but he was VERY sick during the last few months he went to his office. After my initial shock at my mamma's revelation, I wasn't at all surprised they were still doin' it.

If you're lucky it'll be part of YOUR life till you're ninety as well, but Dear LORD, how did they MANAGE this, while one of them was dying and in pain, and the other not doing much better?

I think they knew there wasn't much time left for them on this earth together, and they sure as HELL were NOT going to leave it with their beautiful union broken. These were not people who went quietly into the night.

I knew they were still crazy for each other right up until the end. They had NEVER stopped smooching away in the kitchen—I don't mean little smooches…I mean long gorgeous, passionate kisses that were downright steamy.

Their constant hunger for each other, their flirtatious ways…it was one of the most endearing things about them, and it sure was the most astounding thing I'd ever seen.

After Mommy's remarkable avowal of "no sex in three months," I confided in her. I usually told the folks everything that occurred in my life…unless it was a relationship that was hurting me. I'd always felt I was protecting them, but they knew. They knew. Mommy and Daddy would stay out of it, but they'd do their best to warn me: "Vardzie, you can't save the world. You CANNOT help those who will not help themselves."

I'd never told Mamma THIS one. I was afraid she would have been frightened for me, as it described uncharacteristically reckless behavior, the likes of which I rarely indulged. Truly reckless. I can't believe I had let something like this take place without calling the police. It seems like a dream to me now, but it wasn't. I can't believe I'm gonna tell YOU.

At the time I was slowly beginning to venture into the music world. Little sit-ins, duo types of things. I was still underage, and although I couldn't get into the larger clubs, I'd sneak into smaller ones with friends who were playing, so I could learn. Tony Mason, Paul Geremia, Ed Vadas and later, pals Norman and Suzy were there for me to tag along with, and always kind to me. Thank you, darling pals. I sure owe you ALL.

A year or two of this noodling went on, and I slowly started to go at it full time. I was still underage, but clubs never asked for your ID if you were the talent for the night. It probably never occurred to them.

During this musical birthing period, I shared an apartment with my girlfriend Connie in Bridgeport, Connecticut, and not in a good area. In a couple of years I'd be moving to Mystic, Connecticut, and Connie would move in with a guy named Ray.

One night, maybe three or four in the morning, I was awakened by a sound. There at the foot of my bed, stood a man in a three-piece suit.

He was immaculately dressed. Every hair in place. He looked like he had just walked out of a boardroom, or was a Mob boss. How the heck did I know? I didn't hang with people who looked like him. Why in the world didn't I scream? I had no idea how he had gained entry into our apartment. We had a deadbolt.

He sat next to me on the bed, and put his finger to my lips, saying, "Shhhhh." And strangely I wasn't fearful. No feeling of impending bad things. I felt a little anxious, like just before a math exam, but not threatened in any way.

I calmly watched as he removed his jacket, his vest, and his tie. He said my name (how did he know my name?) and removed my nightie. And I let him. He took off his belt. I was scared for a second...*is he planning something horrible with that?* No, he simply dropped it to the floor. Off came his shoes.

He ran his fingers through my hair, pushed me down on the bed, pulled the rest of his clothing halfway off, and then proceeded to "have" me in an amazingly decisive way.

He whispered things to me. Most is a blur, but the words he said that are burned into my memory are these:

"You HAVE to lose your control. You have to give it to me. GIVE it to me. Let it go. NOW. You'll get it back...I'll give mine to YOU. Open the door. This is the beginning. I said NOW."

Something gave way in my head. I was losing my grip, and afraid. The way he looked at me was demanding, craving, and slightly menacing. I laid down my arms. I answered him with physical obedience and submission, but the look in MY eyes was one of defiance, daring, and not a small degree of insubordination.

I obeyed. I did what I was told, and finally, felt my will crumble, my pride collapse, my eyes soften with longing and I let him see me. Thoroughly conquered. He owned me. He knew it. I knew it.

And I understood.

Do YOU understand? I want YOU to get it. It's not easy to describe, or teach, and I'm not sure if I've been successful in getting it across.

My roommate Connie and I never DID figure out how the mystery man got into our apartment. The door was not jimmied. So HOW?

"Connie, did you give Ray our key? Or anyone ELSE?" She hadn't.

We could not understand how he knew ME, and how he guessed or obviously KNEW when I'd be home. How did he know I would be ALONE? I wasn't seeing anyone at the time. Neither one of us was afraid. Boy, we were really skating on thin ice.

The mystery man appeared again a week later, though not in person. I came home late and found that my entire bed was covered in rose petals. After yelling for Connie, who was asleep in the living room sofa bed, the two of us stood and stared at the "rose" bed incredulously. It resembled a scene from a MOVIE, for gosh sake.

Connie hadn't heard him come in, but we knew it was he. The two of us stood there for a good while puzzling on this, and then Connie noticed there was a piece of paper lying under all the petals. She gingerly picked it up, and we took a look. It was a Shakespearean soliloquy.

This was not my first run in with the Bard of Avon, but it was before I'd been to that Charnovsky class, and I'd never seen this text before.

It was undeniably something he wanted me to understand. I had to read it over and over. I DID understand…and always HAD really, but this was the first time I had seen it in WORDS.

Keep in mind, Shakespeare was firmly planted in Elizabethan society and kept within the accepted restraints of the era when describing the roles of men and women. MEN played all the women's roles in his plays, because in those days, a woman was not allowed to perform. Unlike most writers of this period though, William understood women, and his writing was sympathetic towards them.

In my long-winded way, I'm just trying to tell you…if you're a female reader, just substitute the word "man" where it says woman.

It is long, but please do bear with me if you can.

This is the lesson. The lesson I'd learned from my mommy and daddy, but didn't know how to express. Please read it. Read it again and again. If you can't understand the language, and WANT to understand, call me. I want you to have this.

O, we have made a vow to study, lords,
And in that vow we have forsworn our books.
For when would you, my liege, or you, or you,
In leaden contemplation have found out
Such fiery numbers as the prompting eyes
Of beauty's tutors have enrich'd you with?
Other slow arts entirely keep the brain;
And therefore, finding barren practisers,
Scarce show a harvest of their heavy toil:
But love, first learned in a lady's eyes,
Lives not alone immured in the brain;
But, with the motion of all elements,
Courses as swift as thought in every power,

And gives to every power a double power,
Above their functions and their offices.
It adds a precious seeing to the eye:
A lover's eyes will gaze an eagle blind;
A lover's ear will hear the lowest sound;
Love's tongue proves dainty Bacchus gross in taste:
For valour, is not Love a Hercules,
Still climbing trees in the Hesperides?
Subtle as Sphinx: as sweet and musical,
As bright Apollo's lute, stung with his hair;
And when Love speaks, the voice of all the gods,
Make heaven drowsy with the harmony.
Never durst poet touch a pen to write
Until his ink were temper'd with Love's sighs;
O, then his lines would ravish savage ears,
And plant in tyrants mild humility.
From a woman's eye this doctrine I derive;
They sparkle still the right Promethean fire;
They are the books, the arts, the academes,
That show, contain and nourish all the world;
Else none at all in aught proves excellent.
Then fools you were these women to forswear,
Or keeping what is sworn, you will prove fools.
For wisdom's sake, a word that all men love,
Or for love's sake, a word that loves all men,
Or for men's sake, the authors of these women,
Or for women's sake, by whom we men are men,
Let us once lose our oaths to find ourselves,
Or else we lose ourselves to keep our oaths.

The mystery man disappeared for a month, and then he was back. He came into my life four times altogether and, true to his word he gave his control to me just as he'd taken mine. I owned HIM.

The morning after his last appearance, I found a note on my dresser. The note is long gone, but this is about as close as I can get to the contents:

"Nevard. My warm and lovable coquette. I wanted you to see the foundation of all devotion. I was there to give you awareness that will serve you well. I was not entirely without selfish motives. I made my presence known in an oafish manner, but there was no other way to gain entrance to your boudoir. I will not fit in your life or you in mine. You won't see me again, and I will not forget, but you must erase me. You will not lose what I have taught you. You were my love. Go now…and DANCE."

I ran to look up the word "coquette." I can distinctly remember the phrase "foundation of all devotion" and "Go now, and DANCE." And I was amused by the word boudoir. What did he mean by erasing him? It was all confusing…but I knew one thing. I knew what that Shakespeare stuff meant. I studied and studied it.

I never knew his name, where he was from, or what he did that put him in that Armani-looking suit. I knew nothing about him, except why he was there. To teach me.

After I told my mamma this story, I quoted what I could remember from that monologue, and I asked her:

"Mommy, is it right? I mean what I've felt all these years? I grew up seeing it in you and Daddy. The way you played, the way you sparkled…is this where your interest in LIFE came from? IS IT?"

"Well of course it is, honey. Without THAT, you LOSE the …oh, you know what I mean, you lose what you said…the interest in everything. Daddy and I saw people our age…well, they just withered away. They dried up. We saw that in people much younger than WE were. VARDZIE, you could have been KILLED by that man. I wonder about you sometimes. You'd forget your HEAD if it wasn't attached."

"I fucked like a cowboy, Mommy?"

"Yes, you DID. Nevard Tellalian. Don't you let anything like that happen AGAIN."

Sigh. "I'm pretty certain there won't be any Yummy guys appearing in my bedroom out of nowhere, Mamma."

"Well, you just never know, honey."

"So I AM right? About the passion? About the lust? **If we keep that alive inside, then it feeds our CREATIVE parts? It fuels our curiosity for learning, our energy, it spills into our desire to love, to help, to be compassionate? To keep CARING about the world?**"

"Yes. I never THOUGHT about it, but yes. Of COURSE it does, Vardzie."

"Mamma, is what you had with Daddy…you know, your romancing, the way you played with each other…was it a kind of war?

"Was it a seductive beautiful WAR, and that's what's supposed to be between a man and a woman? Was it a push and pull? WHY IS MY ATTEMPT TO UNDERSTAND, A BAD THING????? It always looked as if you were daring each other. Baiting and chasing each other. WAS IT A DANCE? IS IT A DANCE, MOMMY?"

"YES. SURE that's what your daddy and mommy had. Yes, it is a dance. You knew THAT. What's WRONG? Something is EATING at you…you're like a dog with a bone. What is wrong? Stop your fussing now, baby."

"I can't help it, Mamma. I only found that ONCE in somebody. Do YOU see it in the eyes? Is that where YOU see it?"

"Ya, that's where Daddy had it."

"Mommy, will I EVER see a man like that again?"

"Oh I don't think so, honey. You know there USED to be more men… but even when I met Aram, there weren't many. You're not likely to meet any like THAT nowadays."

"That's great. GOD, you're my NEGATIVE mamma. I feel hopeless."

"Stop that, honey, Mommy's not negative, I'm REALISTIC."

"What's HAPPENING to this world?"

Three months later, my precious mamma was gone.

There were two more losses this year, and both were vicious, and almost disabling. I kept going despite the grieving. I promised I would write this book, and I always keep promises, just as I know Jeff carried out his promise to my daddy. I think he promised my father that he wouldn't let me see him slowly die, and I think he would have kept me from it anyway. He taught me the same thing my folks did. I observed, I loved, I learned. I need to finish this. I need to share the lesson I was instructed to pass on.

By destroying desires, you will destroy your mind.

Put simply, THAT is the lesson. You don't think the word COMPASSIONATE has the word passion in it by accident, do you? It's what keeps you young, keeps you interesting and interested in LIFE.

My parents were never ELDERLY. Ever. As their peers seemed to dry up, and become numb inside, they fell by the wayside.

For the last three thousand years the Indian savants knew it, as did the Greeks and Egyptians. They knew that genius and illumination come from transmuted sexual energy. Freud put it in a different way. He believed that all creative activity arises from of the libido.

As Reich correctly put it, it is anchored in the body, in the libido. He had clearly mentioned this.

But since science has no awareness of a phenomenon that has been in evidence for thousands of years, that it IS this transmutation of sexual energy that leads to creativity, then naturally all current theories about this are incomplete.

HERE IS THE LESSON. NOT ONLY FOR ARTISTS. FOR EVERYONE.

ALL CREATIVE ENERGY COMES FROM THE LIBIDO. THE IMPETUS AND PASSION TO CREATE COMES FROM THAT DESIRE.

I DON'T CARE WHERE IT ENDS UP.

I DON'T CARE IF YOU'RE AIMING FOR THOSE HIGHER CHAKRAS.

I DON'T CARE HOW INTELLECTUAL OR DIVINE YOU AIM TO BE.

I DON'T CARE IF YOUR PASSION IS TO GIVE BIRTH TO THINGS THAT ARE CEREBRAL OR HOLY.

You must never lose desire. It is a powerhouse of a catalyst. A stimulus to creativity, to love and to life.

I'M SAYING IT AGAIN. IT DOES NOT MATTER WHERE IT ENDS UP. IT ALL COMES FROM ONE PLACE.

THIS IS WHERE WE GET IT...THOSE OF US THAT HAVE THE DEVOTION FOR LIVING, LEARNING, AND CREATING.

THIS IS WHERE EVERYTHING STARTS. THIS IS WHERE LIFE ITSELF STARTS.

If your jaws are dropping at the thought of this outrageous theory, or if you find it too simplistic, unspeakable or distasteful, I'd like you to look and listen. Pay attention to all great art.

Look at Renoir. Look at the colors, the sensuous curves. How about Degas and Georgia O'Keeffe? Why am I leaving out gay artists? Michelangelo was a gay artist. Make a close examination of the Sistine Chapel, or his sculpture of David. Look at Picasso, Van Gogh, Frida Kahlo. Can you possibly miss the lusty underpinnings of their work?

Listen to the music of the world. We know about rock and roll already, and that includes blues, jazz and gospel. What's hotter than Rev. Vernard Johnson's sax? ALL American music is infused with hunger, I don't care if it's a Sousa march. Listen to African drums, or Japanese Taiko drums, Irish, Greek and French music. Can you feel erotic stirrings in "Hymne a L'amour" or Jaques Brel's "Port of Amsterdam"? Listen to classical music. Wagner, Verdi's *Otello*, Beethoven, Stravinsky, Mozart. Here are a couple of popular ones—Handel's luscious "Hallelujah Chorus," Schubert's "Ave Maria."

Listen to one EVERYBODY'S heard and performed...geez, Bobby McFerrin SINGS it, and Philip Achille BLOWS it through a harp. For those who don't remember, Procul Harum's "A Whiter Shade of Pale" was based on it. It is Bach's "Air on a G string" from his Orchestral Suite #3. I don't care whether you do it in D or G. Everybody loves it.

Why does everyone love it? Well, it is so romantically lewd-sounding, it's almost uncivilized, that's why. COME ON, PEOPLE, work with me here. If THAT composition doesn't make you want to commit an agonizingly slow and hard fuck with somebody on a sweltering summer night, then you're DEAD. The bass line makes it, and that alone, makes ME want to grow my nails long and CLAW. ALL good music has it.

And so does ALL good writing. Twain, Maugham, Dylan Thomas, Hemmingway, Poe, Dickens, Harper Lee, it goes on and on. Read poetry out loud.

Watch people DANCE. ANY dance. Ballet, modern, I don't care. What the heck do you think the TANGO is all about? Yes, that's right...the tango IS that delicious war. Can you see the look in THEIR eyes?

How about creations of food? Who is the hedonist that invented pizza, or crepe suzette?

LIFE ITSELF A CREATIVE ENDEAVOR. WE ALL HAVE SOMETHING IN US THAT'S WORTH FEEDING WITH PASSION.

> **We have only to keep desire in our lives. If we let that part of us die, we become unable to give to others. We will become numb to our fellow human beings. Numb to the glories that surround us. Numb to our planet. Indifference does not kill in a day, or a week, but eventually an important vitality will die within us. We will lose courage. It is the loving amongst us who are the most daring.**

Good lord, it DOESN'T even matter if you are ALONE. Do you have no MEMORY of that craving, the hunger? One feels suddenly more ALIVE, yes? Ahh, that's the life affirming energy, the seductive and compulsive push. You know where it's coming from by now, don't you?

DON'T BE AFRAID OF IT. GO AHEAD AND TAP INTO IT, FOR GOSH SAKE. LET IT NURTURE YOU. DON'T MISS OUT. STAY YOUNG AND CURIOUS. DO NOT STOP LEARNING. PASS IT ON TO OTHERS.

I spoke in another chapter of people who have lost interest in touching one another. The same dangers hold true for them. Relationships are breaking apart by the millions. Either breaking apart, or the "lovers" involved have been drifting along in an indifferent way, because one or both partners have become PASSIVE. Self-absorbed and lost in an easy solitary satisfaction. DISCONNECTED AND APATHETIC IN THE MOST INEFFECTUAL WAY.

This is the real legacy they have left me.

This is the legacy I want so much to pass on to YOU...to help you travel with caring, passion, laughter, that precious sense of wonder, and an unfettered zest for life.

I want YOU to be able to carry on that legacy of joy, and PASS it to others. I want every day to be an adventure for you to cherish. This is my devout wish for you all.

Here is the eulogy I gave for Mamma:

Mamma was proud to be an honorary Armenian, and she wore that badge mighty proudly, but I think the deepest and truest part of Margo was this:

Mamma was a Southerner. Southernism is mysticism. It's the mist rising over the cypress swamp.

It's the measured speech born of a climate that saps the unwary. It's the opposition of both peace and turmoil.

And it's that mysterious Southern "get right with God" stubbornness that comes only from working with mules.

I thought of what Margo would want to tell you and I think this is what she would say:

I grew up barefoot in red dirt country.

I still climbed trees as a fifteen-year-old and squelched mud between my toes.

I ate pimento and cheese, and boiled peanuts, and never met a catfish fry I didn't cherish.

I was a Southern lady, but I stole watermelon from the farmer's field next door, and I buried it deep in the cold sand to chill it up right, and I cracked it open on the rocks and scooped up the sweet red flesh.

I swam in the cold clear swimming hole, swinging from a vine, my legs flying free in the Mississippi summer, and I didn't flinch at slugs, or fish, or crawdads.

I am a knowledge-loving,
Tennessee Williams devouring,
Thunderstorm-dancing
Wild Southern woman.

Did I get that lesson right? I hope so. Read the Shakespeare. He said it more beautifully than I can.

"From a woman's eye this doctrine I derive;
They sparkle still the right Promethean fire;
They are the books, the arts, the academes,
That show, contain and nourish all the world;
Else none at all in aught proves excellent."
Go ahead...and DO IT. Thunderstorm dancing.
TELL MARGO I SENT YOU.

ACKNOWLEDGEMENTS

Writing a book, is not the solitary task that one would think it is. Once you think you're done with it, you are actually just beginning to START the darn thing. Many patient and kind people are put upon, and actively involved in the thorny process of making it ready to go. Truthfully, it's a scary enterprise, and involves more steps than walking on the moon. Every single time I've read a book, (which used to be about three per week)..the acknowledgements made me laugh, and I'd think..."Why the heck does it take so many people to DO this? Is the writer completely useless? Crikey!" Hmmm…NOW I KNOW, and all I've got to say for myself is a hearty Duuuuh. SO, here it comes.

This book wouldn't have been written, if not for the kindness and wisdom of some amazing friends. I'm talking about the poor sods who actually listened to my writings over the phone. Thank you, my oldest and dearest friend…Bob Halperin, who told me "If you were in the presence of Levon Helm for only ten minutes, he would make you feel as if he was HOLDING you." Yes, he did, and my life was so enriched because of him. You are so very right, Bob. Thank you Claudia, Dawn, Denise and Doug, who unfortunately left this earth, last year. I miss him like the devil. Dear Robin, YOU helped me as well…though you weren't aware of it at the time.

The designer of this book's front cover was Dean Samen, infamous for his particular design genre'…horror. Could he not have painted some blood enticingly trickling out my mouth, or nicely make my eyes a glowing red? HUH? The BACK…oh ok…the BOOTY of the book, as well as the spine, and the front and back flaps on the hardcover version, were thankfully and beautifully done by Tracy Atkins who ALSO formatted the inside, and dealt with difficult photos, a difficult author, and ten million other designer specific things. Tracy works with an equally terrific person named Joel Frielander, who is…um…..well, he's a writer's GURU. THAT'S what he darn well is! And I couldn't thank him enough for his wise counsel if I lived to be a million.

The person I need to thank the MOSTEST (ahh shut it…that IS a word.)…is the man I'd want to become if I were a guy…Burt Kearns. He was the first person to read my manuscript…because I'd trust him with my life…and KNEW that he would tell me if the thing was a pile of poo. He was also darling enough to read the thing AGAIN after I had finished editing it, and shared his thoughts. I wouldn't have been able to name Jeff, if it weren't for Burt. I would heartily suggest that you all read HIS book…the infamous "Tabloid Baby" because he IS a writer, and I'd suggest that you watch the trillion things that he has written, produced, directed, and/or edited. I am MORE than glad that Burt didn't voice the opinions that I gleaned from many book experts. They made me think I was hallucinating, and was back in the music biz.

"This doesn't go in chronological order! It doesn't make SENSE! It's all OVER the place. There's too much of THIS. It needs MORE editing. Ohh THIS thing's weird, and it's gonna be a hard sell!" Here is my answer. NO, I am not a traditionalist. I mostly wrote about life as a musician. Guess WHAT. If you ARE…or would like to be making a living as a musician, NOTHING is in chronological order. Nothing makes sense. You're all over the place, and your LIFE needs editing. You are freakishly NOT IN the middle of any damn ROAD, and therefore you are hard to place within that little box. If your life does not resemble all that, then you are NOT a musician. You are an A.M. Radio Station.

Thank YOU Ross. You don't know how many times you literally lifted me off the ground, threw me into the air and made me giggle…when I felt as if existence was futile. Bless your good and true heart. Oh GOD…Soy Boys! PLEASE don't send me one.

Heartfelt thanks to my Bro-in law, Huw…for coming here after Jeremy left us, and for letting me be on the phone, when he lost his little girl…Jeremy's niece, Emily. You saved me, and all of the sweet people in Jeremy's town…Churwell, took me into their open arms, and saved me as well….Steven M., Janet, Bouncy O., Jo, David, Kath, Sue, Danny, Gary, Aaron, Bryn, Andy, Ian, Steven, Eddie, Emma Williams, Ian, June,

Nick, Clair, Liz and David (RIP), Moira, Gillian, Cuz John, Joe, Glenda,Shirley, Shelly, Stephen, Victoria, Alan, Stephen H., Karen, Mick, David C., Michael R., Jennyfer C., Jason W., Cuz Fiona, Ian H., Andrea D., Julie G., Noel B., Michael M., Graham J., Michelle W., Gary S., Bev J., Tony and Mags, Michael H., Sue W., Richard F., Mark S., Steve and Steph G., Linda B., Andy F., Nick C., Jeff H.,Craig S., Angela G., Julie S., Karen Mc., Stewart L., Lisa S.G., Paul., Lizzie H., Jed H., Debbie &Dave W., Richard B., Warren L., Nigel S., Mark B,Smith, and I hope like hell I haven't missed anyone. I miss you. and hope to be back there sometime soon. I'd start running NOW, if I were you!

I'd like to thank Kimmi Ramone....although I've got NO idea how she got that name. I met her quite a few years ago...and was aware, that she had started an organization...Rock To Cure Cancer. She began in 2009. Wonderful people in different states, put on a concert every year, and the net proceeds from all of those concerts each year...go to the Lymphoma Research Foundation...In honor of Joey Ramone. I believe she was a big fan of his for a long time before she began doing this. NO MATTER WHY. The important thing is...that she DOES IT. If any of you reading this, would like to put on a concert in YOUR town...I'd very much like to invite you to DO IT. Go right ahead to ROCK TO CURE CANCER INC. at Weebly, or on Facebook, and get in touch with Kimmi. She will be happy to guide you. Have a GREAT NIGHT of MUSIC, and help to find a CURE. If you'd like ME to show up, and sell some books, or prance about with no direction known. I'd most likely be more than happy to. Remember, half of the gross proceeds of any books sold will go to the Lymphoma Research Foundation, in honor of Joey Ramone, AND the other half to the Nagourney Institute, founded by a pioneer in the field of assay directed therapy, Robert A. Nagourney, M.D., In honor of Jeremy John Dennis. YOU SHOULD GOOGLE BOTH OF THESE FOUNDATIONS, TO LEARN ABOUT THE WORK THEY DO. Dr. Nagourney is in Long Beach, CA, and you can find out about his laboratory directed cancer treatments at his Rational Therapeutics website
www.rationaltherapeutics.com.

Thank you so very much to Santucci Priori,P.L. , Ft. Lauderdale, FL , who specialize in but are not limited to intellectual property, business and Entertainment law and litigation. They are all quite intelligent AND endlessly entertaining. SINCERE thanks to Atty. Joe Priori, Atty. Daniel Devine, and to my brutha from another mutha Atty. Michael Santucci.

If you have questions for me, are interested in knowing more about this book, or having me present at your event, IN ANY STATE, OR ANY COUNTRY…you may get in touch with me, through Michael Santucci, Esq. You may e-mail him at mis@500law.com

You may also get answers to any questions you may have, or get in touch with me through my Publicist Javier Perez at J.perez@pageturnerpublicity.com

Made in the USA
Middletown, DE
15 September 2018